$18.99

LESSON PLANS & TEACHER'S MANUAL
BUILDING THINKING SKILLS®
Level 3 – Verbal

SERIES TITLES

BUILDING THINKING SKILLS®—BEGINNING FIGURAL
BUILDING THINKING SKILLS®—BEGINNING PHOTO CARDS
BUILDING THINKING SKILLS®—BOOK 1
BUILDING THINKING SKILLS®—BOOK 2
BUILDING THINKING SKILLS®—BOOK 3 FIGURAL
BUILDING THINKING SKILLS®—BOOK 3 VERBAL

SANDRA PARKS AND HOWARD BLACK
edited by Carole Bannes

Purchased From:
EMMANUEL CENTER
4061 Holt Rd.
Holt, MI 48842
517-699-2728-Questions
800-256-5044-Orders

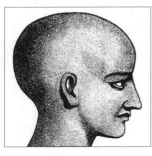

© 1988
CRITICAL THINKING BOOKS & SOFTWARE
www.criticalthinking.com
P.O. Box 448 • Pacific Grove • CA 93950-0448
Phone 800-458-4849 • FAX 831-393-3277
ISBN 0-89455-301-1
Printed in the United States of America
Reproduction rights granted for single-classroom use only.

TABLE OF CONTENTS

EVALUATION RECOMMENDATIONS

1. Any standardized content test currently utilized by your district will reflect increases in students' academic performance that result from better thinking skills and can be used to measure the effectiveness of the Building Thinking Skills® series.

2. Tests are also available to measure growth in cognitive skills specifically. These tests include the following:

Cognitive Abilities Test (Woodcock-Johnson)

Riverside Publishing Company
425 Spring Lake Dr.
Itasca, IL 60143-2079
800-323-9540 • (fax) 630-467-7192 • www.riverpub.com

Differential Aptitude Tests, Otis-Lennon School Ability Test (OLSAT-7), WISC-III

Harcourt Brace Educational Measurement
Psychological Corporation
555 Academic Court
San Antonio, TX 78204
800-228-0752 • (fax) 800-232-1223 • www.harcourt.com

Structure of Intellect Learning Abilities Test

S.O.I. Systems
P.O. Box D
Vida, OR 97488
541-896-3936 • (fax) 541-896-3983 • www.soisystems.com

Test of Cognitive Skills

CTB-McGraw Hill
P.O. Box 150
Monterey, CA 93942-0150
800-538-9547 • (fax) 800-282-0266 • www.ctb.com

INTRODUCTION

ALTERNATIVES FOR USE

The *Building Thinking Skills* books may be used in conjunction with content objectives or as a separate course of study. The decision regarding whether to use thinking skills instruction as a supplement to the existing curriculum objectives, or as a separate course, depends on several factors: (1) how thinking skills instruction can be scheduled in the existing school program; (2) how thinking skills instruction can be managed and evaluated most easily; (3) how much curriculum and staff development time can be committed to the program; (4) whether teachers are more receptive to an additional curriculum or a strategy for existing instructional objectives; (5) the extent to which student proficiency at thinking skills is expected to improve performance in content objectives.

Research in cognitive skills instruction indicates that if content objectives in cognitive skills are taught in the same lesson, the thinking process is likely to be less emphasized than the content objectives. Since teachers and students are held accountable for content information, related cognitive processes are seldom identified or developed. Often, content objectives employ cognitive skills, at which students may be less proficient than expected. Content objectives may presume to be teaching thinking skills when, actually, a lesson is an application of, and not instruction in, the skill that is being addressed.

Content objectives may prescribe a cognitive task, such as classification, without realizing the subtle steps that are involved in the ability to classify. As a result, the teacher has not taught classification, the learner has not perceived that he or she has learned it, and neither understands why the lesson is not effective. Integrating thinking skills totally into content objectives may seem appealing from a curriculum development standpoint, but may be superficial in implementation. Thinking skills instruction totally "hidden" in the content curriculum is difficult to document and evaluate.

Thinking skills instruction as a separate course of study offers an alternative curriculum design. In an independent structured program, teachers know that they are teaching, and students know that they are learning, the cognitive skills required in the academic curriculum. Focusing on teaching a skill encourages adequate explanation and practice. Students recognize their growing competence in the kinds of tasks required in schooling. A structured program is relatively easy to observe and evaluate.

Cognitive skill learning should be tied to applications at school or at home if the learner is to perceive that this instruction is relevant or helpful. Students may not attend conscientiously to a "game" or make the expected connections in academic objectives. The teaching of cognitive skills may be fairly superficial without the reinforcement of use. When thinking skills instruction is perceived as a "separate curriculum," it becomes vulnerable to change in priorities within the school and may be easily eliminated as a "fad." Teachers tend to resist instruction that they do not perceive as relevant to the objectives for which they are already held accountable.

The authors recommend that thinking skills activities be implemented as a structured sequential course of study, offered in conjunction with content objectives. Because content objectives usually apply, rather than develop, thinking skills, the thinking skill instruction should be offered just prior to the corresponding content objective. In this option, the thinking skills course is spread out within the existing school program. Hence, one can be assured of offering an identifiable, structured program as a method for teaching content objectives. The linkage between thinking skills instruction and school performance is accomplished by identifying these skills in the existing school program. The editorial process produces a cognitive skills curriculum tailored to district needs, rather than implementation of a "packaged program." This articulated program allows supervisors to identify and evaluate instruction, but is accepted by teachers because thinking skills instruction makes their existing instruction more effective.

PROGRAM DESIGN

Selection and organization of skills. The cognitive skills developed in this series were selected because of their significance in the academic disciplines. These four skills (similarities and differences, sequencing, classifications, and analogies) are required in all content areas, including the arts. Since improved school performance is an important goal of thinking skills instruction, many variations of the skills are presented.

Four cognitive skills are offered in the same order that the child develops intellectually. Distinguishing similarities and differences is integral to the learner's ability to put things in order, to group items by class, and to think analogously. Skills are presented in figural and verbal form, following the developmental process of conceptualization in concrete, figural form before the development of abstract, verbal reasoning. The organization of this book includes:

Verbal Similarities and Differences
  (Synonyms & Antonyms)
Verbal Sequences
Verbal Classifications
Verbal Analogies
Comparable skills in figural form are presented in *Building Thinking Skills 3—Figural*:
Figural Similarities and Differences
Figural Sequences
Figural Classifications
Figural Analogies

The teacher may select either the figural or the verbal strand as a sequence of instruction, may alternate between the two forms, or may schedule the thinking skills exercises as they occur in content objectives. In any case, similarities and differences in figural and verbal form should be offered early in the course of instruction, since that skill is basic to more complex ones.

Item design. In each strand, exercises have been designed in the manner that the developing child learns: cognition, evaluation, and convergent production. The simplest form of a task is recognizing the correct answer among several choices. These cognition items have the directions: "Select." Next in difficulty is the ability to explain or rank items. This evaluation step clarifies for the learner the relationships between objects or concepts. The evaluation items contain the direction: "Rank" or "Explain."

When the learner must supply a single correct answer from his own background and memory, the task becomes more difficult. This convergent production step is designated by the heading: "Supply." Teachers may find that it becomes helpful to explain concepts in any discipline if they remember the simple "select, explain, then supply" process. Teachers familiar with J. P. Guilford's *Structure of Intellect* model will recognize the cognition, evaluation, and convergent production factors in both figural and verbal form in these exercises.

Vocabulary level. The vocabulary level of *Building Thinking Skills 1* approximates a reading vocabulary of the first thousand words. In practice, this corresponds to the vocabulary typically used in grades 2-4. A few items contain words from the second thousand words. *Building Thinking Skills 1* contains picture forms to allow learners who have limited reading ability to develop more complex thinking skills. *Building Thinking Skills 2* includes the second thousand words with occasional word choices in the third thousand words. This level of difficulty corresponds to the reading vocabulary typically used in grades 4-6.

Building Thinking Skills 3—Verbal includes a vocabulary range up to the sixth thousand words, as specified in the *New Horizon Dictionary of the English Language* (Shaw and Shaw, Signet Publications, 1970). Terms commonly used in elementary school science and social studies texts are also used. *Building Thinking Skills 3—Verbal* is typically used in grades 6-8. Because the vocabulary level is compounded by the thinking skills component, the resulting items may be more difficult than the vocabulary level suggests.

INSTRUCTIONAL METHODS

Piagetian learning theory indicates that the learner proceeds from the concrete, manipulative form of tasks to the semiconcrete, paper-and-pencil form of the task, and finally to the abstract, verbal form. The *Building Thinking Skills* series is based on that progression. Ideally, students should practice each cognitive task in manipulative form. Manipulatives, such as attribute blocks and tangrams, are commonly available or easily made from inexpensive materials.

The student book is the paper-and-pencil form of exercise. Class discussion maximizes student benefit from the paper-and-pencil exercises.

The third step in this process—abstract, verbal expression of the task—is involved in the class discussion of the exercises. This important step reinforces and confirms the thinking processes that the learner used to carry out the task. While there are many subtleties in thinking that we cannot express, the skills in this program are common ones that can be relatively easily discussed. The discussion process clarifies what the learner did to get the answer and differentiates that process from similar ones.

Discussion allows learners to see alternative processing strategies. This technique allows students to understand other ways of getting an answer. For the gifted students, discussion provides insight regarding how other equally bright learners can arrive at correct answers by different analysis. Hence, discussion demonstrates differences in learning styles, a strategy that allows students to recognize and value other people's processes for solving problems.

Discussion reinforces the learner's memory of the thinking process, increasing transfer to similar tasks in the content areas. When the student recognizes that he or she has correctly thought through this kind of task in a nonthreatening learning situation, the learner's confidence in his or her ability to solve similar problems in a different context is enhanced.

Discussion Principles. Discussion is the process by which the learner clarifies subtle aspects of processing the exercises. This clarification distinguishes a task from similar ones and provides alternative and creative ways of getting an answer. Through discussion, the learner ties a task to others in his or her experience and anticipates situations in which that skill is helpful. For effective explanation and transfer of the skill, the explanation should always be **FROM EXPERIENCE TO EXPERIENCE.**

In introducing a skill, the teacher should identify a real world or academic experience in which the learner has used that skill. This reference cues the learner that this task is one with which the learner already has some experience and competence. It signals the learner that the task is useful and reduces anxiety about being able to master it.

After explanation and guided practice, the learner should be asked to tie this skill to another use in his or her experience. This memory aid increases the learner's confidence in reasoning and encourages transfer of the skill.

For learners who have not been successful in school, the relevance and perceived usefulness of thinking skills may be a factor in how thoroughly the learner will attend to the task. While improved thinking skills may improve school performance, low-functioning students seldom expect that effect, and require some extrinsic motive for attempting the exercise.

Because an important goal of thinking skills instruction is improved school performance, both teachers and students should become aware of the applications of thinking skills in the content curriculum. This application reinforces newly mastered skills, improves student confidence, and facilitates new content learning. The focus of thinking skills instruction is improving teaching and learning. That goal is best realized by frequent identification of these four thinking skills whenever teachers and students encounter similar tasks. Thinking skills instruction is a method for improving content learning, as well as a new element of the curriculum.

RATIONALE AND DESCRIPTION OF SKILLS

VERBAL SIMILARITIES AND DIFFERENCES

The VERBAL SIMILARITIES AND DIFFERENCES strand includes synonyms and antonyms. The ability to discern similarity and difference in meaning is integral to reading comprehension, vocabulary development, and writing skills.

Types of exercises in this strand include:

1. Selecting similar and opposite words
2. Selecting how words are alike and how they are different
3. Explaining how words are alike and how they are different
4. Supplying similar and opposite words
5. Recognizing and supplying denotative or connotative meaning

Additional similarities and differences exercises are provided in Midwest Publications' booklets: *Antonyms & Synonyms* and *Antonyms, Synonyms, Similarities, and Differences.*

VERBAL SEQUENCES

Students must recognize word relationships in order to understand subtle differences in meaning, to recognize chronological order, and to organize and retrieve information.

Vocabulary building is the key skill being addressed in the VERBAL SEQUENCES strand. Language arts research indicates that students learn vocabulary effectively through context. Context may be paragraphs or clusters of words that give meaning to the word or words being learned. In the VERBAL SEQUENCES exercises, two of the three words in a series suggest what the degree, size, rank, or order of the third word should be. If the student understands some of the words in the sequence, he or she can infer the meaning of the missing item.

Recognizing degree of meaning fosters correct inference in reading and listening and promotes clarity in writing and speech. Vocabulary and reading comprehension test items frequently involve slight differences in meaning.

Achievement tests also contain items that require the student to number sentences in the order in which they occur. The student may recognize and organize a commonly known sequence or may rely on the context of the passage to determine chronological order.

The first form of word sequence is a game-like exercise called WORD BENDERS™. Word Benders™ are letter systems in which some letters must be changed and others must remain the same. As students follow these rules by deductive reasoning, new words emerge. Students may use clues to decide the correct letter change or to verify the meaning of an unknown word.

The second type of verbal sequence involves following directions regarding sequential action and spatial relationships. Exercises offer the transition from directional perception to map reading. Students confirm skills by writing directions.

Sequential meaning includes distinguishing transitive order. From a written passage, students rank objects or people being compared according to some characteristic (weight, age, height, score, etc.). Transitive order is applied to the solution of deductive reasoning puzzles. Additional practice in this kind of exercise is provided in Midwest Publications' *Mind Benders*® booklets.

Additional degree-of-meaning exercises are provided in Midwest Publications' booklets: *Verbal Sequences A-1, B-1,* and *C-1.*

Sequential analysis of meaning in formal and informal logic involves the use of logic connectives ("and," "or," "not," and "if ... then") and the use of words suggesting cause and effect. By using this series, students gain sufficient background to use basic logic concepts required for Midwest Publications' *Critical Thinking I* and *II,* the secondary school logic course.

Verbal sequences are expressed in computer use as flowcharting. Students practice flowcharting actions, decisions, and cycles.

Time sequence activities allow students to examine common terms regarding time, to convert time zone information to fit local time, and to schedule events.

VERBAL CLASSIFICATIONS

The VERBAL CLASSIFICATION strand features activities to improve students' conceptualization of class and to encourage discernment in word meaning.

Classification provides a basis for storing and retrieving information. Just as a computer stores, organizes, and recalls bits of information, our human memory uses categories or classes to organize and retain otherwise unconnected items and ideas. The learner remembers categories or associations as an aid to recalling details.

Classification also promotes the understanding and recall of the meaning of words. Classes are the categories in any definition of nouns. In the definition of bicycle as "a vehicle having two wheels," "vehicle" is the class and "two wheels" are the descriptors. Describing relations in classes aids the understanding and recall of words.

Classification of collections allows learners to find items or information easily. Commonly, students are introduced to conventional classification systems (library classification systems, biological phyla, the periodic chart). Less often, however, do students learn how to classify. Classification brings order to everyday tasks, such as arranging items on storage shelves, managing the family budget, keeping records, or sorting collections.

Types of items include:
1. Distinguishing parts of a whole
2. Distinguishing between class and members of that class
3. Selecting and explaining common characteristics of a class
4. Explaining the exception to a class
5. Sorting words into classes
6. Using branching diagrams, Venn diagrams, and matrices to depict class relationships
7. Diagraming class arguments
8. Recognizing and writing proper definitions

Additional classifications exercises are provided in the Midwest Publications' booklets: *Verbal Classifications A-1, B-1,* and *C-1.*

VERBAL ANALOGIES

The VERBAL ANALOGIES strand features activities to sharpen students' perceptions of analogous relationships and to develop vocabulary.

The types of analogies include:
1. Synonyms
2. Antonyms
3. Part of
4. Kind of
5. Used to
6. Associations
7. Actions
8. Degree of

Analogy exercises include:
1. Selecting the word to complete an analogy
2. Naming the kind of analogy
3. Supplying the word to complete an analogy
4. Selecting analogous pairs of words to complete an analogy

Additional practice is provided in the Midwest Publications' booklets: *Analogies A, B, C,* and *D.*

GUIDE TO USING THE LESSON PLANS

HEADING
Corresponds to the subhead at the top of each student workbook page.

STRAND
Identifies which of the eight skills is being developed.

PAGES
Identifies corresponding pages in the student workbook.

ADDITIONAL MATERIALS
Lists necessary materials and supplies needed for demonstrating the lesson, e.g., transparencies, models, marking pens.

INTRODUCTION
Indicates where the student has seen or used a similar kind of learning. ***Throughout the Lesson Plans, suggested teacher statements appear in bold italic type.***

OBJECTIVE
Explains to the student what he or she can expect to learn in the lesson.

DEMONSTRATION/EXPLANATION
Offers a concrete form of the task, and/or illustrates by modeling, procedures which students can duplicate. Students may also prepare models or materials similar o those suggested. Facilitators conducting a lesson should verbalize their own thinking process. This modeling provides cues to students for thinking through the task. Procedures for conducting the lessons are printed in standard type.

GUIDED PRACTICE
Controlled practice allows the teacher to identify errors in answers or processes. To check for understanding, **GUIDED PRACTICE** should be followed by **class discussion**. Answers and explanations for individual exercises are included.

INDEPENDENT PRACTICE
Practice exercises for promoting skill mastery.

DISCUSSION TIPS
After students have had to opportunity to complete the exercises, the teacher "debriefs" the class using discussion techniques and stressing the significant terms and concepts suggested in this section. Such discussions should always include the process by which answers were chosen and by which alternate answers were rejected. This verbalization promotes clarification of subtle perceptions in the thinking skill lessons.

ANSWERS
Provides answers and explanations for the **INDEPENDENT PRACTICE** exercises.

FOLLOW-UP REFERENT
Suggests questions and answers to tie the skill into the experience of the student, completing the "from experience back to experience" loop, and cueing the student regarding possible future uses of each skill.

CURRICULUM APPLICATION
Indicates possible content objectives which feature the skill or require it as a prerequisite. These curriculum linkage examples are not intended to be complete, but rather to suggest ideas for applying the skill to specific content areas.

BUILDING THINKING SKILLS®
LESSON PLANS for BOOK 3—VERBAL

VERBAL SIMILARITIES AND DIFFERENCES

ANTONYMS — SELECT

STRAND: Verbal Similarities and Differences   **PAGES:** 1–2

ADDITIONAL MATERIALS
Transparency of student workbook page 1
Washable transparency marker

INTRODUCTION
An antonym is a word that means the opposite of a given word.

OBJECTIVE
In these exercises you will select an antonym for a given word.

DEMONSTRATION / EXPLANATION
You will look for the word choice which is most unlike the given word. When you have selected one, check the other words to confirm that they are not opposites of the given word.
Project exercise **A-1** from the transparency of page 1.
In this exercise you are given the word PRESERVE and three words which might be its opposite: CONSTRUCT, DESTROY, and PROTECT.
Indicate the words as you talk.
PRESERVE means to keep in good condition. An opposite word would mean to put in poor condition. DESTROY means to demolish or tear down and appears to be the opposite of preserve. Check the other two words to make sure that destroy is the choice most unlike preserve. CONSTRUCT means to build, so it is not an opposite. PROTECT means to keep from harm. Since it is similar in meaning to preserve, it can't be an opposite. Destroy is the word choice most opposite preserve.
Underline DESTROY on the transparency.

GUIDED PRACTICE
EXERCISES: **A-2, A-3, A-4**
When the students have had sufficient time to complete these exercises, encourage them to use the demonstration methodology above as they discuss and defend their answers.
ANSWERS:
NOTE: The four given words from each exercise appear in **bold** *type in all answers for this lesson. (Detractors and their definitions are enclosed in parenthesis. An asterisk [*] indicates a word that may be used as a synonym for the given word.)*

A-2   c   **Deposit** means to place, dump, or put away. An opposite word would mean to remove or take out. **Withdraw** means to take out. (**Account** is not an opposite because it means to record transactions. **Spend** is not an opposite because it means to trade money for goods or services.)

15

A-3   b   **Ideal** means without defect. An opposite word would mean having a defect. **Imperfect** means defective or not perfect. (**Desirable** is not an opposite because it means having pleasing qualities. **Worthy** is not an opposite because it means deserving of respect or honor. Something that is ideal may be both desirable and worthy.)

A-4   a   **Idle** means not moving or working. An opposite word would mean moving or working. **Busy** means moving or occupied. (**Complex** is not an opposite because it means intricate or difficult. **Simple** is not an opposite because it means easily understood or uncomplicated.)

INDEPENDENT PRACTICE
Assign exercises **A-5** through **A-24**.

DISCUSSION TIPS
Encourage students to verbalize their definitions and reasons for choosing or rejecting an answer. Class discussion is a valuable technique for having students share their acquired knowledge. Sharing and exchanging information among their classmates leads students to better qualitative, rather than quantitative, thought processes. The brief definitions given by the authors should be modified and tailored to the vocabulary level and needs of the class. The following cues will encourage the discussion procedure demonstrated.
1. Recognize and pronounce given word.
2. Define given word.
3. Define opposite word.
4. Select answer.
5. Eliminate detractors for confirmation.

The detailed answers throughout this lesson also reflect this procedure.

ANSWERS
A-5   b   **Certainty** means something that is sure or accepted unquestionably. An opposite word would mean something that is unsure or questionable. **Doubt** means an uncertainty or a question. (**Belief** means an acceptance of something as true. **Proof** means an establishment of fact by evidence. Neither is an antonym of certainty.)

A-6   b   **Scorn** means to treat with contempt. An opposite word would mean to treat with care or concern. **Honor** means to respect. (**Disregard** means to ignore or pay no attention to. **Reject*** means to refuse or not accept.)

A-7   a   **Treachery** means violation of faith or allegiance. An opposite word would mean maintenance of faith or allegiance. **Loyalty** means reliability and steadfastness. (**Plot** means a secret plan. **Theft** refers to the act of stealing. Treachery might involve a plot for theft.)

A-8   c   **Omit** means to take out or leave out. An opposite word would mean to put in or accept. **Include** means to put in or to have as part of something. (**Avoid** means to stay away from. **Exclude*** also means to leave out.)

A-9   b   **Peculiar** means strange or different from normal. An opposite word would mean familiar or normal. **Ordinary** means common or average. (**Odd*** and **strange*** are not opposites because they also mean different from normal.)

A-10   c   **Conceited** means having an unusually high opinion of one's self. An opposite word would mean having a lower opinion of one's self. **Modest** means to have an unassuming opinion of one's self. (**Capable** is not an opposite because it means having the ability to do something. **Loud** is not an opposite because it means emphatic or urgent. Conceited or modest people may be both capable and loud.)

A-11 c **Resist** means to fight against or abstain from. An opposite word would mean to accept. **Submit** means to give in. (**Oppose*** means to take a position against. **Protest*** means to speak or act against.)

A-12 a **Evident** means visible or noticeable. An opposite word would mean not visible. **Concealed** means hidden from view. (**Obvious*** means in full view or easily understood. **Questionable** means in doubt—neither evident nor concealed.)
ALTERNATE ANSWER: If **evident** is defined as undoubted, then **questionable** [c] may be seen as an antonym; e.g., "His loyalty is evident." vs "His loyalty is questionable."

A-13 b **Domestic** means pertaining to or made in the home or native land. An opposite word would mean imported or not native. **Foreign** means pertaining to or made in another country. (**Exported** refers to goods or services sent out of a country. **Manufactured** refers to goods made by hand or machinery; they may be domestic, foreign, or exported.)

A-14 c **Definite** means certain or clear. An opposite word would mean not certain or not clear. **Vague** means indefinite or ambiguous. (**Complete*** means finished. **Neutral** means belonging to neither one side nor the other.)

A-15 c **Decent** means satisfactory or acceptable. An opposite word would mean unsatisfactory or unacceptable. **Vulgar** means indecent or lacking good taste. (**Insufficient** means not enough. **Proper*** means acceptable or appropriate.)
ALTERNATE ANSWER: If **decent** is defined as a satisfactory amount, then **insufficient** [a] may be seen as an antonym; e.g., "She earns a decent wage." vs "She earns an insufficient wage."

A-16 c **Discharge** means to empty or remove. An opposite word would mean to fill or place. **Load** means to fill or burden. (**Dispel*** means to scatter or banish. **Fire*** means to shoot, explode, or bombard.)

A-17 b **Trivial** means unimportant or small. An opposite word would mean important. **Significant** means vital or valuable. (**Partial** means incomplete or involving only a portion. **Simple*** means having few parts or ordinary.)

A-18 a **Thrill** refers to something exciting, stimulating, or inspiring. An opposite word would mean something dull, depressing, or discouraging. **Bore** refers to something or someone dull or tedious. (**Rally*** and **stir*** both relate to inciting excitement, action, or inspiration.)

A-19 a **Retain** means to keep or hold. An opposite word would mean to let go or release. **Lose** means fail to keep. (**Invest** means to purchase and keep in hopes of earning a profit; it is a form of retaining. In this context, **realize** means to receive a profit.)

A-20 b **Sudden** means happening quickly or without warning. An opposite word would mean happening slowly or gradually. **Prolonged** means occurring over an extended time. (Neither **abrupt*** nor **unexpected*** are opposites; each means quickly or without warning.)

A-21 b **Delay** means to postpone or detain. An opposite word would mean to hurry or push forward. **Hasten** means to hurry. (**Arrest*** means to stop or detain. **Suspend*** means to set aside or stop temporarily.)

A-22 b **Weary** means exhausted or dispirited. An opposite word would mean rested or enthusiastic. **Refreshed** means revived. (**Experienced** means accomplished or knowledgeable. **Worn*** means exhausted.)

A-23 c **Resident** refers to one who lives in an area. An opposite word would mean one who lives elsewhere. **Visitor** refers to a guest, not a resident. (**Citizen*** refers to a person having legal rights and privileges within a prescribed area. **Official** refers to a person involved in enforcing the rules of a government or a game. Both citizens and [government] officials are usually residents of a given area.)

A-24 c **Mingle** means to blend or put together. An opposite word would mean to divide or take apart. **Separate** means to move apart. (**Combine*** means to unite. **Prepare** means to get ready.)

FOLLOW-UP REFERENT

When might you find it helpful to be able to recognize and define a word that means the opposite of another word?

Examples: solving crossword puzzles or cryptograms; giving directions; following reverse directions, e.g., turning left when you go to your friend's house and turning right when you go back home; reassembling models or appliances; understanding oral and/or written communication; recognizing and analyzing analogous relationships involving antonyms

CURRICULUM APPLICATION

Language Arts: vocabulary enrichment activities; antonym exercises; using precise words; writing contrastive paragraphs; describing contrasting characteristics in a work of literature; debating or expressing an opposite opinion

Mathematics: recognizing and using inverse operations; using fractions and reciprocals; recognizing set and set complements; checking basic arithmetic problems by reverse process, e.g., checking subtraction by addition

Science: recognizing reversed processes in experiments; accurately describing differences between objects or concepts; disassembling and reassembling motors, models, or scientific apparatus

Social Studies: contrasting topographic or geographic areas; locating and expressing contrasting details between topics

Enrichment Areas: writing or stating directions for dance movements or art projects; accurately expressing the differences between pieces of music, works of art, dances, or athletic activities

ANTONYMS—SUPPLY

STRAND: Verbal Similarities and Differences   **PAGES:** 3–4

ADDITIONAL MATERIALS

Transparency of student workbook page 3
Washable transparency marker

INTRODUCTION

In the previous lesson you selected an antonym for a given word from a group of three words.

OBJECTIVE

In these exercises you will supply as many antonyms as you can think of for a given word.

DEMONSTRATION/EXPLANATION

Project exercise **A-25** from the transparency of page 3.

In this exercise, the given word is MEND. How would you define this word?
Answer: To fix or repair something.

How many words can you think of that could mean the opposite of MEND?
Possible answers: Break, damage, injure, tear, or rip. Write all suggestions on the transparency, asking the students to confirm each one. Project **A-26**.

What does the word RECKLESS mean?
Answer: Lacking proper cautions, careless.

How many words can you think of that mean the opposite of reckless?
Answers: Careful, cautious, wary, thoughtful, responsible. Again, write all suggestions and ask students to confirm each.

GUIDED PRACTICE

EXERCISES: **A-27**, **A-28**, **A-29**
When the students have had sufficient time to complete these exercises, encourage them to use the demonstration methodology above as they discuss and defend their answers.
ANSWERS:

A-27   *combine:* separate, divide, part, sever, detach, disunite

A-28   *complex:* simple, uncomplicated, easy, clear, obvious, unconfused

A-29   *compliment:* (v.) insult, denounce, condemn, criticize, reproach, censure;
                (n.) insult, condemnation, criticism, censure

INDEPENDENT PRACTICE

Assign exercises **A-30** through **A-48**.

DISCUSSION TIPS

Encourage students to verbalize reasons for choosing their antonyms. Answers provided by the authors should be modified and tailored to the vocabulary level and needs of the students. If students tend to be satisfied with one or two antonym choices, the teacher may need to provide cues to stimulate further answers. You may wish to go through the exercises on two consecutive days to allow students to discover additional antonyms for each given word. Pay particular attention to words that may have multiple definitions or be used as different parts of speech.

ANSWERS

A-30   *initial:* final, last, ultimate, ending, closing, concluding, terminal

A-31   *fixed:* movable, mobile, unsteady, wavering

A-32   *import:* (bring in) export; (significance) unimportance, insignificance

A-33   *minor:* (slight) major, greater, main, important, significant; (under legal age) adult

A-34   *bald:* (hairless) hairy; (bare) overgrown; (undisguised) elaborate, devious

A-35   *innocence:* (guiltlessness) corruption, guilt, sinfulness, viciousness, wickedness;
                (naiveté) guile, cunning, worldliness, sophistication

A-36   *necessity:* luxury, want, desire, triviality

A-37 *freeze:* (cool) melt, thaw, liquefy, soften, heat, cook, warm; (stop) move, hasten

A-38 *remember:* forget, disregard, ignore, neglect, overlook

A-39 *conceal:* reveal, uncover, disclose, expose, display, show

A-40 *construct:* destruct, destroy, demolish, raze, disassemble

A-41 *profit:* (net gain) loss, forfeiture; (advantage) disadvantage, harm, detriment

A-42 *public:* (common) private, personal, individual, exclusive, restricted, closed; (overt) secret, unknown, hidden, unrevealed

A-43 *interior:* exterior, outside, external, coastlands

A-44 *farther:* nearer, closer, imminent, shorter (distance)

A-45 *victor:* loser, defeated, conquered, vanquished

A-46 *reward:* (v.) penalize, punish; (n.) penalty, fine, damages, punishment

A-47 *offense:* (attack) defense, resistance, guard; (insult) praise, respect, politeness

A-48 *temporary:* permanent, lasting, durable, persisting

FOLLOW-UP REFERENT

When might you need to think of antonyms (opposites) for a given word?
Examples: giving directions; following reverse directions, e.g., turning left when you go to your friend's house and turning right when you go back home; reassembling models or appliances; taking vocabulary or essay tests; solving crossword puzzles or cryptograms; stating analogous relationships using antonyms

CURRICULUM APPLICATION

Language Arts: vocabulary enrichment activities; antonym exercises; using precise words; writing contrastive paragraphs; describing contrastive elements in a work of literature; debating or expressing an opposite opinion; creating figures of speech, especially metaphors or similes

Mathematics: recognizing and using inverse operations; using fractions and reciprocals; describing sets and set complements; checking basic arithmetic problems by reverse process, e.g., checking subtraction by addition

Science: recognizing and explaining reversed processes in experiments; accurately describing differences between two objects or concepts; disassembling, reassembling, or describing the actions of motors, gears, or models

Social Studies: contrasting topographic or geographic areas; locating and expressing contrasting details in compared topics

Enrichment Areas: writing or stating directions for dance movements or art projects; accurately expressing the differences between two or more pieces of music, works of art, dances, or athletic activities; scripting computer programs

SYNONYMS—SELECT

STRAND: Verbal Similarities and Differences   **PAGES:** 5–8

ADDITIONAL MATERIALS

Transparency of student workbook page 5
Washable transparency marker

INTRODUCTION

In previous lessons you selected and supplied antonyms for given words.

OBJECTIVE

In these exercises you will select a word which is a synonym for a given word.

DEMONSTRATION / EXPLANATION

You will look for the word which is closest in meaning to the given word. When you have selected a synonym, check the other choices to confirm that they are not more precise synonyms than the word you chose.

Project exercise **A-49** from the transparency of page 5.

In this exercise you are given the word AVERAGE and three words which might mean the same as average: EXCELLENT, NORMAL, and UNUSUAL. Following the pattern of cues that you used in previous lessons, begin by defining the given word. What does AVERAGE mean?

Possible answers: Ordinary, medium, standard, typical, common, or usual.

Which of the word choices has a similar meaning?

Answer: Normal appears to be closest in meaning, since normal also means usual or standard.

Check your answer by defining the remaining words to be sure that the one you chose is the one closest in meaning to the given word.

Answer: Excellent and unusual both name conditions that are not ordinary or usual, so normal is the choice most like average. Underline NORMAL on the transparency.

GUIDED PRACTICE

EXERCISES: **A-50, A-51, A-52**

When the students have had sufficient time to complete these exercises, encourage them to use the demonstration methodology above as they discuss and defend their answers.
ANSWERS:

NOTE: The four given words from each exercise appear in **bold** *type in all answers for this lesson. (Detractors and their definitions are enclosed in parenthesis. An asterisk [*] indicates words that may be used as antonyms for the given word.)*

A-50 b An **error** is something done incorrectly. A **mistake** is an incorrect answer or action. (An **answer** may be correct or incorrect. A **test** is an examination. One might make an error or mistake on a test answer.)

A-51 b **Vast** means of great extent or size. **Immense** means huge. (**Empty** and **open** are frequently used to describe undeveloped or barren land; neither word concerns size.)

A-52 a **Assemble** means to construct or put together. **Build** means to erect or make. (**Replace** means to substitute with another. **Start** means to begin.)

INDEPENDENT PRACTICE

Assign exercises **A-53** through **A-97**.

DISCUSSION TIPS

Encourage students to verbalize their reasons for choosing an answer and to explain why the other words are less precise. Verbally expressing the rationale behind their answers forces students through the thinking processes of comprehension, analysis, synthesis, and evaluation. Each word within a given exercise should be defined as the same part of speech. Pay particular attention to words that may have multiple meanings or be used as various parts of speech. Sometimes the synonym choice does not mean the same thing as the most common definition of the given word. Encourage students to state as many different meanings as they can for each term in each exercise.

The brief definitions given throughout the answer sections should be modified and tailored to the vocabulary level and needs of the students. Use the following cues to encourage the procedures demonstrated in the explanation and followed in the detailed answers.
1. Recognize and pronounce given word.
2. Define given word.
3. Select answer.
4. Define synonym for confirmation.
5. Eliminate detractors.

ANSWERS

A-53 c **Snarl** means to twist or growl. **Tangle** means to intertwine. (A **curve** is a bent line or arc. **Fiber** is a threadlike substance. A fiber may get snarled or tangled.)

A-54 a A **grudge** is a feeling of ill will. A **grievance** is a complaint or reason for unhappiness. (Both **opinion** and **remark** are neutral terms which can express any kind of feeling.)

A-55 a **Spare** means something held in reserve for future use. **Extra** means beyond what is required. (**Lone** means only. **Lost** means not to be found.)

A-56 c **Eliminate** means to get rid of, ignore, or cause to disappear. **Remove** means to take off or take away. (**Finish** means to complete. **Project** can mean to throw, but does not mean to throw away.)

A-57 b A **penalty** is a punishment for violating the law or a legal agreement. A **fine** is money paid as punishment. (A **decision** is a conclusion or judgement. A **reward*** is something given for achievement.)

A-58 c **Linger** means to stay on as if reluctant to leave. **Remain** means to stay or be left behind. (**Arrive** means to reach a place. **Depart*** means to leave.)

A-59 b An **occupation** is a job. A **profession** is a job requiring a high degree of training or education. (A **hobby** is an activity pursued for pleasure rather than money. A **responsibility** is a duty. An occupation or profession may involve many responsibilities.)

A-60 a **Proclaim** means to announce publicly. **Declare** means to make known or make clear. (**Decline** means to refuse. **Devise** means to form in the mind or to plan.)

A-61 b **Glitter** means to gleam or glisten with reflected light. **Sparkle** means to give off flashes of light. (**Gloom*** means darkness, dreariness, or sadness. **Surface** refers to the exterior or superficial aspect of something. A surface may glitter.)

A-62 b A **comment** is a note of explanation, observation, or illustration. A **remark** is a casual observation. (**Meaning** is the sense or significance of a word or statement. A **thought** is a mental activity, reflection, or idea.)

A-63 a **Convert** means to transform or to cause something to change. **Change** means to make different or to alter. (**Introduce** means to make known. **Retreat** means to pull back or withdraw.)

A-64 a **Persuade** means to induce someone to do something. **Convince** means to cause to believe something. (**Doubt** means to hesitate to accept as truth. **Relate** means to tell or narrate.)

A-65 c **Misery** means a condition of great unhappiness or extreme pain. **Suffering** means anguishing or sustaining loss. (**Acceptance** means receiving or agreeing. **Satisfaction*** means gratification of one's needs or desires.)

A-66 b A **rival** is a competitor. An **opponent** is a challenger or enemy. (A **contest** is a game or struggle between two or more players. A **player** is one who participates in a game.)

A-67 c **Readily** means immediately or graciously. **Willingly** means freely offered. (**Rarely** and **scarcely** mean seldom, barely, or hardly.)

A-68 b **Amuse** means to interest, please, or cheer. **Entertain** means to provide enjoyment or hospitality. (**Calm** means to ease or make quiet. **Instruct** means to teach or impart knowledge.)

A-69 a **Despise** means to look down on or dislike. **Reject** means to turn down or cast away as worthless; to disdain). (**Reply** means to answer. **Respect*** means to have high regard or appreciation for the value of something or someone.)

A-70 a **Attain** means to achieve a goal or earn a reward. **Accomplish** means to succeed or achieve the desired ending. (**Attempt** means to make an effort. **Fail*** means to be judged deficient or unsuccessful.)

A-71 c A **cure** is a successful treatment or means of healing. A **remedy** is a means of relief or corrective treatment. (A **disease** is a condition of ill health. An **infection*** is the result of contamination by disease-producing organisms.)

A-72 b An **endeavor** is a serious attempt or an occupation. An **effort** is the conscious exertion of energy. (**Effect** and **result** refer to the outcome of an action.)

A-73 a **Invent** means to devise or create. **Conceive** means to form a concept of or to imagine. (**Conclude** means to end or terminate. **Conform** means to resemble or correspond to specifications.)

NOTE: Exercises **A-74** through **A-97** contain words with multiple meanings. Remind students to read all four words before defining the given word and to make their definitions fit the general category for each exercise.

A-74 b A **peer** (noun) is an equal in talent, rights, or social rank. An **equal** is someone with the same talent, rights, or rank as another. (**Chief** is the highest in rank. A **superior** is one with higher or greater talent or rank.)

A-75 a **Peer** (verb) means to look searchingly. **Gaze** means to look steadily. (**Listen** means to be attentive in order to hear. **Seek** means to search or look for something.)

A-76 c **Project** (verb) means to design or outline. **Plan** means to determine a method or design for attaining an objective. (**Proceed** and **continue** mean to follow the established method in an ongoing action.)

A-77 a A **project** (noun) is a task or assignment. An **enterprise** is an undertaking, especially of a difficult task. (An **ideal** is a concept of perfection. A **judgement** is a reasoned decision or opinion, usually an interpretation of the law.)

A-78 c **Project** (verb) means to transmit, fling, or discharge. **Shoot** means to discharge a missile from a weapon. (**Conclude** means to form a judgement about. [There are other meanings, but this meaning sets the stage for **A-82**.] **Receive** means to take into one's hands or possession.)

A-79 a **Project** (verb) means to describe future conditions or try to determine the outcome in advance. **Forecast** means to prophesy or to anticipate an event or condition. (**Prove** means to show to be true or genuine by evidence or argument. **Solve** means to find the answer.)

A-80 a   **Conclusion** means the working out of an arrangement. **Agreement** means a promise, contract, or settlement. (**Argument** and **negotiation** both refer to processes that may be used to reach a conclusion or agreement.)

A-81 a   **Conclusion** refers to the final state of something. **Finish** refers to the end or termination of something. (**Outset*** refers to the beginning of something. **Route** refers to a course, road, or way.)

A-82 b   **Conclusion** means a determination or decision. **Judgement** means a legal decision or an opinion reached through reasoning. (**Fact** means something that can be proven true. **Reason** is a motive for an action, thought, or belief.)

A-83 b   **Gather** means to bring together in one place or group. **Assemble** means to come together or congregate. (**Announce** means to make known publicly or officially. **Scatter*** means to disperse.)

A-84 c   **Gather** means to deduce or infer. **Understand** means to become aware of or to conclude. (**Confuse** means to perplex, perturb, or bewilder. **Misrepresent** means to give an incorrect or false impression.)

A-85 a   **Gather** means to pick or harvest, as in crops or eggs. **Collect** means to assemble items into a single group or place. (**Discover** means to find out or come upon for the first time. **Disperse*** means to scatter in various directions.)

A-86 a   A **class** (noun) is a category of persons or things with shared characteristics. A **group** is a number of individuals having some unifying relationship. (A **member** is a person within a class or group. A **pupil** is a member of a class in school.)

A-87 c   A **class** refers to a specific category of objects or persons. **Type** also refers to a specific kind, category, or class. (A **characteristic** is a distinctive feature or trait that serves as the basis for classification. A **member** is one who belongs to a particular society, club, class, or category.)

A-88 c   **Class** (verb) means to assign to a category. **Sort** means to arrange according to characteristics. (**Calculate** means to determine by mathematical processes or to compute. **Count** means to itemize or call off one by one.)

A-89 b   **Class** means of a high grade or caliber. **Quality** can refer to high status. (**Item** refers to a single unit within a category. **Volume** refers to the quantity or amount of something, not to its grade or quality.)

A-90 b   A **share** (noun) is a specific part or percent, usually belonging to one person. A **portion** is an allotted part or share of something. (A **collection** is a group or accumulation of objects. **Weight** is a measure of heaviness.)

A-91 a   **Share** (verb) means to determine and give out portions. **Divide** means to separate into portions. (**Prevent** means to keep from happening. **Retain** means to keep or hold.)

A-92 c   **Common** means shared equally among all. **Public** means of, pertaining to, or affecting all of the people. (**Individual*** means belong to a single person. **Private*** means not for public use.)

A-93 a   **Common** means of or relating to the community at large. **General** means involving or affecting the whole. (**Restricted*** means available only to specific groups of people. **Specific*** means distinct and plainly set apart.)

A-94 b   **Common** means plain or usual. **Ordinary** means average or undistinguished. (**Exceptional*** and **remarkable*** mean uncommon or unusual.)

A-95 a **Common** means lacking refinement or quality. **Cheap** means having a low cost or value. (**Valuable*** and **worthy*** mean precious, costly, or of high value.)

A-96 c **Tear** means to move with haste and energy. **Rush** means to hasten or hurry. (**Creep*** means to move slowly. **Remain** means to stay.)

A-97 b **Tear** means to pull apart by force, leaving jagged edges. **Split** means to separate forcibly into parts in a continuous, straight, lengthwise direction. (**Repair*** means to fix or restore to good condition. **Sustain** means to maintain or keep up.)

FOLLOW-UP REFERENT

When might you need to recognize a word that can be substituted for another given word?

Examples: following directions; understanding others' oral or written communication; crossword puzzles or word games; vocabulary or comprehension tests; understanding advertisements and catalog descriptions

CURRICULUM APPLICATION

Language Arts: synonym exercises; vocabulary enrichment; avoiding overused words and trite expressions in compositions; paraphrasing/summarizing written or spoken sentences, paragraphs, or passages; using knowledge of word parts to determine meaning of compound words; using knowledge of prefixes and suffixes to build or comprehend new words

Mathematics: recognizing key words that indicate proper function or order in word problems; reading and understanding directions for solving mathematics problems; recognizing face and place values of numbers; recognizing and using equivalent values of money, time, or measurement

Science: following directions for performing experiments; determining meaning of unfamiliar words using textual definitions or synonym clues

Social Studies: paraphrasing or summarizing key concepts; building content vocabulary using textual definitions or synonym clues; identifying parallel or similar functions of different governmental levels

Enrichment Areas: increasing vocabulary from pleasure reading, e.g., clues from context; recognizing foreign language vocabulary by similarity to native language words; following directions in creative activities, e.g., a work of art, a dance, or a musical composition

SYNONYMS—SUPPLY

STRAND: Verbal Similarities and Differences   **PAGES:** 9–10

ADDITIONAL MATERIALS

Transparency of student workbook page 9
Washable transparency marker

INTRODUCTION

In the previous lesson you selected a synonym for a given word from a group of three words.

OBJECTIVE
In these exercises you will supply as many synonyms as you can think of for a given word.

DEMONSTRATION/EXPLANATION
Project exercise **A-98** from the transparency of page 9.
   What does the word QUANTITY mean?
Answer: The amount, measurement, or number of something.
   What single words can you think of that mean the same as quantity?
Possible answers: Amount, sum, number, measurement, size, volume, extent, proportion.
List all answers on the transparency, encouraging students to use each in an example sentence and to discuss which are closest in meaning to the given word.

GUIDED PRACTICE
EXERCISES: **A-99, A-100, A-101**
When the students have had sufficient time to complete these exercises, encourage them to use the demonstration methodology above as they discuss and defend their answers.
ANSWERS:
A-99   *plunge:* dive, leap, dip, thrust, immerse, submerge, charge, lurch, pitch

A-100   *melt:* thaw, liquefy, dissolve, dispel, fade, evaporate, blend, fuse, soften

A-101   *plead:* beg, appeal, beseech, implore, petition, solicit

INDEPENDENT PRACTICE
Assign exercises **A-102** through **A-121**.

DISCUSSION TIPS
List all student answers on the transparency. Encourage students to discuss which synonyms are closest in meaning to the given word and to explain why other synonyms may be less precise. Answers provided by the authors should be modified and tailored to the vocabulary level and needs of the students. If students tend to be satisfied with one or two synonym choices, the teacher may need to provide cues to stimulate further answers. You may also wish to go through the exercises on two consecutive days to allow students to discover additional synonyms for each given word. Pay particular attention to words that have more than one possible definition or that may be used as various parts of speech. Encourage students to use each given word in an example sentence, then to substitute suggested synonyms for the given word.

ANSWERS
A-102   *oath:* promise, vow, pledge, affirmation, affidavit

A-103   *crease:* fold, wrinkle, pleat, ridge, rumple, crimp

A-104   *horror:* (fear) terror, fright, dread, apprehension, aversion, revulsion
                (cruelty) outrage, inhumanity, crime, atrocity, torment

A-105   *flaw:* (n.) defect, mistake, error, blemish, fault, imperfection, weakness
                (v.) mar, harm, weaken, deface, disfigure

A-106   *verse:* poetry, rhyme, measure, stanza, passage

A-107   *lengthen:* stretch, extend, protract, expand, increase

A-108   *competition:* (personal) rivalry, contention, opposition, struggle
                    (event) contest, match, tournament

A-109   *assist:* (v.) aid, help, collaborate, cooperate, support

            (n.) hand, boost, aid, help, support, cooperation

A-110   *retain:* keep, maintain, hold, memorize, remember

A-111   *imagine:* (pretend) daydream, envision, visualize, fantasize, invent

            (presume) assume, suppose, guess, infer, suspect

A-112   *pursue:* follow, chase, persist, seek

A-113   *corridor:* hall, passageway, aisle, road

A-114   *savage:* untamed, uncivilized, fierce, brutal, wild, barbaric, violent, primitive

A-115   *profession:* (occupation) business, field, vocation, career, position,

            (statement) declaration, announcement, confession, pledge

A-116   *rescue:* save, recover, salvage, liberate, free, release

A-117   *quarrel:* (n.) argument, dispute, conflict, disagreement, objection, contention

            (v.) argue, bicker, disagree, contend

A-118   *sketch:* draw, drawing, outline, summarize, skit, draft (copy)

A-119   *sole:* (only) exclusive, lone, solitary

            (underside, as of a shoe) bottom

A-120   *uncommonly:* rarely, unusually, infrequently, scarcely, exceptionally, supremely

A-121   *contribute:* (give) donate, grant, present, endow

            (advance) influence, forward, promote

FOLLOW-UP REFERENT

When do you find it necessary or useful to be able to provide a synonym for a given word?

Examples: following directions; understanding oral or written communication; crossword puzzles or cryptograms; vocabulary or comprehension tests; choosing words to fit a particular audience or occasion

CURRICULUM APPLICATION

Language Arts: synonym exercises; vocabulary enrichment; avoiding overused words and trite expressions; paraphrasing or summarizing written or spoken sentences, paragraphs, or passages; using knowledge of word parts to determine meaning of compound words; using knowledge of prefixes and suffixes to build or comprehend new words; recognizing denotative and connotative meanings

Mathematics: recognizing key words that indicate the proper function or order in word problems; reading and understanding directions for mathematics problems; recognizing face and place value of numbers; recognizing and using equivalent values of money, time, or measurement

Science: following directions for experiments; determining the meaning of unfamiliar words using textual definitions or synonym clues; making specific statements

Social Studies: paraphrasing or summarizing key concepts; building content vocabulary using textual definitions or synonym clues; identifying parallel or similar functions of different governmental levels

Enrichment Areas: increasing vocabulary from pleasure reading, e.g., clues from context; recognizing foreign language vocabulary by similarity to native language; following directions in creative arts, e.g., a work of art, a dance, or a musical composition

SYNONYMS AND ANTONYMS—SELECT

STRAND: Verbal Similarities and Differences   **PAGES:** 11–12

ADDITIONAL MATERIALS
Transparency of student workbook page 11
Washable transparency marker

INTRODUCTION
In earlier lessons you selected or supplied synonyms or antonyms for specific given words.

OBJECTIVE
In these exercises you will select two words. One should have a meaning similar to the given word (synonym), and a second should have a meaning opposite to the given word (antonym).

DEMONSTRATION / EXPLANATION
Project the **EXAMPLE** from the transparency of page 11.

In this example, you are given the word STOOP and four other words—STRETCH, BEND, and CRAWL. You are to select one of the word choices as an antonym, and one as a synonym for the given word. What does the word STOOP mean?

Answer: To bend the body forward or downward, or to walk or stand in that position. Students may arrive at other definitions, but this one most closely fits the category of the four word choices.

Look for a word which has a meaning opposite to STOOP. When you have selected the antonym, mark an "A" above it. STRETCH, meaning to make tense, tighten, or extend to full length, has been marked with an A in this example.

Indicate the antonym.

Next check the other choices to determine which of the remaining words is most similar in meaning to the given word. When you have selected the synonym, mark an "S" above it. BEND, meaning to make or become crooked or curved, appears to be the word choice closest in meaning to STOOP and is marked with an S. When you stoop down, your posture becomes curved and your back is bent.

Indicate the synonym.

Confirm your answers by checking to see how—or if—the remaining words are related to the given word. CRAWL means to move on one's hands and knees. Although crawling, like bending, requires stooping, it also involves motion from place to place. Neither bend nor stoop indicates any relocation of the body. RELAX means to slacken, loosen, or make less tense. It is related to stretch, rather than to stoop; stretching is often relaxing.

GUIDED PRACTICE
EXERCISES: **A-122, A-123, A-124**
When the students have had sufficient time to complete these exercises, encourage them to use the demonstration methodology above as they discuss and defend their answers.
ANSWERS:
A-122   A: d, youthful; **S:** b, elderly

Aged means ancient or advanced in years. An antonym would mean not old. **Youthful** means being or acting young. A synonym would mean old. **Elderly** refers to later life or those past middle age. (**Ambitious** means desiring success. **Healthy** means being in generally good physical and mental condition.)

A-123   **A:** b, construct; **S:** c, destroy

Wreck means to damage badly or ruin. An antonym would mean to repair or build. **Construct** means to build. A synonym would mean to ravage, shatter, or demolish. **Destroy** means to ruin the structure or existence of something. (**Attempt** means to try. **Direct** means to control or manage.)

A-124   **A:** a, gaze; **S:** b. glimpse

Glance means a quick look. An antonym would mean a stare or long look. **Gaze** means to look steadily. A synonym would mean a short look. **Glimpse** means a momentary look. (**Gloss** refers to the luster of a polished surface. **Glow** means to give off light without flaming.)

INDEPENDENT PRACTICE
Assign exercises **A-125** through **A-148**.

DISCUSSION TIPS
Encourage students to verbalize their reasons for choosing each answer and to explain why the other words are less precise. Class discussion is a valuable technique for having students share their acquired knowledge. The brief definitions given in the answers should be modified and tailored to the vocabulary level and needs of the students. These cues, also followed in the detailed answers, encourage the discussion procedure demonstrated.

1. Recognize and pronounce given word.
2. Define given word.
3. Define antonym.
4. Select antonym answer.
5. Define synonym.
6. Select synonym answer.
7. Eliminate detractors for confirmation.

ANSWERS
A-125   **A:** d, similar; **S:** c, opposite

Contrary means a fact or condition at odds with another. An antonym would mean compatible or alike. **Similar** means having a close resemblance. A synonym would mean incompatible or different. **Opposite** means reversed in character or opinion. (**Changeable** means varying. **Exact** means clear and complete in every detail, precise.)

A-126   **A:** c, stimulating; **S:** a, dull

Boring means unexciting or uninteresting. An antonym would mean exciting or interesting. **Stimulating** means inciting activity or growth. A synonym would mean discouraging. **Dull** means producing little or no interest. (**Lengthy** means long lasting, but not necessarily boring. **Tragic** means sorrowful or disastrous.)

A-127   **A:** c, release; **S:** b, grasp

Clasp means to hold or grip firmly. An antonym would mean to drop or let go. **Release** means to let go. A synonym would mean to keep. **Grasp** means to seize firmly with the hand. (**Agree** means give consent. **Select** means choose.)

A-128   **A:** b, graceful;   **S:** a, clumsy

Awkward means uncoordinated, inconvenient, or unpleasant. An antonym would mean coordinated, convenient, or pleasant. **Graceful** means limber, supple, and attractive. A synonym would mean stiff, graceless, or inelegant. **Clumsy** means ungraceful or cumbersome. (**Steady** means unwavering. **Straight** means unbent. Both words often associated with graceful.)

A-129   **A:** d, unnecessary;   **S:** a, basic

Essential means necessary, fundamental, or indispensable. An antonym would mean incidental, trivial, or optional. **Unnecessary** means not required. A synonym would mean required. **Basic** means vital. (**Distinct** means well-defined. **Terminal** means a boundary, limit, or end.)

A-130   **A:** c, include;   **S:** d, overlook

Omit means to leave out or to neglect. An antonym would mean to add or to remember. **Include** means to involve or take in. A synonym would mean to ignore or exclude. **Overlook** means to fail to notice. (**Edit** means to revise, delete, or add. **Direct** means to point out or indicate.)

A-131   **A:** d, stingy;   **S:** b, generous

Liberal means progressive, tolerant, lavish, or casual. An antonym would mean conservative, bigoted, cheap, or strict. **Stingy** means unwilling to share, spend, or give. A synonym would mean spending or giving freely. **Generous** means unselfish with time, money, or objects. (**Financial** means concerning money or wealth. **Possessed** means owned or controlled.)

A-132   **A:** a, dull;   **S:** d, sharp

Keen means fine, astute, or enthusiastic. An antonym would mean blunt, dense, or apathetic. **Dull** means blunt, stupid, or boring. A synonym would mean edged, smart, or interesting. **Sharp** means intelligent or having a finely honed edge. (**Even** means smooth, but not necessarily sharp. **Extra** means spare or additional.)

A-133   **A:** a, advance;   **S:** d, withdraw

Retreat means to fall back or escape. An antonym would mean to move forward or engage. **Advance** means to go or bring forward. A synonym would mean to go backward. **Withdraw** means to remove, depart, or retire. (**Establish** means to bring into existence. **Prepare** means to get ready.)

A-134   **A:** a, associate;   **S:** c, opponent

A **rival** is a competitor or foe. An antonym would mean a partner or friend. An **associate** is a colleague or fellow employee. A synonym would mean an adversary. An **opponent** is a challenger or an enemy. (A **guest** is a visitor. A **subject** is a person under the control or power of another.)

A-135   **A:** d, neglectful;   **S:** b, considerate

Attentive means mindful or thoughtful. An antonym would mean indifferent or thoughtless. **Neglectful** means careless or inattentive. A synonym would mean careful or observant. **Considerate** means kind or thoughtful of others. (**Attractive** means appealing or charming. **Deceptive** means misleading or dishonest.)

A-136   **A:** a, barely;   **S:** d, totally

Altogether means completely, collectively, or wholly. An antonym would mean partly, separately, or somewhat. **Barely** means scarcely or slightly. A synonym would mean fully or completely. **Totally** means entirely. (**Considerably** means substantially or abundantly. **Practically** means nearly or virtually.)

A-137 **A:** a, ease; **S:** b, exertion

Effort means an expenditure of energy or an attempt. An antonym would mean a lack of energy or an abstention. **Ease** means with little effort or naturally. A synonym would mean with great effort or unnaturally. **Exertion** means requiring power or strength. (**Goal** refers to the objective toward which effort is directed. **Outcome** refers to the result of effort.)

A-138 **A:** c, fearlessness; **S:** d, fright

Dread means anxiety or terror. An antonym would mean confidence or courage. **Fearlessness** means bravery or without fear. A synonym would mean cowardly or fearful. **Fright** means feeling alarm or fear. (**Alertness** means readiness or watchfulness. **Caution** means with care or prudence.)

A-139 **A:** a, future; **S:** d, preceding

Former means past or previous. An antonym would mean present or yet to come. **Future** means a time after the present. A synonym would mean a time before the present. **Preceding** means going before in time, place, or rank. (**Never** means not at any time. **Often** means frequently or repeatedly.)

A-140 **A:** c, permit; **S:** d, prohibit

Forbid means to inhibit, restrain, or disallow. An antonym would mean to encourage or allow. **Permit** means to allow or give consent. A synonym would mean to deny or withhold. **Prohibit** means to disallow or deny permission. (**Discourage** means to cause to lose hope or to express disapproval. **Judge** means to decide, resolve, or appraise.)

A-141 **A:** c, preserve; **S:** b, destruct

Destroy means to tear down or ruin. An antonym would mean to build up, improve, or maintain. **Preserve** means to protect or maintain. A synonym would mean to attack or demolish. **Destruct** means to wreck. (**Damage** means to injure or harm— less severe than destroy. **Treat** means to protect from wear or to repair damage.)

A-142 **A:** a, attract; **S:** c, repulse

Repel means to force back, chase away, resist, or disgust. An antonym would mean to draw forward or please. **Attract** means to draw or interest. A synonym would mean to drive away or spurn. **Repulse** means to drive back or offend. (**Challenge** means to invite to compete or to question. **Sustain** means to uphold or support.)

A-143 **A:** c, doubtful; **S:** b, dependable

Reliable means faithful or worthy of confidence. An antonym would mean unfaithful or untrustworthy. **Doubtful** means uncertain or questionable. A synonym would mean certain or unquestionable. **Dependable** means loyal and trustworthy. (**Conceivable** means possible or thinkable. **Occasional** means happening randomly or without pattern.)

A-144 **A:** d, obscure; **S:** b, evident

Obvious means well-defined or perceptible. An antonym would mean unclear or concealed. **Obscure** means vague or indistinct. A synonym would mean clear or distinct. **Evident** means easily perceived or recognized. (**Acceptable** means favorably received. **Possible** means capable of happening.)

A-145 **A:** d, temporarily; **S:** b, lastingly

Permanently means enduringly, endlessly, or always. An antonym would mean briefly or seldom. **Temporarily** means briefly, transiently, or short-lived. A synonym would mean continuously or long-lived. **Lastingly** means continually or for a long time. (**Currently** means happening presently. **Sometimes** means happening occasionally.)

A-146 **A:** d, unauthorized; **S:** a, approved

Official means formal, sanctioned, or authentic. An antonym would mean casual, unapproved, or invalid. **Unauthorized** means unsanctioned. A synonym would mean legally allowed. **Approved** means formally confirmed or consented to. (**Favorable** means affirmative or advantageous. **Leading** means most influential or significant.)

A-147 **A:** d, subsequent; **S:** b, preceding

Prior means taking precedence in time, order, or importance. An antonym would mean coming after in time, order, or importance. **Subsequent** means following in time, order, or place. A synonym would mean to go before a particular time, order, or place. **Preceding** means coming before in time, rank, or order. (**Instant** refers to a particular point in time. **Present** means current.)

A-148 **A:** b, complex; **S:** d, uncomplicated

Simple means easy, plain, honest, or innocent. An antonym would mean difficult, fancy, insincere, or worldly. **Complex** means complicated or sophisticated. A synonym would mean basic or free from elaboration. **Uncomplicated** means easily understood. (**Complete** means finished or whole. **Observable** means capable of being seen.)

FOLLOW-UP REFERENT

When might you want or need to recognize a synonym for a given word?

Examples: following directions; understanding what others are saying; crossword puzzles or word games; vocabulary or comprehension tests; recognizing verbal relationships

When might you want or need to recognize an antonym for a given word?

Examples: solving crossword puzzles; giving directions; reversing directions for disassembling or reassembling models or appliances; vocabulary or comprehension tests; recognizing verbal relationships

CURRICULUM APPLICATION

Language Arts: antonym or synonym exercises; vocabulary enrichment; avoiding overused words and trite expressions in compositions; paraphrasing/summarizing written or spoken sentences, paragraphs, or passages; using knowledge of word parts to determine meaning of compound words; using knowledge of prefixes and suffixes to build or comprehend new words

Mathematics: recognizing key words that indicate proper function or order in word problems; reading and understanding directions for mathematics problems; recognizing face and place value of numbers; recognizing and using equivalent values of money, time, or measurement

Science: following directions in performing experiments; using textual definitions or synonym clues to determine meaning of unfamiliar words; making specific statements

Social Studies: paraphrasing or summarizing key concepts; building content vocabulary using textual definitions or synonym clues; identifying parallel or similar functions among different governmental levels

Enrichment Areas: increasing vocabulary from pleasure reading, e.g., clues from context; recognizing foreign language vocabulary by similarity to native language; following directions for creative activities, e.g., a work of art, a dance, or a musical composition

SYNONYMS AND ANTONYMS—SUPPLY

STRAND: Verbal Similarities and Differences   **PAGES:** 13–14

ADDITIONAL MATERIALS
Transparency of student workbook page 13
Washable transparency marker

INTRODUCTION
In the previous lesson you selected a synonym and an antonym for a given word from a group of four words.

OBJECTIVE
In these exercises you are given a word and are to supply as many synonyms and antonyms as you can think of for that word.

DEMONSTRATION / EXPLANATION
Project exercise **A-149** from the transparency of page 13.
    What does BOLD mean? Think of as many synonyms and meanings as you can.
Possible answers: Brave, fearless, self-assured, rude, or colorful. Write the responses in the synonym column, asking the class to confirm each answer.
    Now think of words which can be antonyms for BOLD. Look at each word you listed as a synonym, and try to think of a word that means the opposite.
Possible answers: Cowardly, fearful, timid, polite, or colorless. Write the responses in the antonym column, again asking the class to confirm each answer.

GUIDED PRACTICE
EXERCISES: **A-150, A-151, A-152**
When the students have had sufficient time to complete these exercises, encourage them to use the demonstration methodology above as they discuss and defend their answers.
ANSWERS:

		SYNONYMS	ANTONYMS
A-150	*shout*	yell, call, scream, cry	whisper, murmur
A-151	*choose*	pick, select	reject, refuse
A-152	*seldom*	occasionally, rarely	always, often, continually

INDEPENDENT PRACTICE
Assign exercises **A-153** through **A-164**.

ANSWERS

		SYNONYMS	ANTONYMS
A-153	*defend*	protect, guard	attack, oppose
A-154	*tilted*	slanted, inclined, sloping	level, even, straight, upright
A-155	*liberty*	freedom, independence	slavery, restraint
A-156	*profit*	gain, earnings, return, benefit	loss, expense, cost
A-157	*accept*	agree, receive, take	reject, refuse, deny
A-158	*proper*	correct, right, decent	improper, rude, vulgar, wrong

A-159	*dispute*	argument, quarrel	agreement, pact, treaty
A-160	*scarcely*	hardly, barely	totally, completely
A-161	*risk*	danger, chance, dare	safety, security
A-162	*consequence*	result, outcome	cause, origin
A-163	*remember*	recall, recollect	forget, omit
A-164	*lessen*	decrease, lower, reduce	increase, raise, inflate

DISCUSSION TIPS

List all answers on the transparency. Encourage the students to discuss which of the suggested synonyms and antonyms are closest in meaning to the given word and to explain why the others may be less precise. No teacher (or author) can think of as many possible answers as a group of students can. Be accepting of all answers if the student can explain the rationale behind them. Do not just accept an answer, however, even if it's right. Make students explain all answers. Encourage them to explore more than one possible answer by suggesting, discussing, and arguing about possible answers. Continue this process until the students are convinced they have correct and complete (or most nearly so) answers. Answers provided by the authors should be modified and tailored to the vocabulary level and needs of the students.

FOLLOW-UP REFERENT

When might you need to provide a word that means the same as a given word?

Examples: giving clear written or oral directions; understanding others or interpreting for others; crossword puzzles or word games; vocabulary or comprehension tests; seeing relationships between words

When might you need to provide a word that means the opposite of a given word?

Examples: solving crossword puzzles; giving directions; reversing directions when reassembling or disassembling models or appliances; vocabulary or comprehension tests

CURRICULUM APPLICATION

Language Arts: antonym and synonym exercises; vocabulary enrichment; avoiding overused words and trite expressions in compositions; paraphrasing or summarizing written or spoken sentences, paragraphs, or passages; using knowledge of word parts to determine meaning of compound words; using knowledge of prefixes and suffixes to build or comprehend new words; recognizing denotative and connotative meanings; debating or expressing a concurring or opposite opinion

Mathematics: SYNONYMS—recognizing key words that indicate proper function or order in word problems; reading and understanding directions for mathematics problems; recognizing face and place values of numbers; recognizing and using equivalent values of money, time, or measurement; ANTONYMS—recognizing and using inverse operations; using fractions and reciprocals; recognizing set and set complements; checking basic arithmetic problems by reverse processes

Science: SYNONYMS—following directions in performing experiments; determining meaning of unfamiliar words by using textual definitions or synonym clues; ANTONYMS—recognizing reversed processes in experiments; accurately describing differences between two objects or concepts; disassembling and reassembling motors, gears, or models

Social Studies: SYNONYMS—paraphrasing or summarizing key concepts; building content vocabulary using textual definitions or synonym clues; identifying parallel or similar functions among different governmental levels; ANTONYMS—contrasting topographic or geographic areas; locating and expressing contrasting details when comparing topics

Enrichment Areas: increasing vocabulary from pleasure reading, e.g., clues from context; recognizing foreign language vocabulary by similarity to native language words; developing directions for creating a work of art or performing a dance; accurately expressing the similarities and/or differences between two pieces of music, two works of art, two dances, or two athletic activities

HOW ARE THESE WORDS ALIKE?—SELECT

STRAND: Verbal Similarities and Differences

PAGES: 15–17

ADDITIONAL MATERIALS
Transparency of student workbook page 15
Washable transparency marker

INTRODUCTION
In previous lessons you chose or supplied antonyms and/or synonyms for given words.

OBJECTIVE
In these exercises you will identify significant similarities between two terms.

DEMONSTRATION/EXPLANATION
Project exercise **A-165** from the transparency of page 15.
Each exercise contains two terms for comparison. In A-165 you are given the words COPYRIGHT and PATENT and several statements in a column to the right. You are to read each statement and determine whether or not it is true of both given words. Do both COPYRIGHT and PATENT apply to novels?
Answer: No, novels are books, and only copyright applies to books; patent applies to concepts, objects, or machines.
Do both words apply to inventions?
Answer: No, patent applies to inventions; copyright applies to written work. If the student defines "invention" in the broader sense of innovative ideas, then both terms could apply.
Do both words refer to items recorded by a government agency?
Answer: Yes, written works are given an ISBN number; patents are granted by the US Patent Office. Underline sentence **c** on the transparency.
Do both words refer to items that protect legal rights to new ideas?
Answer: Yes, copyrights protect authors and patents protect inventors against piracy of their work. Underline sentence **d** on the transparency.

GUIDED PRACTICE
EXERCISES: **A-166, A-167, A-168**
When the students have had sufficient time to complete these exercises, encourage them to use the demonstration methodology above as they discuss and defend their answers.
ANSWERS:
A-166 b; **A-167** a, c; **A-168** a, b

INDEPENDENT PRACTICE
Assign exercises **A-169** through **A-177**.

DISCUSSION TIPS
Encourage students to discuss their answers and to explain the areas of difference between the two words. Don't assume that all students followed the same reasoning because they arrived at the same answer. Question several students. Some may not know how they arrived at the answer; many times the student gives an intuitive answer. The teacher's role is to help students discover and verbalize the thought processes they followed to arrive at their answer.

ANSWERS
A-169 a, c; **A-170** c; **A-171** a, b; **A-172** a, c; **A-173** b, c;
A-174 a, c; **A-175** a, b; **A-176** b, c; **A-177** b

FOLLOW-UP REFERENT
> *When might you need to determine how two things are alike and how they are different by applying descriptive statements?*

Examples: finding items in a supermarket, hardware store, mall directory, telephone book yellow pages, or classified ads; locating related topics in text books, reference books, or card catalogs; grouping files on a computer disk; making value judgements given different situations, e.g., right/wrong, good/bad; playing word games; test-taking skills, especially essay or objective tests; critical-writing skills

CURRICULUM APPLICATION
Language Arts: choosing proper reference books when researching reports; recognizing parts of speech or types of literature; using an index or table of contents to locate information in books; organizing and writing compare and contrast statements, paragraphs, or papers; recognizing denotative and connotative words or phrases

Mathematics: recognizing numerical or geometrical properties; evaluating or comparing geometric shapes for type and congruence; interpreting word problems and different forms of statistical presentations relating to the same data, e.g., charts, graphs

Science: recognizing and naming attributes of different types of plants, animals, rocks, elements, physical phenomena, clouds, winds, stars, planets; evaluating the characteristics of biological and physical processes

Social Studies: comparing types of architectural structures, governmental divisions, or community institutions according to their function or other attribute; evaluating similarities and differences between particular historical events, eras, people, institutions, or artifacts

Enrichment Areas: recognizing and naming the attributes of types of dance, art, or music; naming functions and attributes of different tools in art, shop, or home economics

HOW ALIKE AND HOW DIFFERENT?

STRAND: Verbal Similarities and Differences   **PAGES:** 18–19

ADDITIONAL MATERIALS
Transparency of student workbook page 18
Washable transparency marker

INTRODUCTION

In the previous lesson you selected phrases which were true of two terms.

OBJECTIVE

In these exercises you will describe how two given terms are alike and how they are different.

DEMONSTRATION/EXPLANATION

Project exercise **A-178** from the transparency of page 18.

In this exercise you are given the words BUSH and VINE. These words name items that are alike in some ways and different in others. How are they alike?

Answer: Both have roots, branches, and leaves. Both are generally smaller than trees. Some bushes and some vines bear fruit.

How are they different?

Answer: A bush is typically low and spreading, with branches starting near the root; a vine is typically long and thin, with branches starting further from the root. Bushes grow into an upright shrub or clump; vines grow into long, slim, creeping plants. A bush supports its own weight; a vine supports itself by entwining around structures or other plants. Bushes spread; vines climb. Bushes usually have one set of roots; vines frequently grow new roots wherever they touch the ground.

GUIDED PRACTICE

EXERCISES: **A-179, A-180**

When the students have had sufficient time to complete these exercises, encourage them to use the demonstration methodology above as they discuss and defend their answers.
ANSWERS:

A-179 garbage/trash

ALIKE: Both are wastes that must be collected and disposed of.

DIFFERENT: Garbage refers to food waste; trash refers to product (paper, plastic, glass, metal) waste.

A-180 borrow/steal

ALIKE: Both refer to possession of something that belongs to another.

DIFFERENT: Borrowing indicates with the owner's permission; stealing means taking without permission. Borrow suggests intent to return to the owner; steal doesn't. Borrowing is legal; stealing isn't.

INDEPENDENT PRACTICE

Assign exercises **A-181** through **A-185**.

DISCUSSION TIPS

Do not assume that something is too obvious to be discussed. Several students may perceive things differently. Be sure that students of varying ability contribute to each analysis, and that all students who have a different answer are comfortable enough to share it with the class. There are many possible answers. Again, write down all answers, but question the rationale behind each. Encourage students to give real-life examples of their areas of similarity and difference for each word and to explore several possible answers. Promote discussion and argument among the members of the class until all students are convinced that the class has arrived at complete and correct answers.

ANSWERS

A-181 alarm/signal
ALIKE: Both concern the sending and receiving of information.
DIFFERENT: A signal is used primarily to convey directional or factual information; an alarm is used primarily to warn, alert, or arouse.

A-182 lumber/wood
ALIKE: Both are tree products, both can be purchased, and both may be used as building materials.
DIFFERENT: Wood is the general class or material; lumber is wood that has been specially dressed to use as building material. Wood, in its natural form, can be burned for fuel; lumber is not primarily used as fuel. Wood regenerates naturally from trees; lumber must be man-made.

A-183 author/composer
ALIKE: Both create new works in their field.
DIFFERENT: An author writes literary works; a composer writes music.

A-184 explorer/pioneer
ALIKE: Both travel into unknown territory and take risks.
DIFFERENT: Explorers travel, chart, and/or claim territories, then return to their point of origin; pioneers travel to an unknown area with the idea of settling there.

A-185 artery/vein
ALIKE: Both carry blood and are part of the circulatory system.
DIFFERENT: Arteries carry blood from the heart; veins carry blood to the heart.

FOLLOW-UP REFERENT

When might you need to identify two things by describing how they are alike and how they are different?

Examples: finding items in a supermarket, hardware store, mall directory, telephone book yellow pages, or classified ads; locating related topics in text books, reference books, or card catalogs; grouping files on a computer disk; making value judgements in different situations, e.g., right/wrong, good/bad; test-taking, especially essay or objective tests; critical-writing skills; describing unfamiliar items or terms by comparison to familiar ones

CURRICULUM APPLICATION

Language Arts: choosing proper reference books when researching reports; recognizing parts of speech or types of literature; using an index or table of contents to locate information in books; organizing and writing compare and contrast statements, paragraphs, or papers; recognizing denotative and connotative words or phrases

Mathematics: recognizing numerical or geometrical properties; evaluating geometric shapes for type and congruence; interpreting word problems, interpreting different forms of statistical presentations, e.g., charts, graphs, pictures, schedules, relating to the same data

Science: naming and recognizing attributes of different types of plants, animals, rocks, elements, physical phenomena, winds, stars, or planets; evaluating characteristics of biological and physical processes

Social Studies: comparing types of architectural structures, governmental divisions, geographic areas, or community institutions according to their functions or other attributes; evaluating similarities and differences between historical events, eras, people, institutions, or artifacts

Enrichment Areas: recognizing and naming the attributes of types of dance, art, or music; naming functions and attributes of different tools in art, shop, or home economics

DENOTATION AND CONNOTATION

STRAND: Verbal Similarities and Differences   **PAGES:** 20–22

ADDITIONAL MATERIALS
Transparency of student workbook page 20
Washable transparency marker

INTRODUCTION
In the previous lesson you discriminated between two terms by stating how they were alike and how they were different.

OBJECTIVE
In these exercises you will identify slight differences in meaning or implication between two given terms and indicate the basic meaning that can be applied to both terms.

DEMONSTRATION / EXPLANATION
The basic meaning of a word is known as its denotation. Denotation is a word or phrase that is neutral and is usually the same from person to person. A word's connotation, on the other hand, may differ from person to person. Connotation refers to the positive or negative interpretations or implications of words.

Project the **EXAMPLE** from the transparency of page 20.

In this example you are given the words CHEAP and INEXPENSIVE. Although both refer to something with a low cost or value, they are slightly different in meaning or implication. CHEAP implies that the item has a poor quality, in addition to a low price or value. INEXPENSIVE implies that the item has an acceptable quality, along with a low price or value. Which of these two words would you consider more positive or flattering?

Answer: Inexpensive is a more flattering term than cheap.

On the first two pages of this lesson, you will underline the word with the more positive or complimentary connotation.

Indicate the underlined answer on the transparency.

What basic meaning, or denotation, can be applied to each of these two words?

Answer: Having a low price. Indicate the answer on the transparency.

You will write the basic meaning for the two given words on the line to the right. The third page of this lesson is to be completed in a slightly different manner. In those exercises you will mark each of three given words—the basic word B, the more positive word P, and the more negative word N.

GUIDED PRACTICE
EXERCISES: A-186 through **A-189, A-207** through **A-209**
When the students have had sufficient time to complete these exercises, encourage them to use the demonstration methodology above as they discuss and defend their answers.
ANSWERS:

NOTE: In exercises ***A-186*** *through* ***A-189****, the word with a more positive connotation is* <u>underlined</u>*; the denotative word or phrase is in* ALL CAPITAL LETTERS.

A-186   criminal, <u>delinquent</u>, LAWBREAKER

A-187 homemaker, housewife, CARETAKER IN THE HOME

A-188 guard, security officer, PROTECTOR

A-189 job, profession, OCCUPATION

A-207 aroma P , odor B , stench N

A-208 cozy P , cramped N , small B

A-209 antique P , old B , worn N

INDEPENDENT PRACTICE

Assign exercises **A-190** through **A-206** and **A-210** through **A-215**.

DISCUSSION TIPS

Use of connotative words is a key factor in recognizing euphemisms and, in some instances, in distinguishing fact from opinion. Students may give example sentences, substituting the connotative form for the basic meaning of the word, to show softened or strengthened interpretations of the same basic meaning. For some sentences the distinction between the connotative form and the basic meaning conveys the difference between fact and opinion. Encourage students to identify the inferred meaning in either case. Encourage students to use their own experiences when identifying positive or negative connotations given to basic meanings of words.

ANSWERS

NOTE: In exercises **A-190** through **A-206**, the word with a more positive connotation is underlined; the denotative word or phrase is in ALL CAPITAL LETTERS.

A-190 blemishes, pimples, SKIN PROBLEM

A-191 lady, female, WOMAN

A-192 dentures, false teeth, ARTIFICIAL TEETH

A-193 pre-owned, used, NOT NEW

A-194 garbage, refuse, WASTE

A-195 kid, youth, YOUNG PERSON

A-196 homely, ugly, UNATTRACTIVE

A-197 disagreement, squabble, ARGUMENT

A-198 pity, sympathy, EMPATHY

A-199 dead, deceased, WITHOUT LIFE

A-200 income, revenue, MONEY

A-201 house, residence, DWELLING

A-202 crippled, handicapped, PHYSICALLY IMPAIRED

A-203 disadvantaged, needy, LACKING

A-204 male, gentleman, MAN

A-205 belly, stomach, ABDOMEN

A-206 choose, prefer, SELECT

A-210 curious P , nosy N , questioning B

A-211 skinny N , slender P , thin B

A-212 behold P , observe B , spy N

A-213 chat N , confer P , talk B

A-214 immature N , young B , youthful P

A-215 little B , miniature P , puny N

FOLLOW-UP REFERENT

When might you need to decide among basic meanings, positive connotations, and negative connotations for a word?

Examples: making value judgements given different situations, e.g., compliment/insult, right/wrong, good/bad; critical-writing skills; recognizing persuasion and propaganda in advertisements, newspaper columns or editorials, and political appeals

CURRICULUM APPLICATION

Language Arts: organizing and writing compare and contrast statements, paragraphs, or papers; recognizing and using desired denotative and connotative words or phrases; distinguishing fact from opinion

Mathematics: —————

Science: distinguishing between factual observation and interpretation

Social Studies: distinguishing between factual observation and interpretation

Enrichment Areas: recognizing interpretative comments or writings regarding the merits of a dance, a musical performance, a work of art, a play, or a sporting event

VERBAL SEQUENCES

WORD BENDERS

STRAND: Verbal Sequences

ADDITIONAL MATERIALS
Transparency of student workbook page 23
Washable transparency marker

INTRODUCTION
In earlier lessons you supplied words which were synonyms or antonyms for a given word.

OBJECTIVE
In these exercises you will complete a letter-sequence puzzle. The answers will be words that have a stated relationship to given words.

DEMONSTRATION/EXPLANATION
Project the Word Bender from the top of the transparency of page 23.

The object of a Word Bender is to make a list of words by changing only certain letters from the previous word. Each new word will have two or more letters the same as those in the word above it. You determine which letters to keep and which to change by following two rules:

1. If there is a blank line, the letter that belongs on that line is the same as the letter directly above it.

2. If there is a circle, the letter that belongs in that circle is different from the letter directly above it.

Point to columns three and four.

Notice that all spaces in the two columns under the S and T in POST are blank lines. How can you determine what letters belong in those blanks?

Answer: Follow the first rule: "If there is a blank line, the letter that belongs on that line is the same as the letter directly above it."

What letters would you put in these blanks?

Answer: An **S** in each third column blank, and a **T** in each fourth column blank.

Looking at the second row, you now have: "Circle, blank, S, T and found." What letter belongs in the blank?

Answer: **O**; the same as the one directly above it. Write an **O** in the blank.

Now the phrase reads: "Circle, O, S, T and found." What letter can be put in the circle to complete the phrase?

Answer: An **L** would make the phrase "LOST AND FOUND." Write an **L** in the circle.

For the third row...

Point as you read.

...you have: "Not first but blank, circle, S, T." What letter belongs in the blank?

Answer: **L**; the same as the one directly above it. Write an **L** in the blank.

Now you have: "Not first but L, circle, S, T." What letter can be put in the circle to complete the phrase?

Answer: **A** completes the phrase "NOT FIRST BUT LAST." Write an **A** in the circle.

For the Word Benders in this lesson, you will need words that are either antonyms (opposite) or synonyms (similar) to a clue word.

GUIDED PRACTICE
EXERCISE: **B-1**
Give students sufficient time to complete these exercises. Then, using the demonstration methodology above, have them discuss and explain their choices.

NOTE: Throughout this section, letters shown in italics are given in the workbook exercise. Circled letters will appear in parenthesis ( ). Letters in regular type are brought down from the letter directly above.

ANSWER:

B-1					
D	*A*	*R*	*K*		GLOOM
(P)	A	R	K		PLAYGROUND
P	A	R	(T)		PORTION
(C)	A	R	T		WAGON
C	A	R	(E)		TEND
(P)	A	R	E		PEEL
(F)	A	R	E		PRICE
F	A	R	(M)		TILL
(H)	A	R	M		HURT
(W)	A	R	M		ENTHUSIASTIC
W	(O)	R	M		FISH BAIT
W	O	R	(N)		THREADBARE
(T)	O	R	N		RIPPED
(B)	O	R	N		BIRTH
B	(U)	R	N		SINGE
(T)	U	R	N		SPIN

INDEPENDENT PRACTICE
Assign exercises **B-2** through **B-9.**

DISCUSSION TIPS
Encourage students to define each word as they discuss their answers. Although these exercises may appear easy, the sequencing skills learned will help students in the more difficult lessons that follow. Students learn thinking skills at different times, in different ways, and at different rates. They will enlarge their concept as they have more practice with a particular skill. Allow everyone a chance to contribute to discussion, and demand that others be good listeners. Eventually, even the shyest students will enter into the discussion process as they feel less threatened and grow more involved.

ANSWERS

B-2									
			S	*I*	*G*	*N*	*A*	*L*	WARNING
	(D)	(E)	S	I	G	N			PATTERN
	D	E	S	I	(R)	(E)			WANT
	D	E	S	(E)	R	(T)			ABANDON
	D	E	S	E	R	(V)	(E)		EARN
	(R)	E	S	E	R	V	E		EXTRA
(C)	(O)	(N)	S	E	R	V	E		PRESERVE
C	O	N	(C)	E	R	(N)			INTEREST
(D)	*(I)*	*(S)*	*C*	*E*	*R*	*N*			RECOGNIZE

B-3

			V	I	S	I	T	O	R		GUEST
			V	I	S	I	(O)	(N)			SIGHT
(P)	(R)	(O)	V	I	S	I	O	N			CONDITION
	P	R	O	V	I	(D)	(E)				GIVE
	P	R	O	(D)	(U)	(C)	E				MAKE
	P	R	O	D	U	C	(T)				OUTPUT
	P	R	O	(J)	(E)	C	T				PLAN
	P	(E)	(R)	(F)	E	C	T				FLAWLESS

B-4

			M	O	T	I	O	N		MOVEMENT
			(N)	O	T	I	O	N		IDEA
			(A)	(C)	T	I	O	N		DOING
(F)	(R)	A	C	T	I	O	N			PART
F	(U)	(N)	C	T	I	O	N			WORK
(J)	U	N	C	T	I	O	N			JOINING
	(S)	(T)	(A)	T	I	O	N			DEPOT
	(N)	A	T	I	O	N				COUNTRY
	(R)	A	T	I	O	N				PORTION
	R	A	T	I	O					FRACTION

B-5

			P	R	E	V	E	N	T	STOP
		(I)	(N)	V	E	N	T			DEVISE
		I	N	(T)	E	N	(D)			MEAN
		(E)	(X)	T	E	N	D			STRETCH
	P	(R)	(E)	T	E	N	D			IMAGINE
	(C)	(O)	(N)	T	E	N	D			MAINTAIN
	C	O	N	T	E	(S)	(T)			GAME
	C	O	N	(S)	E	(N)	T			PERMISSION
(P)	(R)	(E)	S	E	N	T				GIFT
	R	E	S	(I)	(D)	(E)				LIVE
	P	R	E	S	I	D	E			DIRECT
	P	R	E	S	(U)	(M)	E			GUESS
	R	E	S	U	M	E				CONTINUE
(C)	(O)	(N)	S	U	M	E				DEVOUR
	C	O	N	(F)	U	(S)	E			PUZZLE

B-6

		R	E	F	R	A	I	N		WITHHOLD
		(S)	(T)	R	A	I	N			STRESS
(R)	(E)	S	T	R	A	I	N			HOLD BACK
R	E	S	T	R	(I)	(C)	(T)			LIMIT
(D)	(I)	S	T	R	I	C	T			SECTION
D	I	S	T	R	(U)	(S)	T			SUSPECT
D	I	S	T	R	(E)	S	(S)			MISERY
D	I	S	T	R	(A)	(C)	(T)			CONFUSE

(R)	*(E)*	*T*	*R*	*A*	*C*	*T*					RECEDE
	(R)	(E)	A	C	T						RESPOND
		R	E	A	C	(H)					ARRIVE
	(P)	R	E	A	C	H					URGE
(A)	*(P)*	*P*	*R*	*(O)*	*A*	*C*	*H*				COME NEAR

B-7

		D	*E*	*M*	*A*	*N*	*D*				REQUEST
(C)	(O)	(M)	M	A	N	D					FOLLOW
		C	O	M	M	(E)	N	D			REBUKE
(R)	(E)	C	O	M	M	E	N	D			WARN
		C	O	M	M	E	N	(C)	(E)		FINISH
		C	O	M	M	(O)	N				UNUSUAL
		C	O	M	M	O	(T)	(I)	(O)	(N)	QUIET
(P)	(R)	(O)	M	O	T	I	O	N			DEMOTION
		P	R	O	M	O	T	(E)			DISCOURAGE
		P	*R*	*O*	*M*	*(P)*	*T*				TARDY

B-8

I	*N*	*C*	*L*	*U*	*D*	*E*	ELIMINATE
(E)	(X)	C	L	U	D	E	ADMIT
E	X	C	L	(A)	(I)	(M)	WHISPER
(R)	(E)	C	L	A	I	M	DISPOSE
R	E	C	L	(I)	(N)	(E)	STAND
(D)	E	C	L	I	N	E	ACCEPT
D	*E*	*C*	*L*	*(A)*	*(R)*	*E*	DENY

B-9

R	*E*	*S*	*T*	*R*	*A*	*I*	*N*	FREE
R	E	S	T	R	(I)	(C)	(T)	ALLOW
(D)	(I)	S	T	R	(A)	C	T	CONCENTRATE
D	I	S	T	R	(E)	(S)	(S)	COMFORT
D	I	S	T	R	(U)	S	(T)	BELIEVE
D	I	S	T	(I)	(N)	(C)	T	BLURRED
D	I	S	T	(A)	N	C	(E)	VICINITY
D	*I*	*S*	*T*	*A*	*N*	*(T)*		NEAR

FOLLOW-UP REFERENT
When might you need to add letters to complete a word or phrase?
Examples: word games, crossword puzzles, or cryptograms

CURRICULUM APPLICATION
Language Arts: spelling puzzles or games; using prefixes and suffixes to create antonyms; spelling and dictionary exercises; recognizing and using possessives or plurals; completing rhyme schemes

Mathematics: organizing numbers using concepts and categories; adding prefixes and suffixes to root words, e.g., equal/unequal/equality, or division/dividend/divisor; filling in missing or unknown numerals to complete mathematics problems

Science: recognizing, using, and understanding scientific prefixes and suffixes; completing conclusion sentences for experiments; filling in missing parts of a partially listed series, e.g., planets, circulatory system, digestive system, or life cycles

Social Studies: recognizing, using, and understanding prefixes and suffixes common to the study of history, geography, or government, e.g., decade = ten years, biannual = twice a year; filling in the missing parts of a cycle, e.g., how a bill becomes a law, judicial procedures

Enrichment Areas: adding words or notes to change or complete a song, e.g., a parody of a familiar work; vocabulary enrichment exercises in foreign languages; musical improvisations on a theme; adding or subtracting steps in a dance routine

FOLLOWING DIRECTIONS

STRAND: Verbal Sequences

PAGES: 31–38

ADDITIONAL MATERIALS
Transparency of student workbook page 31
Washable transparency marker

INTRODUCTION
Every day you follow directions of some kind. When you ask someone how to get somewhere, they usually give you directions. Sometimes you have to read directions, as when you take a test, fill out a form, or put together a model.

OBJECTIVE
In these exercises you will select the figure that represents given directions.

DEMONSTRATION / EXPLANATION
Project exercise **B-10** from the transparency of page 31.
The directions for this exercise state, "Draw a square. Use the top side of the square as the base of a half circle." Which of the drawn figures contain squares?
Answer: **a**, **b**, and **c**.
Which have some other shape on the top side?
Answer: **a**.
Look at figure a. Is the top side of the square used as the base (bottom) of a half circle?
Answer: Yes.
How do figures b and c differ from the directions?
Answer: Figure **b** has two (not one) half circles on the bottom (not the top) of the square. In figure **c** the side (not the top) of the square is used as part of the half circle.

GUIDED PRACTICE
EXERCISE: **B-11**
Give students sufficient time to complete this exercise. Then, using the demonstration methodology above, have them discuss and explain their choice.
ANSWER:
B-11 c   The triangle is above, not to the left, of the circle in figure **a**. In figure **b** the triangle is to the right, not to the left, of the circle.

INDEPENDENT PRACTICE
Assign exercises **B-12** through **B-25**. (This lesson may be divided **B-12** through **B-15** and **B-16** through **B-25**.)

DISCUSSION TIPS
Ask students to explain why each alternate answer is incorrect. As an extending activity, you may wish to have them practice writing a statement to accurately describe each of the alternate figures. Encourage students to use correct geometric terminology in class discussion and in written statements.

ANSWERS
B-12 c   In figure **a** the square is below the rectangle and the rectangle is not definitely larger than the square. In figure **b** the square is larger than the rectangle.

B-13 b   In figure **a** the rectangle is outside both the circle and the triangle. In figure **c** the triangle is inside the rectangle, rather than vice versa.

B-14 b   The final rectangle in figure **a** is turned the wrong direction; it is wide rather than tall. In figure **c** both rectangles are on the same side of the square, not opposite sides. In figure **d** the rectangles are on touching sides, not opposite sides.

B-15 c   The figure shown in **a** has the square drawn on the wrong side, using the right side of the rectangle rather than left side. Figure **b** shows the rectangle divided with a top left to lower right diagonal, rather than a top right/lower left diagonal.

B-16   **a** lower right; **b** lower left; **c** upper left

B-17   **a** lower right; **b** upper right; **c** lower left; **d** upper left

B-18   **a** striped; **b** checked; **c** striped; **d** black; **e** above

B-19   **a** center; **b** right; **c** upper right; **d** left

B-20   **a** center; **b** lower right; **c** above

B-21   **a** small triangle; **b** large square; **c** small triangle

B-22   **B-23**   **B-24**   **B-25**

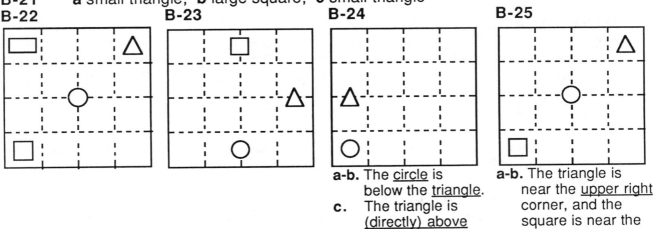

a-b. The <u>circle</u> is below the <u>triangle</u>.
c. The triangle is <u>(directly) above</u> the circle.

a-b. The triangle is near the <u>upper right</u> corner, and the square is near the <u>lower left</u> corner.

FOLLOW-UP REFERENT
When might you need to describe a given location?
Examples: assembling games or models; using computer-tabulated questionnaires or answer sheets; games involving location or direction; giving directions to someone; following directions regarding placement or location of answers; following movement, direction, or placement instructions for square dances, drills, or sports; setting a table

CURRICULUM APPLICATION

Language Arts: diagraming sentences; placing words in sentences according to function or slot, e.g., subject, direct object; following directions for formatting written materials, e.g., business or personal letters, outlines, essays; writing descriptive or instructive paragraphs; proofreading and editing

Mathematics: plotting or connecting graph coordinates; constructing geometric shapes or figures by following directions

Science: plotting or reading a plot of an archaeological dig or ecological study area; seeing and describing strata in natural formations

Social Studies: interpreting and constructing maps, graphs, time lines, or diagrams

Enrichment Areas: test taking; art, physical education, or dance activities involving position or location; following drill, marching band, or sports instructions involving location, direction, or movement

FOLLOWING DIRECTIONS—SUPPLY DESIGNS

STRAND: Verbal Sequences　　　　　　　　　　　　**PAGES:** 39–42

ADDITIONAL MATERIALS
Transparency of student workbook page 39
Washable transparency marker

INTRODUCTION
In previous exercises you matched written directions to the shape that was drawn to represent them.

OBJECTIVE
In these exercises you will draw a group of shapes that accurately reflect given directions.

DEMONSTRATION/EXPLANATION
Project exercise **B-26** from the transparency of page 39.
You are given the following written directions for drawing a group of shapes on a dot grid: "Draw a large rectangle. Draw a small square at the center of the rectangle. Draw a circle near the lower left corner and a triangle near the upper right corner." What should you do first?
Answer: Draw a large rectangle near the center of the grid. Have a student volunteer draw the shape on the transparency.
What is the next step?
Answer: Draw a small square at the center of the rectangle. Have the student continue.
What is the next step?
Answer: Draw a circle near the lower left corner. Have the student continue the drawing.
What is the last step?
Answer: Draw a triangle near the upper right corner.
Does this group of shapes accurately represent the given directions?
Have students confirm the answer by checking each statement against the drawing.

ANSWER: (B-26)

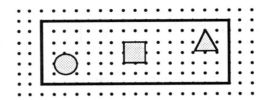

GUIDED PRACTICE
EXERCISE: **B-27**
Give the students sufficient time to complete this exercise. Then, using the demonstration methodology above, have them discuss and explain their drawings.
ANSWER:

B-27

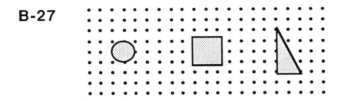

INDEPENDENT PRACTICE
Assign exercise **B-28** through **B-32**.

DISCUSSION TIPS
Encourage students to compare and discuss their answers. Students should recognize that all drawings need not be the same. Individual drawings, although different, may still accurately follow the directions.

ANSWERS
B-28

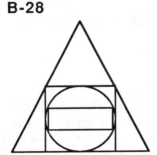

B-29   **B-30**   **B-31**   **B-32**

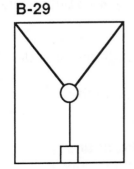 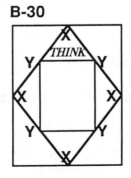 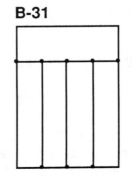 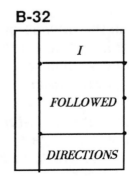

FOLLOW-UP REFERENT

When might you need to follow a series of steps, rules, or directions?
Examples: following directions for errands or chores; following multistep directions for assembling models and toys; following written directions for crafts, sewing, cooking, cleaning, or household repairs; following rules, steps, or directions in games, sports, or stage presentations; creating or using a computer program

CURRICULUM APPLICATION

Language Arts: reading and following directions involving order, number, or position
Mathematics: correctly following multistep operations in solving problems; following the correct sequence in solving word problems
Science: following a series of instructions in laboratory experiments or demonstrations
Social Studies: reading or creating maps, charts, graphs, time lines, or schedules
Enrichment Areas: following classroom procedures; art, drama, music, or physical education activities involving order, number, or position; following dance, drill, or sports instructions

WRITING DIRECTIONS

STRAND: Verbal Sequences   **PAGES:** 43-45

ADDITIONAL MATERIALS

Transparency of student workbook page 43
Washable transparency marker

INTRODUCTION

In the previous lesson you drew and positioned shapes according to written directions.

OBJECTIVE

In these exercises you will reverse the process and write directions for drawing a given figure.

DEMONSTRATION/EXPLANATION

Project exercise **B-33** from the transparency of page 43.
   What shapes do you see in this figure?
Answer: A large circle, a square, and a triangle.
   Is anything special about the alignment of the shapes?
Answer: They are touching or inside one another.
   Is anything else special?
Answer: The bases (bottoms) of the square and triangle are the same line.
   Where is the large circle?
Answer: Outside the square.
   Where is the triangle?
Answer: Inside the square.
   You have described the figure, now you need to write directions for drawing it.
   Remember that the directions you write should provide another person with

the ability to produce a figure that is the same as the given figure. How should the directions begin?

Possible answer: Draw a large circle. As you write the directions on the transparency, have a student draw the figure on the chalkboard.

What should come next?

Possible answer: Inside the circle, draw a square that touches the circle in four points.

Should anything be added to insure that the square will be aligned like the one in the picture?

Possible answer: The bottom of the square should be horizontal.

What should come next?

Possible answer: Use the base (bottom) of the square as the base of the triangle.

What should come next to insure that the triangle will look like the one in the picture?

Possible answer: The top of the triangle should touch the square midpoint in the top line.

ALTERNATE: Draw a large circle. Inside the circle draw a large square touching the circle at four points. The bottom of the square should be horizontal. Draw a line from the lower left corner of the square to the middle of the top line of the square. Draw a line from the lower right corner of the square to the middle of the top line of the square.

ALTERNATE: Draw an equilateral triangle with the base (bottom) parallel to the bottom of the page. Use the base of the triangle as the base of a square that encompasses the triangle. Enclose these figures in a circle that touches the square at all corners.

GUIDED PRACTICE
EXERCISE: **B-34**

Give students sufficient time to complete this exercise. Then, using the demonstration methodology above, have them discuss and explain their choices. Have students read and discuss each other's directions.

ANSWER:

B-34   Draw a rectangle about three times as long as it is high. Use part of the top of the rectangle as the base of a second rectangle, which is just as tall as the first. The second rectangle should be about two-thirds as long as the first and centered. Use part of the top of this smaller rectangle as the base of a square, which is the same height as each of the two rectangles and centered at the top.

INDEPENDENT PRACTICE
Assign exercises **B-35** through **B-38**.

DISCUSSION TIPS
To extend this lesson as a listening-skill exercise, instruct students to create a design with two or three geometric shapes and write directions for drawing each design. Ask each student to read his/her directions aloud and instruct the class to draw the figure as directed. Compare drawings to confirm correct answers and to make suggestions regarding clarification of the directions. Encourage students to discuss their answers.

ANSWERS
B-35   Draw a right triangle with two equal sides. Place the right angle in the lower right corner. Locate the midpoint of each side, then connect these midpoints to form a square inside the triangle.

B-36   Draw a square. Locate the midpoints of the sides. Connect opposite midpoints to form four small squares. Use the top of the large square as the bottom of a rectangle. The rectangle should be as tall as one of the small squares.

ALTERNATE: Draw three equal rectangles stacked on top of one another. Draw a vertical line down the middle of the bottom two rectangles to form four squares.

ALTERNATE: Draw a large vertical (tall) rectangle. Mark points on both vertical sides one-third of the way from the top and bottom. Connect these points with two horizontal lines. Mark the midpoint of each rectangle on its base, then connect the three points with one vertical line to form four squares under the remaining rectangle.

B-37   Construct a rectangular figure three times as long as it is high by connecting three squares. Use the tops of the two squares on the right as the base of a right triangle. The height of the triangle should be the same as the length of its base. The line forming the triangle height should be on the right.

B-38   Draw a large square. Divide the square into two equal rectangles by drawing a vertical line down the center. Divide the left rectangle into two small rectangles by drawing another centered vertical line. Divide the remaining large rectangle on the right into two squares.

FOLLOW-UP REFERENT

When might you need to provide directions for constructing something?

Examples: giving directions, e.g., building projects, assembling toys and bikes, creating craft or sewing projects, repairing household items; giving street directions; telling someone where something is located; writing a computer program for construction of a specific graphic

CURRICULUM APPLICATION

Language Arts: setting an established style for proofreading or editing manuscripts; standardizing formats for business letters, outlines, or essays; establishing layout designs for text; organizing and presenting demonstration speeches

Mathematics: creating geometry constructions and proofs; demonstrating and explaining solutions to mathematics problems

Science: preparing directions for scientific demonstrations; writing scientific processes

Social Studies: creating maps, graphs, or charts

Enrichment Areas: writing or presenting art, industrial arts, or vocational education procedures; developing directions for drill team performances or sports plays; creating stage directions for a dramatic presentation

STACKING SHAPES—SELECT

STRAND: Verbal Sequences   **PAGES:** 46–48

ADDITIONAL MATERIALS

Transparency of student workbook page 46

Shapes cut from colored paper (optional):
- four red squares
- two blue hexagons
- two yellow triangles

INTRODUCTION
In the previous lesson you practiced writing directions for duplicating specific arrangements of shapes or figures.

OBJECTIVE
In these exercises you will select the diagram which correctly represents a stated arrangement of stacked shapes.

DEMONSTRATION / EXPLANATION
Optional Demonstration:
Use the cutout paper shapes to build each of the following stacks: (**1**) square on triangle, (**2**) triangle on square, (**3**) hexagon on square, (**4**) square on hexagon. Hold each stack in place with a staple or paper clip. Hold up stack **1** for students to see.

Describe this stack of shapes.

Answer: The square is on the triangle (or the triangle is under the square). Hold up stack **2**.

Describe this stack.

Answer: The triangle is on the square (or the square is under the triangle). Hold up stack **3**.

Describe this stack.

Answer: The hexagon is on the square (or the square is under the hexagon). Hold up stack **4**.

Describe this stack.

Answer: The square is on the hexagon (or the hexagon is under the square). Place the four stacks, in order, so that the class can see them. (Prop them against a stack of books or tack them on the bulletin board.)

Which stack fits this description: "The square is under the hexagon"?

Answer: Stack **3**.

Which stack fits this description: "The square is on the triangle"?

Answer: Stack **1**.

Which stack fits this description: "The hexagon is under the square"?

Answer: Stack **4**.

Which stack fits this description: "The triangle is on the square"?

Answer: Stack **2**.

When you stack shapes, you can always see all of the shape that is on top of the stack. For example, in this stack...

Hold up stack **2**.

...you can see all of the triangle, but only part of the square. This tells you that the triangle is on the square. In these exercises, try to describe each stack from top to bottom.

Transparency Demonstration:
Project the lettered figure stacks from the bottom of the transparency of page 46.

Which stack matches the statement: "The circle is on the rectangle"?

Answer: **d.**

How do you know that the rectangle isn't on top?

Answer: If the white rectangle were on top, it would be completely visible.

Which stack matches the statement: "The rectangle is on the square"?

Answer: **f.**

How can you be sure that the rectangle is on top of the stack?

Answer: You can see all of the top shape and only part of the bottom shape. In this stack, you can see all of the rectangle and only part of the square, so the rectangle is on top.
> ***Which stack matches the statement: "The square is under the hexagon"?***

Answer: **c.**
> ***How can you be sure that the square is on the bottom of the stack?***

Answer: You can see all of the top shape and only part of the bottom shape. In this stack, you can see all of the hexagon and only part of the square, so the square is on the bottom.

GUIDED PRACTICE
EXERCISES: **B-41, B-42**
Give students sufficient time to complete these exercises. Then, using the demonstration methodology above, have them discuss and explain their choices.
ANSWERS: **B-41** a; **B-42** g

INDEPENDENT PRACTICE
Assign exercises **B-43** through **B-53**.

DISCUSSION TIPS
Encourage students to discuss and defend their answers. These exercises help develop inductive reasoning, visual imagery, visual discrimination, memory, and verbalization of figural concepts.

ANSWERS
B-43 g; **B-44** d; **B-45** b; **B-46** a; **B-47** h; **B-48** e; **B-49** c
B-50 f; **B-51** c; **B-52** b; **B-53** d

FOLLOW-UP REFERENT
> ***When might it be helpful to recognize the order in which representations of two- or three-dimensional objects have been arranged?***

Examples: assembling models or bikes; recreating crafts, sewing, or cooking projects; repairing household items; learning or recognizing pattern plays in sports; using a filing system in an office or at home; locating items, e.g., books in a library, items in a catalog or a supermarket; finding and recognizing errors in computer programs; recognizing and using organizational etiquette, e.g., receiving lines, buffet tables; collating materials

CURRICULUM APPLICATION
Language Arts: following directions in formatting outlines, letters, memos, or layouts; recognizing organizational structures, e.g., type or intent of paragraphs or compositions, organizations of word lists, indexes, or appendices in books
Mathematics: solving multistep problems; recognizing order or position of sequenced numbers or shapes; following geometric constructions and proofs
Science: following and recognizing multistep directions for experiments; recognizing, following, or explaining the sequence of a given system, e.g., circulatory system or electrical system; recognizing and explaining structural differences, e.g., organic and inorganic, mammals and reptiles, cirrus and altostratus clouds, shale and granite rocks
Social Studies: reading or constructing charts, graphs, or maps; determining structural differences in texts or other books, e.g., chronological order v. topical organization
Enrichment Areas: learning a sequence of dance, gymnastics, or skating movements; recognizing a sequence of musical movements; recognizing and following sequential procedures in art, industrial arts, or vocational education projects; learning marching band, drill team, or gymnastic pattern sequences

STACKING SHAPES—SUPPLY

STRAND: Verbal Sequences   **PAGES:** 49–53

ADDITIONAL MATERIALS
Transparencies of Transparency Master (TM) #1 and TM #2
        (All Transparency Masters are located at the end of this book.)
Washable transparency marker
Student handouts of TM #1 and TM #2 (optional)

INTRODUCTION
In the previous lesson you selected a stack of shapes that matched a descriptive statement.

OBJECTIVE
In these exercises you will draw stacks of shapes to represent a description.

DEMONSTRATION / EXPLANATION
Project exercise **A** from the top section of TM #1.
        If the triangle is on the circle, which shape will be completely visible?
Answer: The triangle.
        Which shape will be only partly visible?
Answer: The circle.
        How can you shade the shapes outlined on the transparency to show that the triangle is on the circle?
Answer: Shade in the triangle, as shown below.

Project exercise **B** from TM #1.
        Now the circle is half black. If the triangle is still on the circle, which shape will be completely visible?
Answer: The triangle.
        Which shape will be only partly visible?
Answer: The circle.
        How can you shade the shapes outlined on the transparency to show that the triangle is on the circle?
Pause for student response. Answer:

Project exercise **C** from TM #1.
        If the circle is on the triangle, which shape will be completely visible?
Answer: The circle.
        Which shape will be only partly visible?

Answer: The triangle.

How would you shade the shapes outlined on the transparency to show that the circle is on the triangle?

Pause for student response. Answer:

Now you will try a slight variation of these problems. Let's see if, given an outline of three or four shapes, you can darken some of the parts so the shapes appear to be stacked in a particular order.

Project exercise **A** from TM #2.

If the square is on both the triangle and the circle, which shape or shapes will be completely visible?

Answer: The square.

Which shape or shapes will be only partly visible?

Answer: The circle and triangle.

How can you shade the outline on the transparency to show that the square is on the circle and the triangle?

Pause for student response. Answer:

Project exercise **B** from TM #2.

If the triangle and the circle are both on the square, which shape or shapes will be completely visible?

Answer: The triangle and circle.

Which shape or shapes will be only partly visible?

Answer: The square.

How would you shade the outline on the transparency to show that the triangle and circle are on the square?

Pause for student response. Answer:

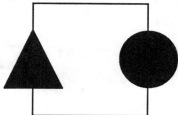

Project exercise **C** from TM #2.

If the triangle is on the square and the square is on the circle, which shape or shapes will be completely visible?

Answer: The triangle.

Which shape or shapes will be only partly visible?

Answer: The square and circle. Have a student volunteer shade the shapes to reflect the proper stacking. Answer:

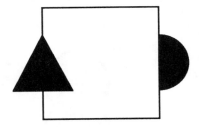

GUIDED PRACTICE
EXERCISES: **B-54, B-59**
Ask students to discuss their answers and to explain their solutions in detail.
ANSWERS:
B-54

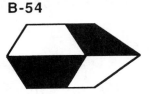

B-59

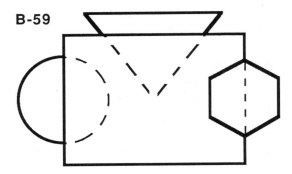

INDEPENDENT PRACTICE
Assign exercises **B-55** through **B-58** and **B-60** through **B-67**.

DISCUSSION TIPS
Encourage students to describe the location of each shape in terms of "on top of" rather than "under." This gives a recognizable sequence from the top to the bottom of a stack. Students should continue to discuss and explain their answers.

ANSWERS

B-55   **B-56**   **B-57**   **B-58**

B-60   **B-61**

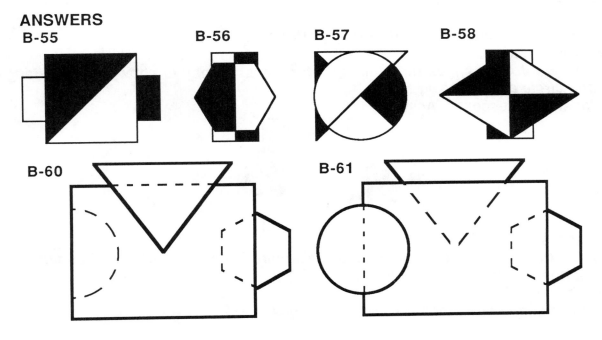

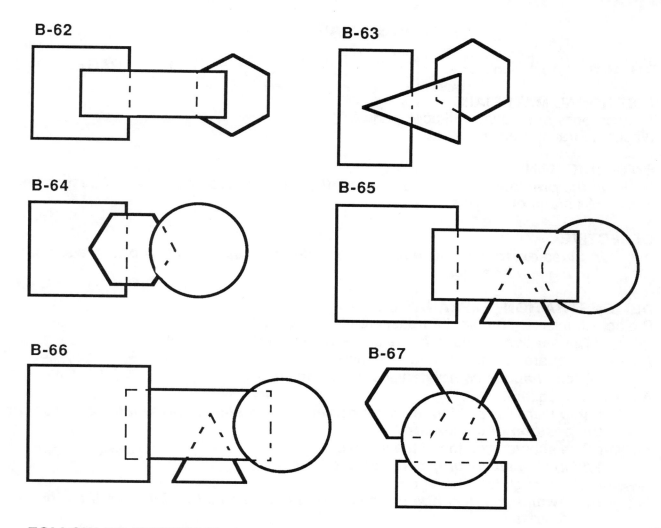

B-62　　　　**B-63**

B-64　　　　**B-65**

B-66　　　　**B-67**

FOLLOW-UP REFERENT

When might you need to follow directions for stacking or arranging something?

Examples: reshelving items, e.g., dishes, records, tools, books; following directions for errands or chores; assembling machinery, models, or toys; following directions for crafts, sewing, cooking, cleaning, or household repairs; arranging notebooks or projects according to specifications; computer programming; efficient arrangement of desk materials or stock inventory; any situation requiring making order out of chaos

CURRICULUM APPLICATION

Language Arts: understanding and following formatting directions, e.g., outlines, letters, memos, writing, essays, layouts

Mathematics: geometry constructions and proofs; arranging algebraic equations

Science: following sequential directions in science demonstrations or experiments; writing equations in chemistry or physics

Social Studies: reading or constructing charts, graphs, or maps

Enrichment Areas: following art, industrial arts, or vocational education procedures; visualizing and learning positions and movements for stage directions, marching band, gymnastics, or drill team formations

STACKING SHAPES—EXPLAIN

STRAND: Verbal Sequences   **PAGES:** 54–61

ADDITIONAL MATERIALS
Transparency of student workbook page 54
Washable transparency marker

INTRODUCTION
In the previous lesson you shaded diagrams to illustrate different descriptions of a stack of shapes.

OBJECTIVE
In these exercises you will write directions for stacking two or three shapes into a given arrangement.

DEMONSTRATION / EXPLANATION
Project exercise **B-68** from the transparency of page 54.
What shapes are used in the stack shown in this exercise?
Answer: A square, a triangle, and a hexagon.
Which shape is completely visible in the stack?
Answer: The square.
If you were describing the arrangement of this stack, how would you describe the position of the square?
Answer: The square is on top of the triangle.
Which shapes are only partly visible?
Answer: The triangle and hexagon.
How would you describe the position of the triangle in relation to the other two shapes?
Answer: The triangle is on top of the hexagon and under the square.
How can you describe the position of the hexagon?
Answer: The hexagon is under the triangle.
Can you think of a single sentence which would describe the stacking order of the three shapes in this figure?
Possible answers: The square is on top of the triangle, which is on top of the hexagon; **or**, the triangle is between the top square and the bottom hexagon; **or**, the hexagon is under the triangle, which is under the square. (The first definition is preferred, since it describes the stack in a sequential order from top to bottom.)

GUIDED PRACTICE
EXERCISES: **B-68, B-69**
Give students sufficient time to complete these exercises. Then, using the demonstration methodology above, have them discuss and explain their choices.
ANSWERS:
B-68 The hexagon is under the (**a**) <u>triangle</u>. The square is on top of the (**b**) <u>triangle</u>.
B-69 The (**a**) <u>circle</u> is the uppermost shape. The rectangle is (**b**) <u>under</u> the circle.

INDEPENDENT PRACTICE
Assign exercises **B-70** through **B-91**.

DISCUSSION TIPS
Encourage students to describe each stack from top to bottom and to discuss their answers using correct geometric terminology.

ANSWERS

B-70   The (**a**) <u>rectangle</u> is on top. The (**b**) <u>circle</u> is on the bottom. The (**c**) <u>triangle</u> is in between.

B-71   The circle is on top of the (**a**) <u>rectangle</u>. The circle is underneath the (**b**) <u>square</u>. The (**c**) <u>hexagon</u> is the uppermost shape.

B-72   The upper layer contains the (**a**) <u>square</u> and the (**b**) <u>hexagon</u>. The lower layer contains the (**c**) <u>triangle</u> and the (**d**) <u>circle</u>.

B-73   Place the circle on the square.

B-74   Place the triangle on the hexagon.

B-75   Place the triangle on the square.

B-76   Place the rectangle on the hexagon.

B-77   Place the right side of the circle on the center of the hexagon.

B-78   Place the circle on the center of the hexagon.

B-79   Place the rectangle on the center of the square.

B-80   Place the circle on the center of the square.

B-81   Place the midpoint of the bottom line of the square on the midpoint of the base of the triangle.

B-82   The circle is on the triangle, and the triangle is on the hexagon.

B-83   The triangle is on the circle, and the circle is on the rectangle.

B-84   The square is on the circle, and the hexagon is on the square.

B-85   The triangle is on the circle, and the circle is on the square.

B-86   The hexagon is on the circle, and the circle is on the square.

B-87   The square is on the rectangle, which is on the circle. The circle is on the triangle.

B-88   The triangle is on the rectangle, which is on the hexagon. The hexagon is on the circle.

B-89   The white circle is on the black circle, which is on the white square. The white square is on the black square. (Either size or color may be used to differentiate between the two circles and the two squares.)

B-90   The white triangle and the square are on the circle. The black triangle is on the square.

B-91   The rectangle is on the hexagon and the circle, and the circle is on the square.

FOLLOW-UP REFERENT
> **When might you need to explain how a series of objects has been arranged or organized?**

Examples: explaining constructions, e.g., models, projects, carpentry, electrical circuits; explaining or giving directions for craft, sewing, cooking, cleaning, or household repair projects; explaining how to find something in a library, store, stockroom, or workshop

CURRICULUM APPLICATION
Language Arts: organizing demonstration speeches; writing or presenting instructions for doing, constructing, or operating something

Mathematics: geometry constructions and proofs; arranging algebraic equations

Science: recognizing and stating instructions for scientific demonstrations or experiments; writing laboratory reports; arranging equations in chemistry or physics

Social Studies: explaining the organization of charts, graphs, schedules, or map legends; recognizing and explaining social or economic factors

Enrichment Areas: recognizing and explaining art, industrial arts, or vocational education procedures; explaining written music; writing directions or descriptions for dance, stage, gymnastic, or drill team formations

PRODUCE A PATTERN AND WRITE DESCRIPTIONS

STRAND: Verbal Sequences   **PAGES:** 62–63

ADDITIONAL MATERIALS
Transparency of student workbook page 62
Washable transparency marker

INTRODUCTION
In the previous lesson you described how shapes were stacked.

OBJECTIVE
In these exercises you will first produce a pattern of shapes then write a description of the arrangement.

DEMONSTRATION/EXPLANATION
Project exercise **B-92** from the transparency of page 62.
First you need to create a stack of shapes. For example, you might darken the rectangle and mark the outlines of the hexagon, square, and circle.
Produce a diagram that looks like this.

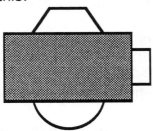

In this figure, which shape is completely visible?
Answer: The rectangle.
What can be said about the location of the rectangle in relation to the other three shapes?
Answer: The rectangle is on top of the other shapes.
Which shapes are only partly visible?
Answer: The hexagon, square, and circle
How might you describe the locations of these three shapes in relation to each other?

Answer: The hexagon is directly above the circle and to the left of the square at the top of the group; the square is to the right of and below the hexagon; the circle is directly below the hexagon and to the left of and below the square.

Can you write a description that would allow someone to visualize this group of shapes?

Answer: A hexagon, a square, and a circle are arranged in a group. The hexagon is at the top of the group, the square is lower than the hexagon and is at the right of the group, and the circle is to the left of and below the square. All three shapes are under a larger, dark rectangle. The rectangle covers about half of each shape.

GUIDED PRACTICE
EXERCISE: **B-93**
ANSWER: Answers will vary depending on how the students shade the patterns.

INDEPENDENT PRACTICE
Assign exercises **B-94** through **B-95**.

DISCUSSION TIPS
As an extension of this activity, have students exchange descriptions and draw their version of the classmate's explanation. Then ask the students to display the two diagrams. If the second drawing turns out to be different than the original, encourage the class to discuss the written description and to determine what may have led to the differences.

ANSWERS
Answers will vary depending on how students shade the patterns and how precisely they write their descriptions.

FOLLOW-UP REFERENT
When might you need to explain how you arranged or organized something?

Examples: explaining your organization of a filing system, school or work project, tool chest or work shop, or file arrangement on a computer disk; explaining an arrangement of flowers, books, clothing, furniture, or tools; explaining constructions, e.g., models, toys, crafts, gears, pulleys; explaining how or where to locate things, e.g., in a library, store, book, or workshop

CURRICULUM APPLICATION
Language Arts: organizing demonstration speeches; writing or presenting instructions for doing, constructing, or operating something

Mathematics: geometry constructions and proofs; arranging or explaining algebraic equations; explaining the process for arriving at a particular solution to a mathematics problem

Science: recognizing and stating multistep instructions for scientific demonstrations or experiments; writing laboratory reports; arranging or explaining chemistry or physics equations

Social Studies: explaining the organization of charts, graphs, schedules, or map legends

Enrichment Areas: recognizing and explaining art, industrial arts, or vocational education procedures; explaining written music; writing directions for stage, dance, or drill team formations; writing instructions for assembling an engine, motor, or other machine type

RECOGNIZING DIRECTION

STRAND: Verbal Sequences   **PAGES:** 64–66

ADDITIONAL MATERIALS
Transparency of student workbook page 64
Washable transparency marker

INTRODUCTION
In previous lessons you made or explained stacked shapes so others could understand the relative position of objects within the stacks.

OBJECTIVE
In these exercises you will use information to determine the direction you are facing and to identify the relative position of shapes as you change directions.

DEMONSTRATION / EXPLANATION
Project the diagram from the transparency of page 64.
You will imagine that you are facing first in one direction and then in another. Look at the lettered arrows in the diagram. Why does the arrow pointing upward have an N on it?
Answer: The N indicates that the arrow is pointing toward the direction north.
Why does the arrow pointing downward have an S on it?
Answer: It is pointing toward the direction south.
Why does the arrow pointing toward the left have a W on it?
Answer: To indicate that it is pointing toward the direction west.
Why does the arrow pointing toward the right have an E on it?
Answer: To indicate that it is pointing toward the direction east. Project the **EXAMPLE** from the transparency.
If you are standing so that the triangle shape is to your right and the hexagon shape is to your left, what shape are you facing?
Answer: The rectangle. Indicate the rectangle under the **FACING SHAPE** column.
What direction are you facing?
Answer: East. Indicate EAST under the **DIRECTION** column. Project exercise **B-96**.
Notice that you are not always given the same information. In exercise B-96, what information are you given?
Answer: Facing shape and shape on right.
What shape are you facing?
Answer: The hexagon.
What shape is to your right?
Answer: The rectangle.
If you are facing the hexagon, what direction are you facing?
Answer: North. Write NORTH in the **DIRECTION** column.
If you are facing the hexagon to the north and the rectangle is to your right, what shape is to your left?
Answer: The square. Draw a square in the **SHAPE ON LEFT** column.

GUIDED PRACTICE
EXERCISES: **B-97, B-98**

Give students sufficient time to complete these exercises. Then, using the demonstration methodology above, have them discuss and explain their choices.

ANSWERS:

NOTE: Answers to be provided by students are underlined throughout this section.

	DIRECTION	FACING SHAPE	SHAPE ON RIGHT	SHAPE ON LEFT
B-97	↓ S	△	☐	▭
B-98	W ←	☐	⬡	△

INDEPENDENT PRACTICE

Assign exercises **B-99** through **B-104**.

DISCUSSION TIPS

Encourage students to use specific geometric and directional terminology when stating and discussing their answers. These exercises lend themselves well to use of the IF-THEN logical connective (see student workbook, page 156).

ANSWERS

	DIRECTION	FACING SHAPE	SHAPE ON RIGHT	SHAPE ON LEFT
B-99	↗ NE	△	☐	◯
B-100	↘ SE	☐	▭	△
B-101	↙ SW	▭	◯	☐
B-102	↘ SE	■	◯	
B-103	NW ↖	●	☐	

B-104   SW

FOLLOW-UP REFERENT
When might you need to recognize changes in relative position?
Examples: following or creating maps; giving oral directions; using a compass or sextant to determine relative location on a map; orienteering or road rallies

CURRICULUM APPLICATION
Language Arts: providing directions to specific locations; writing descriptive paragraphs
Mathematics: spatial orientation exercises; locating and charting points on a graph
Science: using or creating maps to locate stars, planets, or land masses; tracking animal movements
Social Studies: constructing and interpreting maps; recognizing physical or political boundaries
Enrichment Areas: understanding, visualizing, or following stage directions; marking or following instructions for drill team or marching band formations

DESCRIBING LOCATIONS ON A GRID

STRAND: Verbal Sequences   **PAGES:** 67–70

ADDITIONAL MATERIALS
Transparency of student workbook page 67
Washable transparency marker

INTRODUCTION
In the previous lesson you used given information to identify how a change in direction affected the relative position of set objects.

OBJECTIVE
In these exercises you will use a grid to describe directions and locations.

DEMONSTRATION/EXPLANATION
Project exercise **B-105** from the transparency of page 67.
The first instruction for exercise B-105 tells you to put a 1 in the northeast corner of the grid.
Have a student volunteer mark the grid accordingly.
Why did you make the mark in that corner?
Answer: The upward arrow points north, and the arrow pointing to the right indicates east, so the **1** goes in the upper right (northeast) corner.
The next instruction says to mark a 2 in the southwest corner of the grid.
Have a second student mark the grid accordingly.
Why did you chose that corner?

Answer: The downward arrow points south, and the arrow pointing to the left indicates west, so the **2** goes in the lower left corner.

> *How can you describe the relative positions of the 1 and the 2?*

Answer: They are located in opposite corners of the grid.

> *The key word is "opposite." The 1 and the 2 are in opposite corners; 1 is in the northeast corner, and 2 is in the southwest corner. Do you hear the opposites in northeast and southwest? Do you hear the opposites in north**east** and south**west**?*

Indicate the opposite corners as you talk, then project exercise **B-106**.

> *For most exercises in this lesson, you will be asked to follow a path on this grid. As you create a path from point to point, move along the dashed lines and take the path with the least number of turns.*

GUIDED PRACTICE
EXERCISES: **B-105**, **B-106**
ANSWERS:
B-105

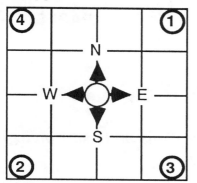

B-106 <u>four</u> units (along the top).

INDEPENDENT PRACTICE
Assign exercises **B-107** through **B-126**.

DISCUSSION TIPS
Emphasize directional relationships during class discussion, e.g., upward represents north, downward represents south, to the right is to the east, and to the left is to the west. Encourage students to use specific directions instead of up, down, left, and right.

ANSWERS

B-107 four units	**B-108** eight units	**B-109** four units	**B-110** four units
B-111 northwest	**B-112** southwest	**B-113** southeast	**B-114** northeast
B-115 to your right	**B-116** behind you		
B-117 southwest	**B-118** southeast	**B-119** northeast	**B-120** northeast
B-121 southwest	**B-122** northwest	**B-123** south	
B-124 southeast	**B-125** southwest	**B-126** northeast	

FOLLOW-UP REFERENT

> *When might you need to recognize general or relational directions?*

Examples: following or making maps; following or giving oral directions; using a compass or sextant to determine relative location on a map; participating in orienteering or road rally races; structural engineering; interior, architectural, or landscape design; organizing or interpreting traffic flow or traffic control

CURRICULUM APPLICATION

Language Arts: providing directions to specific locations

Mathematics: spatial orientation exercises; locating and charting points on a graph

Science: using a map to locate stars or planets; interpreting radar and sonar signals; tracking animal movements

Social Studies: constructing and interpreting maps

Enrichment Areas: understanding, visualizing, or following stage directions; marking or following instructions for gymnastics, drill team, or marching band formations; determining field or court positions from diagrams of patterned sports plays

DESCRIBING LOCATIONS USING MAPS

STRAND: Verbal Sequences   **PAGES:** 71–74

ADDITIONAL MATERIALS
Transparency of TM #3
Washable transparency marker

INTRODUCTION
In the previous lesson you practiced describing directions and paths on a grid.

OBJECTIVE
In these exercises you will describe locations on a map.

DEMONSTRATION/EXPLANATION
Project the map of **MINI-OPOLIS** from the transparency of TM #.
You will use this map of MINI-OPOLIS for these exercises. Whenever you are faced with a map of a new or unknown place, the first thing you should do is become familiar with the markings on the map. In this map of MINI-OPOLIS, what is shown on the left side of the map?
Answer: West Park. Indicate corresponding locations as students respond to the questions.
What is located on the right side of the map?
Answer: East Park.
What is located at the top of the map?
Answer: North Park.
What is located at the bottom of the map?
Answer: South Park.
What are the names of the avenues in MINI-OPOLIS?
Answer: First, Second, Third, Fourth, Fifth, and Sixth Avenues.
In what directions do the avenues run?
Answer: North and south.
What are the names of the streets in MINI-OPOLIS?
Answer: A, B, C, D, and E Streets.

In what direction do the streets run?

Answer: East and west.

> *Now that you are familiar with the map, you will locate some crossings. Mark a P where Third Avenue and B Street cross.*

Ask a student to mark the given intersections on the transparency. After other students verify each answer, have each student mark the answers in his or her book.

> *Mark a Q where Fifth Avenue and C Street cross.*

Pause for students' response.

> *Mark an R where First Avenue and E Street cross.*

Pause for students' response. Answers:

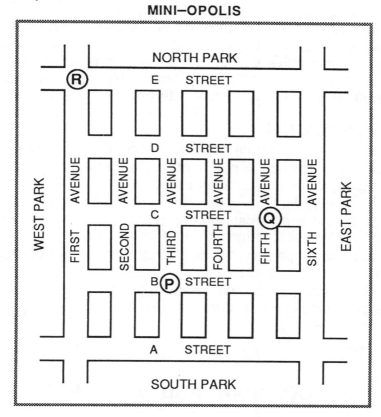

MINI—OPOLIS

GUIDED PRACTICE

EXERCISES: **B-127 a** and **b**

Give students sufficient time to complete these exercises. Then, using the demonstration methodology above, have them discuss and explain their choices.

ANSWERS:

B-127a   The **Q** is closest to East Park.

   b   The **R** is in the northwest corner.

INDEPENDENT PRACTICE

Assign exercises **B-128** through **B-135**.

DISCUSSION TIPS

Encourage students to discuss their answers. Do not assume that something is too obvious to be discussed. Students may perceive things differently. Test for understanding by questioning several students of varying abilities on each exercise.

ANSWERS
B-128   at the intersection of _P_ Street and _FOURTH_ Avenue;   **B-129** at the intersection of _B_ Street and _SECOND_ Avenue

B-130   at the intersection of _D_ Street and _THIRD_ Avenue;   **B-131** _three_ blocks
B-132 at the intersection of _B_ Street and _FOURTH_ Avenue;
B-133 _SECOND AVENUE_

B-134   _three_ blocks _east_ on _B_ Street and _two_ blocks _north_ on _SIXTH_ Avenue
B-135 _four_ blocks _north_ on _FIRST_ Avenue and _five_ blocks _east_ on _E_ Street

FOLLOW-UP REFERENT
When might you need to determine or describe a specific location?
Examples: following or making maps; following or giving oral directions; using a compass or sextant to determine relative location on a map; participating in orienteering or road rally races; structural engineering; interior, architectural, or landscape design; organizing or interpreting traffic flow or traffic control; interpreting radar and sonar signals

CURRICULUM APPLICATION
Language Arts: writing instructional papers; giving demonstration speeches

Mathematics: identifying particular points on a graph; describing an arrangement of geometric shapes; spatial orientation exercises

Science: stating or writing directions for constructing motors or gears; detailing the relative position of a star or planet; locating geophysical phenomena, e.g., fault lines, volcanos, natural gas or oil deposits; tracking animal movements

Social Studies: reading maps, graphs, or charts; describing geographic locations; charting ecological or topographic patterns

Enrichment Areas: creating or following pattern plays in team sports; describing the performance of a dance step or directions for creating an art project; writing or giving stage directions for a play

DESCRIBING LOCATIONS AND DIRECTIONS ON/WITH MAPS

STRAND: Verbal Sequences   **PAGES:** 75–81

ADDITIONAL MATERIALS
Transparency of TM #4
Washable transparency marker

INTRODUCTION
In previous lessons you used small maps and grids to locate and describe locations. Larger cities, however, are sometimes too big to show in detail on a single map. These large cities may be divided into sections, with each section being larger than a small town.

OBJECTIVE
In these exercises you will describe locations on a map of a city that has been divided into sections.

DEMONSTRATION/EXPLANATION

Project the transparency of TM #4.

> *Here you see a map of CAPITAL CITY. Before you begin working with the map, take a few minutes to look at the information it gives. Notice that the city seems to be divided into four sections. These sections are separated by Capital Avenue and Meridian Boulevard, and the city is surrounded by a road called the Beltway. CAPITAL CITY has four parks and two lakes. Locate them on the map and tell me their names.*

Answer: Northwest, Northeast, Southwest, and Southeast are the names of the parks. They are located in the corners corresponding to their names. The two lakes are West Lake and East Lake, located on the west (left) side of the map and the east (right) side of the map respectively.

> *What do you notice about all the streets that run north and south?*

Answer: They are named after letters of the alphabet.

> *What about the east-west streets?*

Answer: They are all numbered streets. Indicate NE 4th St. on the map.

> *Another thing that makes this map different from the others you've used is its use of abbreviations. What does the "St." here stand for?*

Answer: Street.

> *What do you think the "NE" stands for?*

Answer: Northeast.

> *In which section of CAPITAL CITY would you expect to find NW 3rd Street?*

Answer: The northwest (upper left) section.

> *Locate NW 3rd Street and draw a line along it.*

Have a student indicate the street and draw the line on the transparency. Ask all students to mark the answer in their books.

> *Now locate NW B Street and draw a line along it.*

Have another student indicate the street and draw the second line on the transparency, again asking all students to mark the street in their books.

> *Do these two streets share an intersection? Do they cross each other? If they do, mark a Q at their intersection.*

Pause as students locate the intersection, then ask a student to mark the transparency.

> *Now locate SE 1st Street and SE C Street. Draw a line along each.*

Have a student draw a line on the transparency and ask all students to mark the streets in their books.

> *If these two streets share an intersection, mark it with an R.*

Pause for students to locate and mark the intersection, then ask a student to mark it on the transparency.

> *Locate SW 4th Street and SW C Street. Draw a line along each.*

Pause as students locate the streets and draw the lines, then ask a student to mark them on the transparency.

> *Do these two streets cross each other? If they do, mark the intersection with an S.*

Follow the same procedure as above. The completed map is as follows:

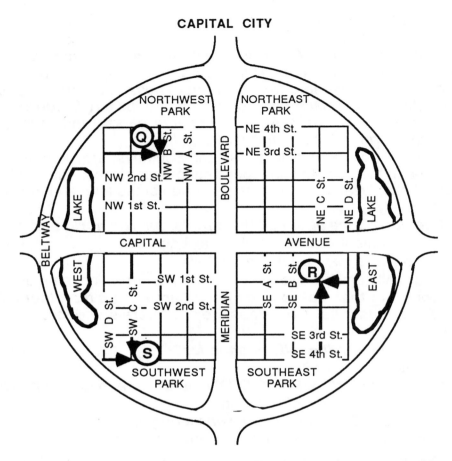

Now, suppose that you wanted to tell a visitor how to get to the town square (the intersection of Capital Avenue and Meridian Boulevard) from point R, what directions could you give?

Encourage students to present many alternative routes and to discuss the merits and drawbacks of each suggestion. If necessary, draw suggested routes on the transparency. Possible answers include "Go north on C Street for one block, then turn left and go three blocks west on Capital Avenue." **OR** "Go west on SE 1st Street for three blocks, then turn right and go one block north on Meridian Boulevard." Note that although other answers are possible, these two present the least complicated directions, thus they would probably be easier for a visitor to follow. Require students to use specific language when they state directions. Additional directions from and to various points on the map may be requested as time permits.

GUIDED PRACTICE
EXERCISES: **B-137, B-138**
ANSWERS: **B-137** <u>three</u> blocks to the <u>east</u>; **B-138** <u>five</u> blocks to the <u>north</u>

INDEPENDENT PRACTICE
Assign exercises **B-139** through **B-159**.

DISCUSSION TIPS
Compare the map of **Capital City** with one of your community. Encourage students to talk about the differences and similarities they find, e.g., your community may designate

streets between numbered avenues or streets *Court* or *Terrace*; all streets in your community may not (in fact, probably will not) run exactly north-south and east-west. Encourage students to identify the north-south or east-west division streets by name and to identify the basis for house numbering systems in your community. Emphasize the importance of drawing arrows in the direction of the motion. The line starts where the motion starts (with the word *from*, as in *from* X Street to Y Street) and ends with the tip of the arrow at the point where the motion stops (with the words following *to*, as in from X Street *to* Y Street).

ANSWERS

B-139 six blocks; **B-140** three blocks west and three blocks south OR three blocks south and three blocks west

B-141 four blocks to the south (along B Street East; the **Y** is at SE 2nd Street and SE B Street); **B-142** eight blocks; **B-143** four blocks east and four blocks south OR four blocks south and four blocks east

B-144 Fresno; **B-145** Santa Barbara; **B-146** Stockton; **B-147** San Bernardino

B-148 northwest; **B-149** south; **B-150** northeast; **B-151** northeast

B-152 Smithsonian; **B-153** Natural History Museum; **B-154** White House **B-155** east along Constitution Avenue; **B-156** southeast; **B-157** west; **B-158** south, then east; **B-159** The Mall

FOLLOW-UP REFERENT

When might you want to describe a path between specific locations? Examples: making or following maps; following or giving street directions; determining alternate routes between locations on a road map; writing or following clues for a "treasure hunt," an orienteering exercise, or a road rally; organizing the sequence of stops on a shopping trip or book locations in a library

CURRICULUM APPLICATION

Language Arts: using references and cross-references in research materials

Mathematics: locating or charting consecutive points on a graph; spatial orientation exercises; connecting points on a geometric plane

Science: using a map to locate stars or planets; using a sextant; constructing gears and pulleys; tracing movements, e.g., animal migrations, changes in microscopic samples

Social Studies: reading maps, graphs, or charts

Enrichment Areas: creating or following pattern plays in team sports; putting a series of dance steps into a sequence; writing or giving stage directions for a play

DEPICTING DIRECTIONS OR DIMENSIONS

STRAND: Verbal Sequences   **PAGES:** 82–85

ADDITIONAL MATERIALS

Transparency of TM #5
Washable transparency marker
Student handouts of TM #5 (optional)

INTRODUCTION
In previous lessons you used maps to describe directions and give locations.

OBJECTIVE
In these exercises you will learn to follow instructions for drawing basic maps or paths.

DEMONSTRATION/EXPLANATION
Cut out the movable rectangle from the transparency of TM #5, then project the grid from the transparency.
Step 1 of the instructions says that you are to place a rectangle on the grid so that its southeast corner falls on point A.
Ask a student to place the rectangle, then ask the class to confirm that it is correctly placed on the grid.
Step 2 directs you to draw a path three units to the east then four units to the south of point A.
After a student has drawn the path, ask the class to confirm its correctness.
In these exercises, each unit on the grids will represent one square mile. What will be the length represented by each side of a unit?
Answer: Each side of a unit will represent one mile.

GUIDED PRACTICE
EXERCISE: **B-160**
Give students sufficient time to complete this exercise. Then, using the demonstration methodology above, have them discuss and explain their answers. Use student discussion to clarify that point **A**, which is the northwest corner in exercise **B-160**, will mark the upper left corner of the rectangular piece of land.
ANSWER:

B-160

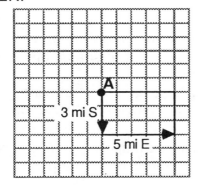

INDEPENDENT PRACTICE
Assign exercises **B-161** through **B-174**.

DISCUSSION TIPS
Remind students that each unit on the grid represents one mile. Confirm that north is toward the top of the page and that east is to the right. Students may express confusion between the English idioms *square mile* and *mile square*. A piece of land having an area of *four square miles* may be a square shape two miles on a side or a rectangular shape, with one set of sides being one mile long and the other set four miles long. A piece of land described as *a four-mile square* has an area of sixteen square miles.

ANSWERS

B-161

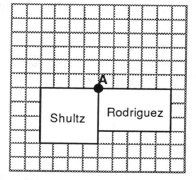

B-162 three (3) miles

B-163 3 + 5 + 3 + 5 = 16 mi

B-164 4 + 4 + 4 + 4 = 16 mi

B-165 3 × 5 = 15 sq mi

B-166 4 × 4 = 16 sq mi

B-167

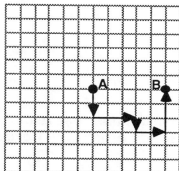

B-168 2 + 3 + 1 + 2 + 3 = 11 mi

B-169 five (5) miles

B-170 The detour is six (6) miles longer
(11 mi − 5 mi = 6 mi)

B-171

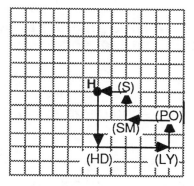

B-172 two (2) miles

B-173 west

B-174 4 + 5 + 2 + 3 + 2 + 2 = 18 mi

FOLLOW-UP REFERENT

When might you need to determine or show the relationship of specific locations on a map or grid?

Examples: indicating specific locations or routes on maps; following or drawing directions between specific locations; telling someone where something is located and/or how to get to a specific location

CURRICULUM APPLICATION

Language Arts: writing instructional papers or giving demonstration speeches; depicting directions integral to the plot of a narrative, e.g. Poe's "The Gold Bug"

Mathematics: identifying particular points on a graph; describing an arrangement of geometric shapes; spatial orientation exercises; solving word problems involving area, perimeter, or direction

Science: stating or writing directions for constructing motors, gears, or pulleys; detailing positions or locations of stars or planets; specifying or depicting locations on topographic, geological, or oceanographic maps

Social Studies: reading or creating maps, graphs, or charts; describing and depicting geographic locations on map outlines; using latitude and longitude to specify locations on maps

Enrichment Areas: creating or following pattern plays in team sports; describing the performance of a dance step or the creation of an art project; writing or giving stage directions; charting marching band or drill team formation positions

TIME SEQUENCE—SELECT

STRAND: Verbal Sequences   **PAGES:** 86–87

ADDITIONAL MATERIALS
Transparency of student workbook page 86
Washable transparency marker

INTRODUCTION
In the previous lesson you followed written instructions for creating a path on a grid. These instructions had to be followed in the order they were stated if you were to end up in the desired location.

OBJECTIVE
In these exercises you will practice putting words into an order of occurrence. You will select the word that continues a given time sequence.

DEMONSTRATION / EXPLANATION
Project exercise **B-175** from the transparency of page 86.

In exercise B-175 you are give the words <u>invasion</u> and <u>combat</u>. What do these words have in common?

Answer: They are both used to talk about war.

The first word you are given is invasion. What is an invasion?

Answer: An invasion occurs when an attacking army enters another country.

What does combat mean?

Answer: A combat is an armed battle or struggle between opposing armies.

The two given events are arranged in time order. An invasion comes before a combat. You are to choose another word from the CHOICE COLUMN that continues this time-order sequence. What does the word attack mean?

Answer: An attack is the beginning of an action, possibly combat.

Could an attack come after a combat?

Answer: Not normally; an attack is the beginning of combat. An attack that follows a particular combat would mark the beginning of the *next* combat.

What does the word battle mean?

Answer: Battle is a synonym for combat.

Could a battle come after a combat?

Answer: No; they would occur at the same time.

What does the word truce mean?

Answer: A suspension of fighting; a cease-fire.

Could a truce come after a combat?

Answer: Yes.

  Look at the words in the CHOICE BOX again. Explain why or how you would eliminate two of the word choices as possible answers.

Answer: Attack and battle can be eliminated. Since they may be synonyms for invasion and combat, they are not the next thing that occurs.

  To confirm your word choice, rephrase the given words. If invasion means "to start a war," then what could you say that combat means?

Answer: To continue a war.

  So the restated sequence is "to start a war, to continue a war, ___blank___." What idea or action might logically come next?

Answer: To stop a war.

  Does the word truce mean "to stop a war"?

Answer: Yes. Write TRUCE in the answer blank for **B-175**, then project exercise **B-176**.

  Look at exercise B-176 and try to determine which word from the CHOICE COLUMN would come next. First you have to determine what the words <u>enroll</u> and <u>attend</u> have in common. Remember that they are already in the correct time order.

Answer: They both refer to going to school.

  Do any of the words in the CHOICE COLUMN have meanings similar to enroll and attend?

Answer: Register and select (selecting courses) are similar to enroll, since they refer to things that must be done when enrolling in school.

  Since both register and select are similar to enroll, they probably do not refer to actions that would take place after attend. This leaves only one word, graduate, as a probability. Check your answer. How can the words enroll and attend be restated in terms of time?

Answer: Enroll means "to start school" and attend means "to continue school."

  If the restated sequence is "to start school, to continue school, <u>blank</u>," what action or concept would come next?

Answer: To finish school.

  When you finish school what do you do?

Answer: Graduate.

  So the next word in this time sequence is graduate.

Write GRADUATE in the answer blank on the transparency.

GUIDED PRACTICE
EXERCISES: **B-177, B-178, B-179**
When students have had sufficient time to complete these exercises, check by discussion to determine that they have used a correct time-order sequence.

NOTE: Definitions marked with an asterisk (*) indicate that the synonym given also appears in the choice column.

ANSWERS:

B-177 till (plow*); plant (sow*); [farming]; harvest (gather crops)
   till, plant, <u>harvest</u>

B-178 larva (egg hatches into larva); pupa (cocoon stage); [development of a butterfly]; adult (the last stage of development); cocoon (home for the pupa); egg (the first stage of development)
   larva, pupa, <u>adult</u>

B-179   initial (original*); intermediate (middle stage); [stages or steps of something]; previous (coming before); terminal (the last stage or end)
initial, intermediate, <u>terminal</u>

INDEPENDENT PRACTICE
Assign exercises **B-180** through **B-188**.

DISCUSSION TIPS
Let the students reach their own conclusions about the words and their time-order sequences. Encourage each student to explain his or her interpretations of the words and to verbalize the relationship(s) they see. Use questions to help students develop their understanding of why some words will not work, as well as why some words do. The following cues will encourage the discussion procedure demonstrated in the explanation:

1. First word (definition or synonym*)
2. Second word (definition or synonym*)
3. To what do the words refer? [topic]
4. Words in choice column (definitions)
5. Final sequence; <u>answer underlined</u>

ANSWERS
NOTE: Definitions marked with an asterisk (*) indicate that this synonym also appears in the choice column.

B-180   sprout (bud*); bloom (blossom*); [development of a plant]; wilt (fade)
sprout, bloom, <u>wilt</u>

B-181   design (conceive* a plan); construct (build*); [stages of building]; occupy (move in)
design, construct, <u>occupy</u>

B-182   attempt (undertake*); pursue (conduct*) ; [stages of trying]; succeed (done well)
attempt, pursue, <u>succeed</u>

B-183   doubt (question*) ; inquire (investigate*); [stages in learning]; determine (finding the answer)
doubt, inquire, <u>determine</u>

B-184   prior (preceding* or previous*); existing (available now); [order of occurrence]; following (coming later)
prior, existing, <u>following</u>

B-185   commence (begin*); continue (proceed*); [order of occurrence]; conclude (finish)
commence, continue, <u>conclude</u>

B-186   income (earnings* or wages*); savings (money not spent); [parts of a budget]; expenditures (money spent)
income, savings, <u>expenditures</u>

B-187   motive (reason* or cause*); deed (action); [cause-effect]; consequence (result)
motive, deed, <u>consequence</u>

B-188   conceive (originate* or introduce*); develop (advance); [stages of planning] ; conclude (finish)
conceive, develop, <u>conclude</u>

FOLLOW-UP REFERENT
When might you need to determine which word indicates later in time than a given word?

Examples: following sequential directions, e.g., at work, in daily life, doing errands or chores; following and making schedules; games involving chronological order, e.g., military board games; telling and understanding jokes, puns, or stories; word puzzles and games; understanding and describing test or game results

CURRICULUM APPLICATION

Language Arts: relating correct chronological order, e.g., writing narratives or letters; relating story plots; understanding and selecting adverbs and verbs to express desired order or time

Mathematics: solving word problems involving transitivity; following directions or explaining the process for solving multistep problems

Science: recognizing and predicting frequency variance; following sequential directions and writing organized reports of science demonstrations; classifying physical phenomena chronologically

Social Studies: recognizing and using chronological order to place historical events

Enrichment Areas: understanding and using correct time-sequence procedures; recognizing and chronologically describing degrees of development

TIME SEQUENCE—RANK

STRAND: Verbal Sequences   **PAGES:** 88–89

ADDITIONAL MATERIALS
Transparency of student workbook page 88
Washable transparency marker

INTRODUCTION
In the previous lesson you selected a word to continued a time sequence.

OBJECTIVE
In these exercises you will rearrange given words into an order of occurrence from earliest to latest.

DEMONSTRATION/EXPLANATION
Project exercise **B-189** from the transparency of page 88.
You are to rearrange these words so that the first word represents the earliest thing in the sequential process and the last word represents the latest. Before you can arrange the terms, however, you will need to determine what the words have in common or what process they refer to. In exercise B-189 you are given three words: <u>memorize</u>, <u>read</u>, and <u>recite</u>. To what general process do these words refer?
Answer: The process of learning something that is to be orally presented.
What type of things might you need to learn before you present them orally?
Answers: Speeches, poems, songs, or a part in a play are all possible answers.
Look at the given words again. Which of the words describes the first step you would take if you were preparing a poem to present orally in class?
Answer: You would read the poem first. Write READ on the answer blank, then cross the word off the given list.

After you had read the poem, which of the remaining words describes what you would probably do next?

Answer: Memorize. Write MEMORIZE next on the answer blank, then cross it off the list.

Only one word, recite, is left, so it must be last.

Write RECITE on the answer blank, then cross it off the given list, too.

You have determined the time-order of these three words by choosing the one that came first, then next, then last. Confirm your answer by saying the order to yourself like this, "First I read, next I memorize, then I recite." Does the order you chose make the sentence true?

Answer: Yes. Project exercise **B-191**.

Sometimes the method you just used doesn't work very well. For example, in exercise B-191 it wouldn't make sense for you to check your answer by saying to yourself "First I afterward." An alternate way of determining the time-order arrangement of a group of words is to arrange them one at a time. For this method you would start by defining and writing down the first word on the list. What does afterward mean?

Answer: Happening later or after some event. Write AFTERWARD in the middle of the answer blank, then write (LATER) above it.

Now look at the next word on the list. What does beforehand mean?

Answer: Happening earlier or before some event.

When you compare this word with the one you have already written, where would it come in time, before or after?

Answer: It would come before the first word. Write BEFOREHAND at the beginning of the answer blank, then write "EARLIER" above it.

You have rearranged two of the words into correct time order from earliest to latest. Now you have to determine where the third word belongs in the process. What does presently mean?

Answer: Happening now or soon.

Where would it occur—before, between, or after the two words you have already arranged?

Answer: Between them. Write PRESENTLY between the two words on the answer blank, then write (NOW) above it.

Confirm your arrangement by looking at the definitions.

Indicate the words you have written in parenthesis as you read them.

Does "earlier, now, and later" reflect a time order from earliest to latest?

Answer: Yes.

So the order of occurrence for this set of words would be: beforehand, now, and afterward. You may use either of these methods to rearrange the words.

GUIDED PRACTICE
EXERCISES: **B-190, B-192, B-193**
When the students have had sufficient time to complete these exercises, use the demonstration methodology above as a guide for discussion.
ANSWERS:
B-190   design (think about); distribute (sell); manufacture (make); [think about; make; sell]
design, manufacture, distribute

B-192   believe (accept as true); deliberate (think about); read (get information); [get information, think about it, accept it as true]
read, deliberate, believe

B-193 choose (pick out); examine (look at); purchase (buy); [pick out, look at, buy]
<u>choose</u>, <u>examine</u>, <u>purchase</u>

ALTERNATE: choose (decide which to buy); examine (look at several); purchase (buy); [look at several, decide which to buy, buy]
<u>examine</u>, <u>choose</u>, <u>purchase</u>

INDEPENDENT PRACTICE
Assign exercises **B-194** through **B-202**.

DISCUSSION TIPS
Encourage students to discuss their answers. Class discussion is a valuable technique for having students share their acquired knowledge and demonstrate verbally the thinking processes they use in problem solving. The following cues will encourage the procedure demonstrated in the explanation:
1. First word (definition or synonym)
2. Second word (definition or synonym)
3. Third word (definition or synonym)
4. [Arrangement of definitions or synonyms into time order]
5. <u>Arrangement</u> <u>of</u> <u>given</u> <u>words</u> <u>into</u> <u>time</u> <u>order</u>

ANSWERS
B-194 action (do something); consequence (result); plan (have an idea); [have an idea, do something, result]
<u>plan</u>, <u>action</u>, <u>consequence</u>

B-195 current (modern); obsolete (long out-of-date, archaic); recent (not long past); [long out-of-date, not long past, modern]
<u>obsolete</u>, <u>recent</u>, <u>current</u>

B-196 cut (segment or divide); mark (indicate the measurement), measure (determine how much); [determine how much, indicate the measurement, segment or divide]
<u>measure</u>, <u>mark</u>, <u>cut</u>

B-197 intermediate (middle grades); primary (beginning grades) secondary (higher grades); [beginning grades, middle grades, higher grades]
<u>primary</u>, <u>intermediate</u>, <u>secondary</u>

B-198 outline (plan); research (investigate); write (complete version); [investigate, plan, complete version]
<u>research</u>, <u>outline</u>, <u>write</u>

B-199 colonization (settling); discovery (finding); exploration (looking for); [looking for, finding, settling]
<u>exploration</u>, <u>discovery</u>, <u>colonization</u>

ALTERNATE: colonization (settling); discovery (finding); exploration (investigating); [finding, investigating, settling]
<u>discovery</u>, <u>exploration</u>, <u>colonization</u>

B-200 contracting (building); designing (general planning); engineering (special planning); [general planning, special planning, building]
<u>designing</u>, <u>engineering</u>, <u>contracting</u>

ALTERNATE: contracting (agreeing); designing (planning); engineering (producing); [planning, agreeing, producing]
<u>designing</u>, <u>contracting</u>, <u>engineering</u>

B-201 crack (start to break); crumble (break into pieces); stress (force or pressure); [force, start to break, break into pieces]
<u>stress</u>, <u>crack</u>, <u>crumble</u>

B-202 cook (prepare for eating), defrost (thaw), serve (place on the plate or table); [thaw, prepare for eating, place on the table]
<u>defrost</u>, <u>cook</u>, <u>serve</u>

FOLLOW-UP REFERENT

When might you need to rearrange words or concepts into a specific sequential time order?

Examples: following sequential directions, e.g., at work, in daily life, doing errands or chores; following and making schedules; games involving chronological order, e.g., military board games; telling and understanding jokes, puns, or stories; word puzzles and games; understanding and describing test or game results

CURRICULUM APPLICATION

Language Arts: relating correct chronological order, e.g., writing narratives or letters; relating story plots; understanding and selecting adverbs and verbs to express desired order or time

Mathematics: solving word problems involving transitivity; following directions or explaining the process for solving multistep problems

Science: recognizing and predicting frequency variance; following sequential directions and writing organized reports of science demonstrations; classifying physical phenomena chronologically

Social Studies: recognizing and using chronological order to place historical events

Enrichment Areas: understanding and using correct time-sequence procedures; recognizing and chronologically describing degrees of development

TIME SEQUENCE—SUPPLY

STRAND: Verbal Sequences   **PAGES:** 90 – 91

ADDITIONAL MATERIALS
Transparency of student workbook page 90
Washable transparency marker

INTRODUCTION
In the previous lesson you arranged three given words according to their order of occurrence.

OBJECTIVE
In these exercises you are given two words which suggest a time sequence. You will need to supply a word which can continue the suggested sequence.

DEMONSTRATION/EXPLANATION
Project exercise **B-203** from the transparency of page 90.
In exercise B-203 you are given the two words <u>departure</u> and <u>flight</u>. To what process do these words refer?

Answer: Air travel.

> *In these exercises the words are arranged so that the first word represents the earlier action or concept, and the second word represents the next thing done in the sequence. First a plane departs or takes off, then it flies. What happens when the flight is over?*

Answer: The plane lands.

> *What word might come after departure and flight to indicate that the flight is over?*

Answer: Arrival or landing. Write the answer on the blank provided.

> *You now have three consecutive actions: departure, flight, and arrival.*

Indicate the three words as you say them. Project exercise **B-204**.

> *The given words in exercise B-204 are <u>lesson</u> and <u>rehearsal</u>. To what process do these two words refer?*

Answer: Preparing for a performance of some kind (music, dancing, singing, acting, swimming, sports, etc.).

> *What action might come after taking lessons and rehearsing?*

Answer: Performing, competing, reciting.

> *What word could go in the blank to continue the sequence begun with lesson and rehearsal.*

Answer: Performance, recital, or competition.

GUIDED PRACTICE
EXERCISES: **B-205, B-206, B-207**
Give students sufficient time to complete these exercises. Then, using the methodology demonstrated above, have them discuss and explain their choices.
ANSWERS:

B-205 *cause, situation*; (course of an event); <u>result</u> or <u>effect</u>

B-206 *early, prompt*; (time of arrival); <u>late</u> or <u>tardy</u>

B-207 *mix, cook*; (food preparation); <u>serve</u> or <u>eat</u>

INDEPENDENT PRACTICE
Assign exercises **B-208** through **B-220**.

DISCUSSION TIPS
Encourage students to provide answers that agree with the given words in number and part of speech. Be sure to allow adequate time for class discussion and alternate answers. The following cue questions will encourage students to use the discussion procedures demonstrated in the explanation.
1. What are the given words? *(Italics)*
2. What process do these words concern? (Topic)
3. What could happen next? <u>Answer</u>

ANSWERS
B-208 *decide, order*; (selecting or buying something); if food–<u>receive</u>, <u>pay</u>, <u>buy</u>, or <u>eat</u>; if something else–<u>receive</u>, <u>buy</u>, or <u>purchase</u>

B-209 *infection, treatment*; (illness); <u>cure</u> or <u>heal</u>

B-210 *problem, action*; (problem solving); <u>solution</u> or <u>answer</u>

B-211 *ancient, old*; (modernization); <u>recent</u>, <u>current</u>, or <u>modern</u>

B-212 *propose, act*; (changing); if a project–<u>complete</u> or <u>finish</u>; if a law–<u>enforce</u>

B-213   *midday, dusk*; (increasing darkness, time of day); <u>evening</u>, <u>dark</u>, or <u>night</u>

B-214   *enter, browse*; (shopping); <u>leave</u>, <u>exit</u>, <u>purchase</u>, or <u>buy</u>

B-215   *former, present*; (time order); <u>future</u>

B-216   *warm, simmer*; (heating food or water); <u>boil</u>

B-217   *question, reason*; (thinking or decision making); <u>answer</u> or <u>solve</u>

B-218   *jog, stumble*; (running); <u>fall</u> or <u>recover</u>

B-219   *arrest, trial*; (judicial procedures); <u>verdict</u>, <u>conviction</u>, <u>dismissal</u>, <u>acquittal</u>, <u>punishment</u>, or <u>release</u>

B-220   *desire, attempt*; (fulfilling wants); <u>result</u>, <u>obtain</u>, <u>outcome</u>, <u>success</u>, or <u>failure</u>

FOLLOW-UP REFERENT

When might you need to supply a word that indicates or names what comes next in time?

Examples: creating sequential directions for work or daily life; following, describing, or making time schedules; games involving chronological order, e.g., military board games; telling or creating jokes, puns, or stories; word puzzles and games; describing test or game results

CURRICULUM APPLICATION

Language Arts: relating correct chronological order, e.g., writing narratives or letters; relating or creating story plots; selecting nouns, verbs, and adverbs to express order or time

Mathematics: solving word problems involving transitivity

Science: recognizing and predicting frequency variance; following sequential directions and writing organized reports of science demonstrations or experiments; classifying physical phenomena chronologically; forming and stating hypotheses

Social Studies: recognizing and using chronological order to place historical events; using historical chronology to project future events

Enrichment Areas: understanding and using correct time-sequence procedures; recognizing and describing degrees of expertise; creating an original recipe; writing instructions for designing, constructing, or disassembling an item

DEGREE OF MEANING — SELECT

STRAND: Verbal Sequences   **PAGES:** 92–93

ADDITIONAL MATERIALS

Transparency of student workbook page 92
Washable transparency marker

INTRODUCTION

In previous lessons you arranged words so they reflected a time sequence, or an order of occurrence, from earliest to latest.

OBJECTIVE

In these exercises you will select a word to continue another sequence type. You will arrange these sequences in increasing order, such as from lowest to

highest or from smallest to largest, or in decreasing order, such as from most to least or from strongest to weakest.

DEMONSTRATION/EXPLANATION

Project exercise **B-221** from the transparency of page 92.

In exercise B-221 the given words are <u>insufficient</u> and <u>adequate</u>. To what do these words refer?

Answer: An amount of something you need or want.

What does <u>insufficient</u> mean?

Answer: In short supply or not enough.

What does <u>adequate</u> mean?

Answer: Having about the right amount.

The given words in these exercises are arranged in increasing order of rank, degree, or size. An <u>adequate</u> amount is greater than an <u>insufficient</u> amount. You are to choose a word from the CHOICE COLUMN that continues this sequence. From what words can you choose?

Answer: Abundant, enough, and scarce.

The word you choose must indicate an amount that is more than adequate. Does one of these words mean "plenty or more than adequate"?

Indicate the words in the CHOICE COLUMN. Answer: Abundant means a large amount.

Before you can be certain of your answer, you need to eliminate the other choices. What does <u>enough</u> mean?

Answer: Enough means "having about the right amount" and is a synonym for adequate.

What does <u>scarce</u> mean?

Answer: Scarce means "hard to find" and is a synonym for insufficient.

Since these words are synonyms for given words, can you eliminate them?

Answer: Yes; since they are synonyms for given words, neither can name or indicate an amount that is more than the two given words. Write ABUNDANT in the answer blank on the transparency, then project exercise **B-222**.

What are the two given words in exercise B-222?

Answer: Admit and ignore.

What does <u>admit</u> mean?

Answer: To recognize or confess.

What does <u>ignore</u> mean?

Answer: To disregard or purposely pass without notice.

To what do these words refer?

Answer: They refer to levels of acknowledgement.

Remember that the two given words are arranged in order. Do they seem to refer to something that is increasing or something that is decreasing?

Answer: They refer to decreasing levels of acknowledgment.

If you substitute definitions for the given words, you have two words that mean "to recognize or confess" and "to disregard or purposefully not recognize." What might the next word in this sequence mean?

Answer: To refuse, contradict, or withhold.

Is there a word in the CHOICE COLUMN that can fit this definition?

Answer: Deny means to refuse or contradict.

Now check your answer by eliminating the other word choices. Do any words in the CHOICE COLUMN have meanings similar to the given words?

Answer: Acknowledge and confirm are similar to admit.

> **Can you eliminate these words as an extension of this sequence? Why or why not?**

Answer: Yes, acknowledge and confirm can be eliminated. Since they are similar to admit, they cannot continue the sequence.

> **Again, you have identified the sequence, chosen a word to continue it, and confirmed your answer by eliminating the other word choices. What word goes in the answer blank?**

Answer: Deny. Write the answer on the transparency.

GUIDED PRACTICE
EXERCISES: **B-223**, **B-224**, **B-225**

Give students sufficient time to complete these exercises. Then, using the methodology demonstrated above, have them discuss and explain their choices.

ANSWERS:

NOTE: Given words from each exercise appear in italic type. If the CHOICE COLUMN contains a synonym for either given word, it is indicated with an asterisk (*). Type and topic for each sequence is given in brackets { }.

B-223 *absurd* (ridiculous*); *possible* (conceivable*); {increasing degree of believability}; actual (factual or real)

B-224 *approval* (agreement*); *admiration* (credit*); {increasing degree of respect}; devotion (strong affection)

B-225 *question* (consider*); *disagree* (challenge*); {increasing degree of debate}; argue (heated debate)

INDEPENDENT PRACTICE
Assign exercises **B-226** through **B-232**.

DISCUSSION TIPS
During class discussion of these exercises, ask students to identify whether the degree or intensity of each sequence is increasing or decreasing. Encourage them to discuss and defend their answers. The following cues will encourage students to use the discussion procedure demonstrated above.

1. Pronounce and define given words in order. (DEFINITION or SYNONYM*)
2. Determine the area of relationship. {TOPIC}
3. Define and select a word that continues the sequence. answer
4. Define any remaining answer choices. (CONFIRMING DEFINITIONS)

ANSWERS
NOTE: Given words from each exercise appear in italic type. If the CHOICE COLUMN contains a synonym for either given word, it will be given and indicated with an asterisk (*).

B-226 *urge* (suggest*); *push* (hustle*); {increasing degree of directing another's actions}; compel (to force, demand, or insist)

B-227 *advance* (attack* or charge*); *maintain* (hold a position); {decreasing degree of confrontation}; retreat (to fall back)

B-228 *fretting* (concerned*); *worried* (anxious*); {increasing degrees of anxiety}; frantic (high anxiety)

B-229 *ordinary* (common*); *rare* (unusual*); {increasing degree of rarity}; unique (one of a kind)

B-230 *irrelevant* (trivial* or nearly useless*); *useful* (functional or helpful); {increasing degree of importance}; <u>essential</u> (necessary)

B-231 *fastened* (bound* or joined*); *loosened* (almost free or untied); {decreasing degree of binding}; <u>untied</u> (loose)

B-232 *suggest* (prompt* or advise); *request* (invite* or ask for); {increasing degree of forcefulness}; <u>order</u> (require or demand)

FOLLOW-UP REFERENT

When might you need to recognize an organizational order of degree, rank, or size and determine what comes next in the sequence?

Examples: games involving rank, e.g., chess, checkers, card games; understanding and describing test or game procedures and results; understanding and telling jokes, puns, or stories; word puzzles; distinguishing the size or worth of objects; understanding consumer product terms describing size or volume

CURRICULUM APPLICATION

Language Arts: using comparative and superlative rank of adjectives or adverbs; writing narratives or letters, relating story plots; selecting nouns and verbs to express order of degree, rank, or placement

Mathematics: solving word problems involving transitivity or inequality; comparing geometric proportions, e.g., angle, size, area, volume

Science: recognizing, predicting, or stating variance in size or frequency; organizing or reporting laboratory processes, demonstrations, or experiments; forming and stating hypotheses

Social Studies: recognizing degrees of meaning in economics, geography, or history texts; recognizing divisions and subdivisions of governmental or political structures; recognizing rank in social, military, or governmental institutions

Enrichment Areas: describing gradations of color or size in art; describing gradations of pitch, rhythm, or volume in music; recognizing and describing degrees of expertise or organizational rank, e.g., military, political, social, or business ranks

DEGREE OF MEANING—RANK

STRAND: Verbal Sequences   **PAGES:** 94–95

ADDITIONAL MATERIALS

Transparency of student workbook page 94
Washable transparency marker

INTRODUCTION

In previous lessons you selected a word to continue a sequenced order of rank, time, degree, or size.

OBJECTIVE

In these exercises you will rearrange a group of words to reflect an increasing order, that is, from lowest to highest or from smallest to largest.

DEMONSTRATION/EXPLANATION

Project the **EXAMPLE** from the transparency of page 94.

In this EXAMPLE you are given the words <u>bellow</u>, <u>cry</u>, and <u>whimper</u>. To what do these words refer?

Answer: Degrees of making sound; loudness.

You need to arrange these words in a sequence so that the first word represents the lowest degree of sound and the last word represents the highest degree of sound. The first given word is <u>bellow</u>. How does bellow compare to the second given word, <u>cry</u>?

Answer: Bellow is louder than cry.

If you needed to arrange these two words in an increasing order, how would they be arranged?

Answer: Cry (softer), then bellow (louder).

Where would the third given word, <u>whimper</u>, fit into this sequence? Remember you are going from lowest to highest degree of sound.

Answer: A whimper is softer than a cry, so it would go first in the three-word sequence, in front of cry.

Arranging the three words in increasing sequential order, then, would produce the answer shown on the answer blank: whimper, cry, bellow.

Point to the given answer, then project exercise **B-233**.

The words in exercise B-233 are <u>limit</u>, <u>prohibit</u>, and <u>regulate</u>. Sometimes you will need to define the given words so you can arrange them in a sequential order. What does <u>limit</u> mean?

Answer: To set a maximum or to restrict.

What does <u>prohibit</u> mean?

Answer: To forbid or prevent.

What does <u>regulate</u> mean?

Answer: To control or adjust.

What do these three words have in common?

Answer: They refer to degrees of restricting or controlling something.

Remember that you are to arrange the words from least to most. Of the first two words, <u>limit</u> and <u>prohibit</u>, which indicates less restriction or interference?

Answer: Limit (setting a maximum or restricting something) indicates less restriction than prohibit (forbidding something).

How would you arrange these two words in increasing order of restriction?

Answer: Limit, then prohibit.

The remaining word is <u>regulate</u>. In a sequence of increasing restriction, would regulate come before, between, or after <u>limit</u> and <u>prohibit</u>?

Answer: Since it indicates the least amount of control, it would come in front of both words.

Arrange the three words from least restrictive to most restrictive.

Answer: Regulate, limit, prohibit. Write the words in order in the answer blank.

GUIDED PRACTICE

EXERCISES: **B-234, B-235, B-236**

Give students sufficient time to complete these exercises. Then, using the methodology demonstrated above, have them discuss and explain their choices.

ANSWERS:

NOTE: Given words for each exercise appear in italic type. Synonyms for given words are marked with an asterisk (*) throughout this lesson.

B-234 *dislike* (not care for); *reject* (deny*); *shun* (avoid*, have no contact with); {degree of acceptance}; [not care for, deny, avoid]; <u>dislike</u>, <u>reject</u>, <u>shun</u>

B-235 *excited* (provoked*); *savage* (brutal*); *violent* (furious*); {degree of agitation}; [provoked, furious, brutal]; <u>excited</u>, <u>violent</u>, <u>savage</u>

B-236 *acceptance* (approval*); *contempt* (scorn*); *criticism* (find fault); {degree of approval}; [scorn, find fault, approval]; <u>contempt</u>, <u>criticism</u>, <u>acceptance</u>

ALTERNATE: {degree of disapproval}; <u>acceptance</u>, <u>criticism</u>, <u>contempt</u>

INDEPENDENT PRACTICE
Assign exercises **B-237** through **B-246**.

DISCUSSION TIPS
The exercises in the lesson stress comprehension, analysis, synthesis, and evaluation of terms. As students express their rationale for each answer and arrangement, the process demonstrated will force them through these steps as they share and exchange information during class discussion. The following cues will encourage students to use the discussion procedure demonstrated in the modeled lesson.

1. State and define the given words. (DEFINITIONS)
2. To what do the words relate? {TOPIC}
3. Arrange the definitions or synonyms. [DEGREE ORDER]
4. Substitute the given words into the degree order. <u>ANSWER</u>

ANSWERS
B-237 *dull* (not bright); *lustrous* (shining); *vivid* (brilliant); {degrees of brilliance}; [not bright, shining, brilliant]; <u>dull</u>, <u>lustrous</u>, <u>vivid</u>

B-238 *vital* (essential); *significant* (important); *urgent* (serious); {degrees of importance}; [important, serious, essential]; <u>significant</u>, <u>urgent</u>, <u>vital</u>

B-239 *baboon* (intermediate-sized primate); *chimpanzee* (small primate); *gorilla* (large primate); {degree of size—primates}; [small, intermediate, large]; <u>chimpanzee</u>, <u>baboon</u>, <u>gorilla</u>

B-240 *beacon* (bright light); *bulb* (medium light); *candle* (dim light); {degrees of brightness or light given off}; [dim, medium, bright]; <u>candle</u>, <u>bulb</u>, <u>beacon</u>

B-241 *citizen* (member of a country); *patriot* (one who loves and supports his own country); *traitor* (one who betrays his own country); {degrees of loyalty}; [betrayer, member, supporter]; <u>traitor</u>, <u>citizen</u>, <u>patriot</u>

B-242 *admirable* (respectable); *ideal* (perfect); *typical* (ordinary); {degrees of worthiness}; [ordinary, respectable, perfect]; <u>typical</u>, <u>admirable</u>, <u>ideal</u>

B-243 *dissatisfied* (unhappy); *grouchy* (grumpy); *hostile* (vicious); {degrees of discontent}; [unhappy, grumpy, vicious]; <u>dissatisfied</u>, <u>grouchy</u>, <u>hostile</u>

B-244 *risk* (jeopardy); *peril* (danger); *security* (safety); {degrees of danger}; [safety, jeopardy, danger]; <u>security</u>, <u>risk</u>, <u>peril</u>

ALTERNATE: {degrees of safety}; <u>peril</u>, <u>risk</u>, <u>security</u>

B-245 *confirm* (approve); *deny* (reject); *suggest* (recommend); {degrees of approval}; [reject, recommend, approve]; <u>deny</u>, <u>suggest</u>, <u>confirm</u>

ALTERNATE: {degrees of rejection}; <u>confirm</u>, <u>suggest</u>, <u>deny</u>

B-246 *extinct* (gone); *common* (plentiful); *rare* (scarce); {degrees of availability}; [gone, scarce, plentiful]; <u>extinct</u>, <u>rare</u>, <u>common</u>

ALTERNATE: {degrees of shortage}; <u>common</u>, <u>rare</u>, <u>extinct</u>

FOLLOW-UP REFERENT
When might you need to recognize and organize words, ideas, or concepts into a given order or rank?
Examples: games involving rank, e.g., chess, checkers, card games; understanding and describing test or game procedures and results; understanding and telling jokes, puns, or stories; word puzzles; distinguishing the size or worth of objects; understanding consumer product terms describing size or volume

CURRICULUM APPLICATION
Language Arts: using comparative and superlative rank of adjectives or adverbs; writing narratives or letters, relating story plots; selecting nouns and verbs to express order of degree, rank, or placement

Mathematics: solving word problems involving transitivity or inequality; comparing geometric proportions, e.g., angle, size, area, volume

Science: recognizing, predicting, or stating variance in size or frequency; organizing or reporting laboratory processes, demonstrations, or experiments; forming and stating hypotheses

Social Studies: recognizing degrees of meaning in economics, geography, or history texts; recognizing divisions and subdivisions of governmental or political structures; recognizing rank in social, military, or governmental institutions

Enrichment Areas: describing gradations of color or size in art; describing gradations of pitch, rhythm, or volume in music; recognizing and describing degrees of expertise or organizational rank, e.g., military, social, political, or business organizations

DEGREE OF MEANING—SUPPLY

STRAND: Verbal Sequences   **PAGES:** 96–97

ADDITIONAL MATERIALS
Transparencies of student workbook pages 96 and 97
Washable transparency marker

INTRODUCTION
In the previous lesson you reorganized given words according to increasing degree of meaning.

OBJECTIVE
In these exercises you will supply a word or words to continue or complete a sequence based upon degree of meaning.

DEMONSTRATION/EXPLANATION
Project the **EXAMPLE** from the transparency of page 96.
In the EXAMPLE sequence you are given the words <u>behind</u> and <u>beside</u>. To what do these words refer?
Answer: Positions or locations.
The given words in these exercises are arranged in order. How does the position <u>behind</u> compare with the position <u>beside</u>?

Answer: Behind means "in back of" and beside means "next to."
　　　This seems to be a sequence of order. If the first word means "in back of," and the second word means "next to," what might the last word in the sequence mean?
Answer: In front of.
　　　Does the word <u>ahead</u> *mean "in front of"?*
Answer: Yes. Indicate the answer on the transparency, then project exercise **B-247**.
　　　In exercise B-247, to what do the words <u>solo</u> *and* <u>duet</u> *refer?*
Answer: They refer to the number of people involved in a dance or a musical number.
　　　How many people are involved in each case?
Answer: A solo is by one person; a duet is by two.
　　　How many people would be referred to by the next word?
Answer: Three.
　　　Can you think of a word that indicates three performers?
Answer: Trio. Write TRIO in the answer blank, then remove the transparency and project the **EXAMPLE** from the transparency of page 97.
　　　These exercises are a little different. In this EXAMPLE you see the words <u>plump</u>, <u>stout</u>, *and* <u>huge</u>. *To what does the given word* <u>stout</u> *refer?*
Answer: A degree of heaviness or obesity.
　　　What word has been used to describe "less than stout"?
Answer: Plump.
　　　What word has been used to describe "more than stout"?
Answer: Huge. Project exercise **B-256**.
　　　<u>*Wet*</u> *is the given word in exercise B-256. To what does the word refer?*
Answer: A degree of dampness or the water content of something.
　　　Can you think of a word that means "slightly wet."
Answer: Damp or moist. Write all student answers in the appropriate column on the transparency.
　　　Now think of a word that means "extremely wet."
Answer: Soggy, soaked, or drenched. Write all student answers in the appropriate column on the transparency.

GUIDED PRACTICE
EXERCISES: **B-248, B-249; B-256, B-257**
Give students sufficient time to complete these exercises. Then, using the methodology demonstrated above, have them discuss and explain their choices.
ANSWERS:

B-248　*faint, loud*; <u>deafening</u>, <u>blaring</u>, <u>thundering</u>, <u>booming</u> {increasing degrees of volume}

B-249　*precede, accompany*; <u>follow</u>, <u>trail</u>; <u>succeed</u>; {order of position}

	LESS IN DEGREE	GIVEN WORD	MORE IN DEGREE
B-257	<u>annoyed</u>, <u>peeved</u>, <u>dissatisfied</u>	*angry*	<u>furious</u>, <u>outraged</u>, <u>enraged</u>
B-258	<u>trickle</u>, <u>seep</u>	*flow*	<u>flood</u>, <u>inundate</u>, <u>cascade</u>, <u>deluge</u>

INDEPENDENT PRACTICE
Assign exercises **B-250** through **B-255** and **B-259** through **B-262**.

DISCUSSION TIPS

Encourage students to discuss their answers and verbalize the reasoning that led to their decisions. Help the students explore multiple definitions and fine degrees of distinction among possible alternate answers. Ask them to identify the direction of the sequence and the area of distinction for each exercise.

Do not assume that something is too obvious to be discussed, for several students may perceive things differently. The teacher's role in such a case is to help students discover and verbalize the thought process so that it can be applied again to similar situations.

ANSWERS

B-250 *hopeless, conceivable*; likely, probable; {increasing degrees of probability}

B-251 *seldom, regularly*; often, frequently, or constantly; {increasing degrees of frequency}

B-252 *more, same*; less, fewer; {decreasing degrees of quantity}

B-253 *scent, odor*; stench, stink; {increasing degrees of smell}

B-254 *possible, probable*; certain, definite, inevitable; {increasing degrees of probability}

B-255 *flicker, glow*; blaze, flare, flame; {increasing degrees of flame}

ALTERNATE: {increasing degrees of light}; glare, intense, brightness

	LESS IN DEGREE	GIVEN WORD	MORE IN DEGREE
B-259	reluctant, resistant	*willing*	eager, enthusiastic
B-260	suggest, hint	*request*	demand, insist
B-261	whimper, moan, complain	*cry*	wail, bellow, scream
B-262	anxious, concerned	*scared*	horrified, terrified

FOLLOW-UP REFERENT

When might you need to recognize gradation in degrees of meaning, then organize, extend, or complete a given order or rank?

Examples: games involving rank, e.g., chess, checkers, card games; understanding and describing test or game processes or results; understanding and telling jokes, puns, or stories; distinguishing the size or worth of objects; understanding consumer product terms describing size or volume; interpreting or creating organizational charts

CURRICULUM APPLICATION

Language Arts: using comparative and superlative rank of adjectives or adverbs; writing narratives, letters, or story plots; selecting nouns and verbs to express order of degree, rank, or placement

Mathematics: solving word problems involving transitivity or inequality; describing geometric proportions, e.g., angle, size, area or volume

Science: recognizing and predicting variance of size or frequency; writing organized reports of science demonstrations; formulating and stating hypothesis

Social Studies: recognizing degrees of meaning patterns in economics, history, or geography texts; recognizing divisions and subdivisions of governmental or political structures; recognizing rank in social, military, or governmental institutions; discerning historical patterns and using them as a basis for projecting future actions or events

Enrichment Areas: describing gradations of color or size in art; describing gradations of pitch, rhythm, or volume in music; recognizing and describing degrees of expertise or organizational rank, e.g., military, political, social, or business organizations

TRANSITIVITY — COMPARISON

STRAND: Verbal Sequences   **PAGES:** 98–100

ADDITIONAL MATERIALS
Transparency of student workbook page 98
Washable transparency marker

INTRODUCTION
In previous lessons you compared words and arranged them according to degrees of meaning.

OBJECTIVE
In these exercises you will compare items and arrange them according to speed, size, or number using information given in a descriptive statement.

DEMONSTRATION/EXPLANATION
Project exercise **B-263** from the transparency of page 98.
You will need to look carefully at the questions and the charts to see whether you are arranging the object in increasing or decreasing order. Read the statement and question in exercise B-263.
Pause while students read to themselves, or ask a volunteer to read the exercise aloud.
What information are you asked to rank?
Answer: Air speeds.
Are the air speeds to be listed in increasing or decreasing order?
Answer: Increasing (from slowest to fastest).
The statement only names two kinds of airplanes, yet there are three blanks to complete on the diagram. What three air speeds are you to compare?
Answer: The speeds of two jet planes (Boeing 707 and Concord) and the official air-speed record.
Which of these speeds is fastest?
Answer: The official air-speed record. Indicate the diagram.
What should you write on the line beside FASTEST?
Answer: The words AIR-SPEED RECORD. Write the answer on the transparency.
The information statement says that the official air-speed record is three times the speed of the 707. What fraction of the air-speed record is the speed of the 707?
Answer: One-third (1/3).
The statement also tells you that the official air-speed record is one and one-half times the speed of the Concord. One and one-half is how many halves?
Answer: Three halves (3/2).
What fraction of the air-speed record speed is the speed of the Concord?
Answer: Two-thirds (2/3).
Now you have a means of comparing the three speeds. You have the air-speed record; the 707, which is one-third the record; and the Concord, which is 2/3 the record. Which is faster, 1/3 the record speed or 2/3 the record speed?
Answer: 2/3.
Which of the two listed jets is faster?

Answer: The Concord is faster than the 707.

> **On which line of the diagram should the Concord be written?**

Answer: The middle line. It is faster than the 707 but slower than the official record. Write CONCORD on the correct line on the transparency.

> **What goes on the top line of the diagram in the slowest position?**

Answer: The 707. Fill in the diagram.

> **Now check the diagram. Does it accurately show the information given?**

Pause for student discussion. Answer:

SLOWEST	Boeing 707
	Concord jet
FASTEST	Air-speed record

GUIDED PRACTICE
EXERCISE: **B-264**
Give students sufficient time to complete this exercise. Then, using the methodology demonstrated above, have them discuss and explain their choices.
ANSWERS:

B-264 **a.** great white shark = 40 ft.

b. whale shark = $1\frac{1}{2}$ × white shark = $1\frac{1}{2}$ × 40 (from **a**) = 60 ft

c. blue whale = $1\frac{1}{2}$ × whale shark = $1\frac{1}{2}$ × 60 (from **b**) = 90 ft

LARGEST	Blue whale (90 ft)
	Whale shark (60 ft)
SMALLEST	White shark (40 ft)

INDEPENDENT PRACTICE
Assign exercises **B-265** through **B-268**.

DISCUSSION TIPS
Encourage students to discuss their answers and to state where they got the information for each decision they made. You may want to split the class into several small groups to work on a problem. Then have each group share their answer with the class to compare and discuss the differences, similarities, and steps to solution.

Do not assume that something is too obvious to be discussed, for several students may perceive things differently. Students who arrive at the same answer may not necessarily have followed the same reasoning. Question several students. Some may not know how they arrived at the answer; they have answered intuitively. The teacher's role in such a case is to help the student discover and verbalize the thought process so that it can be applied again to similar situations. Students may also find it helpful to sketch or diagram information as they proceed through the problem, then assemble the items in order from their diagrams. This process is shown in the detailed answers presented in this section.

ANSWERS
B-265 **a.** The Pentagon (Pe) has twice the volume of the Great Pyramid (Py).

thus Pe = 2 Py, OR Pe > Py

b. The Colosseum (C) has half the volume of the Great Pyramid.

thus C = 1/2 Py, OR C < Py, OR Py > C

    c. St. Peter's Cathedral (St) is larger than the Colosseum.
       thus St > C, OR C < St

    d. St. Peter's is smaller than the Great Pyramid.
       thus St < Py, OR Py > St

    e. Combining **c** and **d**: Py > St > C

    f. Combining **e** and **a**: Pe > Py > St > C

(Statement **b** is not used for the final arrangement, but its information is consistent with the answer.)

LARGEST	Pentagon
	Great Pyramid of Cheops
	St. Peter's Cathedral
SMALLEST	Colosseum

B-266 **a.** A soccer field (S) is larger than a football field (F).
       thus S > F OR F < S

    b. A regulation skating rink* (R) is one-third the size of a football field.
       thus $R = \left(\frac{1}{3}\right)F$, OR R < F OR F > R

    c. An ice skating rink* (R) is about $2\frac{1}{2} \times$ a baseball infield (B).
       thus $R = \left(2\frac{1}{2}\right)B$, OR R > B, OR B < R

  *Students should assume that a regulation skating rink and an ice-skating rink are the same size.

    d. Combine the statements so that all signs indicate "less than" (<).
       F < S (from **a**); R < F (from **b**); and B < R (from **c**)
       thus B < R < F < S

SMALLEST	Baseball infield
	Skating rink
	Football field
LARGEST	Soccer field

B-267 **a.** WW II = 300,000

    b. WW I = 53,500

    c. Civil War = 4 × WW I = 4 × 53,500 = 214,000

    d. Vietnam = 6,000 less than WW I = 53,500 − 6000 = 47,500

	WAR	**NUMBER OF CASUALTIES**
MOST	World War II	300,000
	Civil	214,000
	World War I	53,500
LEAST	Vietnam	47,500

B-268 **a.** Tokyo (T) = 15,500 people per sq km

    b. $T = 2\frac{1}{2} \times$ Chicago (C)
       thus $T = \frac{5}{2}C$, OR $C = \frac{2}{5}T = \frac{2}{5}$ (15,500) [from **a**] = 6,200 people per sq km

c. NYC = 9,300

d. Mexico City (MC) = 2,300 more than New York City (NYC)
thus 2,300 + 9,300 [from **c**] = 12,600

	CITY	PEOPLE PER SQ KM
MOST	Tokyo	15,500
	Mexico City	12,600
	New York City	9,300
LEAST	Chicago	6,200

FOLLOW-UP REFERENT
When might you need to determine order or rank from written information?
Examples: recreational reading; understanding and describing test or game results; distinguishing among size or worth of objects; understanding consumer product terms describing size, volume, or value; interpreting news items or reports involving statistics

CURRICULUM APPLICATION
Language Arts: expressing comparative and superlative rank of adjectives or adverbs; exercises involving order, e.g., writing narratives or letters, relating or writing story plots; selecting words to express desired order of degree, rank, size, or placement
Mathematics: solving word problems involving transitivity or inequality; describing comparative geometric proportions, e.g., angle, size, area, volume
Science: recognizing and predicting variance of size or frequency; writing or presenting reports of science demonstrations or research; making scientific comparisons
Social Studies: recognizing chronological order and using it to place historical events, eras, artifacts, cultures, and people into proper time relationships; recognizing divisions and subdivisions of governmental or political structures; recognizing and/or interpreting rank or order in military, business, social, or political organizations
Enrichment Areas: describing gradations of color or size in art; describing gradations of pitch, rhythm, or volume in music; recognizing and describing degrees of expertise

TRANSITIVITY—TIME ORDER

STRAND: Verbal Sequences   **PAGES:** 101–104

ADDITIONAL MATERIALS
Transparency of student workbook page 101
Washable transparency marker

INTRODUCTION
In the previous lesson you compared and ranked things according to speed, size, or number.

OBJECTIVE
In these exercises you will arrange events according to when they occurred. This type of sequencing is called "time order" or "chronological order."

DEMONSTRATION/EXPLANATION

Project exercise **B-269** from the transparency of page 101.

> *In exercise B-269 you are to arrange four events in the order of occurrence from earliest to latest. What are the four events?*

Answer: The founding of the League of Nations, World War I, World War II, and the founding of the United Nations.

> *What key words in the paragraph suggest a time order?*

Answer: The words "between" and "after."

> *You can use the first sentence—"The League of Nations was formed between World War I and World War II"—to arrange three events in time order. What are the events and what is their order of occurrence?*

Answer: World War I, League of Nations, and World War II, in that order.

> *What is the fourth event and where does it fit in the sequence?*

Answer: The forming of the United Nations was latest of the events.

> *How do you know the U.N. is the most recent event?*

Answer: From the second sentence, which says the United Nations was formed after World War II, which was the most recent of the events listed in the first sentence. Fill in the events on the diagram, asking the students to confirm each answer.

GUIDED PRACTICE

EXERCISE: **B-270**

Give students sufficient time to complete this exercise. Then, using the methodology demonstrated above, have them discuss and explain their choices.

ANSWERS:

B-270 One can draw comparative time lines for the composers' life spans, using B = born and D = died)

    a. Since "Schubert died before Tchaikovsky was born," Schubert's time line should go in front of Tchaikovsky's, and there should be a gap between Schubert's death and Tchaikovsky's birth, as shown below.

        B___Schubert ___D   B___Tchaikovsky___D

    b. Since "Wagner was born during Schubert's lifetime and died during Tchaikovsky's," his time line overlaps the other two.

        B___Schubert ___D   B___Tchaikovsky___D
                B___Wagner___D

    EARLIEST   Schubert
                   Wagner
    LATEST   Tchaikovsky

INDEPENDENT PRACTICE

Assign exercises **B-271** through **B-273**.

DISCUSSION TIPS

Remind students to look for time-indicator words. Encourage them to discuss their answers and to state where they got the information for each decision they made. Do not assume that something is too obvious to be discussed, for several students may perceive things differently. Students who arrive at the same answer may not necessarily have followed the same reasoning. Some may not know how they arrived at the answer. The teacher's role in such a case is to help the student discover and verbalize the thought process so that it can be applied again to similar situations.

ANSWERS

NOTE: The clues are shown with the <u>terms to be listed</u> underlined. The number in parentheses after the clue is the time order of the clue.

B-271 **a.** When the butterfly leaves the cocoon it is a fully developed <u>adult</u>. (5)

The key time clue is "fully developed." This suggests the adult is the latest stage.

b. Upon hatching from the <u>egg</u>, the <u>larva</u> begins to search for food. (2)

The time clue is "upon hatching." This suggests that the larva stage directly follows the egg stage.

c. During the <u>pupa</u> stage, while the forming butterfly is still in the <u>cocoon</u>, the adult wings take shape. (4)

This indicates that the pupa is a stage and that the cocoon is the container in which the pupa lives.

d. The <u>egg</u> stage, which is the first in the development of a butterfly, may last for many months. (1)

The time clue is "first," thus egg is earliest.

e. A day or so before beginning the <u>pupa</u> stage, the <u>larva</u> stops eating and spins a cocoon. (3)

The time clue is "before": larva before pupa.

Collecting all the clues:

From **d** – egg earliest

From **b** – larva follows egg

From **e** – larva before cocoon

From **e** – cocoon before pupa

From **a** – adult butterfly latest

EARLIEST	<u>Egg</u>
	<u>Larva</u>
	<u>Cocoon</u>
	<u>Pupa</u>
LATEST	<u>Adult</u>

B-272 **a.** The earliest <u>analog computer</u> was developed by Lord Kelvin in 1872. (3)

This clue fixes a date: analog computer = 1872.

b. The oldest form of calculating machine is the <u>abacus</u>. (1)

The time clue "oldest" establishes the abacus as the earliest.

c. Charles Babbage, who designed the first <u>digital computer</u>, died in 1872. (2)

This clue indicates that the digital computer was designed before 1872.

d. In 1959 Robert Noyce developed the <u>silicon microchip circuits</u> that allowed the development of the small modern computer. (5)

This establishes that modern computers came after 1959.

e. In 1942 the first <u>electronic computer</u> was developed in the United States. (4)

This fixes another date: electronic computer = 1942.

Significant dates (in order): ancient, pre-1872, 1872, 1942, 1959

	DATE	CALCULATING MACHINE
EARLIEST	Ancient	Abacus
	pre-1872	Digital computer
	1872	Analog computer
	1942	Electronic computer
LATEST	1959	Microchip leading to modern computers

B-273 **a.** The orbital flight of John Glenn occurred during the second year of President Kennedy's term. (4)

b. During President Johnson's second year in office, the Gemini program launched pairs of American astronauts into space, leading to unmanned lunar landings. (5)

c. During January 1961, the first month of President Kennedy's term, a chimpanzee named "Ham" became the first subject launched into space by the United States. (2)

d. The Russians put the space satellite "Sputnik" into orbit during the Eisenhower presidency, about two years before Kennedy was elected. (1)

e. Following the Surveyor missions, Neil Armstrong became the first man to walk on the moon. (7)

f. Because of the successful chimpanzee flight, Alan Sheppard became the first American in space during the first year of Kennedy's administration. (3)

g. Surveyor I made a successful unmanned moon landing during the third year of the Johnson administration. (6)

h. In July 1969 Neil Armstrong broadcast to the American people from the lunar surface and talked with President Nixon from space. (8)

Administrations: Kennedy, Johnson, Eisenhower, Nixon

Events: John Glenn's orbital flight; Gemini program; "Ham" launched; "Sputnik" launched; first man to walk on moon; first American into space; Surveyor I (unmanned lunar landings); Armstrong broadcasts from lunar surface

NOTE: The following steps show one of several possible methods for determining the time order of the given events.

1. Match the events with the proper administration.

Kennedy = **a, c, f**; Johnson = **b, g**; Eisenhower = **d**; Nixon = (**e**), **h** (Although no administration is mentioned in **e**, you know from **h** that Nixon was president when Armstrong walked on the moon.)

2. Arrange the events into time order within each administration.

Kennedy = **c** (first month, January 1961), **f** (first year), **a** (second year)

Johnson = **b** (second year), **g** (third year)

Eisenhower = **d** (two years before Kennedy, i.e., 1960 – 2 = 1958)

Nixon = **e** (Armstrong walks on moon), **h** (1969, broadcast from lunar surface)

3. Arrange administrations in time order and complete the chart.

EARLIEST Eisenhower (1958)

Kennedy (1961)

Johnson (after Kennedy [**f**] and before Nixon [**e** and **g**])

LATEST Nixon (1969)

4. List the space events on the chart in order by chronological administration.

EARLIEST	<u>Sputnik</u>
	<u>"Ham" launched</u> (first American subject in space)
	<u>First American in space</u>
	<u>John Glenn's orbital flight</u>
	<u>Gemini program</u> (pairs of astronauts)
	<u>Surveyor I</u> (unmanned lunar landings)
	<u>Neil Armstrong walks on moon</u>
LATEST	<u>Armstrong broadcasts from moon</u>

FOLLOW-UP REFERENT

When might you need to determine the chronological order of events from written information?

Examples: recreational reading; understanding and describing test or game results; understanding and telling jokes, puns, or stories; distinguishing among size or worth of objects; comparing consumer product terms describing size, volume, value, or ingredients; creating time lines or flow charts; doing genealogical research; solving mysteries; arranging schedules

CURRICULUM APPLICATION

Language Arts: expressing comparative and superlative rank of adjectives or adverbs; exercises involving chronological order, e.g., writing narratives or letters, relating story plots; selecting words to express degree, rank, or order

Mathematics: solving word problems involving transitivity or inequality; describing comparisons of geometric proportions in angle, size, volume, or area

Science: recognizing and predicting variance of size or frequency; writing reports of science demonstrations and experiments; size or development descriptions in comparing plants or animals

Social Studies: recognizing chronological order and using it to place historical events, eras, artifacts, cultures, and people into proper time relationships; recognizing divisions and subdivisions of governmental, political, or social structures

Enrichment Areas: describing gradations of color or size in art; describing gradations of pitch, rhythm, or volume in music; recognizing and describing degrees of expertise

TRANSITIVITY—MULTIPLE TIME LINES

STRAND: Verbal Sequences   **PAGES:** 104–110

ADDITIONAL MATERIALS
Transparency of student workbook page 104
Washable transparency marker

INTRODUCTION

In the previous lesson you used written information to arrange events according to their time of occurrence.

OBJECTIVE

In these exercises you will use written information to connect events in two different fields. You will first identify the events, then group them according to type, then arrange each group in chronological order. Finally, you will place this information on a single time line to see how the events in the two groups fit together chronologically.

DEMONSTRATION/EXPLANATION

Project the transparency of page 104.

In the last exercise you were given these sentences about the space program and the presidential administrations in which they occurred. You used the information in the sentences to put the space events and the presidents' terms in chronological order. Do you remember that order?

As students re-establish the order of the space events and presidential administrations, write the list on the transparency.

You might see more correlation between the people and the events if they were listed on a single scale. Use the information from the transparency to complete the multiple time line in exercise B-274.

GUIDED PRACTICE

EXERCISE: **B-274**

Since these events occurred before today's students were born, the correlation between the two lists may not be as obvious to them as to adults. Encourage students to draw inferences about the various administrations and the milestones in space that occurred during each period. For example, they might note the shortness of President Kennedy's term. The significant inference to be discussed in this lesson is the effect of each president's leadership on the promotion and implementation of the space program.

Encourage students to recall and record other events which they may connect to each time period. A key insight for students is the awareness of surprising time connections, which may be made more obvious by use of the time line. For example, students often marvel that the U.S. effort to put a man on the moon was accomplished in twelve years, just about the lifespan of some students using this book and an amazingly short period for the necessary technological development.

ANSWER:

B-274

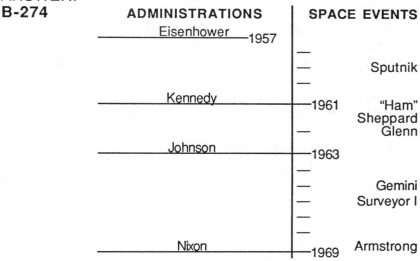

INDEPENDENT PRACTICE
Assign exercises **B-275** through **B-277**.

DISCUSSION TIPS
Encourage students to discuss their answers and check their completed charts against the information in the paragraph. They should always be asked to state where they found the information on which they based their decision or answer.

Multiple time lines allow comparative data to be placed into chronological perspective. Avoid cause-effect connections, rather encourage students to draw inferences and to express unexpected connections which they may see among time-related occurrences. For example, a discussion might develop around the following theme:

> *It seems surprising to some people that antibiotics, used so commonly to fight infection today, were unheard of until after World War II. What other time correlations shown by these exercises do you find surprising?*

Answers might include:
- Many nations that are major powers in today's world did not exist until after World War II.
- Mickey Mouse and Snow White were familiar around the world long before people had television sets in their homes.
- Over 13 million immigrants came into this country during a relatively short period of our history.
- The atomic bomb is the same age as synthetic vitamin A and actually older than most antibiotics.

As an extending activity, students may wish to research other political and scientific events to add to their time line. They might also wish to extend the timespan in either or both directions or to choose a different time period for comparison.

ANSWERS

B-275

POLITICAL EVENTS	YEAR	SCIENTIFIC EVENTS
End of Word War II	— 1945 —	Atomic bomb (Alamogordo) Vitamin A synthesized
First meeting of U.N. General Assembly	— 1946 —	Electronic brain (Penn. U.) Xerography (Chester Carlson)
Marshall Plan India's independence	— 1947 —	Transistor
Gandhi assassinated Israel established	— 1948 —	Aueromycin and Chloromycetin introduced
Vietnam established Chiang Kai-shek to Formosa Mao Tse-tung on mainland China	— 1949 —	Cortisone and neomycin produced
Korean War	— 1950 —	

B-276

TELEVISION	YEAR	DISNEY
	— 1890 —	
Cathode-ray tube	— 1892 —	
	— 1895 —	
	— 1900 —	
	— 1901 —	Disney born
	— 1905 —	

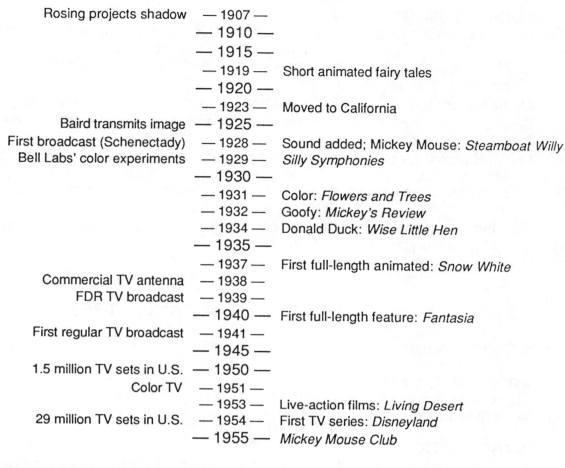

Rosing projects shadow	— 1907 —	
	— 1910 —	
	— 1915 —	
	— 1919 —	Short animated fairy tales
	— 1920 —	
	— 1923 —	Moved to California
Baird transmits image	— 1925 —	
First broadcast (Schenectady)	— 1928 —	Sound added; Mickey Mouse: *Steamboat Willy*
Bell Labs' color experiments	— 1929 —	*Silly Symphonies*
	— 1930 —	
	— 1931 —	Color: *Flowers and Trees*
	— 1932 —	Goofy: *Mickey's Review*
	— 1934 —	Donald Duck: *Wise Little Hen*
	— 1935 —	
	— 1937 —	First full-length animated: *Snow White*
Commercial TV antenna	— 1938 —	
FDR TV broadcast	— 1939 —	
	— 1940 —	First full-length feature: *Fantasia*
First regular TV broadcast	— 1941 —	
	— 1945 —	
1.5 million TV sets in U.S.	— 1950 —	
Color TV	— 1951 —	
	— 1953 —	Live-action films: *Living Desert*
29 million TV sets in U.S.	— 1954 —	First TV series: *Disneyland*
	— 1955 —	*Mickey Mouse Club*

B-277

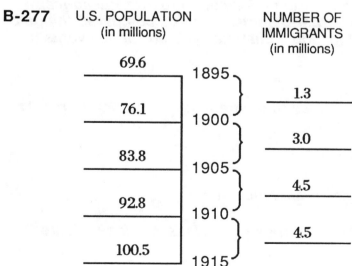

U.S. POPULATION (in millions)

NUMBER OF IMMIGRANTS (in millions)

69.6	1895	
		1.3
76.1	1900	
		3.0
83.8	1905	
		4.5
92.8	1910	
		4.5
100.5	1915	

FOLLOW-UP REFERENT

When might you need to connect events according to the time period in which they happened?

Examples: putting world events on television or in the newspaper into historical context; recreational reading; study techniques

CURRICULUM APPLICATION

Language Arts: exercises involving chronological order, e.g., writing research papers, narratives, or letters, relating story plots; selecting words to express desired chronological order; correlating literature and literary schools with historical, political, social, and/or economic events

Mathematics: transferring verbal, numerical, or statistical information to graphs

Science: correlating scientific developments with historical, political, literary, social, or economic events

Social Studies: recognizing chronological order and using it to place historical events, eras, artifacts, cultures, and people into time relationships; correlating historical, sociological, economic, artistic, or political events from different cultures, countries, or time periods

Enrichment Areas: correlating musical or artistic developments with historical, political, social, literary, or economic events

TRANSITIVITY—FAMILY TREE

STRAND: Verbal Sequences   **PAGES:** 111–114

ADDITIONAL MATERIALS
Transparencies of student workbook page 111 and TM #6
Washable transparency marker

INTRODUCTION
In previous exercises you used written information to arrange concepts, people, or events into specific orders. Sometimes you compared things by size, rank, or degree of meaning, and sometimes you arranged events in chronological order.

OBJECTIVE
In these exercises you will use clues to diagram several generations of a family tree.

DEMONSTRATION/EXPLANATION
Project the transparency of page 111.
    Diagrams of this type are called "branching diagrams."
Point to the circles.
    In the diagrams that you will use for these exercises, circles indicate that the person represented is a female.
Point to the squares.
    Squares indicate that the person represented is a male.
Indicate horizontal lines.
    A horizontal line connecting a square and a circle means the man and woman are married.
Indicate vertical lines.
    A vertical line connects the husband and wife to their children.
Project the transparency of TM #6. Point to the rows of the diagram.

> *This family tree diagram shows three rows. If this were a diagram of your family, what generation would the bottom row represent?*

Answer: The most recent generation, usually the children in the family. Write CHILDREN beside the bottom row.

> *How would those represented by the middle row be related to the children?*

Answer: They would be parents of the children. Write PARENTS beside the middle row.

> *How would those represented by the top row be related to the children?*

Answer: They would be grandparents of the children (father's parents). Write GRANDPARENTS beside the top row.

> *The paragraph at the top of the transparency gives you clues to help you complete this family-tree diagram. What is the first sentence, and what information does it give you?*

Answer: The first sentence states, "Juan and Rosita have the same names as their grandparents." The names of two of the children (bottom row) and the names of the grandparents (top row) are Juan and Rosita.

> *Where would you put this information on the diagram?*

Answer: In the top row, put JUAN in the square (grandfather) and ROSITA (grandmother) in the circle. In the bottom row, put JUAN in the square and ROSITA in one of the circles. Fill in this information on the transparency as students explain the name placement.

> *The next sentence tells you that Marie has the same name as her mother. How many mother-daughter relationships can you see on the chart?*

Answer: One; between the parent-child rows. (The grandparent-parent row shows only a parent-son relationship.)

> *What new information do you now have, and where does it go on the chart?*

Answer: There are at least two females names Marie in the family and they are mother and daughter. Put MARIE in the circle in the middle row (mother), and in the remaining circle in the bottom row (daughter).

> *Only one shape remains blank. How can you determine what name belongs in the last empty square?*

Answer: The last sentence states that one of Jose's daughters has the same name as Jose's mother. Since Jose is a new name, write JOSE in the empty square.

> *You can confirm that Jose's name belongs in the square by looking back at the diagram. What is the name of Jose's mother?*

Answer: Rosita. Point to the circle in the top row.

> *What is the name of one of Jose's daughters?*

Answer: Rosita. Point to the correct circle in the bottom row.

> *The completed diagram agrees with the clues.*

Indicate the comparable parts of the diagram as you read each clue from the paragraph. As you read, ask students to confirm that each clue is represented on the diagram.

GUIDED PRACTICE
EXERCISE: B-278
Give students sufficient time to complete this exercise. Then, using the demonstration methodology above, have them discuss and explain their choices.
ANSWER:
B-278   **a.** Barbara Winston
        b. Winston
        c. Leon Winston

DETAILED SOLUTION

Clue 1: "James and Sarah Levy have a son named Harry," is not sufficient to decide which of the two married couples is James and Sarah, since both have a son.

Clue 2: "**Harry** has an aunt named **Mary**" implies that either Harry's mother or father has a sister named Mary. Since only one nephew-aunt relationship is indicated, you can put Harry's name in the square in the bottom row and Mary's name in the first circle from the right in the middle row (**2**).

Clue 3: "Mary has a brother named **Leon**" fills in the right-hand square in the middle row, since Mary has only one brother shown (**3**).

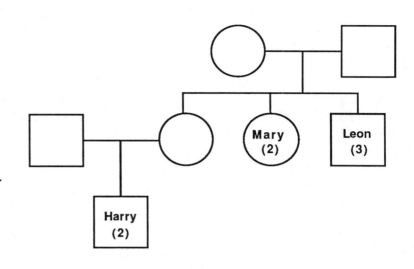

Clue 4: "Leon's father and mother are **Walter** and **Barbara Winston**" allows these names to be entered in the top row (**4**).

Completion: By referring back to Clue 1, you can now place **James** and **Sarah** (**1b**) as the parents of Harry.

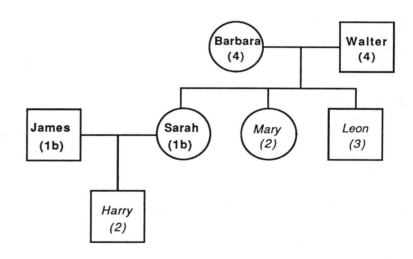

INDEPENDENT PRACTICE
Assign exercises **B-279** and **B-280**.

DISCUSSION TIPS
Students should discuss their answers and check their completed diagrams against the clues. Encourage them to identify which clue gave them each indicated piece of information. The teacher might wish to play "devil's advocate" to encourage students to develop and verbalize their reasoning. For example, the teacher might read Clue 1 from exercise **B-278** and say, "Okay, James and Sarah Levy have a son named Harry. I see that the married couple in the top row have a son, so I'm going to put James and Sarah as their names, and Harry in the square for their son." If this does not elicit an immediate

reaction from the students, draw them out by questioning individual students; e.g., "Is that what you have, John?" (Hopefully, he'll say no.) "Where did you put James and Sarah?" "Oh, really? Why did you put them there?" This technique should stimulate discussion and cause students to defend their decisions.

ANSWERS

NOTE: In all answers, the clue numbers that give you the information to complete each section of the diagram are indicated in bold in both the clue analysis and in the diagrams.

B-279

Clue 1: "Ivan Jones married Betty Green, and they have two children named Charles and Helen." No information in this clue can be placed on the diagram at this point, since two of the three married couples on the diagram have two children. It does, however, create two possible places for the four names [Ivan Jones, Betty Green, Charles (Jones), and Helen (Jones)].

Clue 2: "Charles Jones was named for his grandfather on his dad's side of the family." Since there is only one *paternal* grandfather-grandson relationship shown, place the name **Charles Jones I (2)** in the top square (paternal side)(**2**). Now, by reference to *Clue 1*, you can add the names given there. You know that **Ivan Jones** and **Betty Green** are the parents of **Charles II (2)** and **Helen Jones (1b)**. The chart at this point should look like the one below.

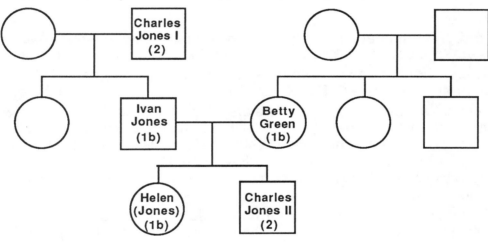

Clue 3: "Helen Jones was named for **her mother's sister**." There are two ways to place this clue. Since you know where both Helen Jones and her mother, Betty Green Jones, are in the chart, look for the circle representing Betty's sister and put **Helen (Green)**'s name there (**3**). As a double check, there is only one sister-sister relationship shown on the chart: middle row, maternal side.

Clue 4: "Ivan's sister and mother have the same name." Since you have already placed Ivan's name on the chart, this clue is helpful in telling you that the same name goes in the top- and middle-row circles on the paternal side—but it doesn't tell you what that name is. No new information can be placed on the chart at this time.

Clue 5: "Charles has an aunt named **Elizabeth**." This clue enables you to put Elizabeth in the remaining circle in the middle row, since it indicates Charles's only remaining aunt (**5**). By referring back to *Clue 4* now, you can put **Elizabeth** in the circle for the paternal grandmother (**4b**), also.

Clue 6: "Arthur and Grace Green have three children." Since only one set of parents shown on the diagram has three children, put **Arthur** and **Grace Green** in the remaining square and circle in the grandparents' row (**6**).

Clue 7: "Betty Green has a brother named **David**." Since Betty Green has only one brother shown on the diagram, put David (Green) in the remaining square of the middle row (**7**). The completed chart is shown below.

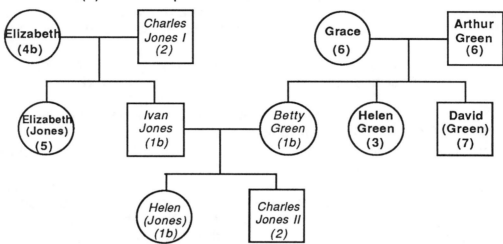

B-280

Clue 1: "**Fred Williams** has three sisters." Since only one male (square) shows three sisters (circles) on the chart, put Fred (**1**) in the square in the bottom row.

Clue 2: "**Grace Thomas** has two brothers." As in Clue 1, only one female (circle) shows two brothers (squares). Put Grace Thomas in the (**2**) circle on the diagram.

Clue 3: "**Harold Williams, Jr.,** has two sisters." This clue, like the previous two, gives you direct information allowing you to fill in one name: the father of Fred is the only male (square) on the diagram (**3**) showing two sisters. In addition, however, you can infer one additional piece of information: Harold Williams' father's name is also **Harold** (**3**), since the "Jr." on the name indicates that the father has the same name as the son.

Clue 4: "Fred Williams has a grandfather named John." This clue allows you to put **John** (**Thomas**) in the last (maternal grandfather) square on the top row (**4**), since Fred has only one remaining unnamed grandfather.

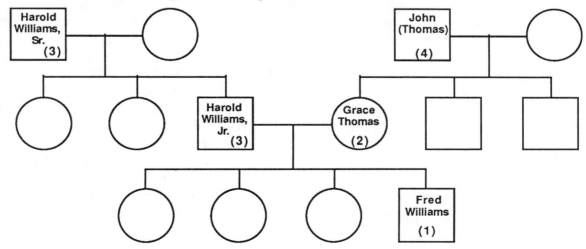

108

Clue 5: "Fred Williams has a sister, an aunt, and a grandmother named **Lillian**." This clue allows you to fill in one circle (**5**) in the bottom row (Fred's sister) and one circle (**5**) in the middle row (Fred's aunt). Since the only females who remain unidentified in the middle row are on the paternal side, one of Harold Jr.'s sisters must be named Lillian. At this point you can conjecture that Fred's paternal grandmother is probably named Lillian, but there is no proof. (The Williams and Thomas families might have been good friends before their children married, so it is possible that the Williams named one of their children Lillian after their good friend, John Thomas's wife.)

Clue 6: "**Irene Williams** has an aunt named **Nancy** and an uncle named **David**." From this clue you can complete three more sections of the diagram. Only the children of Harold and Grace show aunt or uncle relationships on the diagram, therefore one of the girls in the bottom row is named Irene (**6**). Since Irene has only one unidentified aunt (on the paternal side), put Nancy in the remaining circle (**6**) of the middle row. She also only has uncles on the maternal side of the family, so put David in one of the remaining squares (**6**).

Clue 7: "Fred Williams was named for an uncle." Since Fred W. has only one uncle who is still unidentified, put **Fred (Thomas)** in the remaining square (**7**) on the maternal side of the middle row.

Clue 8: "Pauline Williams was named for her grandmother Pauline Thomas." Although there are two grandmother-granddaughter relationships yet to be identified, the fact that Pauline-the-grandmother's last name is Thomas tells you that she is married to John Thomas. Put **Pauline Williams** in the remaining circle in the bottom row (**8**) and **Pauline Thomas** in the maternal grandmother's circle in the top row (**8**).

Completion:

By referring back to *Clue 5,* you can complete the chart by putting **Lillian** in the one remaining circle, the paternal grandmother (**5b**).

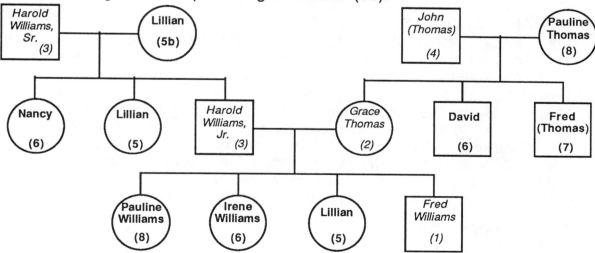

FOLLOW-UP REFERENT

When might you need to identify family relationships or arrange names into generations from written clues?

Examples: recording or explaining family histories; gathering information for medical records; making or reading branching diagrams

CURRICULUM APPLICATION

Language Arts: comprehending family relationships in literature; using branching diagrams in transformational grammar

Mathematics: tracking and recording generations; making and utilizing branching diagrams when solving mathematical problems

Science: diagramming genetics research or relationships; using branching diagrams to illustrate zoological or botanical phyla

Social Studies: tracing historical families; tracing technological or industrial developments

Enrichment Areas: diagramming historical or organizational development of various vocations; understanding or diagramming computer programs; developing or reading business organizational charts

DEDUCTIVE REASONING

STRAND: Verbal Sequences   **PAGES:** 115–122

ADDITIONAL MATERIALS

Transparencies of student workbook pages 115 and 116
Transparency of TM #7

INTRODUCTION

In the previous lesson you used clues to organize and chart information regarding the order of family generations.

OBJECTIVE

In these exercises you will also use clues to chart information and answer related questions.

DEMONSTRATION / EXPLANATION

Sometimes you have lots of information that you need to sort out or arrange to answer specific questions. Using a chart or a matrix may help you see relationships that are hard to find from reading information.

Project the transparency of page 115.

This example illustrates one way of organizing information to make it more accessible. You are asked to identify the owners of three different pets by marking the clues from the paragraph onto a chart. Some clues are not specific, so you will have to deduce the information for the chart.

Follow the **EXAMPLE** through the step-by-step process demonstrated on the transparencies, indicating the charted information as you read.

GUIDED PRACTICE

EXERCISE: **B-281**

NOTE: The transparency of TM #7 can be used as an aid when discussing these exercises and charting the information. Clue identification is in bold type throughout the solutions.

ANSWER:

B-281   Bob is in grade 4.
Christy is in grade 6.
Freddy is in grade 2.
Joe is in grade 1.

DETAILED SOLUTION
If "Joe is three years younger than Bob," (**b**) and if
"No student has been held back or skipped a grade,"
(**a**) then look for two grades that are three years
apart; i.e., grades 1 and 4. So Joe is in grade 1 and
Bob is in grade 4. Put Y's (Yes) in the proper cells
and add N's (No) to complete the rows and columns
as shown to the right.

	B	C	F	J
1	N	N	N	Y
2	N			N
4	Y	N	N	N
6	N			N

If "Christy is four years older than Freddy," (**c**) then
Christy is in grade 6 and Freddy is in grade 2.
Complete the chart as shown to the right.

	B	C	F	J
1	N	N	N	Y
2	N	N	Y	N
4	Y	N	N	N
6	N	Y	N	N

INDEPENDENT PRACTICE
Assign exercises **B-282** through **B-289**.

DISCUSSION TIPS
Use the DETAILED SOLUTIONS given in the answer sections for discussion focus and
techniques. Be certain students know why and how they arrived at each specific answer.

ANSWERS
B-282　The <u>Crusader</u> has the <u>49 mm</u> gun.
　　　　　The <u>Sherman has</u> the <u>75 mm</u> gun.
　　　　　The <u>SU-100</u> has the <u>100 mm</u> gun.
　　　　　The <u>Tiger</u> has the <u>88 mm</u> gun.

DETAILED SOLUTION
If "The Tiger tank has a larger gun than [two other
tanks]," (**a**) then it cannot have the smallest (49mm)
or the second smallest (75mm) guns. Put N's in the
T-49 and T-75 cells. If "The SU-100 has the most
powerful gun," (**c**) then it must have the 100mm gun.
Place a Y in the SU-100 cell, and fill in the 100 row
and SU column with N's. (If the 100mm gun belongs
to the SU, then it cannot belong to any other tank,
and if the SU has a 100mm gun then it cannot have
any other size. This logic applies to all deductive
reasoning activities in this section.) Since there is
now only one cell blank in the T column, the Tiger
must have an 88mm gun.

	C	Sh	SU	T
49			N	N
75			N	N
88	N	N	N	Y
100	N	N	Y	N

Only the 75mm and 88mm tanks are not identified
at this point. Clue **d** says, "The Crusader, a British
tank, has the least powerful gun." Thus, the 75mm
gun belongs to the Sherman tank and the 88mm gun
belongs to the Tiger.

	C	Sh	SU	T
49	Y	N	N	N
75	N	Y	N	N
88	N	N	N	Y
100	N	N	Y	N

B-283   The <u>elephant</u> runs <u>38</u> km/hr.
The <u>fox</u> runs <u>64</u> km/hr.
The <u>deer</u> runs <u>79</u> km/hr.
The <u>cheetah</u> runs <u>112</u> km/hr.

DETAILED SOLUTION
Since "The largest animal (elephant) is the slowest," (**a**) put a Y in the E-38 cell and fill in the E row and the 38 column with N's as shown. Since "The fastest weighs less than half as much as a deer," (**b**) the deer, by implication, is not the fastest. Put an N in the D-112 cell. Clue **c** implies that the fox is not the fastest animal, for it cannot catch two of the others. Put an N in the F-112 cell. The chart looks like this.

	Running Speed			
	38	64	79	112
C	N			
D	N			N
E	Y	N	N	N
F	N			N

This leaves only one animal open to be the fastest: the cheetah. Place a Y in the C-112 cell and fill in the C row. There are now two animals left, the deer and the fox, and two running speeds that have not yet been matched, 64 kph and 79 kph. Since clue **c** implies that the fox is slower than the deer, place Y's in the F-64 and D-79 cells and complete the chart.

	Running Speed			
	38	64	79	112
C	N	N	N	Y
D	N	N	Y	N
E	Y	N	N	N
F	N	Y	N	N

B-284   <u>Mercury</u> has an orbit time of <u>1/4</u> year.
<u>Venus</u> has an orbit time of <u>2/3</u> year.
<u>Jupiter</u> has an orbit time of <u>11</u> years.
<u>Pluto</u> has an orbit time of <u>248</u> years.

DETAILED SOLUTION
Since Jupiter has neither the longest nor the shortest orbit time (**a**), put N's in the J-1/4 (shortest) and J-248 (longest) cells. If "Pluto has an orbit time 22.5 times that of Jupiter" (**b**), Pluto must have an orbit time of 248 years to Jupiter's 11 years. (No other pair of orbit times fits the 22.5 ratio.) Put Y's in the P-248 and J-11 cells, and fill in the N's as indicated.

	Orbit time in yrs.			
	1/4	2/3	11	248
J	N	N	Y	N
M			N	N
P	N	N	N	Y
V			N	N

Since "Mercury has a shorter orbit time than Venus" (**c**), put Y's in the M-1/4 and V-2/3 cells and complete the chart.

	Orbit time in yrs.			
	1/4	2/3	11	248
J	N	N	Y	N
M	Y	N	N	N
P	N	N	N	Y
V	N	Y	N	N

B-285   <u>Kavana</u> lives in <u>Zambia</u>.
           <u>Schleinstein</u> lives in <u>Czechoslovakia</u>.
           <u>Totino</u> lives in the <u>U.S.S.R.</u>
           <u>Warpenburg</u> lives in <u>Chile</u>.

DETAILED SOLUTION

NOTE: Students may wish to consult an atlas to locate the countries in this exercise.)

If "Kavana's country has no sea coast" (**a**), then Kavana must live in either Czechoslovakia or Zambia, for both Chile and the U.S.S.R. have sea coasts. Put N's in the K-Chile and K-USSR cells. Clue **b** states that "Schleinstein's country is not in South America," so Schleinstein is not from Chile, which is in South America. Put an N in the S-Chile cell. Since "Totino does not live in the southern hemisphere" (**c**),Totino lives in neither Chile nor Zambia. When the chart is filled in with the above information, there are three N's in the Chile column, thus Warpenburg is from Chile.

	K	S	T	W
Ch	N	N	N	Y
Cz				N
USSR	N			N
Z			N	N

Clue **c** also says that Kavana lives in the southern hemisphere (Chile or Zambia). Since Warpenburg lives in Chile, Kavana must live in Zambia. Put a Y in the K-Zambia cell and fill in the N's as indicated. The last clue (**d**) says that "Totino's country is farther north than Schleinstein's." Since the only remaining countries are Czechoslovakia and the U.S.S.R, and since the U.S.S.R. extends to both the north and south of Czechoslovakia, Totino must be from the U.S.S.R. and Schleinstein is from Czechoslovakia. Complete the chart as shown to the right.

	K	S	T	W
Ch	*N*	*N*	*N*	Y
Cz	N	Y	N	*N*
USSR	*N*	N	Y	*N*
Z	Y	N	*N*	*N*

B-286   <u>Mr. Jaworski</u> owns the <u>Collie</u>.
           <u>Miss Roberts</u> owns the <u>Dachshund</u>.
           <u>Mrs. Bradley</u> owns the <u>German Shepherd</u>.
           <u>Mr. Forsythe</u> owns the <u>Great Dane</u>.

DETAILED SOLUTION

Since "Miss Roberts does not own a dog that has fleas" (**a**), and since "German Shepherds and Great Danes have fleas" (**e**), you can infer that Roberts owns neither the German Shepherd nor the Great Dane. Put N's in the R-Gr. Shep. and R-Gr. Dane cells. Since neither Jaworski nor Bradley owns the Great Dane (**b**), put N's in the J-Gr. Dane and B-Gr. Dane cells. If "Mr. Forsythe knows the German Shepherd and Dachshund owners" (**c**), and he does not know Mr. Jaworski (**d**), then it can be inferred that neither he nor Mr. Jaworski is the owner of either dog. Fill in the chart accordingly.

	B	F	J	R
Collie				
Gr. Dane	N		N	N
Gr. Shep.		N	N	N
Dach		N	N	

Referring to the chart, there is only one person who can own the Great Dane (Forsythe), one person who can own the German Shepherd (Bradley), and only one type of dog (the Collie) can belong to Jaworski. Mark this information on the chart, filling in the correct cells with Y's and N's. By elimination, Miss Roberts must own the Dachshund.

	B	F	J	R
Collie	N	N	Y	N
Gr. Dane	N	Y	N	N
Gr. Shep.	Y	N	N	N
Dach	N	N	N	Y

B-287 Betty is married to Fred.
Lora is married to Tim.
Mary is married to Ken.
Pam is married to Ross.

DETAILED SOLUTION
Clues **b** and **e** combine to tell you that "Ross's best friend is Fred" and that "Betty and Ross's best friend (Fred) are married." Put a Y in the F-B cell and add N's to the B row and the F column. Since Ross is an only child (**c**), he did not marry (**d**) Pam's sister (Mary, from **a**) or (**f**) Lora, because both of their husbands have brothers. Put N's in the R-M and R-L cells. Since "Pam's sister (Mary) married Tim's brother" (**d**), Mary did not marry Tim. Put an N in the M-T cell.

	F	K	R	T
B	Y	N	N	N
L	N		N	
M	N		N	N
P	N			N

Looking at the R column, Ross can only be married to Pam. Put a Y in the R-P cell and add N's to the P row. Now look at the T column. Tim must be married to Lora. By elimination, Ken and Mary are married.

	F	K	R	T
B	Y	N	N	N
L	N	N	N	Y
M	N	Y	N	N
P	N	N	Y	N

B-288 Beaumont is from England.
Phillipe is from France.
Cicero is from Greece.
Letitia is from Spain.

DETAILED SOLUTION
"P is older than L but younger than C" (**a**), thus C > P > L, and "B is older than C" (**b**). So the age arrangement is B > C > P > L:

Clue **c** tells you that "The oldest (Beaumont) is not from Greece or Spain." Put N's in the B-G and B-S cells. From clue **d** you learn that "The youngest (Letitia) is not from England or France. If "The second oldest (Cicero) visited Athens" (**e**), and since you know that each recently visited their home country, you can deduce that Cicero was born in Greece. Fill in the chart accordingly.

OLDEST	1931	Beaumont
	1935	Cicero
	1942	Phillipe
YOUNGEST	1946	Letitia

	E	F	G	S
B			N	N
C	N	N	Y	N
L	N	N	N	
P			N	

Looking at the L row, Letitia must be from Spain. Put a Y in the L-S cell. If Letitia is from Spain, Phillipe is not. Put an N in the P-S cell. Clue **f** says that "The second youngest (Phillipe) is not from England." Put an N in the P-E cell. Looking at the P row, Phillipe must be from France. By elimination, Beaumont is from England.

	E	F	G	S
B	Y	N	*N*	*N*
C	*N*	*N*	Y	*N*
L	*N*	*N*	*N*	Y
P	N	Y	*N*	N

B-289

SPORT	FIRST NAME	LAST NAME
Basketball	Jim	Wolfe
Football	George	Roberts
Swimming	Sam	Carey

DETAILED SOLUTION

If "George and Carey do not go to basketball" (**a**), then there should be N's in the B-G and B-C cells. Since "Sam and Wolfe do not go to football" (**b**), put N's in the F-S and F-W cells. "Jim and Roberts do not go swimming" (**c**), so put N's in the S-J and S-R cells.

FIRST NAMES			SPORT	LAST NAMES		
G	J	S		C	R	W
N			Basketball	N		
	N	N	Football	N		N
	N		Swimming		N	

Clue **d** says that "Jim and Carey do not go to football." Put N's in the F-J and F-C cells. Looking at the chart, you can determine that GR goes to football, C to swimming, and J to basketball. (In each case two of the three cells in a row or column were filled.) At this point, by elimination, it appears that S goes to swimming and W to basketball.

FIRST NAMES			SPORT	LAST NAMES		
G	J	S		C	R	W
N	Y	N	Basketball	*N*	N	Y
Y	*N*	*N*	Football	*N*	Y	*N*
N	*N*	Y	Swimming	Y	*N*	N

FOLLOW-UP REFERENT

When might you need to deduce information from clues?

Examples: games or puzzles requiring deductive reasoning, e.g., card games, mystery games, logic puzzles; recreational reading, especially detective novels or mysteries; comparison shopping; interpreting chronological events in news articles, television shows, movies, or plays; applying deductive reasoning to everyday life, e.g., using deductive reasoning to estimate solutions to problems at work or at school

CURRICULUM APPLICATION

Language Arts: comprehension exercises involving transitive order or process of elimination; determining chronological events in stories or dramatizations

Mathematics: transitivity or inequality exercises; solving word problems

Science: evaluating and charting experiment results; making genetics charts

Social Studies: comprehending chronological order; comparing statistics

Enrichment Areas: interpreting chronological events in dramatic productions

NEGATION—DETERMINING YES-NO RULES

STRAND: Verbal Sequences   **PAGES:** 123–124

ADDITIONAL MATERIALS
Transparency of TM #8
Washable transparency marker
Student handouts of TM #8 (optional)

INTRODUCTION
In a previous lesson you used clues in the form of yes-no statements to solve deductive reasoning problems.

OBJECTIVE
In these exercises you will describe a path of color changes by following a set of yes-no rules.

DEMONSTRATION / EXPLANATION
Project TM #8 and indicate the **RULE BOX** at the top of the sheet.
As you follow the path from start to finish, you are to write "Yes" or "No" on each arrow that joins two circles. What you will write depends upon the shading of the circles. If they are the same color, you will write "Yes" on the arrow. If they are not the same color, you will write "No."
Point to the **START** circle, the first arrow, then the second circle.
For example, this first arrow should be marked "No," since the two circles it joins are not the same color.
Write NO on the arrow, then point to the second arrow.
How should you mark this arrow, and why would you mark it that way?
Answer: "No;" since the two circles it joins are not the same color. Write NO on the second arrow, then point to the third arrow.
How would you mark this arrow and why would you mark it that way?
Answer: The arrow should be marked "Yes." The two circles it joins are the same color. Write yes along the arrow. Continue this line of questioning until each arrow has been marked as shown below, or duplicate TM #8 as a student handout.

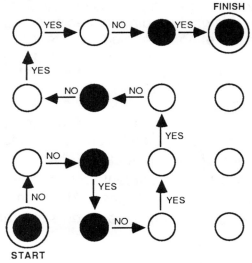

GUIDED PRACTICE
EXERCISE: **B-290**
ANSWER:
B-290

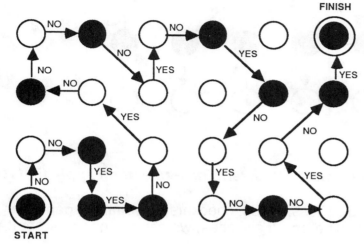

INDEPENDENT PRACTICE
Assign exercises **B-291** and **B-292**.

DISCUSSION TIPS
Students may sometimes confuse *negation* with *opposite*. When two statements **negate** each other, they must have opposite truth values; i.e., one **must** be true and the other **must** be false. Although opposite statements **may** have opposite truth values, this does not always happen. For example, the statement "The gas tank is full" is not necessarily negated by a sentence with an opposite meaning, i.e., "The gas tank is empty." Although these two sentences **may** have opposite truth values, it is not true that they **must** have opposite truth values. They may both be false if, for example, the gas tank is half-full! The statement can, however, be negated by adding the word *not*, e.g., "It is *not* true that the gas tank is full" or "The gas tank is *not* full."

Encourage students to use negation sentences when they state "No" rules in these exercises. They should say, for example, "The two circles are *not* the same color," rather than "The first circle is black and the second circle is white."

ANSWERS
B-291

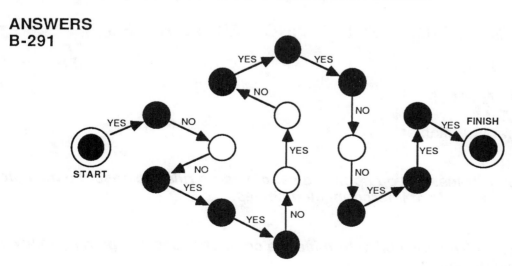

B-292

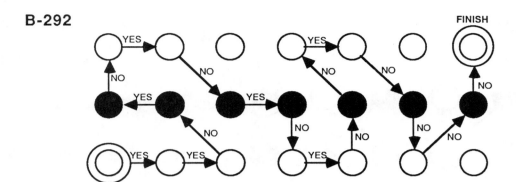

FOLLOW-UP REFERENT
When might you use examples to determine a rule, then apply that rule to further examples?

Examples: strategy games, e.g., chess, cards, checkers; assembling games or models involving multistep directions; using on-off switches; watching a game or sport with which you are unfamiliar

CURRICULUM APPLICATION

Language Arts: determining whether usage, spelling, grammar, or paragraph construction examples follow a given set of rules

Mathematics: recognizing correctly completed multistep operations; recognizing similarities among word problems that call for similar solutions; recognizing similarity and congruence in geometric shapes

Science: explaining basic experimental reactions and their causes; recognizing the change of a single variable in science demonstrations

Social Studies: placing artifacts according to usage, era, or culture; determining specifics from a map, e.g., type of road, size of city, elevations, points of interest; deductive reasoning involving truth value

Enrichment Areas: deciding the time signature for a piece of music from written samples of the music; learning the rules of a game by playing rather than by reading instructions; playing hidden-rule games on a computer or video

NEGATION—FOLLOWING YES-NO RULES

STRAND: Verbal Sequences   **PAGES:** 125–126

ADDITIONAL MATERIALS
Transparency of TM #9
Washable transparency marker

INTRODUCTION
In the previous lesson you applied a set of yes-no rules to describe the color changes in a series of interconnected circles.

OBJECTIVE
In these exercises you will determine the color changes in a path by following a set of yes-no rules.

DEMONSTRATION/EXPLANATION

Project TM #9 and indicate the **RULE BOX**.

> *According to the RULE BOX, what is true if "Yes" is written on an arrow?*

Answer: The circle toward which the arrow points is the same color as the previous circle.

> *What if "No" is written on an arrow?*

Answer: The circle toward which the arrow points is not the same color as the previous circle. Point to the **START** circle.

> *The circle in the START position is black, and the arrow that leads from it to the next circle has a "No" on it. According to the RULE BOX, what color should this second circle be?*

Answer: White (or any color that is not black). Point to the second arrow.

> *How is the second arrow marked?*

Answer: "Yes." Point to the second and third circles.

> *What color should the third circle be if it follows the yes-no rule above?*

Answer: It should be the same color as the previous circle (white).

> *What should be done to the third circle on this path?*

Answer: Nothing, it should stay white so it will be the same as the second circle. Continue this line of questioning until the path is complete as shown below.

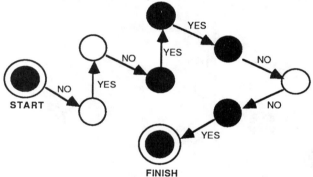

GUIDED PRACTICE

EXERCISE: **B-293**

Give students sufficient time to complete this exercise. Then, using the demonstration methodology above, have them discuss and explain their choices.

ANSWER:

B-293

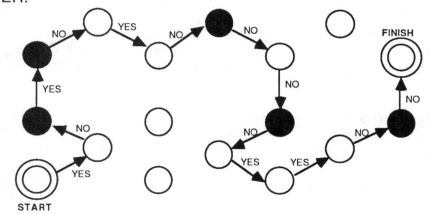

INDEPENDENT PRACTICE

Assign exercises **B-294** through **B-295**.

DISCUSSION TIPS
Encourage students to use negation statements as they discuss their answers. Class discussion is a valuable technique for having students share their acquired knowledge and verbalize the reasoning behind their decisions.

ANSWERS
B-294

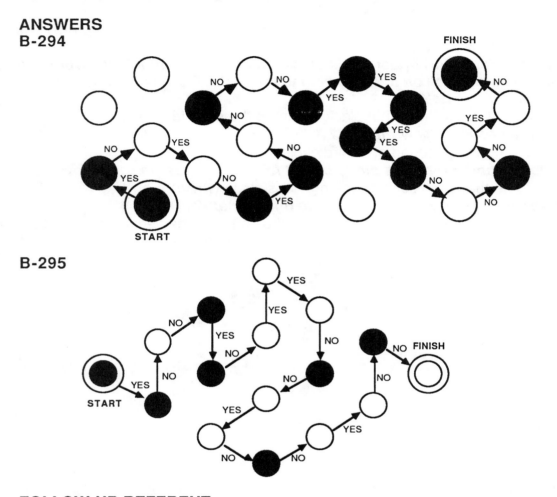

B-295

FOLLOW-UP REFERENT
When might you find it necessary or helpful to apply given rules to a series of consecutive steps?

Examples: strategy games, e.g., chess, cards, checkers; following multistep directions in assembling games or models; using a series or chain of on-off switches; determining the truth value of true-false or yes-no statements; deductive reasoning or logical exercises involving truth value

CURRICULUM APPLICATION
Language Arts: arranging topics into a two- or three-step outline; recognizing the effect of *no* or *not* on meaning; interpreting double negatives; following rules of capitalization or punctuation

Mathematics: applying multistep operations in mathematics problems; analyzing or applying geometric proofs

Science: recognizing the change of a single variable in science demonstrations or experiments; tracing the path of an electrical circuit; applying laws of physics or chemistry to a series of events or to multistep experiments

Social Studies: following or creating a chart or mapping a route; applying yes-no statements to historical, geographic, social, or economic events

Enrichment Areas: understanding or creating computer programs or applications; learning or duplicating a series of dance steps; learning and duplicating pattern plays in organized sports or games; following a sequence of instructions for art, needlework, or craft projects

NEGATION—SUPPLY THE RULE

STRAND: Verbal Sequences   **PAGE:** 127

ADDITIONAL MATERIALS
Transparency of student workbook page 127
Washable transparency marker

INTRODUCTION
In previous lessons you determined or followed yes-no statements as applied to color changes in a sequence of circles.

OBJECTIVE
In these exercises you will identify the rule shown by a path of circles.

DEMONSTRATION/EXPLANATION
Project the transparency of page 127.

In each exercise there are three paths from START to finish. One path is dotted (o o o), one path is solid (———) and one path is dashed (— — —). You are to identify the rule that each path illustrates. Look at the dotted path. How do the circles along this path compare with each other?

Answer: They are all the same color, black.

If you were to follow the rules in the rule box and mark the arrows along the dotted path, how would they be marked?

Answer: Each arrow would be marked "Yes."

Since each arrow would be marked "Yes," you would say that the dotted path follows the Yes rule.

Indicate the answer on the transparency, then point to the first several circles along the solid path.

Now look at the circles along the solid path. How do these circles compare with each other?

Answer: Some of the circles are white and some are black.

Do you see any particular pattern to the color sequence?

Answer: The pattern of color repetition is black-white-white.

How would you mark the arrows along the solid path?

Answer: Write YES or NO on each arrow in the sequence as students give the rule.

What pattern do you see to the arrow markings?

Answer: The No's and Yes's alternate.

What rule would you say that the solid path follows?

Answer: It follows the Yes-No rule. Write the answer beside the solid line in the **RULE** space on the transparency.

GUIDED PRACTICE
EXERCISE: **B-296**
ANSWER:
B-296 Since the circles along the dashed path (– – –) alternate in color, each arrow would be marked "No." The path follows the No rule.

INDEPENDENT PRACTICE
Assign exercise **B-297**.

DISCUSSION TIPS
Encourage students to discuss their answers. Class discussion is a valuable technique for having students share their acquired knowledge and verbalize the reasoning they used to make their decision. Often their words will communicate in a more meaningful way than words a teacher may use.

ANSWERS
B-297 ———— The solid path follows an alternating Yes-No rule.

o o o o The dotted path follows the Yes rule.

– – – – The dashed path follows the No rule.

FOLLOW-UP REFERENT
   When might you determine a rule by examining examples of that rule?
Examples: strategy games, e.g., chess, cards, checkers; assembling games or models involving multistep directions; using on-off switches; watching a game or sport with which you are unfamiliar

CURRICULUM APPLICATION
Language Arts: determining whether usage, spelling, grammar, or paragraph construction examples follow a given set of rules

Mathematics: recognizing correctly completed multistep operations; recognizing similarities among word problems that call for similar solutions; recognizing similarity and congruence in geometric shapes

Science: explaining basic experimental reactions and their causes; recognizing the change of a single variable in science demonstrations

Social Studies: placing artifacts according to usage, era, or culture; determining specifics from a map, e.g., type of road, size of city, elevations, points of interest; deductive reasoning involving truth value

Enrichment Areas: deciding the time signature for a piece of music from written samples of the music; learning the rules of a game by playing rather than by reading instructions; playing hidden-rule games on a computer or video

NEGATION—COMPLETING TRUE-FALSE TABLES—A

STRAND: Verbal Sequences   **PAGES:** 128–129

ADDITIONAL MATERIALS
Transparency of TM #10
Washable transparency marker

INTRODUCTION

In previous lessons you identified and followed yes-no rules as applied to paths of colored circles. You have also used yes-no statements to determine facts from a series of clues in deductive reasoning exercises.

OBJECTIVE

Sometimes "true" and "false" can be used for "yes" and "no." In these exercises you will complete a matrix by deciding whether a statement is true or false when applied to a given shape.

DEMONSTRATION/EXPLANATION

Project TM #10.

Do you remember exercises like this from Figural Classifications? In those exercises there were no words at the top of the column, but you filled in the matrix by using clues gathered from the cells that had been filled in. This matrix, like those in the figural activities, has rows, columns, and cells.

Indicate rows, columns, and cells. Indicate the specific locations as you talk.

This particular kind of matrix is called a TRUE-FALSE TABLE. What is the heading for Column 1?

Answer: IT IS STRIPED.

What is the heading for Column 2?

Answer: IT IS CHECKED.

What is the heading for Column 3?

Answer: IT IS SQUARE.

How would you describe the figure at the beginning of Row 1?

Answer: It is a striped square.

As you move across this row, you will write "true" if the statement at the head of that column is true for a striped square and "false" if the statement is not true for a striped square. Look at the heading of Column 1. Is the statement "It is striped" true for the striped square?

Answer: Yes.

What should you write in the Row 1, Column 1 cell?

Answer: True, because the statement is true for a striped square. Write TRUE in the Row 1, Column 1 cell on the transparency.

Now move to the next column in Row 1. What is the heading?

Answer: IT IS CHECKED.

Is the statement "It is checked" true for a striped square?

Answer: No.

What should be written in the Row 1, Column 2 cell?

Answer: False, because the statement is *not* true for a striped square. Write FALSE in the Row 1, Column 2 cell on the transparency.

Now move to Column 3 in Row 1. What is the heading?

Answer: IT IS SQUARE.

Is the statement "It is square" true for a striped square?

Answer: Yes.

What should be written in the Row 1, Column 3 cell?

Answer: True, because the statement is true for a striped square. Write TRUE in the cell.

Repeat this line of questioning until all cells in the table have been filled as shown below.

		COLUMN 1 IT IS STRIPED	COLUMN 2 IT IS CHECKED	COLUMN 3 IT IS SQUARE
ROW 1	▨	TRUE	FALSE	TRUE
ROW 2	⊕	FALSE	TRUE	FALSE
ROW 3	▦	FALSE	TRUE	TRUE

GUIDED PRACTICE
EXERCISE: **B-298**
ANSWER: **B-298**

	IT IS WHITE	IT IS CHECKED	IT IS NOT WHITE	IT IS NOT CHECKED
▦	*FALSE*	TRUE	TRUE	FALSE
●	FALSE	FALSE	TRUE	*TRUE*
△	TRUE	FALSE	*FALSE*	TRUE
○	*TRUE*	FALSE	FALSE	TRUE
■	FALSE	*FALSE*	TRUE	TRUE
◬	FALSE	*TRUE*	TRUE	FALSE

INDEPENDENT PRACTICE
Assign exercise **B-299**.

DISCUSSION TIPS
Some students may have difficulty determining the truth value of negative statements. The italicized explanations shown in the answer to exercise **B-299** may help explain these "double negatives." Encourage students to discuss, explain, and defend their answers.

ANSWER
B-299

There are two PATTERNS: BLACK and CHECKED.
There are two SHAPES: SQUARES and TRIANGLES.
There are two SIZES: LARGE and SMALL.

SHAPE	IT IS NOT LARGE	IT IS NOT SQUARE	IT IS NOT CHECKED
▲	FALSE (If it is FALSE that it is NOT large, then it is large.)	TRUE (If it is TRUE that it is NOT square, it must be a triangle.)	TRUE (If it is TRUE that it is NOT checked, it must be black.)
■	TRUE (If it is TRUE that it is NOT large, it must be small.)	FALSE (If it is FALSE that it is NOT square, it must be square.)	TRUE (If it is TRUE that it is NOT checked, it must be black.)
◭	FALSE (If it is FALSE that it is NOT large, then it is large.)	TRUE (If it is TRUE that it is NOT square, it must be a triangle.)	FALSE (If it is FALSE that it is NOT checked, it must be checked.)

FOLLOW-UP REFERENT

When might you need to determine whether a statement is true or false when applied to a particular object or concept?

Examples: observing that operating instructions or directions have been correctly followed; recognizing whether recipes or directions for taking medicine are being correctly followed; answering true/false questions on a test; recognizing that negative statements can be either true or false; observing whether given safety rules and procedures are followed on the job and at home or school

CURRICULUM APPLICATION

Language Arts: proofreading papers for errors in spelling, grammar, or punctuation; answering true/false questions about a specific aspect of a story or selection; judging whether formatting instructions have been followed

Mathematics: checking computations to determine if correct procedures were followed; choosing correct answer sets to a problem; checking computations by estimation

Science: verifying animal or plant characteristics in laboratory demonstrations; reading or completing genetic probability charts

Social Studies: finding facts to support or negate statements; determining correct time in different time zones; deductive reasoning involving truth value

Enrichment Areas: determining whether instructions and/or rules have been followed in sports or recreation activities

NEGATION—COMPLETING TRUE-FALSE TABLES—B

STRAND: Verbal Sequences   **PAGES:** 130–136

ADDITIONAL MATERIALS

Transparencies of student workbook pages 130 and 131
Washable transparency marker

INTRODUCTION

In the previous lesson you completed true-false tables by deciding whether statements applied to specific figures were true or false.

OBJECTIVE

In these exercises you will also complete true-false tables, but you will have to follow a number of rules or conditions.

DEMONSTRATION / EXPLANATION

Project the transparency of page 130.

In this true-false matrix, the shapes at the top of each column must be shaded so that each meets all the conditions described in the box above the matrix. Only the patterns shown in the rectangles at the beginning of each row may be used to shade the shapes. The shapes are the same for each exercise in this section: a large and a small square, a large and a small hexagon, and a large circle.

Project the transparency of page 131, following the **EXAMPLE** step-by-step and indicating the charted information as you read.

GUIDED PRACTICE
EXERCISE: **B-300**

NOTE: A transparency of the blank matrix on the bottom part of TM #10 may be used with all activities in this section. Clue numbers are given in parenthesis within each cell. The boxed statements under each matrix will explain how each pattern was determined from the conditions.

ANSWER:

B-300

Clue 1: "Squares are not striped." Write an **F** (false) in the striped row under each square.

Clue 2: "The circle is not checked." Write an **F** in the checked row under the circle.

Clue 3: "No large figure is gray." Write an **F** in the gray row under each large figure.

Clue 4: "No small figure is checked." Write an **F** under each small figure in the checked row.

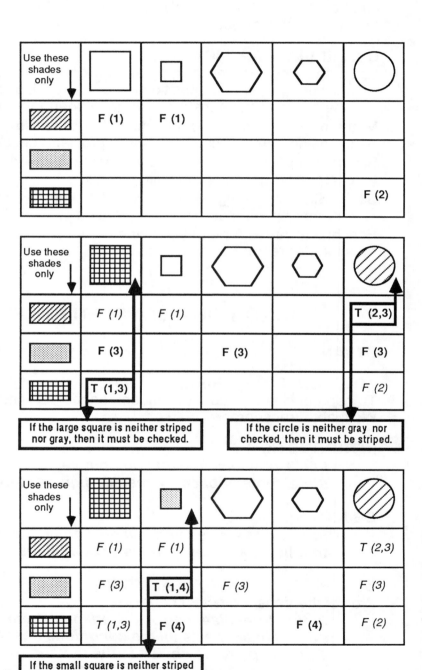

If the large square is neither striped nor gray, then it must be checked.

If the circle is neither gray nor checked, then it must be striped.

If the small square is neither striped nor checked, then it must be gray.

Clue 5: "No hexagon is striped." Write an **F** in the striped row under each hexagon.

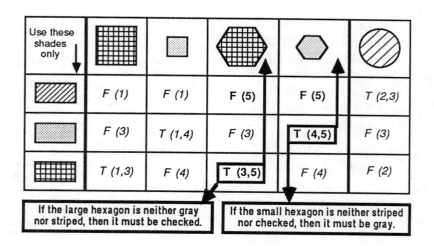

Use these shades only ↓	▦	▪	⬡	⬡	⊘
▨	F (1)	F (1)	F (5)	F (5)	T (2,3)
▩	F (3)	T (1,4)	F (3)	T (4,5)	F (3)
▦	T (1,3)	F (4)	T (3,5)	F (4)	F (2)

If the large hexagon is neither gray nor striped, then it must be checked.	If the small hexagon is neither striped nor checked, then it must be gray.

INDEPENDENT PRACTICE
Assign exercises **B-301** through **B-304**.

DISCUSSION TIPS
A transparency of the blank matrix from the bottom part of TM #10 may be used with all activities in this section. Students may have difficulty in determining the truth value of a negative statement. Encourage them to use Yes-No questions ("Is this statement true of a _____ _____ ?") to arrive at their decisions.

Students should discuss and explain their answers, identifying the clue(s) they used to determine the pattern of each shape and using sentences similar to the boxed statements under each table when they give their reasons for choosing a particular pattern. The solutions presented in the **ANSWER** sections are intended to show one progression of steps. Other progressions are possible, but the solutions should be the same.

ANSWERS
NOTE: Clue numbers are given in parenthesis within each cell. The boxed statements under each matrix will explain how each pattern was determined from the conditions.

B-301
Clue 1: "Polygons are not gray." Since only the circle is not a polygon, write an **F** in the gray row for each shape except the circle.

Clue 2: "Small figures are not striped." Write an **F** in the striped row under each small figure.

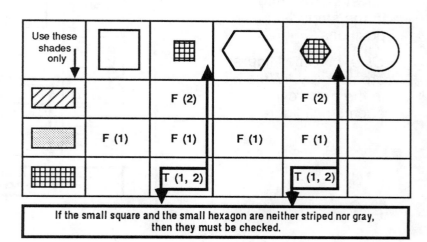

Use these shades only ↓	☐	▦	⬡	⬡	◯
▨		F (2)		F (2)	
▩	F (1)	F (1)	F (1)	F (1)	
▦		T (1, 2)		T (1, 2)	

If the small square and the small hexagon are neither striped nor gray, then they must be checked.

Clue 4: "Large polygons are not striped." Write an **F** in the striped row under the large square and the large hexagon (polygons).

Clue 3: "There is only one gray figure."

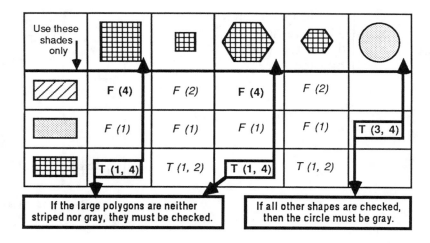

B-302

Clue 1: "It is not true that the circle is gray." Put an **F** in the gray row under the circle.

Clue 2: "Large figures are not checked." Put an **F** in the checked row under each large figure.

Clue 3: "Squares are not striped." Write **F**'s in the striped-square positions.

Clue 4: "Small figures are not gray." Write **F**'s in the gray row under each small figure.

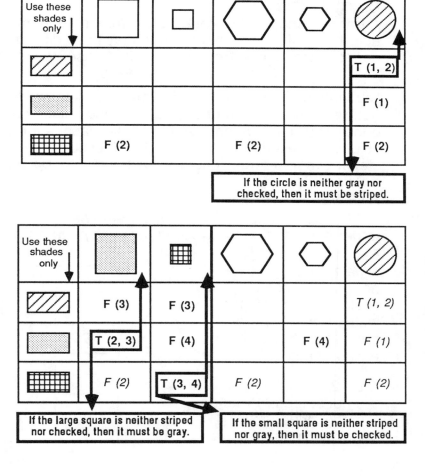

Clue 5: "Hexagons are not striped." Write **F**'s in the striped row under each hexagon.

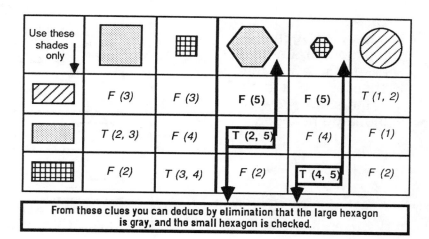

From these clues you can deduce by elimination that the large hexagon is gray, and the small hexagon is checked.

B-303

Clue 1: "Small figures are not striped." Put an **F** in the striped row under each small figure.

Clue 2: "No figure is gray." Put an **F** under every figure in the gray row.

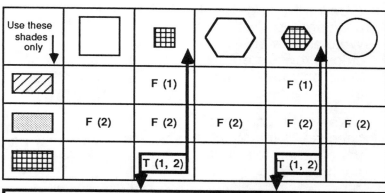

If the small square and the small hexagon are neither striped nor gray, then both must be checked.

Clue 3: "Non-polygons (circles) are striped." Put a **T** in the striped row and an **F** in the checked row under the circle. (If the circle is striped, it cannot be checked.)

Clue 4: "The squares are not shaded alike." Put an **F** under the square in the checked row. (Since the small square IS checked, the large square CANNOT be checked.)

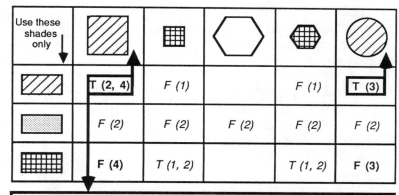

If the small square is checked, and the large square is neither the same as the small square (checked) nor gray, then the large square must be striped.

Clue 5: "The non-square polygons (hexagons) are shaded alike." Put a **T** in the checked row and an **F** in the striped row under the large hexagon.

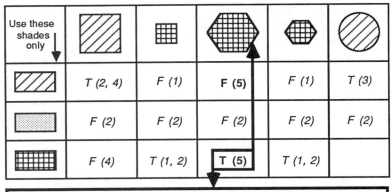

B-304

Clue 1: "No large polygon is striped." Write an **F** in the striped row under the large polygons (square and hexagon).

Clue 4: "No square is checked." Write an **F** in the checked row under each square.

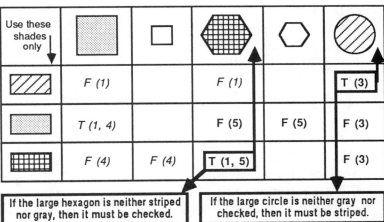

Clue 5: "No hexagon is gray." Write an **F** in the gray row under each hexagon.

Clue 3: "Large figures are not shaded the same." Write an **F** in both the checked and gray rows under the circle.

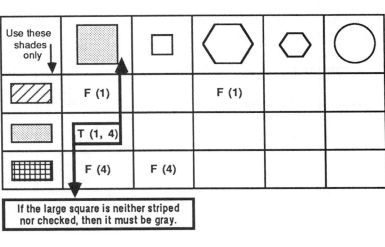

Clue 6: "No small figure is striped." Write **F**'s in the striped row under the small square and small hexagon.

[*Clue 2*, "Small figures are not shaded the same," has not been used in the above illustration, but it is satisfied by the solution.]

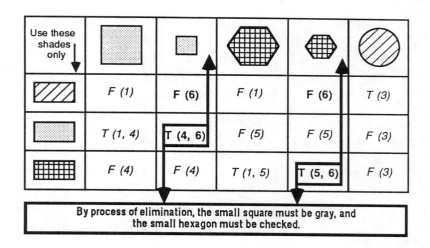

By process of elimination, the small square must be gray, and the small hexagon must be checked.

FOLLOW-UP REFERENT
When might you need to apply a series of conditions to determine whether a statement is true or false?

Examples: observing whether directions have been correctly followed, e.g., medication directions, recipes, operating instructions; answering true/false questions on a test; recognizing that negative statements can be either true or false

CURRICULUM APPLICATION
Language Arts: proofreading papers for errors in spelling, grammar, or punctuation; answering true/false questions over an aspect of a story or selection; judging when formatting instructions have been followed

Mathematics: checking computations to determine if correct procedures were followed; choosing correct answer sets to a problem; checking computations by estimation

Science: verifying animal or plant characteristics in laboratory demonstrations; reading or completing genetic probability charts; using charts to illustrate cross-characteristics in plants, animals, or elements

Social Studies: finding facts to support or negate statements; determining correct time in different time zones; deductive reasoning involving truth value

Enrichment Areas: determining whether instructions and/or rules have been followed in sports or recreation activities

CONJUNCTION—FOLLOWING "AND" RULES

STRAND: Verbal Sequences   **PAGES:** 137–139

ADDITIONAL MATERIALS
Transparencies of TM #11 and TM #12
Washable transparency marker

INTRODUCTION
In previous lessons you studied the way the word NOT affected the meaning of a statement.

Answer:

Repeat the process with the remaining statements on the transparency.
Answer (Draw the squares that contain a checked figure and are not gray.):

Answer (Draw the squares that are not white and do not contain a gray figure.):

GUIDED PRACTICE
EXERCISE: **B-305**.
When students have had sufficient time to complete this exercise, use the discussion techniques demonstrated above to verify and correct their answers.
ANSWERS:
B-305 **a** No; **b** No; **c** Yes; **d** No; **e** Yes; **f** No; **g** Yes; **h** No; **i** Yes

INDEPENDENT PRACTICE
Assign exercises **B-306** through **B-310**.

DISCUSSION TIPS
To introduce the effect of the connective "AND" on meaning, ask students to confirm that BOTH stated characteristics concerning a given item or figure are true. If necessary, have them break each AND statement into two equal statements, then apply each new statement to the chosen figures. For example, if the statement is "Figure A is small and white," the two parts of the statement are "Figure A is small" and "Figure A is white." If each part of the statement is true of a given figure, then the AND statement is true.

The position of NOT in a sentence also affects the meaning. Remind students that they are using two concepts of negation. One is the effect of NOT on the meaning of the sentence; the other is whether the sentence is true or false. Students may have difficulty with negative statements that are false. These distinctions can be clarified by using relevant, real-life experiences. Students will enlarge on this concept and grasp it more readily as they practice using connectives.

As an extending activity, encourage students to restate the relationships in items **5** through **8** on TM #11 by changing the connective or by inserting the word "NOT," then identifying whether the restatement has the same meaning as the original. For statement 5, for example, you might start the discussion by asking:
* *What would happen if you changed the word AND to BUT within the statement?*
* *Would it change the meaning of the statement?*
* *Would the original answer to statement 5 still be true?*
* *What about moving the NOT around in the statement: "Figure E is NOT small AND white"? Does this mean the same as the original statement?*

ANSWERS
B-306 **a** No; **b** Yes; **c** Yes; **d** Yes; **e** No; **f** No; **g** Yes; **h** No; **i** Yes

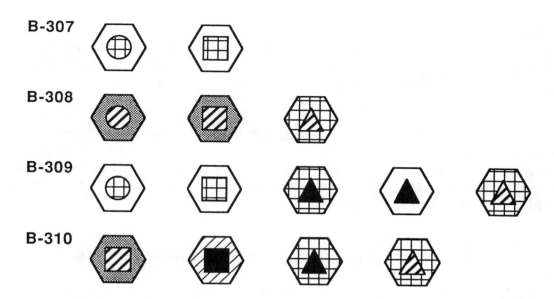

FOLLOW-UP REFERENT

When might you need to decide whether both parts of a two-part statement are true when applied to a given object or situation?

Examples: observing whether two-part operating instructions or directions have been correctly followed; recognizing whether multistep recipes or two-part directions for taking medicine are being correctly followed; answering true/false questions (especially those using a connective); recognizing that negative statements can be either true or false; deductive reasoning involving truth value

CURRICULUM APPLICATION

Language Arts: proofreading compositions for errors in spelling, grammar, or punctuation; answering true/false questions over an aspect of a story or selection; judging whether formatting instructions have been followed

Mathematics: checking computations to determine if correct procedures were followed; choosing correct answer sets to a problem; checking computations by estimation

Science: verifying animal or plant characteristics in laboratory demonstrations; reading or completing probability charts; applying facts to determine the validity of a hypothesis

Social Studies: finding facts to support or negate a statement; transferring written information to charts, graphs, or maps

Enrichment Areas: determining whether instructions and/or rules have been followed in sports or recreation activities; trouble-shooting computer programs

CONJUNCTION—INTERPRETING "AND" RULES

STRAND: Verbal Sequences

PAGES: 140–142

ADDITIONAL MATERIALS
Transparency of TM #13
Washable transparency marker

INTRODUCTION
In the previous lesson you studied the effect of the words AND and NOT on the meaning of statements. You also investigated how the position of these words within each statement affects the truth of the statement.

OBJECTIVE
The effect of AND on a statement's meaning can be illustrated by comparing the statement to the flow of water through a pipe with more than one control valve. In these exercises you will look at different combinations of two valves and determine if each combination would allow water to flow through a pipe so some water comes out the other side.

DEMONSTRATION / EXPLANATION
NOTE: For emphasis and clarity, you may wish to use a blue washable marker on the transparency to represent each pipe's water flow.

Project the top section from the transparency of TM #13, covering the problems at the bottom of the sheet.

These diagrams represent water flowing through a pipe into valves. The arrows indicate the direction that the water is flowing. These symbols represent valves. When the valve is open, water will flow out the pipe. When the valve is closed, no water will exit from the pipe.

Project exercise 1.

In this example, Valve A is open and Valve B is open. If water enters the pipe from the west (left side), will it flow through this combination of valves and exit into the pipe on the east (right side)?

Answer: Yes; since both valves are open, the water will flow completely through the pipe. Project example **2**.

What are the positions of these two valves?

Answer: Valve A is open and Valve B is closed.

From which direction is the water entering the pipe?

Answer: The water is entering from the west (left).

Will water flow through this combination of valves and continue into the pipe extending to the east (right)?

Answer: No.

What makes you think so?

Answer: Although Valve A is open and will allow water to pass through it, Valve B is closed. No water can enter the exit pipe. Project example **3**.

Will water flow through this combination of valves? Why or why not?

Answer: No; Since Valve A is closed, no water can get to the exit pipe. The fact that Valve B is open has no bearing on the water flow, since no water gets to that point.

GUIDED PRACTICE
EXERCISES: **B-311, B-312, B-313**
When students have had sufficient time to complete these exercises, use the discussion techniques demonstrated above to verify their answers.
ANSWERS: **B-311** No;   **B-312** Yes;   **B-313** No

INDEPENDENT PRACTICE
Assign exercises **B-314** through **B-319**.

DISCUSSION TIPS

Using water flow or electricity conduction gives students a concrete example of the effect of the connective "AND" on meaning. Students see clearly that both statements must be true for the sentence to be true. Just as one "NO" valve would stop the flow of water, one FALSE component in a sentence results in a conjunction statement that is false. This is particularly helpful for Hispanic students, since negative indicators in Spanish have different meanings.

Because complex conditions are so significant in the personal choice-making of students, encourage them to relate this principle to real-life situations. The value of the connectives results in students' clearly conceptualizing the meaning of *and* as used in various English sentence structures. Encourage students to search magazines and newspapers for examples of complex sentences containing connectives. Use the sentences they find as an extending and reinforcing activity, asking what the consequence would be if any component of the sentence under consideration were false.

Encourage students to think of examples of conditional statements with two antecedents, both of which must be true before a consequence can happen. For example, the statement, "If we finish the math lesson *and* put all the materials away, we will see a movie," might lead to such questions as "If we do *not* finish the math lesson, will we see the movie?" or "If we *don't* put the materials away, will we see the movie?"

ANSWERS

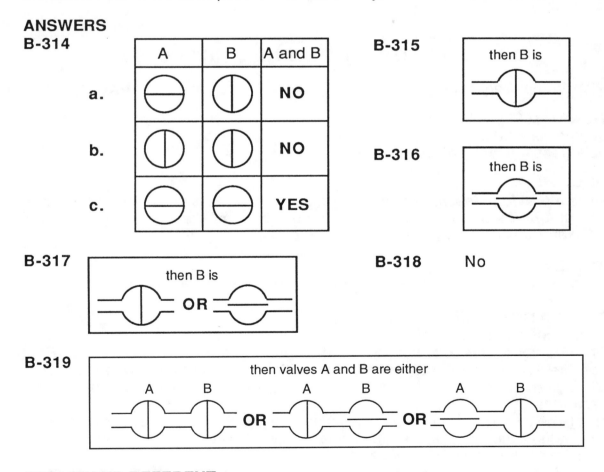

B-314

	A	B	A and B
a.			NO
b.			NO
c.			YES

B-315

then B is

B-316

then B is

B-317

then B is

OR

B-318   No

B-319

then valves A and B are either

A   B   A   B   A   B

OR   OR

FOLLOW-UP REFERENT

When might you need to determine whether a multipart statement is true or false by examining each part?

Examples: observing whether two-part operating instructions or directions have been correctly followed; recognizing whether multistep recipes or two-part directions for taking medicine are being correctly followed; answering true/false questions (especially those using a connective); recognizing that negative statements can be either true or false; deductive reasoning involving truth value

CURRICULUM APPLICATION

Language Arts: proofreading compositions for errors in spelling, grammar, or punctuation; answering true/false questions regarding a specific aspect of a story or selection; judging whether formatting instructions have been followed

Mathematics: checking computations to determine if correct procedures were followed; choosing correct answer sets to a problem; checking computations by estimation

Science: verifying animal or plant characteristics in laboratory demonstrations; reading or completing genetic probability charts; applying facts to determine the validity of a hypothesis

Social Studies: finding facts to support or negate a statement; transferring written information to charts, graphs, or maps

Enrichment Areas: determining whether instructions and/or rules have been followed in sports or recreation activities; trouble-shooting computer programs

CONJUNCTION—APPLYING "AND" RULES

STRAND: Verbal Sequences   **PAGES:** 143–145

ADDITIONAL MATERIALS
Transparency of student workbook page 143
Washable transparency marker

INTRODUCTION
In the previous lesson you studied the effect of the word AND on the meaning of multipart statements by comparing the parts of the statement to the flow of water through a pipe with more than one control valve.

OBJECTIVE
In this exercise you will apply AND rules to solve maze puzzles.

DEMONSTRATION/EXPLANATION
Project the transparency of page 143.
The object of this exercise is to mark a path that goes from START to FINISH on the figure maze by obeying the conditions stated at the top of the page. This particular maze has three possible types of moves along the path. What are they?

Answer: 1) The two figures must have the same size and the same shape; OR 2) The two figures must have the same shape and the same pattern; OR 3) The two figures must have the same pattern and the same size.

The first two moves are shown. Why is the first move, from a large black square to a small black square, allowed?

Why is the next move, from a small black square to a small black circle, okay?
Answer: The move obeys the condition in the third statement: the two figures have the same pattern (black) and the same size (small).

Is it possible to continue upward for the next move?
Answer: No, only the shapes of the two figures are the same. Although the two figures are the same shape (circle), they are not the same size or the same color. According to the statements, two attributes must be the same before a move can be made.

Is it possible to move from the small black circle to the figure at its left?
Answer: No; this would be from a small black circle to a small striped square; since only the attribute of size is the same, this would not be a possible move.

Is it possible to move from the small black circle to the figure at its right?
Answer: Yes; this would be from a small black circle to a small white circle. The attributes of size (small) and shape (circle) are the same, so the move is allowed according to the first statement. Continue this line of questioning until students are ready to complete the maze puzzle on their own. Always ask students to explain the basis for their decisions.

GUIDED PRACTICE
EXERCISE: Remainder of **B-320**
ANSWER:

B-320

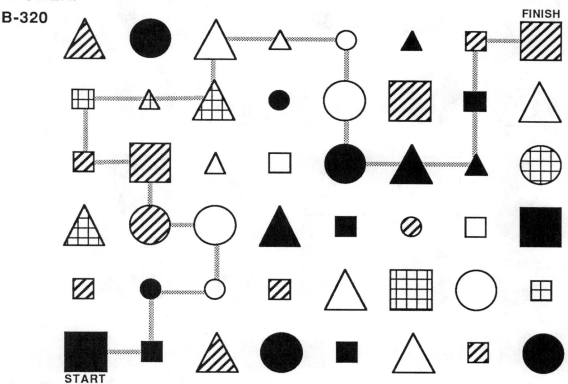

INDEPENDENT PRACTICE
Assign exercises **B-321** and **B-322**.

DISCUSSION TIPS
This game format offers practice in using AND statements. Emphasize that each statement describes two conditions and that both must be met in order to "follow the rule." Ask students to support each move along the path by stating the rule that supports it.

Encourage students to produce original maze puzzles for their classmates to solve. Students will produce a variety of drawings for exercise **B-322**. Their mazes should be checked carefully to be sure the directions were followed exactly. Ask individual students to describe the figure s(he) drew at each intersection, specifying size, shape, and pattern.

ANSWERS

B-321

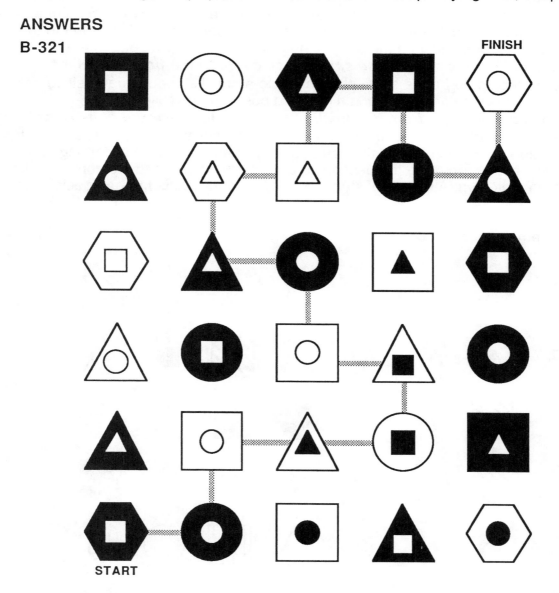

B-322 Answers will vary.

FOLLOW-UP REFERENT

When might you need to decide whether a multipart statement is being correctly followed?

Examples: observing whether operating instructions or directions have been correctly followed; recognizing whether recipes or directions for taking medicine are being correctly followed; determining whether rules of a game are being correctly applied or interpreted

CURRICULUM APPLICATION

Language Arts: proofreading compositions for errors in spelling, grammar, or punctuation; judging whether formatting instructions have been followed; constructing complex sentences, paragraphs, and arguments

Mathematics: checking computations to determine if correct procedures were followed; checking computations by estimation

Science: verifying animal or plant characteristics in laboratory demonstrations; reading or completing genetic probability charts; verifying facts that test a hypothesis; verifying chemical and physical equations

Social Studies: determining whether facts support or negate statements; deductive reasoning involving truth value; comparing written information with corresponding charts, graphs, or maps

Enrichment Areas: determining whether instructions and/or rules have been followed in sports or recreation activities; verifying steps in a computer program

DISJUNCTION—INTERPRETING "AND/OR" RULES

STRAND: Verbal Sequences

PAGES: 146–148

ADDITIONAL MATERIALS
Transparency master of TM #14
Blue washable transparency marker

INTRODUCTION
In an earlier lesson you thought about AND *statements as if they were valves in a single, continuous water pipe.*

OBJECTIVE
In these exercises you will use water valves to think about AND/OR *statements. This time the incoming water branches, feeds into two valved pipes, and comes back together into a single exit pipe.*

DEMONSTRATION/EXPLANATION
NOTE: For emphasis and clarity, you may wish to use a blue washable marker on the transparency to represent each pipes' water flow.
Project the top section from the transparency of TM #14.
> *The* AND/OR *connective can be represented by water flowing through a divided pipe as shown here. The water flow is controlled by valves, marked on the transparency as A and B. How do you know which direction the water is flowing through this pipe?*
Answer: The arrows indicate the direction of water-flow; in this case it is flowing from west (left) to east (right).
> *In this diagram the upper valve (A) is open, permitting water to flow through the pipe it controls. What is the position of the lower valve (B)?*
Answer: Valve **B** is closed.
> *If any particular valve is closed, will water flow through the pipe it controls?*
Answer: No.

In your mind, trace the flow of water through the diagrammed system. Will any water flow from the exit pipe?

Answer: Yes; although valve **B** is closed, water will flow through valve **A** and out the right side of the pipe.

Project the lower portion of the transparency and continue the discussion, asking students to explain the diagram using the methodology demonstrated above. (Water flows from west (left) to east (right) through valve **B**. Valve **A** is closed. Water will flow out the exit pipe as long as at least one valve remains open.)

GUIDED PRACTICE
EXERCISES: **B-323, B-324, B-325**
When students have had sufficient time to complete these exercises, use the discussion techniques demonstrated above to verify and correct their answers.
ANSWERS: **B-323** Yes;   **B-324** No;   **B-325** Yes

INDEPENDENT PRACTICE
Assign exercises **B-326** through **B-332**.

DISCUSSION TIPS
In the English language, the "AND/OR" connective suggests that at least one, and possibly both, conditions of a given statement are true. In the case of flowing water, the water will go through the pipes if one or both of the valves are open. This is called the **inclusive OR**. In common English usage OR is sometimes taken to mean either one or the other is true, but *not* both. This meaning of OR is called the **exclusive OR**. Students may believe that OR always suggests "one or the other, but not both." This exercise allows students to understand that *both* OR statements may be true unless the speaker adds the condition "but not both."

As students become proficient at recognizing the effect of AND/OR statements, ask them to compare these and their resulting diagrams with those illustrating the AND statements (workbook pages 140–142). As an extending activity, encourage students to search newspapers and magazines for examples of complex sentences containing connectives.

ANSWERS

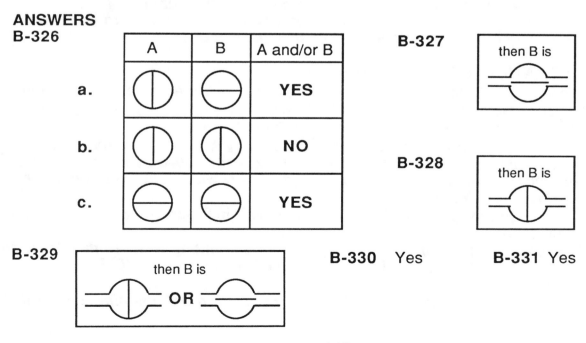

	A	B	A and/or B
a.			**YES**
b.			**NO**
c.			**YES**

B-326

B-327 then B is

B-328 then B is

B-329 then B is   OR

B-330 Yes   **B-331** Yes

B-332

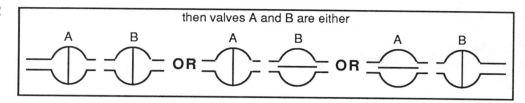

then valves A and B are either

FOLLOW-UP REFERENT

When might you need to decide whether a complex statement using the AND/OR connective is true or false?

Examples: observing whether operating instructions or directions have been correctly followed; following recipes with optional steps or ingredients; recognizing that directions for taking medication are being correctly followed; answering true/false questions on a test; recognizing that negative statements can be either true or false

CURRICULUM APPLICATION

Language Arts: proofreading compositions for errors in spelling, grammar, or punctuation; answering true/false questions regarding a specific aspect of a literature selection; checking formatting against written instructions

Mathematics: checking computations to determine if correct procedures were followed; choosing correct answer sets to a problem; checking computations by estimation

Science: verifying animal or plant characteristics in laboratory demonstrations; reading or completing genetic probability charts; applying facts to determine the validity of a hypothesis

Social Studies: finding facts to support or negate a statement; transferring written information to charts, graphs, or maps

Enrichment Areas: determining whether instructions and/or rules have been followed in sports or recreation activities; trouble-shooting computer programs

DISJUNCTION—FOLLOWING "AND/OR" RULES

STRAND: Verbal Sequences

PAGES: 149–155

ADDITIONAL MATERIALS

Transparency master of TM #15
Washable transparency marker

INTRODUCTION

In the previous lesson you thought about AND/OR statements as if they were valves in a branching water line.

OBJECTIVE

In these exercises you will learn to follow AND/OR rules to sort a group of shaded figures.

DEMONSTRATION/EXPLANATION

Project the **CHOICE BOX** from the transparency of TM #15.

Answer: Since all of the figures appear to be about the same size, probably only shape and pattern (color) will be considered.
Project the **EXAMPLE** problem from the transparency.

What characteristics are you asked to use to sort the figures?

Answer: Shape and pattern.

What shape and what pattern will you use?

Answer: Triangles for shape; checked for pattern.

How would you phrase an AND/ OR rule to describe the figures inside the box?

Answer: The statement would read "The figures are triangles AND/OR checked."

The completed box contains two checked figures and two triangles. Does each of these figures meet the conditions of the statement?

Answer: Yes; each is either a triangle or a checked figure.

Notice that those figures that are not part of the "triangles AND/ OR checked" group are placed to the right of the box under the heading FIGURES NOT USED. Can you think of an AND/ OR statement to describe this group?

Answer: Each figure outside the box can be described as "not-triangle" and "not-checked." A possible disjunction statement might be "The figures are not triangles AND/OR not checked." Project exercise **A** from the transparency.

What disjunction statement describes the group of figures that should be placed inside this box?

Answer: "The figures are circles AND/OR striped."

Take a few minutes to decide which figures from the CHOICE BOX you would place inside the box. Remember that each chosen figure must meet one of the two conditions, but it may meet both.

Give students time to think about their choices, then ask for volunteers to draw an answer figure on the transparency until all figures are placed either inside or outside the box. Use the techniques demonstrated above as students confirm their answers.

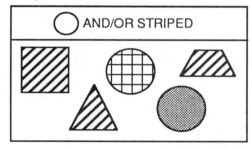

FIGURES NOT USED

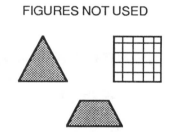

GUIDED PRACTICE
EXERCISE: **B-333**
When students have had sufficient time to complete this exercise, use the discussion techniques demonstrated above to verify and correct their answers.
ANSWERS:

B-333

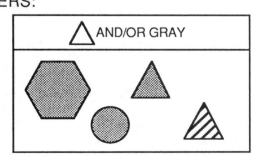

FIGURES NOT USED

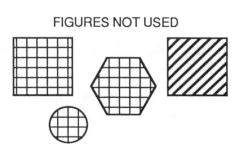

INDEPENDENT PRACTICE
Assign exercises **B-334** through **B-347**.

DISCUSSION TIPS
In the English language, the connective AND/OR suggests that at least one, and possibly both, conditions of a given statement are true. In the case of flowing water, the water will go through the pipes if one or both of the valves are open. This is called the **inclusive** OR. In common English usage OR is sometimes taken to mean either one or the other is true, but *not* both. This meaning of OR is called the **exclusive** OR. Students may believe that OR always suggests "one or the other, but not both." This exercise allows students to understand that *both* OR statements may be true unless the speaker adds the condition "but not both."

The value of the connectives results in students' clearly conceptualizing the meaning of English sentences involving such connectives as AND, AND/OR, NOT, or IF-THEN. As an extending activity, encourage students to search newspapers and magazines for examples of complex sentences containing connectives. Using sentences they have found, ask what the consequence would be if any part of the sentence were false.

ANSWERS

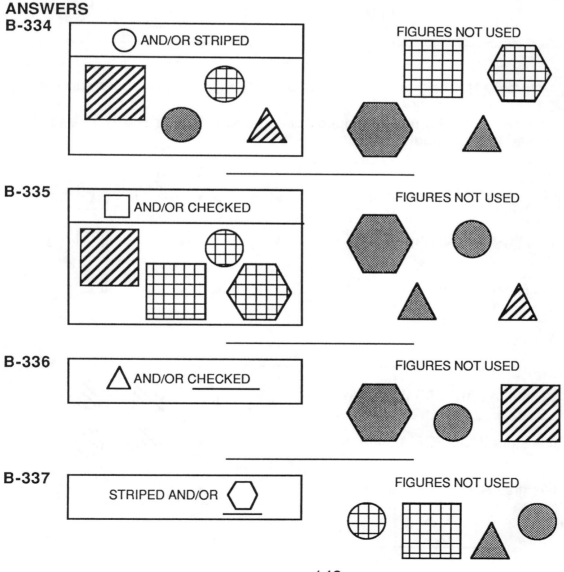

143

B-338 ☐ AND/OR <u>GRAY</u>

B-339 ◯ AND/OR <u>STRIPED</u>

B-340 ⬡ AND/OR <u>STRIPED</u>

B-341 △ AND/OR <u>STRIPED</u>

B-342 ◯ AND/OR <u>CHECKED</u>

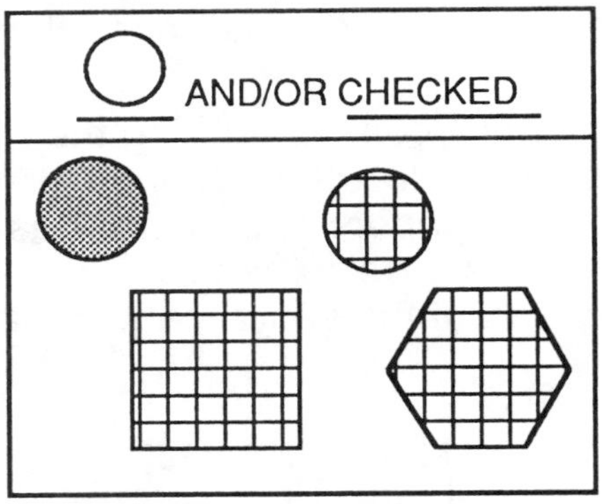

B-343 ☐ AND/OR <u>GRAY</u>

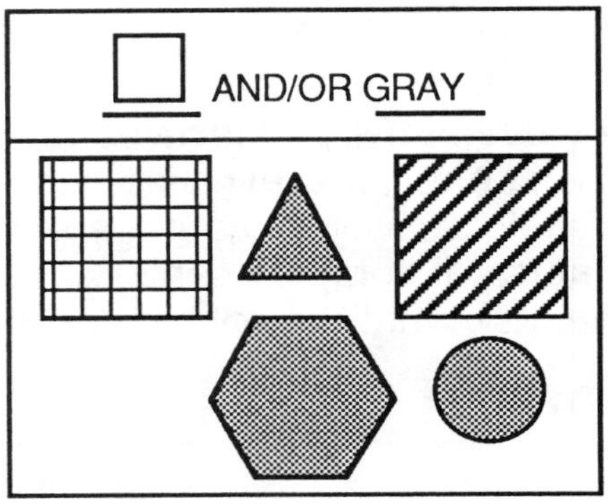

B-344 <u>Yes</u> (gray); <u>No</u> (neither a triangle nor striped); <u>Yes</u> (both a square and gray); <u>No</u> (neither a circle nor striped)

B-345 <u>Yes</u> (checked); <u>No</u> (neither striped nor a square); <u>Yes</u> (triangle); <u>Yes</u> (both checked and a triangle)

B-346 It is gray AND/OR a square.

It is checked AND/OR a circle.

It is checked AND/OR a triangle.

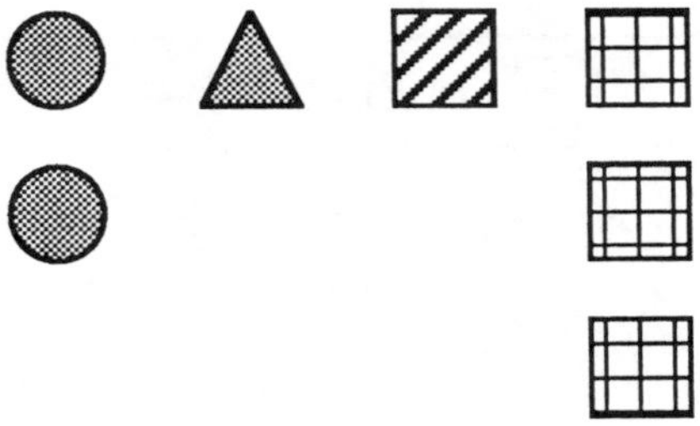

Answer: _____

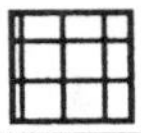

B-347 It is striped AND/OR a triangle.

It is striped AND/OR a square.

It is gray AND/OR a triangle.

Answer: _____

FOLLOW-UP REFERENT

When might you need to determine what objects or situations are described by an AND/OR statement?

Examples: observing whether operating instructions or directions are been correctly given or followed; recognizing whether recipes or directions for taking medication are being correctly followed; following requirements for building construction, additions, or improvements; verifying the truth value of complex statements

CURRICULUM APPLICATION

Language Arts: applying proofreading rules when checking for errors in spelling, grammar, or punctuation; applying AND/OR statements to an aspect of a literature selection; following formatting instructions

Mathematics: following correct procedures when solving multistep problems; choosing correct answer sets to a problem; checking computations by estimation; comprehending and/or interpreting word problems

Science: verifying animal or plant characteristics; choosing facts to verify or negate an hypothesis; interpreting laboratory experiment results

Social Studies: choosing facts to verify or negate historical hypotheses; comparing written information to corresponding charts, graphs, pictures, or maps

Enrichment Areas: following AND/OR rules or instructions in sports, games, or recreational activities; comparing written descriptions of architectural, musical, or artistic schools to specific works

IMPLICATION—INTERPRETING "IF-THEN" RULES

STRAND: Verbal Sequences

PAGES: 156–164

ADDITIONAL MATERIALS

Transparencies of TM #16 and TM #17
Red, green, and purple washable transparency markers

INTRODUCTION

In the previous lesson you followed an AND/OR rule to sort a group of shaded figures to accurately reflect the truth of each statement. Remember that in an AND/OR statement, at least one condition must be true, and it is possible that all conditions are true.

OBJECTIVE

In these exercises you will learn to understand and follow statements called IF-THEN rules.

DEMONSTRATION/EXPLANATION

Project figure **A** from the transparency of TM #16.

IF-THEN statements, like the connectives you have studied previously, are composed of two parts, or conditions. In this case, you have an IF condition,

Indicate the first part of the statement as you read it.

"If the shape is square,..." and a THEN condition,

Indicate the second part of the statement as you read.

> *"...then it is checked." The IF part of the statement tells you what figures are covered by the rule. It directs your attention to a single attribute, in this case, square shapes. For the purposes of this exercise, therefore, forget about the triangles and the circles; we're talking only about squares. To help focus your attention on the squares, we'll use one color to draw circles around the IF statement and the figures it concerns, the squares.*

Project figure **B** from the transparency and trace an outline around the IF statement and the squares with a red transparency marker. Ask students to verify that the IF statement applies to the figures inside the outlined section.

> *The THEN statement, "...then it is checked," defines those figures covered by the rule that meet both conditions of the IF-THEN statement. We'll focus attention on the checked figures by drawing a different colored box around the THEN statement and those figures COVERED BY THE RULE which meet the limitations stated in the THEN statement.*

Project figure **C** from the transparency. Draw a circle around the THEN statement and trace the outline around the checked figures with a green marker.

> *When you use the entire IF-THEN statement, it says that OF THE SHAPES COVERED BY THE RULE—the squares—*

Indicate the squares.

> *only the checked ones correctly follow this IF-THEN rule.*

Indicate the checked figures.

> *Which figures follow the rule? Which are enclosed by both colors.*

Answer: The checked square.

> *Only figures described by both the IF and the THEN statements "fit the rule." The directions tell you to cross out the shapes that do not fit the rule.*

Indicate the crossed-out squares.

> *The circles and triangles are not mentioned in the IF statement, therefore, they are not covered by the rule. Since they are not governed by the rule, they cannot either follow or not follow the rule, and they are not crossed out.*

NOTE: This is a complex concept. If the class appears to have difficulty grasping the concept of IF-THEN statements, the examples on student workbook pages 156 and 157 may help. The method used on these example pages model a different way of interpreting conditional statements.

When students are comfortable interpreting IF-THEN statements, project the problem from the top of TM #17.

> *These exercises are similar to those you have been doing, except that the figures are not arranged in a matrix style. Each row and column may contain figures with different shapes and/or different patterns. You do these exercises, however, in much the same way.*

Indicate the IF-THEN statement at the top of the transparency.

> *You are to determine which group of figures, those in box a, those in box b, those in both boxes, or those in neither box, all fit the stated rule, "If the shape is checked, then it is a square." What do you do first when you apply a conditional statement to a group of figures?*

Answer: Circle the IF statement and all of the figures it concerns, in this case, the checked figures. Use a red marker to enclose the checked figures on the transparency, or ask a student volunteer to do the drawing. When other students have agreed that the figures marked on the transparency represent the IF statement, project the answer from the transparency for confirmation.

*NOTE: You may have to remind students that the statement is to apply to **both** groups of shapes. When determining the figures governed by the statement, they may wish to ignore the boxes that indicate the group separation, treating all eight figures as if they were a single group.*

> **The THEN statement says, "...then it is a square." How do you indicate this on the diagram?**

Answer: Circle the THEN statement and the *checked* figures (each figure already circled) that makes the statement true (the checked squares). Use a green marker to draw these circles, or ask a student volunteer to mark the figures. Again, it may be necessary to remind students that they are to consider the figures in both boxes, *but only those governed by the rule.*

> **The figures that follow the rule are enclosed by both colors. Figures that are supposed to follow the rule, but don't, are circled in the same color as the IF statement. Are there any figures in these boxes that do not follow the rule?**

Answer: Yes; the checked circle in box **b** does not fit the rule. It is checked, so it is one of the figures that is governed by the rule. It is not, however, square. It does not follow the THEN statement.

> **How do you indicate figures that should, but do not, fit the rule?**

Answer: You cross them out. Project the answer from the bottom of the transparency.

> **What true statement can you make about this IF-THEN rule and groups a and b?**

Answer: All the figures in group **a** follow the rule.

> **Remember that although some figures in group a do not follow the rule, the rule does not apply to them. It applies ONLY to those figures identified by the IF statement.**

*NOTE; If students need further practice on this skill, you may use a transparency of student workbook page 161. Use the above demonstration technique as you follow the exercise on the transparency. See the **DISCUSSION TIPS** section of this lesson plan for further clarification of conditional statements.*

GUIDED PRACTICE
EXERCISES: **B-348, B-349**
When students have had sufficient time to complete these exercises, use the discussion techniques demonstrated above to verify and correct their answers.
ANSWERS:

B-348 (If the shape is checked,) ⟨then it is a triangle.⟩

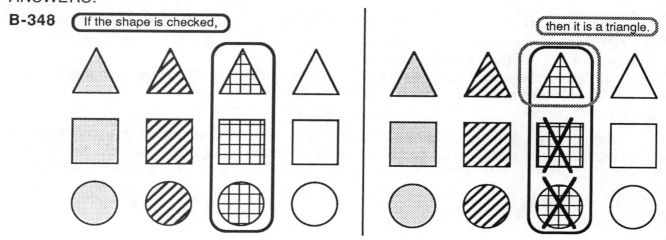

B-349   If the shape is not a circle,   then it is white.

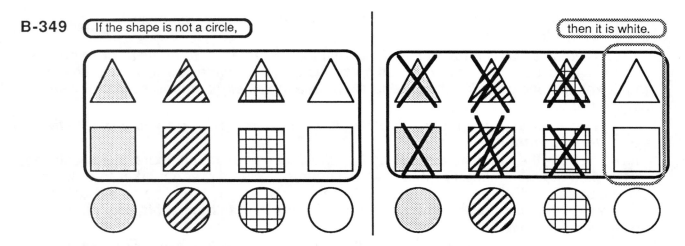

INDEPENDENT PRACTICE
Assign exercises **B-350** through **B-357**.

DISCUSSION TIPS
Conditionals (a.k.a. "implication" or IF-THEN statements) is often a difficult concept for students — as well as for teachers — to master. If you, as a teacher, find it difficult, let the students know that you do. This will keep them from being discouraged and let them know that this particular concept may be more confusing, and may take more time and effort to understand, but that together you can work it out. Ask the students what questions they have, and encourage active class discussion. Do not assume they understand this logical connective just because they aren't asking questions. Students frequently experience difficulty ignoring the figures that are not governed by the rule. The following discussion may help clarify this concept.

Can you think of an example of a rule or law that applies to people who live in one city but does not apply to people who live in another?

Encourage varied answers. Some suggestions might be hours during which stores or restaurants may be open; varying city speed limits; rules covering public land use.

Can you restate those rules as IF-THEN statements?

Possibilities: "IF you are in Megatropolis, THEN the stores close at 11:00 p.m." "IF you are in Microtropolis, THEN the speed limit is 23 mph." "IF you live in Beachside City, THEN you can swim in the city pool for $2.00."

Do these rules apply to everyone in all cities?

Allow ample time for class discussion. Students should realize that only those people who are in the city that has the rule are covered by the rule. For example, stores in the city of Microtropolis may or may not close at 11:00 p.m., but they are not under the control of the rules or laws of the city of Megatropolis.

Describe someone who might not follow this rule: "If you are in Megatropolis, then the stores are open until 11:00 p.m."

Answers: A store in Megatropolis that closes at any time other than 11:00 p.m.

The discussion may be extended to rules that govern various games, rules at home and at school, rules at work, social customs in various countries or ethnic groups, and differing forms of government among city, state, and federal levels or among different countries.

ANSWERS

B-350 (If the shape is a triangle,) (then it is not checked)

B-351 (If the shape is not a square,) (then it is checked.)

B-352 (If the shape is a circle,) (then it is not striped.)

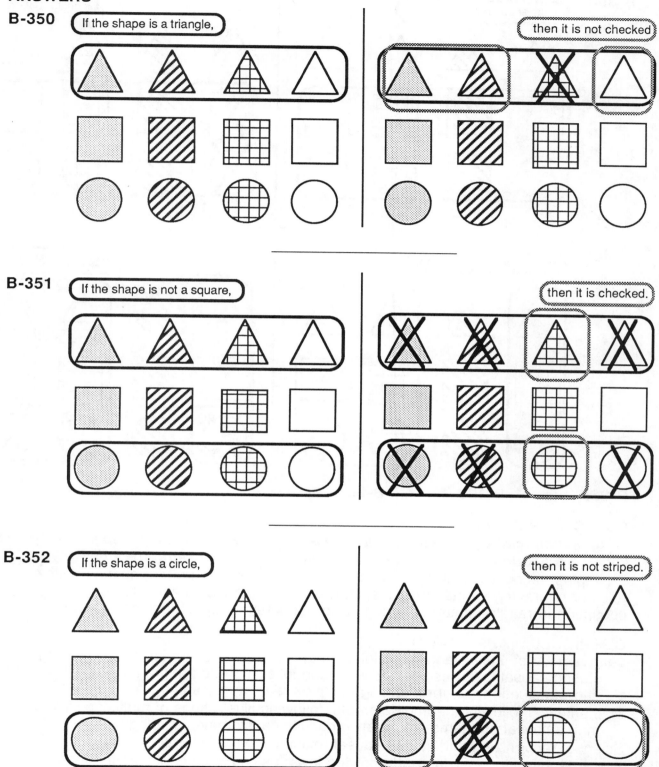

B-353

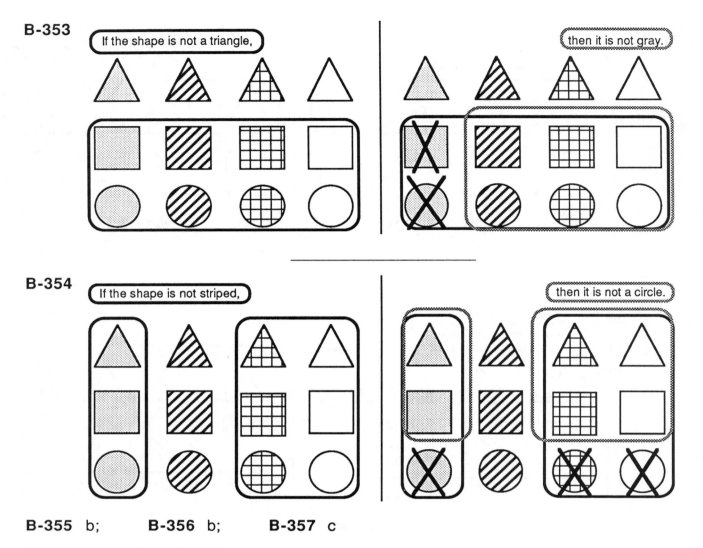

B-354

B-355 b;   **B-356** b;   **B-357** c

FOLLOW-UP REFERENT

When might you need to determine which members of a group are covered by a rule and which of those who are covered are following the rule?

Examples: recognizing and following parliamentary procedure in meetings; following rules or refereeing sports or games; knowing if and how laws apply to you; recognizing causation in reading material; recognizing and interpreting conditional statements

CURRICULUM APPLICATION

Language Arts: understanding conditional and exclusive statements; recognizing and stating causal relationships; knowing and following rules of grammar, spelling, usage, and punctuation; comprehending complex reading materials

Mathematics: following geometric proofs; following illustrations of multistep solutions for mathematical problems; interpreting conditional statements in logic or statistics

Science: recognizing and stating causal relationships in laboratory reports

Social Studies: recognizing and applying laws; using conditional statements for sociological or psychological hypotheses

Enrichment Areas: understanding stated consequences for actions; matching tools or materials to correct usages; recognizing and correctly interpreting conditional statements or situations in artistic areas

IMPLICATION—APPLYING "IF-THEN" RULES

STRAND: Verbal Sequences   **PAGES:** 165–167

ADDITIONAL MATERIALS
Transparency of TM #18
Red and black washable transparency markers
Damp cloth for cleaning transparency (optional)
Transparency of student workbook page 165 (optional)

INTRODUCTION
In the previous lesson you identified figures and groups of figures which followed a specific IF-THEN rule.

OBJECTIVE
In these exercises you will apply IF-THEN statements by marking blank figures to make them follow the rule.

DEMONSTRATION/EXPLANATION
Project the exercise from the top of the transparency of TM #18.
In these exercises you are to shade the shapes in each group so that all of them follow the given IF-THEN rule. The rule for these figures is, "If the shape is not a circle, then it is checked." How will you start?
Answer: Locate and circle all the shapes covered by the IF statement.
To which shapes does the IF statement direct your attention?
Answer: Those that are not circles. Project the middle figure from the transparency, indicating the enclosed figures. You may wish to trace the enclosing line with a marker.
How does the THEN statement define these selected shapes?
Answer: They are checked. Project the bottom figure from the transparency, indicating the checked figures.
Are the figures in this box shaded so that all of them follow the IF-THEN rule?
Answer: Yes; all shapes that are not circles (the IF statement) are checked (the THEN statement).
What pattern can the circles have?
Answer: Since the circles are not restricted by the rule, they can have any pattern, including checked.

NOTE: As an optional extending activity, project the blank group of shapes at the top of the transparency again. Provide a different conditional statement regarding shape and pattern, asking students to make all the figures fit the statement. Repeat the activity as often as necessary or as time permits.

If students need further practice, make a transparency of student workbook page 165 and follow the demonstrated procedure through the exercise.

GUIDED PRACTICE
EXERCISE: **B-358**
When students have had sufficient time to complete this exercise, use the discussion techniques demonstrated above to verify and correct their answers.

ANSWER:

B-358

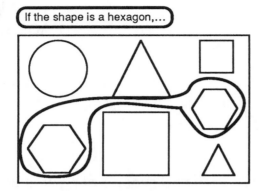

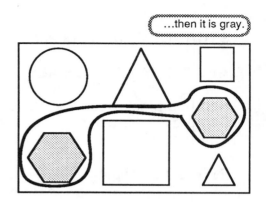

INDEPENDENT PRACTICE
Assign exercises **B-359** through **B-361**.

DISCUSSION TIPS
Do not assume that students understand the concept of conditional statements just because they aren't asking questions. Ask specific students what questions they have, and encourage active class discussion. Students sometimes have difficulty ignoring those figures that are not governed by the rule. Remind them that not all laws or rules apply to all people; for example, rules that apply to the basketball team cannot be applied to members of the student council (unless they are also members of the basketball team).

ANSWERS

B-359

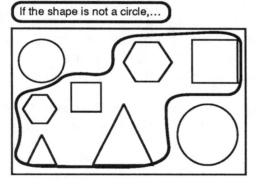

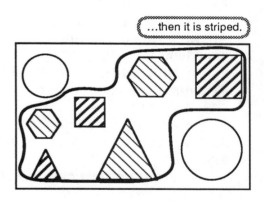

B-360

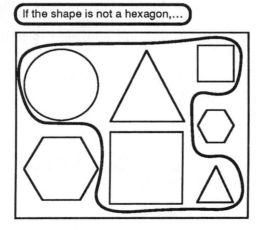

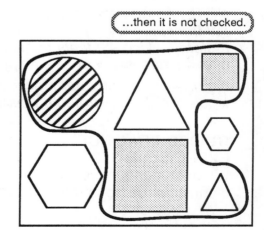

B-361

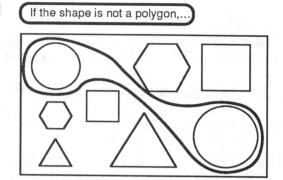

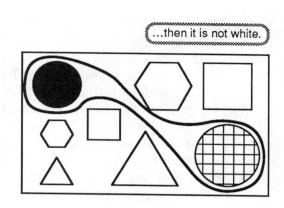

FOLLOW-UP REFERENT

When might you need to determine which members of a group are affected by a rule, then apply that rule to those members?

Examples: following parliamentary procedure in meetings; following or applying rules in sports; refereeing sports matches; knowing if and how laws apply to you

CURRICULUM APPLICATION

Language Arts: understanding conditional and exclusive statements; recognizing and stating causal relationships; knowing and following rules of grammar, spelling, usage, and punctuation

Mathematics: recognizing and understanding geometric proofs; distinguishing necessary conditions and sufficient conditions

Science: stating causal relationships in laboratory reports; setting up laboratory experiments; forming hypotheses

Social Studies: developing deductive reasoning involving conditional statements; recognizing and applying laws; comparing governments, societies, legal systems, or religions and their varying effects on history; interpreting map or chart legends

Enrichment Areas: understanding causal relationships; matching tools or materials to correct usages

IMPLICATION—FOLLOWING "IF-THEN" RULES

STRAND: Verbal Sequences

PAGES: 168–170

ADDITIONAL MATERIALS

Transparency of student workbook page 168
Two different colors of washable transparency markers

INTRODUCTION

In previous lessons you selected and marked figures to make them follow specific IF-THEN rules.

OBJECTIVE

In these exercises you will select from a group of cards those that do not follow a given IF-THEN rule.

DEMONSTRATION / EXPLANATION

Project the numbered cards from the transparency of page 168.

> *You will use this group of nine cards, each containing two figures, to complete these exercises. Notice that each card has either a triangle, a hexagon, or a circle drawn in each half.*

Pause to give the students a chance to become familiar with the markings on the cards, then project the **EXAMPLE** statement.

> *In these exercises you are to draw only those cards that do NOT follow the IF-THEN rule. What is the rule you will apply in this exercise?*

Answer: "If there is a hexagon in the lower half, then there is a circle in the upper half."

> *Remember that the IF-statement singles out those cards affected by the rule. Which of the cards at the top are affected by this statement?*

Give students several minutes to make their choices, then circle those cards they have chosen. Ask students to verify that each of the chosen cards follows the IF statement's qualification: it must have a hexagon-shape in the lower half of the card. Project the center section of the page from the transparency (**Step 1**) to confirm their answers.

> *Now look at the THEN-statement, "...then there is a circle in the upper half." Of the three cards chosen in Step 1, which follow the rule?*

Answer: Card 9. Use a different color to circle card 9 a second time.

> *The cards covered by the rule that DO NOT follow the rule are circled with only one color. Remember that since there are no restrictions placed on those cards that do not have a hexagon in the bottom half, they also follow the rule and are not marked.*

Project **Step 2** from the transparency to confirm that cards 1 and 5 are the two cards that do not fit the IF-THEN rule.

GUIDED PRACTICE

EXERCISE: **B-362**
ANSWER:

B-362   The IF-statement, "If there is a triangle in the lower half,..." directs attention to cards 2, 3, and 7. Other cards are not affected by the rule.

   2   3   7

The THEN-statement, "...then there is a hexagon in the upper half," selects card 3 **of those cards covered by the rule** as the card that follows the rule. Since students are to draw the cards that **do not** follow the rule, the final answer is cards 2 and 7.

   2   7

INDEPENDENT PRACTICE

Assign exercises **B-363** through **B-367**.

DISCUSSION TIPS

Ask the students what questions they have, and encourage active class discussion. Do not assume they understand the concept just because they aren't asking questions. If students have difficulty ignoring figures not governed by the rule, the following example may help clarify this concept.

Can you think of an example of a rule or a law that applies to some people but not to others?

Answers might include rules that apply to participants of particular activities (band, service or political organizations, art,...), members of particular teams (volleyball, basketball, debate,...), or people from particular locations (citizens of a town, state, or country).

What are some rules that a school band might have?

Possible answers might include that uniforms must be cleaned and pressed for each band performance; band instruments must be taken home from school every night; all performed music must be memorized; each member must attend sectional rehearsals.

To whom do these rules apply?

Answer: These rules apply only to members of the school band at that particular school.

Might these rules be applied to members of some other organization?

Answer: No; some organizations might have some rules that are the same or similar, but they are not governed by the band's rules. (For example, it would make no sense to tell members of the chorus to take his or her band instrument home from school every night.)

Can you give some examples of someone who is NOT following each of the rules you mentioned.

Students should use the phrase "A member of the school band who..." as the first part of each statement. If they fail to use this limiting designation (saying, for example, "Someone who..."), call their attention to the omission; e.g., "I don't memorize music to perform. Does this mean I'm not following the rule?"

How could these rules be phrased as IF-THEN statements?

All student answers should have the antecedent (IF-statement) "If you are a member of the band,..." and should contain a consequent (THEN-statement).

NOTE: This type of discussion can be repeated as often as desired or necessary. Choose from different activities, teams, or governmental divisions for each discussion.

ANSWERS

B-363 The IF-statement, "If there is no triangle in the lower half,..." eliminates any card that **does** have a triangle. Six cards remain to which the statement applies.

The THEN-statement, "...then there is a hexagon in the upper half," indicates that cards 5 and 8 fit the rule. The remaining cards (1, 4, 6, and 9) **do not** fit the rule and should be drawn in the answer space.

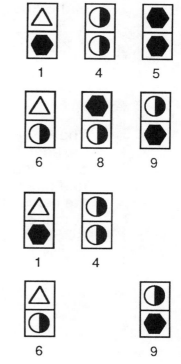

B-364　The IF-statement, "If there is a circle in the upper half,…" indicates that only cards 2, 4, and 9 are governed by the rule.

The THEN-statement, "…then there is a triangle in the lower half," limits those that comply with the rule to one card (2). Cards 4 and 9 should be drawn to indicate that they are the two cards that **do not** follow the rule.

B-365　The IF-statement, "If there is a circle in the upper half,…" indicates that the same set of cards is governed by this rule as was governed by the rule in **B-364**.

The THEN-statement, "…then there is no triangle is the lower half," is contradictory to the then statement in **B-364**. Therefore, cards 4 and 9 follow the rule, and card 2 is the only card that **does not** follow it.

B-366　The IF-statement, "If there is no circle in the upper half,…" is the opposite of the previous two conditionals and directs attention to the set of cards not chosen in exercises **B-364** and **B-365** (1, 3, 5, 6, 7, and 8).

The THEN-statement, "…then there is a hexagon in the lower half," completes the conditional. Since cards 1 and 5 follow the rule (they have a hexagon in the lower half), the cards that **do not** follow the rule are 3, 6, 7, and 8.

156

B-367 The IF-statement, "If there is no circle in the upper half,..." select the same set of cards as those selected in exercise **B-366**.

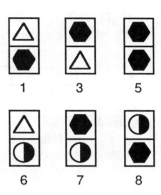

The THEN-statement, however, is contradictory to the previous exercise, "...then there is no hexagon in the lower half." This selects the cards that did not follow the previous rule (3, 6, 7, and 8) as those that do follow this rule, and the cards that did follow the previous rule (1 and 5) as those that **do not** follow this rule.

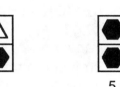

FOLLOW-UP REFERENT
When might you need to determine what members of a group are affected by a rule and, of those affected, which are not following the rule?
Examples: following parliamentary procedure in meetings; following rules for sports; refereeing sports matches; knowing if and how laws apply to you

CURRICULUM APPLICATION
Language Arts: understanding conditional and exclusive statements; recognizing and stating causal relationships; knowing and following rules of grammar, spelling, usage, and punctuation
Mathematics: recognizing and understanding geometric proofs; distinguishing necessary conditions and sufficient conditions
Science: stating causal relationships in laboratory reports
Social Studies: developing deductive reasoning involving conditional statements; recognizing and applying laws; comparing governments, political parties, social mores, or cultures
Enrichment Areas: understanding stated consequences for actions; matching tools or materials to correct usages

INTERPRETING THREE CONNECTIVES

STRAND: Verbal Sequences   **PAGES:** 171–174

ADDITIONAL MATERIALS
Transparency of student workbook page 171
Transparency of TM #19
Washable transparency marker

INTRODUCTION

In earlier lessons you thought of AND *statements by comparing them to several valves controlling the flow of water through a single pipe. You also compared* AND/OR *statements to valves controlling water flow through branching pipes.*

OBJECTIVE

In these exercises you are going to think about three connectives by comparing statements to three valves and their effect on the flow of water through a branching pipe.

DEMONSTRATION/EXPLANATION

NOTE: For emphasis and clarity, you may wish to use a blue washable marker on the transparency to represent each pipe's water flow.

Project the transparency of page 171. After students have read the information at the top of the page, go over the introduction with them, stressing that, from this point on, the symbol ∧ will be used for the connective AND, and the symbol ∨ will be used for the connective AND/OR. Indicate the pipe in exercise **B-368**.

> *Remember how two valves in a single pipe affect the flow of water through that pipe? Summarize those ideas.*

Answer: If either valve A or valve B is closed, water will not flow. If both valve A and valve B are open, then water will flow.

> *What English connective is represented by valves arranged in this manner?*

Answer: They illustrate AND statements. Indicate the branching pipe in exercise **B-369**.

> *These two valves control the flow of water through a branching pipe. How is the flow of water affected by these valves?*

Answer: If both valve A and valve B are closed, water will not flow. If either valve A or valve B is open, water will flow.

> *What English connective do valves in this arrangement represent?*

Answer: They illustrate AND/OR statements. Project the transparency of TM #19.

> *There are several ways to locate three valves on a branching pipe. Two of those are illustrated on this transparency.*

Indicate problem **A**.

> *If water flows into this pipe from the west side, and if the valves are in the positions shown in this example, will water flow out the east side of the pipe?*

Answer: Yes; valve 1 is open so the water enters the two branches. Although the water is stopped by valve 3 in the lower branch, it is allowed to flow through the the upper branch because valve 2 is open.

Indicate the symbolic statement under problem **A**.

> *This valve arrangement can be described by the statement, "If valve 1 and valve 2 and/or valve 3 are open, water will flow through the pipe."*

Indicate problem **B**.

> *Now look at example B. If water enters this pipe from the west, will it flow through this pipe?*

Answer: Yes; water enters the two branches and, although it is stopped by valve 3 in the lower branch, it is allowed to flow in the the upper branch because valve 1 is open.

> *What statement would best describe this valve arrangement?*

Answer: "If valve 1 and/or valves 2 and 3 are open, water will flow through the pipe."

GUIDED PRACTICE
EXERCISES: **B-368, B-369, B-370**
When students have had sufficient time to complete these exercises, use the discussion techniques demonstrated above to verify and correct their answers.
ANSWERS:

B-368 **a** No;   **b** No;   **c** No

B-369 **a** Yes;   **b** Yes;   **c** No

B-370 **a** Yes;   **b** No;   **c** Yes;   **d** No;
          e Yes;   **f** No;   **g** No;   **h** No

INDEPENDENT PRACTICE
Assign exercises **B-371** through **B-377**.

DISCUSSION TIPS
Using multiple connectives is more complex than the simple water-flow problems suggest. The key to deciding whether the complete statement is true (that water will flow through) is the use of parenthesis. If students have had prealgebra instruction involving the use of parenthesis, they can readily transfer that type of grouping to these logic activities. If students have not practiced using parenthesis, you may need to explain that items grouped inside parenthesis are treated as a unit. The value of these connective exercises lies in students' clear conceptualization of the meaning of English sentences involving such connectives as AND, AND/OR, NOT, or IF-THEN. Encourage students to search magazines for examples of complex sentences containing the connectives. Using sentences they have found, ask what the consequence would be if any components of the sentence were false.

ANSWERS
B-371 **a** Yes;   **b** Yes;   **c** Yes;   **d** No;
          e Yes;   **f** No;   **g** Yes;   **h** No

B-372 ⊖ ⊖ ⊖ or ⊖ ⦶ ⊖ or ⊖ ⊖ ⦶
          A B C   A B C   A B C

B-373 ⊖ ⊖ ⊖ or ⦶ ⊖ ⊖ or ⊖ ⦶ ⦶ or
          A B C   A B C   A B C

          ⊖ ⦶ ⊖ or ⊖ ⊖ ⦶
          A B C   A B C

B-374 ⊖ ⊖ ⊖ ⊖ or ⊖ ⦶ ⊖ ⊖ or
          A B C D   A B C D

          ⊖ ⊖ ⦶ ⦶ or ⊖ ⊖ ⦶ ⊖ or
          A B C D   A B C D

          ⊖ ⊖ ⊖ ⦶
          A B C D

159

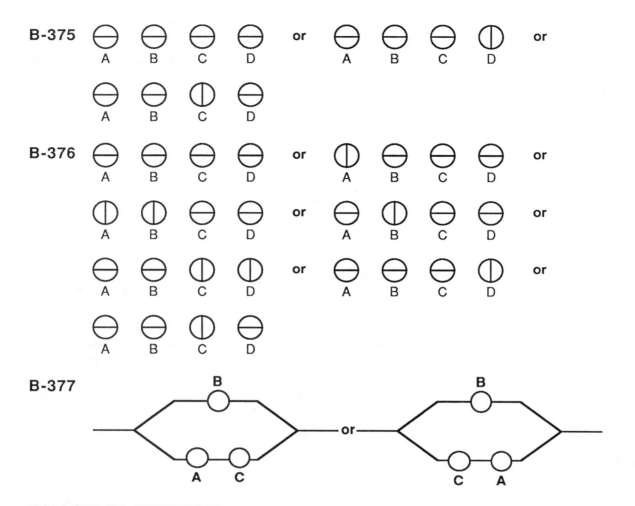

FOLLOW-UP REFERENT
When might you need to decide whether a complex statement using three connectives is true or false?
Examples: observing whether operating instructions or directions have been correctly followed; recognizing whether recipes or directions for taking medicine are being correctly followed; answering true/false questions on a test; recognizing that negative statements can be either true or false

CURRICULUM APPLICATION
Language Arts: proofreading papers for errors in spelling, grammar, or punctuation; answering true/false questions over an aspect of a story or selection; judging when formatting instructions have been followed

Mathematics: the use of parenthesis in algebra; checking computations to determine if correct procedures were followed; choosing correct answer sets to a problem; checking computations by estimation

Science: verifying animal or plant characteristics in laboratory demonstrations; reading or completing genetic probability charts

Social Studies: finding facts to support or negate statements; deductive reasoning involving truth value

Enrichment Areas: determining whether instructions or rules have been followed in sports or recreation activities; evaluating procedures, e.g., governmental or managerial

USING THREE CONNECTIVES

STRAND: Verbal Sequences   **PAGES:** 175–178

ADDITIONAL MATERIALS
Transparency of TM #20
Washable transparency marker

INTRODUCTION
In the previous lesson you used three valves controlling the water flow in a branching pipe to illustrate statements containing three connectives.

OBJECTIVE
In these exercises you will use the idea of three connectives to sort a group of shaded shapes.

DEMONSTRATION/EXPLANATION
Project the **CHOICE BOX** and the **EXAMPLE** from the transparency of TM #20.

The object of these exercises is to find the one shape in the CHOICE BOX for which all three statements are true. Begin by choosing shapes from the CHOICE BOX that meet the rule stated in the first sentence. In this example, the white circle, the black square, and the black circle are shown as meeting the requirements for the statement "It is black and/or it is a circle." What kind of connective is used in this sentence?

Answer: It is the AND/OR (disjunction) connective.

How does each of the chosen shapes follow the rule?

Answer: The white circle fulfills the second part of the statement (it is a circle); the black square fulfills the first part of the statement (it is black); and the black circle fulfills both parts of the statement (it is both black and a circle).

Which of the shapes in the CHOICE BOX is not included in this group and why is it left out?

Answer: The white square is omitted because it does not meet either requirement of the AND/OR statement: it is not black, and it is not a circle.

The second AND/OR statement helps you narrow the field of possible shapes. Instead of going back to the CHOICE BOX to make your choices, refer to the shapes you chose for statement 1. The white circle and the black square are shown here as meeting the requirements for the statement "It is white and/or it is a square." How does each of these shapes follow the given rule?

Answer: The white circle fulfills the first part of the statement (it is white), and the black square fulfills the second part of the statement (it is a square).

Which shape is eliminated and why?

Answer: The black circle is eliminated because it does not meet the requirements of either part of the AND/OR statement: it is not white, and it is not a square.

Remember that you are to choose the answer for each step from the shapes in the answer to the previous step. You are not to go back to the CHOICE BOX for statements 2 or 3. The black square is shown as being the only shape from step 2 that follows the third AND/OR statement. How does it fulfill the requirements, and why was the white circle not chosen?

Answer: The black square fulfills both parts of the AND/OR statement: it is black AND it is a square. The white circle fulfills neither part of the statement: it is NEITHER black NOR a square. Project the **practice** exercise from the bottom of the transparency.

    Try this one in your mind, then we'll work it out on the transparency.

Allow ample time for all students to reach a mental solution before proceeding with the steps demonstrated above. It may be necessary to remind students that they are trying to choose ONE shape that meets all three rules. To do this, they must automatically eliminate any shape that is not a member of the set that fulfills the preceding rule, for if a shape does not meet the requirements for any one rule, it cannot meet the requirements for all rules.

Answer:

1. It is white and/or a square.

2. It is black and/or a circle.

3. It is white and/or a circle.

GUIDED PRACTICE
EXERCISES: **B-378**, **B-379**
When students have had sufficient time to complete these exercises, use the discussion techniques demonstrated above to verify and correct their answers.
ANSWERS:

B-378   1. It is black and/or it is a hexagon.

          2. It is white and/or it is a triangle.

          3. It is black and/or it is a triangle.

B-379   1. It is black and/or it is a hexagon.

          2. It is white and/or it is a triangle.

          3. It is white and/or it is a hexagon.

INDEPENDENT PRACTICE
Assign exercises **B-380** through **B-384**.

DISCUSSION TIPS

These exercises transfer the use of connectives from the flow-of-water examples to the form in which students commonly use them, i.e., common English sentences. The student must decide which figures are described by the true meaning of each sentence. By taking all three sentences to be true of the same figure, the student eliminates all but one of the geometric figures in the **CHOICE BOX.** The difficulty of the item is compounded by the deductive reasoning required in each example. The student eliminates figures based on the conditions of each sentence. As an extending activity, play a version of "Twenty Questions" in which students cite two conditions using connectives and negations, i.e., AND, AND/OR, IF-THEN, and NOT.

ANSWERS

B-380   1. It is not white and/or not a triangle.

2. It is not black and/or not a triangle.

3. It is not white and/or not a hexagon.

B-381   1. It is not white and/or not a triangle.

2. It is not black and/or not a triangle.

3. It is not black and/or not a hexagon.

B-382 **a** Region 4;   **b** Region 2;   **c** Region 3;
          d Regions 1, 2, 3;   **e** Regions 2, 3, 4

B-383 **a** Yes;   **b** No;   **c** No;   **d** Yes;   **e** No;   **f** Yes;   **g** Yes;   **h** No

B-384 **a** No;   **b** Yes;   **c** No;   **d** Yes;   **e** Yes;   **f** No;   **g** Yes

FOLLOW-UP REFERENT

When might you need to decide whether a complex statement is true or false when applied to a specific group or item?

Examples: applying operating instructions or construction directions; recognizing whether directions for medication are being correctly followed; answering true/false questions on a test; recognizing that negative statements can be either true or false; applying construction requirements and rules to new buildings, remodeling projects, or renovations

CURRICULUM APPLICATION

Language Arts: applying rules of spelling, grammar, or punctuation when proofreading papers; answering complex true/false questions over an aspect of a story or selection;

applying formatting instructions in journalism or composition; preparing cause-effect compositions or arguments

Mathematics: applying complex instructions for solving problems; choosing correct answer sets to a problem

Science: applying characteristics to identify various animals or plants; reading or completing genetic probability charts; applying facts to test or support a hypothesis

Social Studies: comparing written characteristics to various artifacts, events, eras to establish their category; finding facts to support or negate statements; recognizing cause-effect relationships

Enrichment Areas: applying formatting instructions, e.g., typewritten or computer generated forms, tables, letters; determining whether instructions and/or rules have been followed in sports or recreation activities; completing forms, e.g., job or loan application forms, governmental forms, requisition or request forms

APPLYING THREE CONNECTIVES

STRAND: Verbal Sequences   **PAGES:** 179–180

ADDITIONAL MATERIALS
Transparency of TM #21
Washable transparency marker

INTRODUCTION
In earlier lessons you interpreted statements containing three connectives and used them to identify nonconforming members of a group.

OBJECTIVE
In these exercises you will apply a three-connective statement to find a path through a maze.

DEMONSTRATION / EXPLANATION
Cut apart the transparency of TM #21 as indicated, then project figure **A**.

Every maze has rules. The instructions for this maze say that you are to find the shortest path to the exit that follows a specific rule. What is the rule for this maze?

Answer: "If you are on a white field, then the next field you enter is striped." Remove figure **A** from the projector, replacing it with figure **B**.

Let's try some solutions for this maze. Does the beginning of this path follow the rule? The first move is from a white field into a striped field. Is this a "legal" move?

Answer: Yes; the rule says that if you are on a white field, then the next field you enter must be striped.

The next move is from a striped field into a white field. Is that a "legal" move?

Answer: Yes; the move is "legal" because there is no rule governing it. (Since moves *from* a striped field are not covered by the rule, they cannot break the rule.)

Where might the next move be?

Allow ample time for covert thinking and active class discussion. Encourage students to state reasons for each move they suggest or reject. They should arrive at the conclusion that no legal move is possible from the top-left (white) field. You may need to remind them that they cannot move backward along the same path or diagonally; only forward vertical or horizontal moves are allowed.

Repeat the procedure with figure **C**, then figure **D**, asking students to confirm the "legality" of each move. When this has been completed, project figures **A** and **D** simultaneously.

Can anyone find an alternate path through the maze?

Allow time for discussion, drawing suggested paths onto figure **A**. Have students confirm each suggested move and state the reason for its acceptability or inacceptability.

Answer:

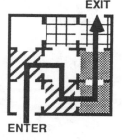

Is this path a better choice than the one shown in figure D?

Answer: No; this path takes more moves (goes through more fields) than the path shown in figure **D**. The instructions say to find the shortest path.

GUIDED PRACTICE
EXERCISE: **B-385**

Give students sufficient time to complete these exercises. Then, using the demonstration methodology above, have them discuss and explain their choices.
ANSWERS:

B-385

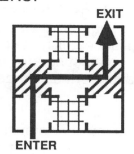

INDEPENDENT PRACTICE
Assign exercises **B-386** through **B-391**.

DISCUSSION TIPS
The maze activities allow students to apply what they have learned about the effect of connectives in a game-like format. Stress the connective words when making conditional statements, and encourage students to use IF-THEN connectives in other content areas

As a follow-up activity, encourage students to make their own mazes involving a path governed by an IF-THEN rule. Remind them to make sure their puzzle is solvable, then have them trade puzzles with classmates. Complexity will increase if they add more fields to the maze and/or more connectives to the rules.

ANSWERS

NOTE: One path is shown. Others may be possible, but they are not shorter.

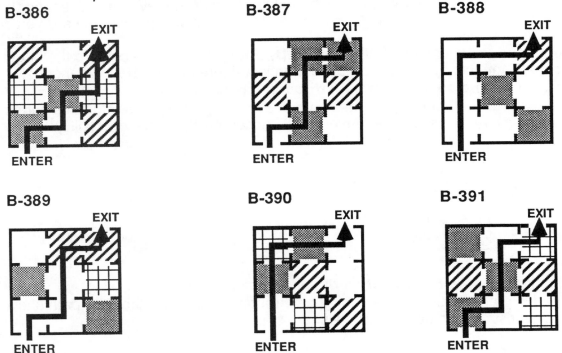

B-386 **B-387** **B-388**

B-389 **B-390** **B-391**

FOLLOW-UP REFERENT

When might you need to interpret a complex rule, then apply the rule to a specific task?

Examples: interpreting and following parliamentary rules for meetings; interpreting and following rules for taking medication; interpreting and following sequential steps in preparing recipes, building models, or assembling toys or appliances; filing tax information or forms; interpreting and following instructions for completing any form, e.g., applications forms for employment or loans, insurance information forms, accident reports

CURRICULUM APPLICATION

Language Arts: interpreting and following rules for spelling, grammar, or punctuation; interpreting and answering true/false questions over an aspect of a story or selection; interpreting and following formatting instructions, e.g., journalism assignments, composition or homework directions, business or personal letters

Mathematics: interpreting and following multistep procedures for mathematics, algebra, or geometry problems; applying theorems in geometry proofs; interpreting word problems and applying correct procedures for solving them

Science: interpreting animal or plant characteristics and identifying animals or plants by correctly applying the interpretation; reading or completing genetic probability charts

Social Studies: reading or constructing maps, graphs, or charts according to specific rules or instructions; interpreting and obeying laws which apply to you; applying information from primary sources to a given situation, e.g., reading and interpreting the U.S. Constitution by applying it to a real or imaginary legal case

Enrichment Areas: interpreting and following established rules for sports or recreation activities; interpreting and following any set of sequential steps

CAUSE-EFFECT WORDS—SELECT

STRAND: Verbal Sequences   **PAGES:** 181–182

ADDITIONAL MATERIALS
Transparency of student workbook page 181 (optional)
Washable transparency marker

INTRODUCTION
In previous exercises you rearranged words within a specified sequence according to degrees of meaning or time of occurrence. Sometimes a time sequence also suggested that one event or condition caused or resulted in another. This type of relationship is called a "cause-effect" relationship.

OBJECTIVE
In these exercises you will be given two words. You are to determine whether the word pair illustrates a cause-effect relationship.

DEMONSTRATION/EXPLANATION
Project the top half of the transparency of page 181.

Here you see three sample word pairs. If the first word of each pair names a common cause for the second word, you are to mark the pair "C-E" to indicate their cause-effect relationship. If the the first word does not name something that commonly causes the second, mark the pair "NO."

Indicate the first word pair from the **EXAMPLE**.

In the first example, fear often results in flight, and the pair has been marked C-E (cause-effect).

Indicate the second word pair from the **EXAMPLE**.

In the second pair, fear does not commonly cause fright. This pair has been marked "NO" to indicate that they do not show a cause-effect relationship. What is the relationship shown by this word pair?

Answer: They mean the same thing; they have a synonym relationship. Indicate the third **EXAMPLE** example.

The third pair, fear and height, is also marked "NO" to indicate that it is not a cause-effect relationship. Why isn't it marked "C-E"?

Answer: One may be afraid of heights, but fear does not commonly cause height.

If this pair of words were reversed, then a cause-effect relationship might exist; being at great heights may result in fear. Be sure you consider each word pair in the order they are given, not reversed. The first word must cause or result in the second, not vice versa.

GUIDED PRACTICE
EXERCISE: **B-392 a**, **b**, and **c**
Give students sufficient time to complete these exercises. Then, using the demonstration methodology above, have them discuss and explain their choices.
ANSWERS:

B-392   **a**   C-E   Achievement commonly results in recognition.

        b   NO   "Taste" does not result in "honey." Although the phrase "taste of honey" is common, it does not have a cause-effect relationship.

(Students may note that a C-E relationship might be possible if the word pair were reversed, i.e., the use of honey may give a taste to something.)

c   C-E   Vibrations create sound.

INDEPENDENT PRACTICE
Assign exercises **B-392 d–j** and **B-393**.

DISCUSSION TIPS
Encourage students to identify the relationship shown by those word pairs that do not have cause-effect relationships. Listen carefully for the verbs that students use in describing cause-effect relationships. These might include produces, builds, creates, results in, brings about, and makes. Mark each new word on a chart, then use the chart to help students identify cause-effect clues in reading, literature, or social studies lessons.

Encourage students to identify cause-effect relationships drawn from their own experience, but help them identify and avoid faulty reasoning. This might be a good place to introduce them to "faulty cause," a common error in reasoning (also known as "after this, therefore because of this"). Examples of this type of logical error might be shown by such word pairs as "robin-spring" ("After the robins appear in our area, the weather gets warmer and the days get longer; therefore, the robins cause spring to arrive.") or "clean car-rain" ("Every time I wash my car it rains; therefore, my washing the car causes rain.")

ANSWERS

B-392			
	d	NO	The terms are synonyms.
	e	NO	The terms are synonyms.
	f	C-E	A flood commonly produces damage.
	g	NO	"A quart of liquid" is a common phrase, but quarts do not cause liquids.
	h	C-E	Running builds stamina.
	i	C-E	A violation results in a fine.
	j	C-E	Salt produces thirst.
B-393	**a**	C-E	Gravity commonly causes things to fall.
	b	C-E	A mystery results in suspense.
	c	NO	Music is a kind of sound.
	d	NO	The terms are synonyms.
	e	C-E	Hunger is a result of famine.
	f	NO	The terms are synonyms.
	g	NO	The words are reversed; hoarseness may cause whispering.
	h	C-E	Misconduct commonly results in punishment.
	i	C-E	Cold causes numbness.
	j	NO	The terms are synonyms.
	k	C-E	The result of a blow will frequently be a bruise.
	l	C-E	A virus causes illness.
	m	NO	Parts are not caused by a sum; they make up a sum.
	n	C-E	Suffering causes distress.
	o	NO	The terms are synonyms.

FOLLOW-UP REFERENT

When might you need to recognize that two terms or actions have a cause-effect relationship, then distinguish the cause from the effect?

Examples: interpreting newspaper articles or television news commentaries and stories; understanding cause-effect relationships in social situations; reaching valid conclusions from a given set of facts; distinguishing cause from coincidence; analyzing advertising techniques

CURRICULUM APPLICATION

Language Arts: interpreting and using conditional statements; recognizing and stating causal relationships in literature and composition; identifying the turning point or alternatives in a literary work; identifying consequences of a character's actions

Mathematics: recognizing and understanding geometric proofs; recognizing whether a change in one aspect of a problem will affect an answer

Science: recognizing and stating causal relationships in laboratory reports; recognizing and stating causal relationships between chemical elements; interpreting animal behavior

Social Studies: recognizing and applying laws; analyzing propaganda; recognizing supply-demand relationships in economics

Enrichment Areas: understanding and evaluating stated consequences for actions; analyzing computer programs; recognizing the consequences of breaking the law or the rules of a game or sport; evaluating causes of changes in production in agriculture or manufacturing

CAUSE-EFFECT WORDS—SUPPLY

STRAND: Verbal Sequences

PAGES: 183–184

ADDITIONAL MATERIALS

Transparencies of student workbook pages 183 and 184

INTRODUCTION

In the previous lesson you identified word pairs that illustrated a cause-effect relationship.

OBJECTIVE

In these exercises you are given one part of a cause-effect word pair. You will supply a word or words to complete the relationship.

DEMONSTRATION / EXPLANATION

Project the transparency of page 183.

In the EXAMPLE you are given the word "worry" in the CAUSES/REASONS column. The answers, shown in the EFFECTS/RESULTS column, are "tension" and "frown." Do you agree that worry often results in tension or frowning? What other common or possible results can you think of?

Pause for discussion. Encourage additional answers that might complete the relationship, but ask each provider to explain his or her answer.

Now look at B-394. You are given the word "fire" as a cause. What are some common effects or results of fire?

Possible answers: Ashes, smoke, destruction, burns. Replace the transparency with the one of page 184.

In these exercises you are given an effect, such as the word "health" in the EXAMPLE. You are to supply a reason or cause for the given effect. "Nutrition" and "exercise" often cause a person to have good health and are given as possible answers. Can you think of others?

Pause for discussion. Students may wish to provide answers that affect health in a negative way. You may remind them that such answers would cause illness, not health.

Now look at B-406. You have the given effect, "fragrance." What causes can you think of for fragrance?

Possible answers: Flowers, perfume, baking bread.

GUIDED PRACTICE
EXERCISES: **B-395, B-396, B-407, B-408**
Give students sufficient time to complete these exercises. Then, using the demonstration methodology above, have them discuss and explain their choices.
NOTE: Given words appear in italics throughout the answers in this section.

ANSWERS:

	CAUSES/REASONS	EFFECTS/RESULTS
B-395	*quality*	pleasure; long-lastedness
B-396	*imbalance*	falls, unevenness
B-407	left-overs; by-products	*waste*
B-408	war; accidents; fires	*casualties*

INDEPENDENT PRACTICE
Assign exercises **B-397** through **B-405** and **B-409** through **B-416**.

DISCUSSION TIPS
Encourage students to identify the relationship shown by those word pairs that do not have cause-effect relationships. Listen carefully for the verbs that students use in describing cause-effect relationships. These might include produces, builds, creates, results in, brings about, and makes. Mark each new word on a chart, then use the chart to help students identify cause-effect clues in reading, literature, or social studies lessons.

Encourage students to identify cause-effect relationships drawn from their experience and to recognize those occasions when there is no cause-effect relationship.

ANSWERS

	CAUSES/REASONS	EFFECTS/RESULTS
B-397	*practice*	perfection; improvement
B-398	*hurricane*	damage; rain
B-399	*reading*	pleasure; information
B-400	*supply*	price control; availability
B-401	*stretch*	extra room; greater size; relaxation
B-402	*noise*	confusion; irritation; aggravation

B-403	*spices*	tastiness; change in color, taste, or aroma
B-404	*emotion*	tears; laughter; anxiety
B-405	*speeding*	tickets; accidents; increased fuel; consumption; fear

B-409	spinning; illness; heights	*dizziness*
B-410	uncertainty; fear; insecurity	*hesitation*
B-411	work; exercise; heat; nervousness	*perspiration*
B-412	strangers; uncertainty; egocentricity	*shyness*
B-413	sun; electricity; combustion	*light*
B-414	germs; viruses; uncleanliness	*infection*
B-415	tickling; pleasure; humor; hysteria	*laughter*
B-416	work; exercise; lack of rest; stress; poor nutrition	*fatigue*

FOLLOW-UP REFERENT

When might you need to complete or supply words for a cause-effect relationship?

Examples: interpreting news articles or television commentaries; interpreting cause-effect relationships in social situations; understanding reactions to one's own behavior or statements; determining the effects that various decisions have on one's own (or another's) physical, mental, or economic health; recognizing and avoiding faulty cause-effect reasoning; organizing answers to cause-effect essay questions; analyzing advertising techniques; understanding stated consequences for actions

CURRICULUM APPLICATION

Language Arts: interpreting and using conditional statements; recognizing and stating causal relationships in literature and composition; identifying the turning point or alternatives in a literary work; identifying consequences of a character's actions; organizing cause-effect compositions; recognizing and using cause-effect arguments in debates

Mathematics: recognizing and understanding geometric proofs; recognizing whether a change in one aspect of a problem will affect an answer

Science: recognizing and stating causal relationships in laboratory reports; recognizing and stating causal relationships between chemical elements; developing and stating cause-effect hypotheses for experiments; predicting outcomes; interpreting human or animal behaviors

Social Studies: recognizing and applying laws; analyzing propaganda; recognizing the causes and effects (and distinguishing between them) of various historical, social, economic, or governmental acts; recognizing and interpreting rules of supply and demand in economics

Enrichment Areas: analyzing computer programs; recognizing consequences of breaking a law or rules of a game or sport; recognizing causes and effects of production changes in argiculture or manufacturing

SIGNAL WORDS—SELECT

STRAND: Verbal Sequences   **PAGE:** 185

ADDITIONAL MATERIALS
Blank transparency sheet (optional)
Washable transparency marker (optional)

INTRODUCTION
In previous lessons you identified and completed word pairs that had cause-effect relationships.

OBJECTIVE
In these exercises you will look at words used to signal various relationships. You will use these words to help determine whether the relationship between two parts of a given sentence is time-order, contradiction, or cause-effect.

DEMONSTRATION / EXPLANATION
Write the following three sentences on the chalkboard or a transparency.
  • Juarez stopped at the library before he went home.
  • Juarez wanted to stop at the library, but he needed to go directly home.
  • Juarez stopped at the library because he needed information for his research paper.
> *As you learned in previous exercises, not all time-order statements are also cause-effect statements. Some statements simply tell the order in which things happen.*

Indicate the first sentence you wrote.
> *For example, the statement "Juarez stopped at the library before he went home" simply tells the order in which Juarez acted. He didn't go home BECAUSE he went to the library, nor did he stop at the library BECAUSE he went home. Although the two actions are related by time order, they are not related by cause and effect. What other time-order statements can you think of that do not illustrate cause-effect relationships?*

As students become proficient at time-order statements, ask them to increase the number of steps taken, e.g., "Before Kai went home from school, she attended cheerleading practice, then bought an ice cream cone." Ask them to identify which part of each statement happened first, which second, etc.
> *Sometimes a statement starts by suggesting one action, but the result is something else.*

Indicate the second sentence on the chalkboard or the transparency.
> *Look, for example, at the statement "Juarez wanted to stop at the library, but he needed to go directly home." Such sentences are called contradictory statements. The condition in one part of the sentence cannot be accomplished because of the condition in the other part of the sentence. What other examples can you think of that would illustrate contradictory statements?*

As various students respond, ask the class to verity that the given statement is, indeed, a contradiction rather than a cause-effect or time-order statement.
> *Cause-effect statements may also suggest a time order, but one action causes the other.*

Indicate the third sentence on the chalkboard or transparency.

For example, "Juarez stopped at the library because he needed information for his research paper." In this sentence, his need for information caused him to stop at the library. Can you think of other cause-effect statements?

As students supply examples of cause-effect sentences, have them identify which part of the statement is the cause and which the effect.

Each of these sentences contains a signal word as a clue to help the reader establish whether a time-order relationship, a contradiction relationship, or a cause-effect relationship is being expressed. What signal words are used in the sentences?

Answer: Before (time-order), but (contradiction), and because (cause-effect).

What other words might signal a time-order relationship?

As students suggest signal words for each type of statement, ask them to supply sentences to illustrate their suggestions. Possible answers: Then, before, after, later, earlier, next.

What signal words or phrases might you use for contradictory statements?

Again, ask for illustrative sentences. Possible answers: However, contrary to, although, nevertheless.

What words might you use to signal a cause-effect relationship?

Possible answers: Since, because, for, consequently.

The signal words are underlined in these exercises. You are to mark the sentence T-O if the signal word suggests a time-order relationship, CON for a contradictory relationship, or C-E for a cause-effect relationship.

GUIDED PRACTICE
EXERCISES: **B-417, B-418, B-419**
Give students sufficient time to complete these exercises. Then, using the demonstration methodology above, have them discuss and explain their choices.
ANSWERS:

B-417   C-E   The signal word *consequently* means "as a result."

B-418   T-O   *Eventually* means "at some future time," suggesting time-order.

B-419   CON   The signal word *although* warns the reader that the sense of the first clause is likely to be reversed in the second.

INDEPENDENT PRACTICE
Assign exercises **B-420** through **B-424**.

DISCUSSION TIPS
Make three columns on a chart. Label the first "time-order," the second "contradiction," and the third "cause-effect." List words students use to indicate each relationship category. Ask students to suggest a single situation, such as Margo's studying for her chemistry course in items **B-417** through **B-424**, then add signal words and new clauses to express different concepts. See how many sentences your class can develop using these three types of signal words.

Extend this prewriting activity to other lessons by developing a "Signal-word Bulletin Board," offering students a lasting visual reminder of these sentence connectives. In subsequent writing lessons ask students to select signal words to connect short sentences into more complex ones. Ask students to make their own complex sentences, then change their wording and composition structure to show example of the different sentence types.

ANSWERS

B-420 C-E   The signal word *since* means "as a result."

B-421 CON   The phrase *on the contrary* indicates that the fact is opposite from what was expected.

B-422 C-E   The signal word *for* means "because."

B-423 CON   The signal word *while* in this sentence does not indicate time; rather it is a synonym for "although."

B-424 T-O   In this sentence, the signal word *while* does indicate the passage of time.

FOLLOW-UP REFERENT

When might you use signal words to recognize or indicate time-order, contradiction, or cause-effect statements?

Examples: interpreting or creating news articles or television commentaries; interpreting or explaining cause-effect relationships in social situations; understanding reactions to one's own behavior or statements; determining and stating the effects of various decisions on one's own (or another's) physical, mental, or economic health; recognizing and avoiding faulty cause-effect reasoning; organizing and writing answers to essay questions, especially those calling for chronological order, contradictory statements, or cause-effect analysis; analyzing advertising techniques

CURRICULUM APPLICATION

Language Arts: understanding conditional statements; recognizing and stating desired relationships; identifying the turning point or alternatives in a story; prewriting exercises; combining short sentences to form more complex ones

Mathematics: recognizing and understanding geometric proofs

Science: stating causal relationships in laboratory reports; following directions properly

Social Studies: recognizing and applying laws; analyzing propaganda; recognizing contradictory purpose in light of subsequent action

Enrichment Areas: understanding stated consequences for actions; following directions in home economics, art, music, and industrial arts

FLOWCHARTING—SEQUENCES AND PLANS

STRAND: Verbal Sequences   **PAGES:** 186–193

ADDITIONAL MATERIALS

Transparencies of student workbook pages 186,187, and 192
Transparencies of other workbook pages (optional)
Washable transparency marker (optional)

INTRODUCTION

In previous lessons you arranged words and events into specific orders. You also learned to interpret IF-THEN statements.

OBJECTIVE

In these exercises you will arrange a series of events using flowchart diagrams. Diagrams like these can be used to organize solutions to problems, as well as to illustrate a sequence or a plan of action.

DEMONSTRATION / EXPLANATION

Project the transparency of page 186, uncovering each step as you talk about it.

Here you see an example of a simple flowchart showing steps in writing a report. First you pick a topic for your report. What might you do next?

Allow time for discussion and predictions, then project the second step.

Might you go to the library to find resource material on your topic? What would you do with the resource material?

Project the third step from the chart, asking students to confirm that taking notes would probably follow the previous step. Remove the cover from the transparency to project the entire chart. Indicate each step as you verbalize the process.

When you believe you have gathered enough information, you organize your notes in the order that the information will appear in your paper, prepare your preliminary draft, discuss it with your teacher, and make any necessary corrections or additions. Last, you write your final report.

Replace the transparency with the one of page 187.

Computer programmers use a standard set of symbols to help the reader quickly understand the flow of thought represented by the chart. They use rectangles to indicate actions or activities, and ovals to show START and STOP points. The diagram at the bottom of the page shows standard flowchart form. Other than a computer program, what types of information or sequences can you think of that might be charted using ovals and rectangles?

Possible answers: Any event involving a series of steps, e.g., getting ready for school, after school chores, preparing for an exam, cleaning the house, preparing dinner, planning a shop project, preparing for a performance, getting ready for a date.

On page 188 you have an example of a basic flowchart applied to a math problem. What is the problem, and what are they trying to find out?

If you have made a transparency of this page, project it as you explain the flowchart. Answer: "Find the cost of eight gallons of gasoline if the price per gallon is $1.35." They want to know the total price of 8 gallons of gasoline at a specific price per gallon.

Your starting point is indicated by the oval. The rectangle indicates the first action: multiply the number of gallons times the cost per gallon. The open shape to the right of the rectangle can be used for notes or calculations. The answer, $10.80, is written in the trapezoid. Once you find the answer, the process is finished. Indicate this ending with another oval.

Project the transparency of page 192, indicating the parts as you describe the process.

Complex sequences, those involving decisions which can be answered "yes" or "no," require additional symbols. Here you see that diamonds appear to be used to symbolize decision spots or questions. Circles follow the diamonds and contain the possible choices (the "yes" or "no" answers). What process does this flowchart seem to illustrate?

Answer: Placing a call from a pay phone.

Let's look at the flowchart. You start by finding a telephone, as indicated in the rectangle. Your first decision, shown in the diamond, is whether or not you have the correct change for placing the call. If the answer is "no," as shown in the circle, then you must get change (rectangle). When you have the correct change ("yes" circle), you insert the money into the phone and dial the number (rectangle). Your next decision is whether or not you have reached the correct number (diamond). If the answer is no, then you dial the operator (rectangle), who will return your money (rectangle), which will be in the correct change ("yes" circle). What do you do next?

Answer: The refund creates a loop back to the correct change question, and you go through the process again. When you reach the correct number, you talk, then hang up. ***The process ends with the STOP in the bottom oval.***

GUIDED PRACTICE
EXERCISES: **B-425**, **B-426**, **B-427**
ANSWERS:

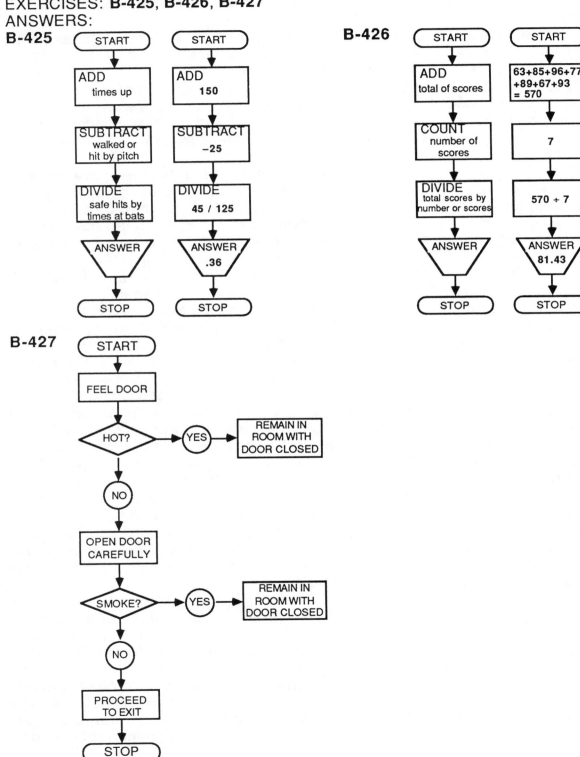

B-425

B-426

B-427

INDEPENDENT PRACTICE
Assign exercises **B-428** through **B-431**.

DISCUSSION TIPS
As an extending activity, you may ask students to illustrate a recent homework or project assignment using a flowchart. These are especially applicable to mathematics word problems and to composition, report, or project assignments. Be sure students understand and use the correct flowcharting symbols, then ask them to depict real-life sequences involving decision points.

ANSWERS

B-428

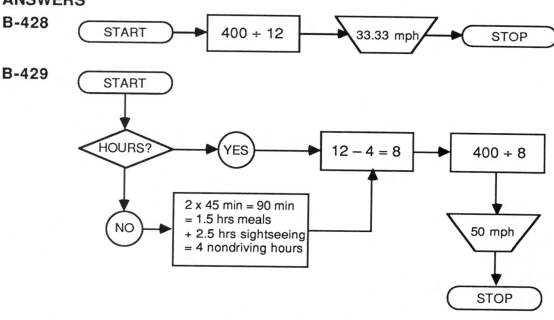

B-429

B-430

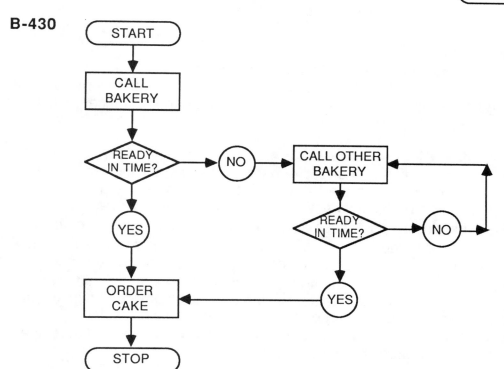

B-431

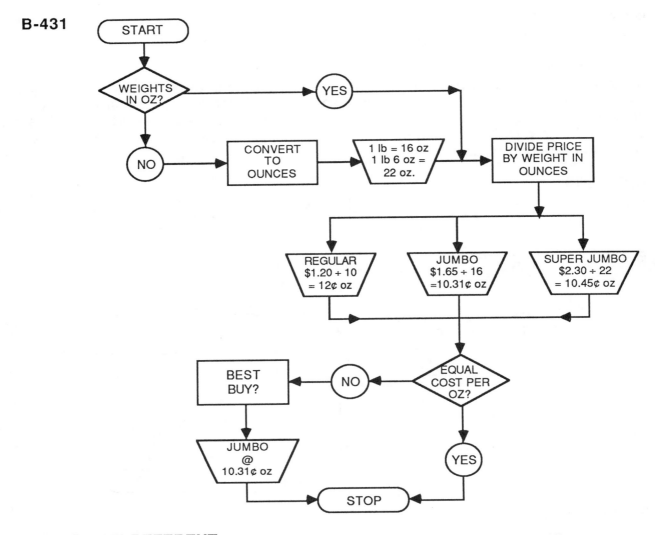

FOLLOW-UP REFERENT
When might it be helpful to use a flowchart diagram?
Examples: to understand types of decisions and consequences of actions involved in a situation; organizing or planning events and schedules, e.g., parties, dances, elections, work projects; illustrating or organizing a "chain-of-command," e.g., clubs, businesses

CURRICULUM APPLICATION
Language Arts: writing descriptive or instructive paragraphs; organizing proofreading and editing tasks; sequencing writing projects; depicting complex literary plots; checking plots for contradictions or implausible actions, particularly mystery or adventure novels

Mathematics: depicting multistep processes; charting processes for word problems

Science: depicting the steps in laboratory experiments, chemistry, or physical science problems; charting any sequential developments, e.g., stages of human development

Social Studies: interpreting and constructing maps, graphs, time lines, or diagrams; depicting consequences of historic events; tracing the development of significant trends or legislative actions; projecting or predicting sociological results

Enrichment Areas: test taking skills; depicting computer programs; diagraming stage directions or actions for a marching band or drill team

FLOWCHARTING A CYCLE

STRAND: Verbal Sequences   **PAGES:** 197–201

ADDITIONAL MATERIALS
Transparency of student workbook page 197 (optional)

INTRODUCTION
In previous lessons you used flowchart diagrams to show sequences of steps and plans of action. You also used flowcharts to depict the consequences of yes-no decisions.

OBJECTIVE
In these exercises you will use flowcharting to depict cycles.

DEMONSTRATION/EXPLANATION
Project the transparency of page 197. Indicate the process sections as you talk.

This water cycle illustrates the usefulness of cycle diagrams. Such cycles really have no beginning or end; they are repeating events. If you start at the top of the diagram, you see that as large bodies of water are heated by the sun, water evaporates and forms clouds over the water. As clouds move inland over cooler land formations, the difference in heat results in precipitation. What happens next in this process?

Answer: Rainwater trickles into streams and rivers, which flow into larger bodies of water.

Then the cycle begins again. The water vapor cycle involves simple steps. Cycle diagrams may also, however, include yes-no decisions. These create branches and loops similar to those we saw in the previous lesson.

GUIDED PRACTICE
EXERCISES: **B-432, B-433**

Give students sufficient time to complete these exercises. Then, using the demonstration methodology above, have them discuss and explain their choices.

ANSWERS:

B-432   (1) A corn plant is nourished by organic material in the soil.
           (4) Some corn is eaten by corn borer insects.
           (6) Insects are eaten by a sparrow.
           (2) A fox eats a sparrow.
           (5) After the fox dies, the carcass is decomposed by bacteria.
           (3) The decomposing action of bacteria replenishes the soil with organic material.

B-433

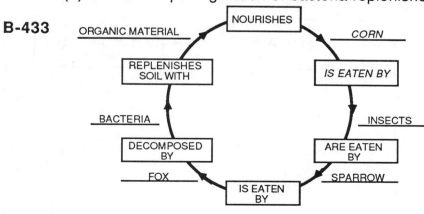

INDEPENDENT PRACTICE
Assign exercises **B-434** and **B-435**.

DISCUSSION TIPS
Have students verbalize their charts as you draw them on the chalkboard or transparency. As they become familiar with the decision-making symbols, ask students to depict real-life sequences and cycles with flowchart diagrams. Flowcharting is especially useful for English grammar and composition, historical events, and scientific cycles.

ANSWERS
B-434

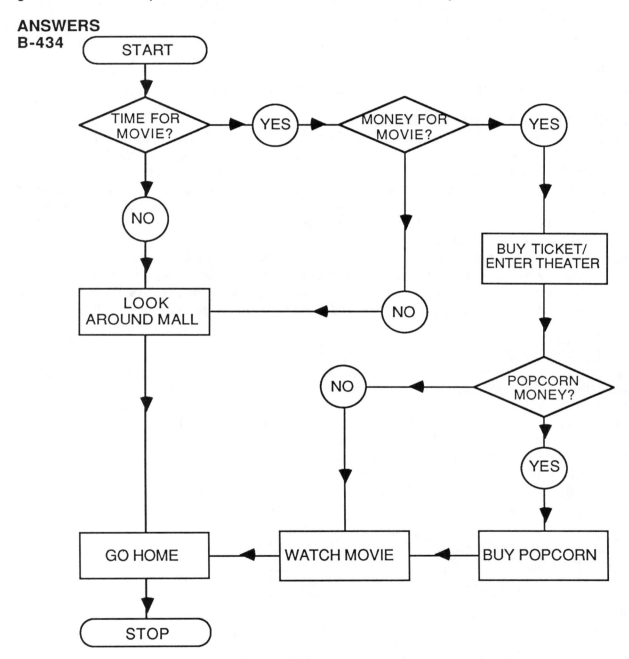

B-435

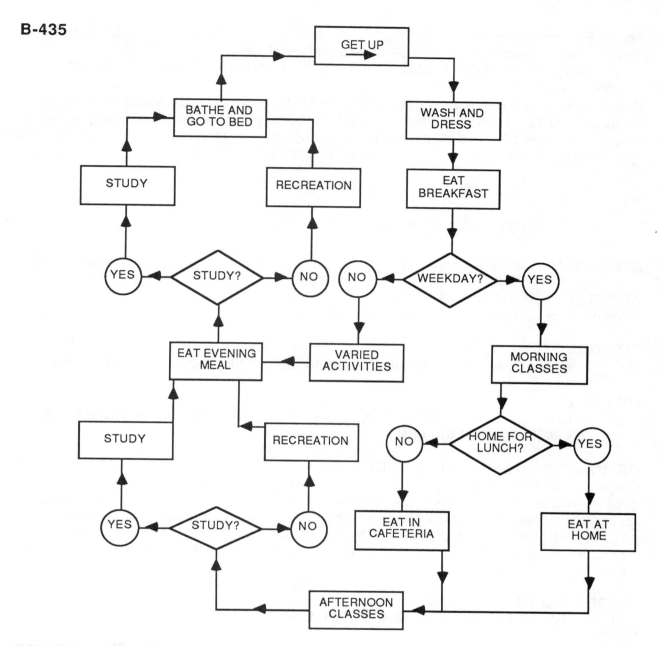

FOLLOW-UP REFERENT

When might you use a flowchart to show a cycle of events or a sequence?

Examples: clarifying or illustrating an organizational structure that is difficult to describe in words; communicating changes or alternatives in activities or structure; organizing and planning to reduce wasted time and minimize confusion; using flow charts to explore possible alternatives

CURRICULUM APPLICATION

Language Arts: illustrating plot structures; using flowcharts for sentence analysis, composition organization, and report planning

Mathematics: creating and depicting a sequence of steps for problem solving

Science: depicting biological or physical cycles; illustrating steps and/or decision points in a laboratory experiment

Social Studies: depicting cyclical trends or hierarchical decision-making processes in economics; illustrating the steps or decisions that led to the rise and/or fall of civilizations; depicting political events, sociological trends, and governmental processes

Enrichment Areas: depicting cycles within computer programs; depicting staging, set design, or plot actions in dramatic presentations; planning and organizing social or political events, e.g., dances, elections, activities; reorganizing written instructions into a series or sequence of steps for home or business projects

TIME INTERVALS OF A DAY—SELECT/SUPPLY

STRAND: Verbal Sequences   **PAGES:** 202–206

ADDITIONAL MATERIALS
Transparency of student workbook page 202

INTRODUCTION
In several previous lessons you arranged events according to time order.

OBJECTIVE
In these exercises you will apply commonly held definitions of time intervals to clarify parts of the day.

DEMONSTRATION/EXPLANATION
Project the definitions from the transparency of page 202. If necessary, go over the definitions with the class, encouraging them to use their own words and to be as specific as possible when defining the time intervals. You may wish to leave the transparency projected as students complete the exercises in this lesson. This will keep them from having to leaf through the book to refer to the definitions. It may also be helpful to use two circle diagrams to depict the a.m. and p.m. terms.

GUIDED PRACTICE
EXERCISES: **B-436, B-437, B-438, B-439, B-440**
ANSWERS:

B-436 b, c, f	**B-437** a, b, e	**B-438** b, d
B-439 b, c	**B-440** a, d	

INDEPENDENT PRACTICE
Assign exercises **B-441** through **B-453**.

DISCUSSION TIPS
Discussion of these terms may reveal some regional differences in interpretation. This is a good time to clarify how regional usage compares with standard usage. Latitudinal location and time of year will influence the hours of the day that your students consider dusk or dawn, sunrise or sunset. This presents a good opportunity to confirm students' understanding of the effect of latitude on the numbers of hours of daylight at various times of the year.

ANSWERS

NOTE: Given words within each exercise appear in italics throughout this section.

B-441   b, c   **B-442**   b   **B-443**   d

B-444   *6:00 a.m.*, <u>9:00 a.m.</u>, *12:00 noon, 3:00 p.m.,* <u>6:00 p.m.</u>, *9:00 p.m.* (three-hour intervals)

B-445   <u>9:20 p.m.</u>, *9:40 p.m., 10:00 p.m.,* <u>10:20 p.m.</u>, *10:40 p.m.* (twenty-minute intervals)

B-446   *12:00 noon, 9:00 p.m.,* <u>6:00 a.m.</u>, <u>3:00 p.m.</u>, *12:00 midnight* (nine-hour intervals)

B-447   <u>2:30 p.m.</u>, <u>3:15 p.m.</u>, <u>4:00 p.m.</u>, *4:45 p.m., 5:30 p.m.* (forty-five minute intervals)

B-448   *1:00 a.m., 7:00 p.m.,* <u>1:00 p.m.</u>, *7:00 a.m.,* <u>1:00 a.m.</u> (eighteen-hour intervals)

B-449   The time between high and low tide is about six hours.

B-450   The time between one high tide and the next high tide is about thirteen hours.

B-451   High tide should be about one hour later tomorrow than it was today.

B-452   a.   *a.m.* — (ante meridiem) Between 12:00 midnight and 12:00 noon.

   b.   *night* — Technically, between sunset and midnight, but more commonly considered as the dark hours between sunset and sunrise.

   c.   *dawn or daybreak* — Between the first appearance of light and sunrise (actual time varies according to latitude and time of year).

   d.   *midafternoon* — About 3:00 p.m.; i.e., the middle of the afternoon period.

   e.   *dusk or twilight* — Sometimes defined as one hour before dark, but commonly defined as the period between sunset and darkness (actual time varies with latitude and time of year).

   f.   *p.m.* — (post meridiem) Between 12:00 noon and 12:00 midnight.

   g.   *forenoon* — Between sunrise and 12:00 noon.

   h.   *daylight* — Between dawn and dusk (actual time varies with latitude and time of year).

   i.   *midmorning* — About 9:00 a.m., i.e., the middle of the morning period.

   j.   *evening* — Usually between sunset (or the last meal of the day) and bedtime, i.e., late day and early night.

   k.   *midday* — Usually between 11:00 a.m. and 1:00 p.m ; i.e., the middle of the day.

B-453   a.   *2:45 p.m.* — midafternoon

   b.   *noon to midnight* — p.m.

   c.   *sunrise to noon* — morning or forenoon

   d.   *12:00 a.m.* — midnight

   e.   *7:00 p.m.* — evening; possible dusk or twilight

   f.   *10:10 a.m.* — midmorning

   g.   *midnight to noon* — a.m.

   h.   *sunset to sunrise* — night

   i.   *daylight to dusk* — day or daytime

   j.   *sunset to darkness* — dusk or twilight

   k.   *dawn to noon* — morning or forenoon

FOLLOW-UP REFERENT

When might you need to clarify or generalize the time intervals of a day?
Examples: following directions for medication, treatment, or health maintenance; establishing schedules; giving directions for the care and feeding of pets or domestic animals; following time regulations or restrictions when fishing or hunting; using tide tables to predict high or low tides; obeying parking regulations; keeping appointments; following travel time tables; creating, using, or interpreting time lines

CURRICULUM APPLICATION

Language Arts: clarifying and comprehending time frames within a plot; accurately reflecting chronology in compositions, speeches, or class discussions of literature

Mathematics: recognizing and understanding time intervals in word problems

Science: relating time passage to the earth's rotation on its axis (one day) and to its revolution around the sun (one year); clarifying terms involving the appearance of stars or planets

Social Studies: clarifying the effect of time of year on the length of days and of latitude on the number of daylight hours

Enrichment Areas: understanding changes in music theory or dance choreography; understanding game divisions in sports, e.g., periods, quarters, halves, innings

LONG-TERM INTERVALS—SUPPLY

STRAND: Verbal Sequences   **PAGES:** 207–213

ADDITIONAL MATERIALS
Transparency of student workbook page 207

INTRODUCTION
In the previous lesson you interpreted and applied terms to common time intervals in a day.

OBJECTIVE
In these exercises you will interpret and apply common terms regarding time intervals in a year or longer.

DEMONSTRATION / EXPLANATION
Project the transparency of page 207, and review the interval definitions with the class. Since these terms may not be so familiar to the students, encourage them to use their own words and to be as specific as possible when defining the time intervals. You may wish to leave the transparency projected as students complete the exercises in this lesson. This will keep them from having to leaf through the book to refer to the definitions.

GUIDED PRACTICE
EXERCISES: **B-454**
ANSWERS:

B-454 a.   *biannually* — Occurring twice a year, not necessarily at equal intervals. "The board of directors for our club meets *biannually*."

    b.   *biennially* — Occurring every two years.
"In some states you must renew your driver's license *biennially.*"

    c.   *bimonthly* — Occurring every two months.
"We get a *bimonthly* bill for the water we use."

    d.   *biweekly* — Occurring every two weeks.
"The student council has scheduled *biweekly* meetings for the remainder of the school year."

    e.   *centennial* — A 100-year anniversary.
"The United States celebrated its *centennial* in 1876.

    f.   *century* — A period of 100 years.
"The eighteenth *century* includes the years 1701 through 1800."

    g.   *decade* — A period of 10 years.
"The 1960's were a *decade* characterized by student rebellion in many parts of the country."

    h.   *era* — An unspecified number of years having historical significance and bound together by some common bond, e.g., a war (the Vietnam Era), a single national ruler (the Kennedy Era, the Victorian Era), a specific geological time (the Paleozoic Era).
"William Shakespeare and Walter Raleigh lived during the Elizabethan *Era.*"

    i.   *millennium* — A period of 1,000 years.
"It may take me a *millennium* to finish this book!"

INDEPENDENT PRACTICE
Assign exercises **B-455** through **B-468**.

DISCUSSION TIPS
Emphasize the difference between the two prefixes *bi-* and *semi-*. Also note the difference between *biannual* and *biennial*. Slight regional or colloquial differences may occur in interpretations of these terms.

As an extending activity, you may wish to start a list of events commonly associated with each of these time intervals. For example, under *annually* you might list such things as annual sports events (the World Series, the Super Bowl), political events (the State of the Union Address), school events (homecoming parade, honor society inductions), and natural events (the first frost). As students become aware of more applications for each term, have them added to the list.

ANSWERS
B-455 a.   *month* — One-twelfth of a year; about 4 1/3 weeks; about 30 days.
"One *month* from today school will be out for the summer."

    b.   *monthly* — Occurring once a month.
"Since Iona only works a few hours each week, she gets paid *monthly.*"

    c.   *perennial* — Occurring year after year.
"He is a *perennial* candidate for city council."

    d.   *score* — A period of 20 years.
"One of the most famous documents of American history begins with the words, 'Four *score* and seven years ago,...'."

e.   *season* — A period of 3 months; 1/4 of a year.
"Although yesterday was the official end of the summer *season*, the temperature seems hotter than ever."

f.   *semiannually* — Occurring twice a year at equal intervals, usually every six months.
"According to the advertisement, this store places its entire stock of merchandise on sale *semiannually*."

g.   *semimonthly* — Occurring twice a month, usually at equal intervals.
"The Jones' have started making their mortgage payments on a *semimonthly* basis, which should save them over $20,000 in interest payments over the life of the loan."

h.   *semiweekly* — Occurring twice a week.
"Mrs. Kirch has gone to the bank to make the *semiweekly* deposit."

i.   *week* — A period of 7 days; 1/52 of a year.
"I have three reports due this *week*."

B-456   [earliest (1) to latest (12)]

a.	7	midday	**g.**	3	4:19 a.m.
b.	8	1:30 p.m.	**h.**	12	11:34 p.m.
c.	2	2:15 a.m.	**i.**	4	dawn
d.	1	12:02 a.m.	**j.**	6	midmorning
e.	11	dusk	**k.**	5	sunrise
f.	10	midafternoon	**l.**	9	2:15 p.m.

B-457   [shortest (1) to longest (14)]

a.	3	hour	**h.**	6	day
b.	10	year	**i.**	9	season
c.	7	week	**j.**	2	minute
d.	1	second	**k.**	5	daylight
e.	4	morning	**l.**	8	month
f.	11	decade	**m.**	13	century
g.	14	millennium	**n.**	12	score

B-458   [least often (1) to most often (10)]

a.	10	hourly	**f.**	1	biennially
b.	8	semiweekly	**g.**	2	annually
c.	6	monthly	**h.**	9	daily
d.	4	quarterly	**i.**	7	semimonthly
e.	5	bimonthly	**j.**	3	semiannually

B-459	annually	**B-460**	hourly
B-461	monthly	**B-462**	quarterly
B-463	weekly	**B-464**	semiweekly
B-465	biweekly; semimonthly	**B-466**	daily

B-467a.   vernal equinox (March 21) and autumnal equinox (September 21)

b.   fall; autumn   **c.**   spring

d.   winter   **e.**   summer

B-468 (Times given as answers here are based on averages for the continental United States and, as such, are only approximate. Local newspapers or weather reports will provide more exact times for specific areas.)

a. 5:00 – 6:00 p.m.

b. 4:30 a.m. (5:30 a.m. daylight savings time)

c. 7:00 – 8:00 p.m.

d. 7:00 p.m.– 5:00 a.m.

e. 9:00 p.m. – 5:00 a.m.

FOLLOW-UP REFERENT
When might you need to recognize, identify, or rank the meaning of words concerning time intervals of longer than a day?
Examples: recognizing and budgeting for regularly scheduled bills, e.g., quarterly insurance premiums, income and property taxes; predicting and planning for regularly scheduled events, e.g., family celebrations, sports events, hunting or fishing seasons; keeping track of regularly scheduled appointments, e.g., semiannual medical or dental exams, monthly club or organization meetings; semester breaks; annual vacations

CURRICULUM APPLICATION
Language Arts: comprehending time structure in a literary work; using accurate terminology when discussing or writing about time intervals
Mathematics: recognizing and understanding time intervals in word problems
Science: understanding and explaining the relationship between movement in our solar system and time elements; clarifying terms involving seasonal appearance of stars or planets; recognizing and interpreting time intervals in geological periods
Social Studies: recognizing and interpreting time intervals in history, geography, economics, and the social sciences
Enrichment Areas: recognizing seasons for plant care and availability of produce; relating sports seasons and events to the calendar

TIME ZONES

STRAND: Verbal Sequences

PAGES: 214–217

ADDITIONAL MATERIALS
Transparency of student workbook page 214

INTRODUCTION
In a previous lesson you identified and classified terms that concerned the various intervals of the day.

OBJECTIVE
Daily time designations become more complicated as we realize that cities around the world do not have the same time as we do. For example, when it's 3:00 a.m. in New York City, it's 9:00 a.m. in Rome, Italy. These exercises involve recognizing the time differences among zones in the United States.

DEMONSTRATION / EXPLANATION

Project the map depicting the time zones across the continental United States from the transparency of page 214.

> *The continental United States is divided into four standard time zones, as shown here and on page 214 in your workbooks. Each time zone to the west...*

Indicate the Central, Mountain, and Pacific time zones in turn.

> *...is one hour earlier than its neighbor to the east. If it is 4:00 p.m. in Maine, it it 1:00 p.m. in California. If you are going from west to east, the reverse will be true; each time zone will be one hour later than its neighbor to the west. For example, let's say it is midnight in San Francisco. What time is it in Raleigh, North Carolina?*

Answer: 3:00 a.m.

> *What time is it in Columbus, Ohio?*

Answer: 2:00 a.m.

> *In Denver, Colorado?*

Answer: 1:00 a.m. Repeat this type of oral exercise until students seem comfortable with the concept of changing time zones.

> *Refer to this diagram as you complete the exercises in this lesson. They all concern the differences in time between American cities.*

GUIDED PRACTICE

EXERCISES: **B-469**, **B-470**, **B-471**, **B-472**
ANSWERS:

B-469	2:05 p.m. PST	**B-470**	8:05 p.m. EST
B-471	11:45 a.m. MST	**B-472**	1:45 p.m. CST

INDEPENDENT PRACTICE

Assign exercises **B-473** through **B-483**.

DISCUSSION TIPS

Encourage students to identify the general band of states within their own time zone and to relate how many hours earlier or later it will be in other time zones. Use time reports in televised news items to confirm time differences. Discuss, for example, why sports events telecast live during daylight hours may reach the viewer during darkness.

As an extending exercise, have the students work with world time zones and the international date line. This type of exercise may be as extensive as you wish, with maps, references, art, and mathematics all being utilized curricular areas.

ANSWERS

B-473	10:20 a.m. EST	**B-474**	8:20 a.m. CST	**B-475**	11:15 p.m. PST
B-476	11:25 a.m. MST	**B-477**	3:25 p.m. EST		

B-478   11:00 a.m. EST (although Gina may wish to stay on the good side of Grandma and call a little later!)

B-479   4 hours and 15 minutes air time
SOLUTION: Convert both times to PST (4:30 p.m. EST = 1:30 p.m. PST)
Depart CA 9:15 a.m. PST
Arrive GA 1:30 p.m. PST
Convert to military time (24-hour clock) and subtract earlier time from later time:

$$1:30 \text{ p.m.} = 13:30 \text{ military time}$$
$$9:15 \text{ a.m.} = \underline{09:15 \text{ military time}}$$

$$4:15 = 4 \text{ hours and 15 minutes flying time}$$

ALTERNATE: Convert both times to EST and follow the same steps.

B-480　Her mother will be in Houston from 1:43 to 2:50 p.m. EST, although Kimberly will probably want to avoid the first and last 15 minutes of the time period to allow deplaning and boarding time for her mother. The best time for Kimberly to actually reach her mother would probably be between 2:00 and 2:20 p.m., EST.

B-481　Mr. Horowitz spent 5 hours and 50 minutes in the air. (Find the solution by using either method suggested in **B-479**.)

B-482　He would be able to place calls from 3:00–11:00 p.m., EST.

B-483　They would be able to place calls from 3:00–11:00 a.m., HST.

FOLLOW-UP REFERENT

When might you need to clarify or determine time difference across the country?

Examples: respecting the convenience or habits of friends or relatives in another part of the country whom you wish to call; awareness of time differences when making business calls to another part of the country; planning airline flights; understanding and preventing jet lag; predicting time of arrival for trips that cross time zones

CURRICULUM APPLICATION

Language Arts: ——————————

Mathematics: understanding and interpreting time differences as an element in mathematics word problems

Science: clarification of time differences involved in astrological observations

Social Studies: recognizing the effect of longitude on global time designations; interpreting and correlating news happening in other parts of the world; understanding the effect of the international date line

Enrichment Areas: ——————————

SCHEDULES

STRAND: Verbal Sequences　　　　　　　　　　　　　**PAGES:** 218–224

ADDITIONAL MATERIALS
Transparency of student workbook page 218

INTRODUCTION
In previous lessons you arranged events into time order, used flowcharts to show a sequence of events, and interpreted differences in time.

OBJECTIVE
In these exercises you will combine these skills to create time schedules.

DEMONSTRATION/EXPLANATION

Project the problem description from the top of the transparency of page 218.

> *You are to use the information given in this paragraph to depict a schedule of Marta's meetings during a day. You will record the name of each person Marta met next to the time of each appointment. Let's follow the events and record each as we go along. The first time mentioned in the paragraph is 11:00 a.m. "Before going to her 11:00 a.m. dance class with Helen" tells us that she met Helen at 11:00.*

On the line next to 11:00, write "HELEN (dance class)."

> *The next clause gives us the names of two more people that Marta met. Who were they, and when did she meet them?*

Answer: She met Jenna, then Sandy, and she met both of them before 11:00 a.m.

> *What other information do you have about these meetings?*

Answer: Each of these two meetings lasted one hour.

> *If she met Jenna first, then Sandy; and if each meeting was for one hour, at what times did these meetings occur?*

Answers: She met with Jenna at 9:00 and Sandy at 10:00. Write "JENNA" on the 9:00 line and "SANDY" beside 10:00.

> *"Following a lunch date with Carol" tells us that she probably met Carol at 12:00 noon.*

Write "CAROL (lunch)" beside 12:00.

> *Following lunch, she went to the mall with Shawn.*

Write "SHAWN (mall)" beside 1:00.

> *"After an hour with Shawn she worked on her research paper at the library with Catherine. This tells us that she met Catherine at 2:00 at the library.*

Write "CATHERINE (library)" beside 2:00.

> *Finally we learn that Catherine's brother Fred gave Marta a ride home after the library. Since the only time remaining on the schedule outline is 3:00, you can infer that she rode home at that time.*

Write "FRED (ride)" at 3:00.

GUIDED PRACTICE

EXERCISE: **B-485**

Give students sufficient time to complete these exercises. Then, using the demonstration methodology above, have them discuss and explain their choices.

ANSWERS:

B-485 1) 3:30 – 4:00 Pick up brother from day-care center
2) 4:00 – 5:00 Do homework
3) 5:00 – 6:00 Prepare supper
4) 6:00 – 6:30 Eat supper
5)* 6:30 – 7:00 Clean bedroom
6) 7:00 – 7:30 Help brother get ready for bed
7)* 7:30 – 8:00 Put away clothes
* Steps 5 and 7 are interchangeable.

INDEPENDENT PRACTICE

Assign exercises **B-486** through **B-490**.

DISCUSSION TIPS

Encourage students to discuss differences between their schedules and those of other members of the class. There is usually more than one way to arrange a schedule, but some things may be better placed at one time than at another. Have students defend their placements. When they have become accustomed to arranging hypothetical schedules, ask them to use the diagrams offered in this chapter to illustrate school or family schedules, to record television watching, or to plan extracurricular project schedules.

ANSWERS
B-486

Gordon's jobs*	Two-person jobs	Tad's jobs*
carry in paint (10 min)	——————————	sweep garage (30 min)
carry in tools (20 min)	——————————	——————————
——————————	move lathe (20 min)**	——————————
——————————	move drill press (10 min)**	——————————
——————————	move workbench (20 min)**	fill workbench with tools (40 min)
carry in lumber (20 min)**	——————————	
paint cans onto shelf (20 min)**	——————————	

*   Jobs are not restricted to any particular mover. These columns are interchangeable, as long as the times are equal.

**   These jobs are interchangeable. They need not be performed in this order.

B-487

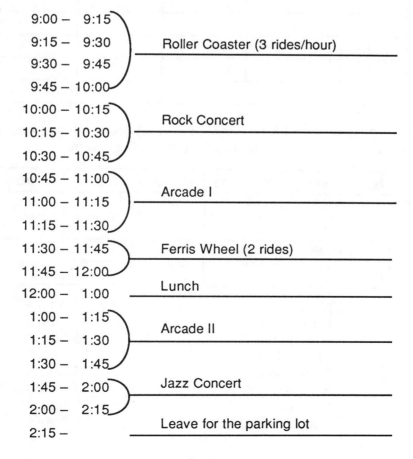

9:00 – 9:15	
9:15 – 9:30	Roller Coaster (3 rides/hour)
9:30 – 9:45	
9:45 – 10:00	
10:00 – 10:15	
10:15 – 10:30	Rock Concert
10:30 – 10:45	
10:45 – 11:00	
11:00 – 11:15	Arcade I
11:15 – 11:30	
11:30 – 11:45	Ferris Wheel (2 rides)
11:45 – 12:00	
12:00 – 1:00	Lunch
1:00 – 1:15	
1:15 – 1:30	Arcade II
1:30 – 1:45	
1:45 – 2:00	Jazz Concert
2:00 – 2:15	
2:15 –	Leave for the parking lot

B-488 This is one of several possible schedules.

	Monday	Tuesday	Wednesday	Thursday	Friday
8–9	◄——————————————— LANGUAGE ARTS ———————————————►				
9–10	◄——————————————— MATH ———————————————►				
10–11	GYM	SCIENCE ▲▼	GYM	SCIENCE ▲▼	GYM
11–12	ART		ART		TYPING
12–1	◄——————————————— LUNCH ———————————————►				
1–2	COMPUTER	MUSIC	COMPUTER	MUSIC	COMPUTER
2–3	◄——————————— SOCIAL STUDIES ———————————►				AV

B-489

TIME	FLUIDS	DECONG.	ASPRIN	ANTIBIOTIC	VAPORIZER
6:00 a.m.	√				√
8:00 a.m.	√	√*		√	
10:00 a.m.	√		√		√
12:00 noon	√			√	
2:00 p.m.	√		√		√
4:00 p.m.	√	√			
6:00 p.m.	√		√	√	√
8:00 p.m.	√				
10:00 p.m.	√		√		√
12:00 midnight	√	√			

B-490 Many schedules are possible with the given information. If all workers are given an equal number of hours, this is one way of scheduling them.

	Sunday	Monday	Tuesday	Wednesday	Thursday	Friday	Saturday
A M	Dino Cheryl Monroe	Anita Cheryl	Anita Pam	Josh Pam	Josh Pam	Leslie Monroe	Dino Leslie Pam
P M	Dino Cheryl Monroe	Anita Cheryl	Anita Kim	Josh Kim	Josh Kim	Leslie Monroe	Dino Leslie Kim

Anita	Mon, Tues	16 hours
Cheryl	Sun, Mon	16 hours
Dino	Sat, Sun	16 hours
Josh	Wed, Thur	16 hours
Kim	Tues, Wed, Thur, Sat	16 hours
Leslie	Fri, Sat	16 hours
Monroe	Fri, Sun	16 hours
Pam	Tues, Wed, Thur, Sat	16 hours

Suppose that Juan has two full-time workers (Anita and Cheryl), and the others are part-time? Then the schedule might look like this.

	Sunday	Monday	Tuesday	Wednesday	Thursday	Friday	Saturday
A M	Cheryl Leslie Monroe	Anita Cheryl	Anita Cheryl	Anita Cheryl	Anita Pam	Anita Pam	Cheryl Dino Josh
P M	Cheryl Leslie Monroe	Anita Cheryl	Anita Cheryl	Anita Cheryl	Anita Kim	Anita Kim	Cheryl Dino Josh

Anita	Mon–Fri	40 hours
Cheryl	Sun–Wed, Sat	40 hours
Dino	Sat	8 hours
Josh	Sat	8 hours
Kim	Thur, Fri	8 hours
Leslie	Sun	8 hours
Monroe	Sun	8 hours
Pam	Thur, Fri	8 hours

FOLLOW-UP REFERENT

When might you need to create a time schedule?

Examples: recording daily activities to evaluate one's time use; planning group work projects or excursions; summarizing medical instructions; eliminating family or group misunderstandings regarding chores and curfews; planning and recording class schedules; planning vacations, travel itineraries, or field trips

CURRICULUM APPLICATION

Language Arts: charting action sequences for complex story or novel plots; outlining action sequences for creative writing or journalism assignments

Mathematics: complex word problems involving time order or transitivity

Science: planning laboratory schedules; organizing laboratory experiments

Social Studies: developing time lines

Enrichment Areas: care and feeding schedules for plants or animals; organizing schedules for food preparation; scheduling equipment usage in shop, art, and home economics classes; creating practice schedules for teams or groups

SCHEDULES—TOURNAMENTS

STRAND: Verbal Sequences

PAGES: 225–228

ADDITIONAL MATERIALS

Transparency of student workbook page 225
Washable transparency marker

INTRODUCTION

In the previous lesson you created time schedules to illustrate how various blocks of time could be used for specific purposes.

OBJECTIVE

In these exercises you will complete a competition schedule. Such schedules are frequently used to depict the opponents and results of games in elimination tournaments.

DEMONSTRATION/EXPLANATION

Project the transparency of page 225.

You are given three clues to help you determine the results of an eight-team holiday basketball tournament. The bracket at the bottom will help you organize the results and determine the winner of each game.

Indicate clue 1.

The first clue tells you that Washington H.S. and Roberto Clemente H.S. won no games. From this, you can deduce that they were beaten by their opponents in the first round of play. Referring to the bracket, can you determine who beat them?

Answer: Yes, Washington H.S. lost to St. Mary's H.S., and Roberto Clemente H.S. lost to Martin L. King H.S.

How do you record the results of these games on the bracket?

Answer: Write the names of the winning teams on the lines extending from the bracket that shows each game of the first round. Write ST. MARY'S on the second line from the top and M. L. KING on the third line from the top.

The second clue tells you that only South H.S. won two games. Does this mean they won the tournament?

Answer: No; the team that won the tournament had to win a total of three games.

If South won two games, which two did they win?

Answer: They won their first and second round games, but lost the final game. Write SOUTH on the appropriate lines of the bracket.

Clue 3 says that Susan B. Anthony H.S. won the championship. What does that tell you about the games they played?

Answer: They won each game they played, and they played three games. Write S.B. ANTHONY on each remaining line on the bracket. The completed schedule should look like this.

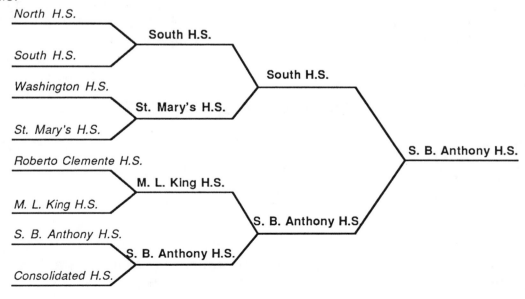

Now go back and check the diagram against the clues. Is each clue true of the schedule shown? Could any results be different, given this set of clues?
Allow time for students to confirm the answers and discuss the results. They should conclude that the results shown are the only ones possible using the given clues.

INDEPENDENT PRACTICE
Assign exercises **B-492** through **B-494**.

DISCUSSION TIPS
Students should always confirm their results by checking the completed diagram against the given clues. If differences arise among results, let the students present the reasoning that led to their answers. Encourage students to use branching diagrams to depict elimination processes. By rotating the diagram one position to the left, one can use it to illustrate such concepts as class-subclass divisions or growth from a single factor. Rotating the branching diagram one position to the right will result in a diagram that might be used to illustrate a family tree.

ANSWERS
B-492

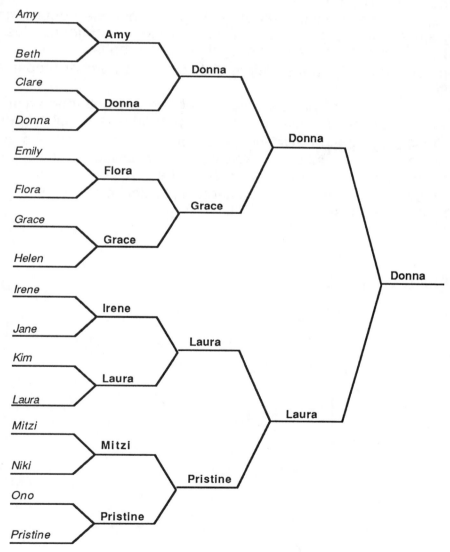

B-493 a. List the girls whose names belong in each of the following categories.

Won No Matches		Won 1 Match	Won 2 Matches	Won 3 Matches
Beth	Emily	Amy	Grace	Laura
Jane	Helen	Flora	Pristine	
Niki	Kim	Irene		
Clare	Ono	Mitzi		

    b. Donna was not listed.

    c. She was the only one to win more than 3 matches; she won 4, and the tournament.

B-494 Answers and clues will vary.

FOLLOW-UP REFERENT
When might you need to design or complete a branching diagram?
Examples: depicting stages in elimination tournaments; illustrating family trees; recording committee members, telephone "trees," or sales teams

CURRICULUM APPLICATION
Language Arts: depicting the development of the English language from its many sources; differentiating among literary genres and types of works within genre; classifying examples of figures of speech, parts of speech, or paragraphs

Mathematics: representing factor trees; differentiating among number properties and problem types

Science: differentiating among phyla, classes, and orders of plants and animals; classifying elements or compounds according to properties and subproperties

Social Studies: classifying types of dwellings, weapons, household articles, or tools belonging to various eras or cultures; depicting responsibilities of various governmental, social, political, or economic structures

Enrichment Areas: classifying music, art, architectural, or dance styles by era, culture, or type, or historical influences

VERBAL CLASSIFICATIONS

PARTS OF A WHOLE—SELECT

STRAND: Verbal Classifications

PAGES: 229–233

ADDITIONAL MATERIALS
Transparency of student workbook page 229
Jigsaw puzzle with 5–10 large pieces (optional)

INTRODUCTION

In the section on Similarities and Differences, you compared the meanings of words to determine how they were alike and how they were different. Sometimes these words were different parts of some item or system.

OBJECTIVE

In these exercises you will examine a group of words to determine which one names the whole and which words name parts of that whole.

DEMONSTRATION/EXPLANATION

(Optional Demonstration)
Place a piece of the jigsaw puzzle on a table or overhead projector so that the class can see the outline clearly.

This puzzle piece by itself has little meaning.

Place the other pieces near the original piece, also so the outlines can be seen.

Even several pieces of a puzzle have little meaning, taken individually.

Begin moving the pieces around and fitting them together.

When you begin to combine the pieces, however, a relationship gradually emerges. As you add more and more pieces, you gain a better idea of the total picture. The more pieces you have, the more easily you recognize how a single piece relates to the whole. We call this type of relationship "parts of a whole."

(Transparency Demonstration)
Project the EXAMPLE problem from the transparency of page 229, but keep the answers covered.

In this example, you are given the words CLOSING, GREETING, LETTER, and SIGNATURE. The task is to identify which of the given words names the whole and which words name parts of that whole. Begin by comparing pairs of words. Is a "closing" part of a "greeting"?

Answer: No, a closing is at the end and a greeting is at the beginning.

Is a closing part of a letter?

Answer: Yes, a closing would be at the end of a letter.

You have found one part-whole relationship. Which of these two words names a part, and which names the whole?

Answer: "Closing" names the part; "letter" names the whole.

Do the remaining words, "greeting" and "signature," also name parts of a letter?

Answer: Yes.

Then what is the whole?

Answer: The letter.

What are the parts?

Answer: The closing, greeting, and signature. Project the solution to confirm answers.

197

GUIDED PRACTICE

EXERCISES: **C-1, C-2, C-3, C-4**
Give students sufficient time to complete these exercises. Then, using the demonstration methodology above, have them discuss and explain their choices.
ANSWERS:

C-1	WHOLE: globe	PARTS: equator, latitude, longitude
C-2	WHOLE: face	PARTS: brow, cheek, chin
C-3	WHOLE: hammer	PARTS: claw, handle, head
C-4	WHOLE: expressway	PARTS: median, ramp, shoulder

INDEPENDENT PRACTICE

Assign exercises **C-5** through **C-30**.

DISCUSSION TIPS

Encourage students to discuss their answers and to distinguish each part according to its function, location, or material. In discussing a letter, for example, the greeting identifies the person to whom the letter is sent, the closing conveys personal regards, and the signature identifies the writer. By making these fine distinctions, students will gain vocabulary precision, a major objective of these exercises.

It is sometimes difficult for younger children to distinguish between parts of a whole and members of a class, for in each of these relationships a smaller item is compared to a larger item or a group. To reinforce part-whole and class-subclass concepts, identify these relationships as they occur in content lessons, use them to create bulletin board displays, and discuss their application to classroom objects.

ANSWERS

C-5	WHOLE: jacket	PARTS: hem, lapel, seam
C-6	WHOLE: pants	PARTS: cuff, inseam, waistband
C-7	WHOLE: fruit	PARTS: core, peel, pulp
C-8	WHOLE: shoe	PARTS: heel, shank, sole
C-9	WHOLE: bicycle	PARTS: chain, fork, frame
C-10	WHOLE: safety pin	PARTS: clasp, coil, shafts
C-11	WHOLE: pen	PARTS: barrel, cartridge, point
C-12	WHOLE: typewriter	PARTS: carriage, keyboard, ribbon
C-13	WHOLE: camera	PARTS: body, film, lens
C-14	WHOLE: book	PARTS: margin, spine, text
C-15	WHOLE: piano	PARTS: hammer, keys, strings
C-16	WHOLE: wheel	PARTS: hub, rim, spoke
C-17	WHOLE: sink	PARTS: bowl, drain, spigot
C-18	WHOLE: stove	PARTS: burner, broiler, oven
C-19	WHOLE: steak	PARTS: bone, fat, tissue
C-20	WHOLE: celery	PARTS: leaf, stalk, stem
C-21	WHOLE: sundae	PARTS: ice cream, sauce, topping
C-22	WHOLE: bottle	PARTS: lip, neck, shoulder
C-23	WHOLE: bed	PARTS: frame, mattress, spring

C-24	WHOLE: watch	PARTS: band, case, face
C-25	WHOLE: zipper	PARTS: tab, tape, teeth
C-26	WHOLE: eyeglasses	PARTS: frame, hinge, lens
C-27	WHOLE: umbrella	PARTS: panel, rib, shaft
C-28	WHOLE: blind	PARTS: pulley, slat, tape
C-29	WHOLE: shade	PARTS: hem, pull, roller
C-30	WHOLE: stapler	PARTS: base, cap, spring

FOLLOW-UP REFERENT

When might you need to distinguish between a whole and its parts?

Examples: assembling or disassembling models, appliances, or construction toys; examining, assembling, or repairing household objects; gathering ingredients for recipes and materials for construction; assembling small appliances or tools, especially when different parts are used for different purposes, e.g., food processors, mixers, electronic drills, ratchet wrenches

CURRICULUM APPLICATION

Language Arts: identifying parts of speech, parts of a book, parts of a letter; identifying the topic sentence and its supporting statements from a paragraph; utilizing heads and subheads in outlines; constructing elements of a poem or screenplay; writing specific definitions or descriptive paragraphs

Mathematics: identifying components of arithmetic problems, e.g., addends and sums in an addition problem

Science: identifying significant parts of living organisms; observing components of constellations, stars, planets, or solar systems

Social Studies: examining dwellings, artifacts, costumes, communities, and governments to identify component parts; using keys or legends to identify map components

Enrichment Areas: recognizing component parts of written music, e.g., the concepts of measures, phrases, notes; planning, preparing for, and creating the parts of a project, e.g., gathering necessary materials, planning and using such concepts as positive and negative space, focal point, and elements of composition; identifying pattern pieces for constructions or projects

CLASS AND MEMBERS—SELECT

STRAND: Verbal Classifications

PAGES: 234–236

ADDITIONAL MATERIALS

Transparency of student workbook page 234
Examples of several different types of fruit (optional)

INTRODUCTION

In the previous lesson you distinguished among words that identified a whole and those that named parts of a whole.

OBJECTIVE

In these exercises you will determine which of a given group of words names the class to which the other items or concepts belong.

DEMONSTRATION/EXPLANATION
(Optional Demonstration)
Place the fruit on a table so students can see the individual items.

>*Can you identify these items?*

Allow time for the students to identify each fruit represented.

>*What general name, sort of like a "generic name," can you think of that would include every item on the table?*

Write each answer on the chalkboard without judging it for correctness at this point. If students are too general ("food," for example), accept the answer, but ask them if they can be a little more specific and still include all the items. After several suggestions, ask the class to evaluate the suggested names and to determine which is the most specific, but still includes every item on the table.

>*What you just did with these pieces of fruit is very similar to the exercises you will be doing today. You named a general class, fruit, and several members of that class.*

(Transparency Demonstration)
Project the EXAMPLE problem from the transparency of page 234, keeping the answers covered.

>*Given the words CUPCAKE, DESSERT, PIE, and SUNDAE, you are to decide which word names the class to which the other items belong. As you did in the last lesson, begin by comparing pairs of words. Is a cupcake a type of dessert?*

Answer: Yes.

>*When you determine a possible class-subclass relationship, see if the other given words are also correct answers to the same question. For example, is pie a type of dessert?*

Answer: Yes.

>*Is a sundae a type of dessert?*

Answer: Yes.

>*When you have "yes" answers to all the questions, you have determined that the class "dessert" contains the members "cupcake," "pie," and "sundae."*

Project the answers for student confirmation.

>*The key difference between part-whole and class-subclass relationships are shown by the words "part of" and the words "type of" in the comparison questions. For example, is a sundae a part of a dessert or a type of dessert?*

Answer: A sundae is a type of dessert.

>*Since it is not a "part of," you know that the relationship is not part-whole, but rather class-subclass.*

GUIDED PRACTICE
EXERCISES: **C-31, C-32, C-33**
Give students sufficient time to complete these exercises. Then, using the demonstration methodology above, have them discuss and explain their choices.
ANSWERS:

C-31 CLASS: indicators   MEMBERS: gauges, meters, registers

C-32 CLASS: folds   MEMBERS: gathers, pleats, tucks

C-33 CLASS: appliances   MEMBERS: blenders, juicers, processors

INDEPENDENT PRACTICE
Assign exercises **C-34** through **C-49**.

DISCUSSION TIPS

Encourage students to discuss their answers and to distinguish among the members of each class according to their function, location, or material. Although the specific language may seem tedious, a basic objective of this lesson is to teach students to use precise words in describing common terms. This language precision fosters clarity of thinking and is a necessary tool for developing vocabulary and clear expression.

To reinforce this concept, use the process of naming characteristics and special qualities whenever you or your students need to define terms. Identify classroom objects by general classes (e.g., tools, texts, furniture, paper products, objects which can be magnetized, building materials) and by members. When writing definitions of nouns, students should identify the category (general class) and the characteristics that distinguish this particular member from others in that class using the format:

A _____ is a _____ that _____ .
    (noun)   (general class)   (specific characteristics)

For example: A mallard is a duck that is characterized by the male's green head and black neckband. Use the questioning technique demonstrated in this lesson to define words in other curriculum areas.

ANSWERS

C-34 CLASS: styles   MEMBERS: bangs, braids, flips
C-35 CLASS: agreements   MEMBERS: contracts, pacts, treaties

C-36 CLASS: hobby   MEMBERS: collection, craft, game
C-37 CLASS: culture   MEMBERS: custom, language, religion
C-38 CLASS: decomposer   MEMBERS: bacteria, mold, yeast
C-39 CLASS: debt   MEMBERS: i.o.u., lien, mortgage
C-40 CLASS: distance   MEMBERS: inch, foot, mile
C-41 CLASS: volume   MEMBERS: gallon, pint, quart
C-42 CLASS: luggage   MEMBERS: tote bag, handbag, suitcase

C-43 CLASS: monument   MEMBERS: statue, tomb, tower
C-44 CLASS: vessel   MEMBERS: barge, ferry, freighter
C-45 CLASS: symbol   MEMBERS: abbreviation, flag, trademark
C-46 CLASS: unit   MEMBERS: ounce, pound, ton
C-47 CLASS: business   MEMBERS: manufacturing, sales, service
C-48 CLASS: reference book   MEMBERS: almanac, atlas, directory
C-49 CLASS: employee   MEMBERS: agent, clerk, secretary

FOLLOW-UP REFERENT

When might you need to identify something by naming the class to which it belongs?

Examples: finding items in a supermarket, hardware store, mall directory, telephone book yellow pages, or classified ads; answering identification questions on essay tests; using the Dewey Decimal System to locate sources in a library; classifying lumber, farm implements, or tools according to function or use

CURRICULUM APPLICATION

Language Arts: using proper form when defining nouns, i.e., stating the general class and the characteristics that distinguish it within that class; using reference books to locate information on a topic, e.g., Reader's Guide, encyclopedias, atlases

Mathematics: using cue words to determine functions for solving word problems; using set theory and grouping techniques

Science: describing phyla; identifying natural objects in the same manner as nouns, i.e., name, general class, distinguishing characteristics

Social Studies: defining terms; identifying people, events, artifacts, groups, or eras

Enrichment Areas: classifying music according to type, e.g., classical, jazz, operatic; classifying paintings by given characteristics, e.g., the artist's techniques, type of medium used; classifying dances according to style, e.g., folk, modern, tap, jazz, ballroom, ballet; organizing displays for fairs, art galleries, museums, or arboretums

SENTENCES CONTAINING CLASSES AND SUBCLASSES—SELECT

STRAND: Verbal Classifications   **PAGES:** 237–238

ADDITIONAL MATERIALS
Transparency of student workbook page 237
Washable transparency marker

INTRODUCTION
In the previous lesson you identified the word which named the class to which a group of things belonged.

OBJECTIVE
In these exercises you will select words which name members of a common class, then arrange those words from the most general to the most specific.

DEMONSTRATION/EXPLANATION
Project the EXAMPLE sentence from the transparency of page 237, but keep the solution covered. Discuss each vocabulary item with the students to assure that everyone has a clear definition of each term.

Each exercise is a sentence containing three words that name members of a class. You are to identify the members of the class, then arrange them from the most general to the most specific class. In this sentence, which three words name the classes?

Answer: Orange, citrus, and fruit. (You may need to help students identify citrus as a kind of fruit.)

Which of these words names the most general class? Which class contains the other two classes?

Answer: Fruit. Both an orange and citrus are types of fruit.

Which of the remaining words, orange or citrus, is more specific? That is, which is an example of the other?

Answer: Orange. An orange is an example of a citrus fruit. Project the answers for confirmation.

The most general word, fruit, has been written on line one; the most specific word, orange, has been written on line three; and the remaining word, citrus, has been written on line two. To check that the answer is correct, ask yourself if answer three (3) is a member of (type of) class two (2) and if answer two (2) is a member of (type of) class one (1).

Answer: Yes, an orange is a type of citrus fruit, and yes, citrus is a type of fruit.

GUIDED PRACTICE
EXERCISES: **C-50, C-51, C-52**
Give students sufficient time to complete these exercises. Then, using the demonstration methodology above, have them discuss and explain their choices.
ANSWERS:

C-50   (1) warning; (2) signal; (3) flares

C-51   (1) weather; (2) precipitation; (3) hail

C-52   (1) grammar; (2) punctuation; (3) commas **OR**
(1) book; (2) chapter; (3) rules (lists of)

INDEPENDENT PRACTICE
Assign exercises **C-53** through **C-59**.

DISCUSSION TIPS
Encourage students to discuss their answers. When writing definitions of nouns, students should identify the category (general class) and the characteristics that distinguish it from others in that class using the format:

A _____ is a _____ that _____
  (noun)   (general class)   (specific characteristics)

To identify terms from the most general to the most specific, students should continue to follow the procedure of identifying the class and specific characteristics. This allows clear conceptualization of terms used in academic areas. Develop the habit of using this technique in defining words and in accepting student responses.

• A <u>duck</u> is a <u>water bird</u> that <u>has webbed feet and a flattened beak</u>.

• A <u>mallard</u> is a <u>duck</u> that <u>is characterized by the male's green head and black neckband</u>. The concept mallard has been developed from the general concept bird with sufficient distinction that the learner can follow the differentiation

bird → duck → mallard

By using this classification and definition technique, the learner will realize that the mallard is a species of the duck family and belongs to the bird class. It does not belong in a separate category (family) of bird.

ANSWERS

C-53   (1) wildcat; (2) panther; (3) Florida (panther) **OR**
(1) endangered species; (2) wildcat; (3) Florida panther

C-54   (1) mathematics; (2) algebra; (3) (quadratic) equations

C-55   (1) marketing; (2) advertising; (3) commercials

C-56   (1) investment; (2) stock; (3) shares

C-57   (1) containers; (2) bottles; (3) flask

C-58   (1) pie; (2) custard; (3) quiche
C-59   (1) crafts; (2) textile design; (3) tie-dying

FOLLOW-UP REFERENT
When might you need to find information, then arrange it from most general to most specific?
Examples: finding items in a supermarket, hardware store, mall directory, telephone book yellow pages, or classified ads; answering identification or definition questions on essay tests; using the Dewey Decimal System to locate sources in a library; locating related topics in books, reference sources, or card catalogs; differentiating among tools or utensils for specific jobs; organizing any complex procedure

CURRICULUM APPLICATION
Language Arts: using proper form when defining nouns, i.e., stating the general class and the characteristics that distinguish each member within that class; organizing and writing descriptive paragraphs; organizing topic or passage outlines
Mathematics: using cue words to determine functions for solving word problems; using set theory and grouping techniques; using number decomposition
Science: describing phyla; identifying natural objects in the same manner as nouns, e.g., name, general class, distinguishing characteristics
Social Studies: defining terms or identifying people, events, artifacts, groups, or eras; recognizing specific studies within general social science areas, e.g., geography includes the study of maps, physical features, climates, and natural resources
Enrichment Areas: classifying music according to type, e.g., classical, jazz, operatic; classifying paintings by given characteristics, e.g., the artist's techniques, type of medium used; classifying dances according to style, e.g., folk, modern, tap, jazz, ballet

GENERAL TO SPECIFIC—RANK

STRAND: Verbal Classifications   **PAGES:** 239–240

ADDITIONAL MATERIALS
Transparency of student workbook page 237
Washable transparency marker
Set of plastic nesting toys (optional)

INTRODUCTION
In the previous exercise you identified and arranged classes from the most general to the most specific, based on the context of a sentence.

OBJECTIVE
In these exercises you will rank given words from the most general to the most specific based on your knowledge of the terms.

DEMONSTRATION/EXPLANATION
(Optional Demonstration)
Hold up the assembled set of nesting toys (e.g., plastic nesting eggs or barrels) so the class can see the outside item clearly.

Remember when you were very young and used to play with toys like this?
Take the outside item off, displaying an inner, nested item. Keep removing sections as you talk until each item is visible.

Young children can spend hours taking these apart and putting them back together. They are amazed that for each layer they take away, another layer appears. The relationship you are going to determine in today's lesson is very similar to the concept shown by this nesting toy.
Hold up one half of the largest section, then fit the next size into it.

If you think of this large section as being a general class, you can think of the next size down as being a subclass.
Continue fitting the halves inside each other.

Each subclass contains a specific class, each specific class contains a more specific class, and so on.
Begin fitting the matching halves together and enclosing each interior item within the largest, layer by layer.

When this "class of items" is assembled, you see that each smaller item is entirely within the next larger one. General-to-specific relationships are like this, too. Members of each specific class are all included in the next larger class. How is this different from the part-whole and class-subclass relationships you studied a few lessons ago?
Answer: In part-whole, each piece fits into or on a single item, making it complete. The pieces were related only in that they were parts of the same whole; each of them contributed some aspect to a common item or concept. *NOTE: You may illustrate this relationship by fitting together two matching parts of one section of the nesting toy.* In class-subclass, there were many parallel subclasses. Each subclass was separate and distinct from each other subclass, not contained within. *NOTE: This relationship may be illustrated by separately assembling the sections of the nesting toy. If students have difficulty expressing the distinctions among these relationships, draw the following diagrams on the chalkboard, labeling each as indicated.*

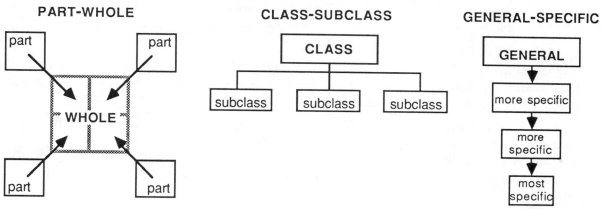

PART-WHOLE   CLASS-SUBCLASS   GENERAL-SPECIFIC

(Transparency Demonstration)
Project the EXAMPLE problem from the transparency of page 239, keeping the solution covered.

The given words in this example are <u>dog</u>, <u>canine</u>, and <u>terrier</u>. Which names the most general class; that is, which names a class that contains the other two?
Answer: Canine, which includes dogs and other dog-like animals, such as wolves, is the most general.

Which of the two remaining words, "dog" or "terrier," names the more general class?

Answer: A terrier is a type of dog. Therefore, dog is the more general class. Project the solution so students can confirm the answer.

Check your answers by asking class-subclass questions. In this case, you would ask, "Is terrier (specific class) a type of dog (subclass)? Is dog (subclass) a type of canine (general class)?" If the answer to each question is "Yes," then you have confirmed your answers.

GUIDED PRACTICE

EXERCISES: **C-60, C-61, C-62**

Give students sufficient time to complete these exercises. Then, using the demonstration methodology above, have them discuss and explain their choices.

ANSWERS:

C-60	footwear (general class)	shoe (subclass)	sneaker (specific class)
C-61	currency (general class)	coin (subclass)	peso (specific class)
C-62	seed (general class)	nut (subclass)	almond (specific class)

INDEPENDENT PRACTICE

Assign exercises **C-63** through **C-73**.

DISCUSSION TIPS

Encourage students to discuss their answers and to be specific in their definitions of terms. In discussing the canine → dog → terrier progression from the demonstration lesson, for example, a student might use the following statements.

- A <u>dog</u> is a type of <u>canine</u> that <u>is usually domesticated and kept as a pet</u>.

- A <u>terrier</u> is a type of <u>dog</u> that <u>is typically small, active, intelligent, and originally used to burrow after small game.</u>

By developing each class-subclass distinction in this manner, the learner reinforces the distinctions among the members of a class and recognizes that each succeeding specific class is a member of the preceding subclass, not a separate subclass.

Question students extensively regarding distinguishing characteristics. If they cannot think of specific descriptors, encourage them to find and use resource books to add to their definitions. This type of exercise also reinforces clear, concise sentence structure and extensive use of the logical connectives on pages 123–180 in the student workbook.

ANSWERS

C-63	fluid (general class)	beverage (subclass)	tea (specific class)
C-64	communication (general class)	media (subclass)	television (specific class)
C-65	transportation (general class)	automobile (subclass)	taxi (specific class)

C-66	groceries (general class)	produce (subclass)	vegetables (specific class)
C-67	rules (general class)	laws (subclass)	ordinances (specific class)
C-68	sound (general class)	music (subclass)	harmony (specific class)
C-69	storage (general class)	furniture (subclass)	cabinet (specific class)
C-70	hobbies (general class)	games (subclass)	cards (specific class)
C-71	chemical (general class)	cleaner (subclass)	detergent (specific class)
C-72	Asian (general class)	Oriental (subclass)	Korean (specific class)
C-73	polygon (general class)	quadrilateral (subclass)	parallelogram (specific class)
	rectangle (more specific class)	square (most specific class)	

FOLLOW-UP REFERENT

When might you need to arrange terms or categories from most general to most specific?

Examples: organizing files and filing information in an office or on a computer disk; answering identification or definition questions on essay tests; using the Dewey Decimal System to classify and locate sources in a library; recognizing related topics in books, reference sources, or card catalogs; organizing tools or utensils for specific projects; creating or using a subject index

CURRICULUM APPLICATION

Language Arts: defining nouns, i.e., stating the noun, the class to which the noun belongs, and the characteristics that distinguish it within that class; organizing and writing descriptive paragraphs; organizing information for outlines or diagrams; narrowing a composition or speech topic to suit the audience or the assignment

Mathematics: using cue words to determine functions for solving word problems; using set theory; verbally distinguishing among similar geometric shapes

Science: recognizing and using classification techniques common in biology, zoology, and botany; identifying natural objects in the same manner as nouns, e.g., name → general class → distinguishing characteristics; identifying machine types in physics; identifying and categorizing compounds and mixtures according to their elements

Social Studies: defining social studies terms or identifying people, events, artifacts, groups, or eras; recognizing specific examples of general social science categories, e.g., social science → geography → maps → physical features

Enrichment Areas: classifying music, art, or dance using general → specific relationships, e.g., music → classical → instrumental → piano → concerto → "Concerto in C# Minor;" organizing or writing descriptions of displays, e.g., art exhibits, collections, conventions

DISTINGUISHING RELATIONSHIPS

STRAND: Verbal Classifications   **PAGES:** 241–244

ADDITIONAL MATERIALS
Transparency of student workbook page 241

INTRODUCTION
In previous exercises you identified groups of words or sentences that expressed part-whole relationships and class-subclass relationships. You also arranged given words from the most general class to the most specific class.

OBJECTIVE
In these exercises you will identify which of those relationships—part-whole, class-subclass, or general-specific—describes the relationship among a given group of words.

DEMONSTRATION/EXPLANATION
Project the top section from the transparency of page 241.

Each exercise contains a word group that is related in one of the following ways. You are to identify the relationship, then write each word and label it according to its identification.

Indicate the part-whole (**P/W**) example.

Remember the pieces of puzzle? They all fit together to make up a whole picture. The four words shown in this example have that same relationship. "Head," "trunk," and "foot" all name parts of an "animal." Notice that the relationship is indicated on the blank in front of the word group and that each word is marked according to its category within the relationship.

Indicate the class-subclass (**C/S**) example.

Remember the basket of fruit? Each fruit was different from the others in several ways, but they were all examples of the general class "fruit." These four words also have a class-subclass relationship. "Protist," "invertebrate," and "vertebrate" each name a separate and distinct type of "animal." They are not parts of an animal, nor can they be arranged so that each is a subclass of another. Again, notice that the relationship is indicated and that each word's category is marked.

Indicate the general-specific (**G/Sp**) example.

Remember the nesting toy? Each smaller piece was completely included in the next larger piece. These words show that type of relationship. A "dog" is a specific type of "mammal," "mammals" are specific types of "vertebrates," and "vertebrates" are specific types of the general class "animals." The relationship type is indicated, each word is labeled according to its category, and the arrows point from most general to most specific.

Project the EXAMPLE exercise from the bottom of the page, but keep the category labels covered.

What type of relationship has been indicated for this group of words?

Answer: They have a class-subclass relationship.

How can you determine which word names the class and which name the subclasses?

Answer: Compare pairs of words using the format "Is (___) a type of (___)?"
Is an ant a type of bee, a type of grasshopper, or a type of insect?
Answer: An ant is a type of insect.
Do the other words, bee and grasshopper, also name types of insects?
Allow time for discussion and decision, then project the category labels for confirmation of the answer.

GUIDED PRACTICE
EXERCISES: **C-74, C-75, C-76**
Give students sufficient time to complete these exercises. Then, using the demonstration methodology above, have them discuss and explain their choices.
ANSWERS:

C-74 C/S vertebrate (class) amphibian (subclass) fish (subclass) reptile (subclass)

C-75 G/Sp animal → (general class) invertebrate → (subclass 1) bivalve → (more specific subclass) clam (most specific subclass)

C-76 P/W insect (whole) antenna (part) thorax (part) wings (part)

INDEPENDENT PRACTICE
Assign exercises **C-77** through **C-95**.

DISCUSSION TIPS
Encourage students to discuss their answers. When writing proper definitions of nouns, students should identify the category (general class) and the characteristics that distinguish it from others in that class. Use this format:

A _____ is a _____ that _____ .
(noun) (general class) (specific characteristics)

For example:

• A duck is a water bird that has webbed feet and a flattened beak.
• A mallard is a duck that is characterized by the male's green head and black neckband.

This exercise compels the student to clarify animal phyla and communications concepts. Encourage students to depict these relationships graphically. Select a similar body of knowledge from science, mathematics, social studies, or English, and allow students to write a "classification teaser" for other students to answer. By assembling students' classification teasers you compile a review of content requiring more sensitive analysis skills than students are likely to use when learning the factual content.

ANSWERS

C-77 C/S reptile (class) lizard (subclass) snake (subclass) turtle (subclass)

C-78 P/W snake (whole) fang (part) rattle (part) scale (part)

C-79 C/S crustacean (class) crab (subclass) lobster (subclass) shrimp (subclass)

C-80 C/S invertebrate (class) crab (subclass) insect (subclass) spider (subclass)

209

C-81	G/Sp	animal → (general class)	vertebrate → (subclass 1)	reptile → (more specific subclass)	lizard (most specific subclass)
C-82	G/Sp	animal → (general class)	vertebrate → (subclass 1)	amphibian → (more specific subclass)	frog (most specific subclass)
C-83	P/W	fish (whole)	fin (part)	gill (part)	scale (part)
C-84	P/W	sentence (whole)	predicate (part)	punctuation (part)	subject (part)
C-85	C/S	communication (class)	discussion (subclass)	media (subclass)	writing (subclass)
C-86	G/Sp	communication → (general class)	speaking → (subclass 1)	discussion → (more specific subclass)	debate (most specific subclass)
C-87	C/S	humor (class)	irony (subclass)	pun (subclass)	satire (subclass)
C-88	P/W	poetry (whole)	images (part)	rhyme (part)	rhythm (part)
C-89	G/Sp	communication → (general class)	speech → (subclass 1)	language → (more specific subclass)	dialect (most specific subclass)
C-90	C/S	sentence (class)	exclamation (subclass)	question (subclass)	statement (subclass)
C-91	G/Sp	narrative → (general class)	fiction → (subclass 1)	novel → (more specific subclass)	mystery (most specific subclass)
C-92	C/S	lesson (class)	fable (subclass)	parable (subclass)	sermon (subclass)
C-93	P/W	letter (whole)	body (part)	heading (part)	signature (part)
C-94	C/S	fiction (class)	fantasy (subclass)	mystery (subclass)	romance (subclass)
C-95	C/S	autobiography (class)	diary (subclass)	letter (subclass)	journal (subclass)

FOLLOW-UP REFERENT

When might you need to identify the relationship among given items, then rank or arrange those items according to their classification?

Examples: determining where items might be located in a supermarket, hardware store, mall directory, telephone book yellow pages, or classified ads; answering identification or definition questions on essay tests; using the Dewey Decimal System to locate sources in a library; locating related topics in books, reference sources, or card catalogs; differentiating among tools or utensils for specific jobs; arranging and organizing collections, e.g., stamps, rocks, coins, insects; arranging and organizing household supplies, recipes, clothing, or food; organizing and using hierarchical filing systems, such as those on computers; selecting desired or necessary courses that fulfill graduation requirements; planning and organizing group and community events or activities; analyzing a branching diagram to determine the relationship shown

CURRICULUM APPLICATION

Language Arts: using proper form and relationships when defining nouns, i.e., stating the general class and the characteristics that distinguish it within that class; organizing and writing descriptive paragraphs; organizing topic or passage outlines; narrowing a composition or speech topic to suit the requirements and the audience; choosing words which express the desired mood in creative writing

Mathematics: using cue words to determine functions for solving word problems; using set theory; distinguishing verbally among similar geometric shapes

Science: determining and describing phyla; identifying natural objects in the same manner as nouns, e.g., name, general class, distinguishing characteristics

Social Studies: defining social studies terms or identifying people, events, artifacts, groups, or eras; recognizing specific examples of general social science categories, e.g., geography includes the study of maps, physical features, climates, and natural resources

Enrichment Areas: classifying music according to type, e.g., classical, jazz, operatic; classifying paintings by given characteristics, e.g., artist's techniques, type of medium used; classifying dances according to style, e.g., folk, modern, tap, jazz, ballet, ballroom; recognizing and describing subclasses within school or art or music; recognizing part-whole relationships in works of art, musical compositions, film, or stage productions

HOW ARE THESE WORDS ALIKE?—SELECT

STRAND: Verbal Classifications

PAGES: 245–252

ADDITIONAL MATERIALS

Transparency of student workbook page 245
Washable transparency marker

INTRODUCTION

In the previous lesson you identified the relationship shown by a group of words and arranged the words according to class and subclass.

OBJECTIVE

In these exercises you will look at similarities among three given words, then choose the term or phrase that best describes the class to which all three words belong.

DEMONSTRATION/EXPLANATION

Project exercise **C-96** from the transparency of page 245.

You are given the words CHECKED, PLAID, and STRIPED. From the column on the right, you are to choose the term or phrase which best describes the class to which all three words belong. Are CHECKED, PLAID, and STRIPED types of fabric?

Answer: No. (They are patterns found in fabric and other materials, but fabric is not made of them. Wool, cotton, and silk are examples of types of fabric.)

Are CHECKED, PLAID, and STRIPED types of lined patterns?

Answer: Yes, each is a pattern using lines as part of their design.

Are *CHECKED,* *PLAID,* *and* *STRIPED* ***types of thread?***
Answer: No. (Threads may be woven in such a way as to produce these lined patterns, but the threads themselves are not checked, plaid, or striped.)
Remember that you are looking for a word or phrase which can be used to describe a class to which each of the given words can belong.

GUIDED PRACTICE
EXERCISES: **C-97, C-98, C-99**
Give students sufficient time to complete these exercises. Then, using the demonstration methodology above, have them discuss and explain their choices.
ANSWERS:

C-97 b (mixing device) A whisk is neither an appliance nor a spoon.

C-98 a (lifting device) None of the three given words can be described as either a type of motor or a weighing device, although any of them might use a motor or be a part of a weighing device.

C-99 a (facial hair) A strand of hair may be part of a beard or mustache, but it cannot be used to name either; style may be used to specify the type of beard or mustache, but cannot be applied to whisker.

INDEPENDENT PRACTICE
Assign exercises **C-100** through **C-183**.

DISCUSSION TIPS
Encourage students to discuss their answers and to share their definitions. Be certain that all students understand and can define the terms clearly. Ask them to explain why the unchosen answers are less specific or incorrect.

ANSWERS
C-100 b (control device) A dial, selector, or switch may select a channel or a frequency.

C-101 b (consumer of goods or services) Advertisers and merchants are suppliers of goods or services.

C-102 c (stream flowing into a river) Both bank and current are parts of a branch, fork, or tributary.

C-103 c (turbulence or fast water motion in a river) Water changes direction when traveling through a cataract, rapid, or waterfall. Landforms cause these water motions.

C-104 c (wetland of a river) None of the given words can be classified as either a branch or a channel of a river.

C-105 c (part of a river) The bed refers to the bottom of a river and not to a river bank. None of the given words describes a river flow, although all may direct a river's flow.

C-106 c (landform cut by a river) Neither delta nor flood plain applies to any of the given words.

C-107 b (body of water partially surrounded by land) A gulf is another member of this class. Although these bodies of water may be spawning grounds for fish, that is not the best identification for their common class.

C-108 c (inward curve) None of the given words represent shapes containing angles or circles.

C-109 b (curved part of a building) Although arches, domes, and vaults contain curved lines, they are not members of either the class "curved lines" or "curved roads."

C-110 a (curved object) A radius is a straight line and, as such, has no relationship to the given words; a wave might be another member of the class.

C-111 b (curve) None of the given words are types of angles or circles.

C-112 a (irregular bend) A spiral winds around a fixed point and produces a regular pattern; a maze is an intricate network of winding paths or a puzzle produced by such a network. Crimps, dents, or wrinkles produce no regular pattern, have changing angles or curves, and possess no recognizable paths.

C-113 b (rounded shape) Neither alternative names a class to which the words belong.

C-114 lift (to encourage, comfort, or help someone should give them a "lift")

C-115	follow	C-116	like	C-117	first
C-118	soft	C-119	follow	C-120	first
C-121	soft	C-122	lift	C-123	first
C-124	soft	C-125	like		

C-126	complete	C-127	rare	C-128	common
C-129	complete	C-130	common	C-131	complete
C-132	rare	C-133	complete	C-134	common
C-135	common	C-136	complete	C-137	rare
C-138	common				

C-139	result	C-140	start	C-141	plan
C-142	start	C-143	result	C-144	plan
C-145	result	C-146	start	C-147	plan
C-148	plan	C-149	result	C-150	plan
C-151	start	C-152	plan	C-153	result
C-154	plan	C-155	start		

C-156	heavy	C-157	track	C-158	direct
C-159	open	C-160	track	C-161	open
C-162	heavy	C-163	track	C-164	direct
C-165	open	C-166	direct	C-167	open
C-168	heavy	C-169	direct		

C-170	control	C-171	relieve	C-172	strain
C-173	observe	C-174	control	C-175	relieve
C-176	strain	C-177	observe	C-178	strain
C-179	relieve	C-180	strain	C-181	observe
C-182	strain	C-183	observe		

FOLLOW-UP REFERENT

When might you need to identify a class name for several individual items?

Examples: asking the location of items in a supermarket, hardware store, or shopping mall; looking for information in a mall directory, telephone book yellow pages, classified ads, textbooks, reference books, or card catalogs; developing a hierarchical filing system, e.g., grouping files on a computer disk or in a filing cabinet

CURRICULUM APPLICATION

Language Arts: diagraming sentences according to functions of words; choosing proper reference books when researching reports; recognizing parts of speech or types of literature; using an index or table of contents to locate information in books

Mathematics: distinguishing among types of arithmetic problems; recognizing numerical or geometrical properties; grouping numbers according to place or face values

Science: naming and recognizing attributes of different phyla of plants or animals; naming and recognizing properties of various elements or compounds

Social Studies: classifying types of architectural structures, governmental divisions, or community institutions according to their functions or other attributes

Enrichment Areas: naming similar attributes among types of dance, art, or music; naming similarities in functions and attributes of different tools in art, shop, or home economics

HOW ARE THESE WORDS ALIKE?—EXPLAIN

STRAND: Verbal Classifications   **PAGES:** 253–256

ADDITIONAL MATERIALS
Transparency of student workbook page 253

INTRODUCTION
In the previous lesson you chose the word or phrase which best described the class to which three given words belonged.

OBJECTIVE
In these exercises you will look for the similarities among a set of given words and explain how the words are alike.

DEMONSTRATION/EXPLANATION
Project the EXAMPLE problem from the transparency of page 253, but keep the answer blank covered.

The given words for this example are NEWSPAPER, RADIO, and TELEVISION. You are to explain what these words have in common or how they are related. Before you can determine how things are alike, you must describe each of them. What is a newspaper?

Answer: A newspaper is a print medium for news and entertainment. If students have difficulty with this definition, ask them to name the different sections of a newspaper, then identify the function of each section, i.e., to persuade, to entertain, to inform.

What is radio?

Answer: Radio is an audio medium for news and entertainment.

What is television?

Answer: Television is a video medium for news and entertainment.

What do all three things have in common?

Answer: They all provide news and entertainment. Project the answers for confirmation.

GUIDED PRACTICE
EXERCISES: **C-184, C-185, C-185**
ANSWERS:
C-184 They all mean clearly seen or understood.
C-185 They all indicate walking without a goal or direction.
C-186 All are related to theater or film productions.

INDEPENDENT PRACTICE
Assign exercises **C-187** through **C-222**.

DISCUSSION TIPS
An effective classroom technique for these exercises is to break the class into small groups of three or four for problem solving, then reassemble the large group to compare and defend their answers. Encourage students to discuss their answers and to be specific in their definitions. Requiring them to look for and state subtle similarities will force examination of various relationships among the words in each group. Encourage alternate answers if students can defend their reasoning.

As an extending activity for vocabulary development, ask students to supply words that might be added to each group and to support their additions. You might also ask them to state the subtle differences in meanings among the words in each group.

ANSWERS
C-187 All are terms for large, usually expensive, homes.
C-188 The words describe retiring, quiet individuals.
C-189 All describe speed.
C-190 The words all indicate strength.

C-191 All are types of passenger vehicles made to run on snow or ice.
C-192 All name places where animals are protected and displayed.
C-193 All the words are associated with raising something to a higher elevation.
C-194 All name computer components.
C-195 All name commonly used substitutes for cash.
C-196 All express the idea that something will be true.
C-197 All name hot weather.
C-198 All are names for types of music.

C-199 All are terms commonly used to describe a being with high intelligence.
C-200 All concern looking into the future or predicting occurrences.
C-201 All are terms used to measure value or worth.
C-202 All are kinds of fruit. (**ALTERNATE:** shades of orange)
C-203 All are words used to describe great size.
C-204 All are used to carry or contain money.
C-205 All indicate that something is to be expected.
C-206 All the words name a means of making larger or more extensive.

C-207 bright red with pink or purple tones

C-208 dark brown

C-209 medium to dark gray

C-210 yellow

C-211 black

C-212 bright red

C-213 pink-orange

C-214 white

C-215 light gray

C-216 brown with orange tones

C-217 blue

C-218 white with yellow tones

C-219 deep red with brown tones

C-220 green

C-221 blue-green

C-222 soft black; black with gray tones

FOLLOW-UP REFERENT

When might you need to recognize what several items have in common and explain how they are related?

Examples: recognizing and explaining categories used for grouping, e.g., filing systems, libraries, department stores, grocery and hardware stores; recognizing connotation differences among synonyms; choosing exact words when expressing an idea or describing an item or concept; organizing and writing essay answers to questions that ask for comparisons between or among items or concepts

CURRICULUM APPLICATION

Language Arts: classifying words in a sentence according to function and/or part of speech; choosing and using correct terminology when discussing or writing about literature; recognizing the effects of prefixes and suffixes on root words; recognizing and explaining similarities within word or language families; organizing and writing comparative essays

Mathematics: grouping like terms in algebraic equations; recognizing and using correct terminology for parts of problems, e.g., dividend, divisor, quotient, remainder; recognizing classifications of geometric shapes and angles; classifying information for statistical analysis

Science: recognizing and explaining phenetic similarities among plants or animals; recognizing similarities or parallel developments in such areas as weather patterns, rock formations, molecular structures, or evolutionary changes

Social Studies: recognizing and stating parallels in historic, economic, sociologic, or governmental cycles; recognizing and explaining similarities in different political, economic, governmental, or social structures; recognizing and stating geographic similarities among different regions

Enrichment Areas: recognizing and explaining similarities among works of art or music; recognizing and stating similarities among or between films and dramatic productions; recognizing and using similarities in computer programs or applications; recognizing and/or explaining similarities in construction of clothing, furniture, or craft projects

EXPLAIN THE EXCEPTION

STRAND: Verbal Classifications

PAGES: 257–260

ADDITIONAL MATERIALS
Transparency of student workbook page 257

INTRODUCTION
In the previous lesson you explained how three given words could fit into the same class by stating how they were alike.

OBJECTIVE
In these exercises you will look at the similarities and differences among four given words, then explain how three of the words are alike and how the fourth word is different.

DEMONSTRATION / EXPLANATION
Project the EXAMPLE problem from the transparency of page 257, but keep the answer section covered.

In this example exercise you have the given words AREA, MEASUREMENT, PERIMETER, and VOLUME. Before you can see the similarities and differences among these words, you must understand what each of them means. How would you define AREA?

Answer: Area is the measure of a surface enclosed within a set of lines and measured in square units.

Define MEASUREMENT.

Answer: Determining the dimensions or capacity of an object or figure.

Define PERIMETER.

Answer: The sum of the length of all sides of a polygon; the distance around such a figure as measured in linear units.

Define VOLUME.

Answer: The amount of space occupied by a three-dimensional figure and measured in cubic units.

What is the general topic for these four words?

Answer: They all concern measuring or measurements.

Which three of the four words seem to fit most readily into a single class?

Answer: Area, perimeter, and volume are all methods of distinguishing the size of some figure; all concern measurement and are determined by mathematical processes.

Which of the four words is the exception to the class?

Answer: Measurement is the act of determining length, weight, area, volume, or time. It is a general class of which the other are subclasses and is the exception to the class "types of measurement."

GUIDED PRACTICE
EXERCISES: C-223, C-224, C-225

Give students sufficient time to complete these exercises. Then, using the demonstration methodology above, have them discuss and explain their choices.

ANSWERS:

C-223   *Quotient* refers to division and is the exception to the class of words concerning multiplication. A *product* is the answer obtained by *multiplying* two *factors*.

C-224   *Continent*, a large land mass, is the exception to the class of words related to weather. *Climate* describes long-term *temperature* and *weather* conditions.

C-225   *Character*, a description of mental and ethical traits, is the exception to the class of words describing physical traits. *Force*, *might*, and *strength* describe endurance and capacity for physical work.

C-226   *Value* refers to the monetary worth of something and is the exception to the class of words describing the arrangement of objects or qualities to reflect a continuity of progression. *Order*, *sequence*, and *ranking* refer to the act of organizing items or concepts in a hierarchical arrangement according to specified criteria.

INDEPENDENT PRACTICE
Assign exercises **C-227** through **C-241**.

DISCUSSION TIPS
Small group-large group class arrangements are well-suited to this type of activity. Ask students to discuss their answers, to be specific in their definitions, and to look for and state subtle differences among the members of a class. Encourage alternative answers, but require students to defend their reasoning. As an extending activity for vocabulary development, ask students to supply words that might be added to each class and to support their additions.

ANSWERS
C-227   *Turkey*, a bird frequently used for food and sometimes domesticated, is the exception to the class. *Buzzard*, *eagle*, and *hawk* are all members of the class birds of prey; they are not normally used for food. (general class: bird)

C-228   *Elevate* means to lift all of something to a higher place and is the exception. *Incline*, *slant*, and *tilt* all belong to the class of words meaning to place at an angle, with one end higher than the other. (general class: raise)

C-229   A *tunnel* is a roofed, man-made, underground passageway and is the exception to the class. *Canyon*, *ditch*, and *gully* all describe open, natural cracks or depressions in the earth. (general class: passageways lower than the surface)

C-230   *Pupil*, which is within the eye, is the exception to the class. *Brow*, *lashes*, and *lid* all name external parts of the eye. (general class: parts of the eye)

C-231   *Ocean*, a large mass of water, is the exception to the class. *Continent*, *island*, and *peninsula* all name types of land masses. (general class: geographic formations)

C-232   *Calculating*, which results in precise answers, is the exception to the class. *Averaging*, *estimating*, and *rounding* are processes which result in less than exact answers. (general class: mathematical processes)

C-233   A *frog* is an amphibian and is the exception to the class reptile, represented by *alligator*, *lizard*, and *turtle*. (general class: vertebrates)

C-234   *Population*, defined by the number of people in a region or area, is the exception to the class. *Depression*, *poverty*, and *unemployment* all describe economic conditions that may affect various segments of a population. (general class: socioeconomic terms)

C-235   *Liter*, a metric volume-measuring unit, is the exception to the class English units of measuring volume, represented by *gallon*, *pint*, and *quart*. (general class: units of measuring volume)

C-236 *Decide* is the final step in decision making; *inquire, question,* and *research* are all steps in the decision-making process. (general class: decision making)

C-237 *Egg* relates to animal reproduction and is the exception to the class of words related to plant reproduction, i.e., *pollen, seed,* and *spore.* (general class: reproduction)

C-238 *Parallel,* a geometric term describing lines or planes that never intersect, is the exception to the class. *Acute, obtuse,* and *right* are all geometric terms describing angles or triangles. (general class: geometric terms)

C-239 *Pastel,* meaning pale or light in color, is the exception to the class. *Intense, rich,* and *vivid* are all adjectives applied to deep or dark colors. (general class: adjectives applied to color intensity)

C-240 *Period,* a punctuation mark at the end of a sentence, is the exception. *Colon, comma,* and *dash* are all punctuation marks used within a sentence. (general class: punctuation marks)

C-241 A *bus,* which runs on roads, is the exception to the class. *Monorail, subway,* and *trains* all travel on tracks. (general class: mass transit vehicles)

FOLLOW-UP REFERENT

When might it be important to identify which member does not fit a group, then explain the similarities and differences among the members?

Examples: choosing exact words to express desired meanings; recognizing positive and negative connotations among similar words; explaining library organization, filing systems, or classifications in any area, e.g., items in stores, categories in newspaper classified ads; eliminating impossible answers from the group of multiple-choice options

CURRICULUM APPLICATION

Language Arts: recognizing and explaining variations of pronunciation among words with common letter combinations, e.g., thorough, through, bough, bought; recognizing, using, and explaining irregular verb conjugations and uncommon noun plurals; recognizing and explaining etymological differences among words that appear to be of similar derivation; recognizing and avoiding inconsistencies in original creative writing, e.g., character development, mood, plot, meter; recognizing and avoiding inconsistencies in expository writing, e.g., changes in tense or style, irrelevant or contradictory statements; making an outline as a prewriting exercise by choosing those subheads or points which support the main idea

Mathematics: identifying and continuing number of figure sequences; distinguishing among operations in arithmetic problems; distinguishing among similar polygons or among polygons with the same number of sides; grouping numbers according to place or face values

Science: identifying plants or animals that do not belong in a particular phyla; identifying differing properties of elements or compounds; classifying foods according to basic food groups or nutritional values; distinguishing among various rock formations, mineral compounds, or chemical compounds

Social Studies: eliminating architectural structures, artifacts, governmental divisions, or community institutions that do not fit a given class according to function or other attribute; identifying geographic similarities and distinctions among continents, countries, regions, or areas

Enrichment Areas: recognizing types of dance, art, or music that do not fit stated criteria; eliminating inappropriate tools for art, shop, or home economics projects

SORTING INTO CLASSES

STRAND: Verbal Classifications   **PAGES:** 261–267

ADDITIONAL MATERIALS
Transparency of student workbook page 261
Washable transparency marker

INTRODUCTION
In your daily life you often choose a group of items, then sort or classify them into two or more categories or classifications. For example, suppose it's time to buy some new clothes, and you want to give the clothes you have outgrown to your younger sister or brother. To do this, you go to your closet and divide your clothing into two groups: clothes that fit and clothes that are too small.

OBJECTIVE
In these exercises you will sort a group of words according to three or more given classes.

DEMONSTRATION / EXPLANATION
Project the transparency of page 261.

The Choice Box at the top of this chart contains twenty-four words. You are to place each word into one of the three given classes: words that name people, words that name places, and words that name things. The first word is <u>clinic</u>. What is a clinic?

Answer: A clinic is a place for outpatient medical treatment.

Into which of the three categories on the chart would you place clinic?

Answer: **PLACES**; write CLINIC in the **PLACES** column.

The next word is <u>consultation</u>. What is a consultation?

Answer: A consultation is the act of seeking professional help or advice.

Does consultation refer to a person, a place, or a thing?

Answer: Thing; write CONSULTATION in the **THINGS** column.

NOTE: Students may confuse consultation, which is an act, with consultant, who is the person giving the advice.

The third word is <u>contract</u>. What is a contract?

Answer: A contract is a legally binding, written agreement between two or more parties.

Is a contract a person, a place, or a thing?

Answer: Thing; write CONTRACT in the **THINGS** column.

NOTE: Students may suggest the verb form <u>contract</u>, meaning "to reduce in size." Although using this definition would still place the term in the THING column, you might point out that all words in the CHOICE BOX are in noun form. The noun form for "reduction in size" would be contraction.

The fourth word is contractor. What is a contractor?

Answer: A contractor is one who agrees to supply materials or services for a set price.

Into which class does contractor fit?

Answer: **PEOPLE**; write CONTRACTOR in the **PEOPLE** column.

GUIDED PRACTICE
EXERCISE: Remainder of **C-242**
Give students sufficient time to complete these exercises. Then, using the demonstration methodology above, have them discuss and explain their choices.
ANSWERS:
C-242

PEOPLE	PLACES	THINGS
contractor	clinic	consultation
curator	mountains	contract
engineer	museum	equipment
governor	planet	instrument
mechanic	theater	investment
passenger		lecture
reporter		license
secretary		software
teller		telescope
		textbook

INDEPENDENT PRACTICE
Assign exercises **C-243** through **C-248**.

DISCUSSION TIPS
These exercises are excellent for utilizing small-group decision making and large-group discussion techniques. Some words in each exercise may fit into more than a one given category, depending upon the definitions chosen. Require students to state their reasons for any classification alternates to those shown in the answers throughout this lesson. Encourage them to use each word only once and to choose the classifications carefully. Make sure students understand that they will be required to defend their choices.

Encourage students to use reference books and other appropriate source materials to aid in their definitions and to support their classification decisions throughout this lesson.

ANSWERS
C-243

COOKING	CUTTING	FLAVORING	MIXING
boil	chop	pickle	beat
broil	dice	season	blend
grill	grate	sweeten	combine
poach	grind		fold
roast	shred		whip
simmer	slice		
steam			

C-244

HERBIVORES	CARNIVORES	OMNIVORES
butterflies	coyotes	bears
cattle	foxes	chickens
deer	frogs	humans
grasshoppers	lions	
mice	seals	
rabbits	wolves	
squirrels		

C-245

CUTTING	HOLDING	MAKING HOLES	MEASURING	TURNING
axe	clamp	drill	gauge	lathe
cleaver	pliers	needle	yardstick	screwdriver
knife	tape	punch		wrench
saw	tweezer			
snips	vice			

C-246

PAST	PRESENT	FUTURE
bygone	contemporary	afterward
former	current	following
obsolete	existing	hereafter
once	instant	later
preceding	modern	proceeding
	nowadays	succeeding

C-247

COMPARISON	EXCEPTION	RESULT
better than	although	because
different from	but	due to
equally	however	for
hardly	in spite of	if ... then
in the same way	instead of	since
just as	not	therefore
larger than	only	thus
like		
same as		
similar to		

C-248

TIME	LOCATION/POSITION		ADDITION
after	above	lower	again
at the same	across	next	also
time	among	off	and
during	around	on	another
finally	away	out	as well as
later	before	over	besides
meanwhile	behind	second	extra
now	below	through	
once	beneath	toward	
soon	beside	under	
then	between	upon	
until	higher		
while	in front of		

FOLLOW-UP REFERENT

When might it be necessary or useful to sort a given list of items into predetermined classes?

Examples: sorting or organizing tools, utensils, toys, clothes, coupons, records, or books for storage and easy retrieval; organizing a shopping list; making lists for special projects or occasions, e.g., Hanukkah, Christmas, planning a party or school project; organizing or filing office records or letters; organizing or sorting items at work, e.g., for a department store or supermarket display or warehouse, reshelving items in a library, bookstore, or record shop

CURRICULUM APPLICATION

Language Arts: differentiating among literary genres and types of works within genre; classifying figures of speech, parts of speech, or paragraph types; recognizing sentence connectives which influence meaning; organizing and classifying articles and/or pictures for journalism projects, e.g., according to yearbook or newspaper sections, according to genre for creative writing publications

Mathematics: differentiating among number properties or problem types; grouping like terms in equations; organizing information for statistical analysis or probability studies

Science: classifying plants or animals according to phyla or other predetermined characteristics; classifying elements or compounds according to properties; mixing formulas; establishing experimental procedures; determining nutritional needs

Social Studies: classifying types of dwellings, weapons, household articles, or tools according to era or culture; classifying items from psychological profiles according to specific behaviors; classifying social, economic, political, or governmental actions, behaviors, or processes within a given society

Enrichment Areas: classifying music, art, architecture, or dance according to era, culture, or type; selecting appropriate tools for art, shop, or home economics projects; organizing sports teams by players and positions; selecting music, art, flowers, decorations, or fashions appropriate to the occasion

SUPPLY THE CLASSES

STRAND: Verbal Classifications   **PAGES:** 268–270

ADDITIONAL MATERIALS
Transparency of student workbook page 268
Washable transparency marker

INTRODUCTION
In the preceding lesson you sorted a given list of items into specified classes.

OBJECTIVE
In these exercises you are also provided a list of items, but you will determine your own classification criteria.

DEMONSTRATION / EXPLANATION
Project the transparency of page 268.
You are given a group of words to sort into classes. Before you can sort them, however, you must decide what significant characteristics you will use as general classes. What do all these items have in common?
Answer: They are all foods.
One way to classify foods is to categorize them according to how they grow. Almonds, for example, grow on trees.

Write GROW ON TREES as the heading for the first class at the bottom of the transparency, then write ALMONDS under it.

How do bananas grow?

Allow time for student opinions, since this is a more confusing question than it appears. If students think that bananas grow on trees, suggest that they check a reference book. (Answer: Bananas grow from stalks on low plants.) Write the answer in an appropriate column on the transparency.

Do beans grow on trees?

Answer: No, most beans grow on bushes, although some (pole beans, for example) grow on climbing vines. Allow the class to determine by discussion what class they will use for beans, then write the heading and the word on the transparency. Be sure that students who express a preference state the reasoning behind their choice.

Do beets grow on trees? On bushes (vines)?

Answer: No, beets grow underground like a bulb. Write GROW UNDERGROUND as a class designation, then write BEETS in the new class.

What about the next food, broccoli? How does it grow?

Answer: Broccoli grows on stalks from a plant. Allow adequate time for students to discuss the classification and to determine whether they want to establish another class (GROW ON STALKS) or use an existing class. Continue classifying items in this manner until all words on the list are sorted.

Possible Solution:

GROW ON TREES	GROW ON VINES	GROW UNDERGROUND	GROW ON STALKS
almonds	beans	beets	bananas
lemons	cantaloupe	carrots	broccoli
oranges	cucumbers	radishes	cabbage
peaches	peas	yams	cauliflower
pears	pumpkins		corn
pecans	strawberries		lettuce
walnuts			rhubarb
			spinach

GUIDED PRACTICE

EXERCISE: **C-249**

Divide the class into small groups, then ask each group to do **C-249** again using different criteria, e.g., type of food (fruits, vegetables, nuts), edible part (seed, root, pod, stalk, leaf), color (brown, green, yellow, red). When all groups have completed the exercise, bring the larger group together. Ask each small group to present, explain, and defend its answer.

POSSIBLE ANSWER:

C-249

[Classified by food group (not plant class)]

FRUITS	NUTS	VEGETABLES	
bananas	almonds	beans	cucumbers
cantaloupe	pecans	beets	lettuce
lemons	walnuts	broccoli	peas
oranges		cabbage	pumpkins
peaches		carrots	radishes
pears		cauliflower	spinach
rhubarb		corn	yams
strawberries			

INDEPENDENT PRACTICE
Assign exercises **C-250** and **C-251**.

DISCUSSION TIPS
Ask individual students or groups to present, explain, and defend their class and classification decisions. Classification exercises such as these encourage students to visualize various relationships that exist among items in a group and to demonstrate these relationships graphically. Discourage artificial categories that bear no relationship to word meanings, e.g., by number of letters in the words, by initial letter.

As an extending activity, encourage students to add words and/or categories to their original charts. They might even wish to make a wall display using newsprint or butcher paper to display various ways of classifying the same list.

ANSWERS
C-250
(Classified by "Units that measure _____ .")

AREA	LENGTH	NUMBER	VOLUME	WEIGHT
acre	centimeter	dozen	cubic yard	gram
square foot	kilometer	score	cup	kilogram
square mile	meter		liter	milligram
square yard	mile		milliliter	ounce
	millimeter		pint	pound
	yard		quart	ton

(Classified by "Units of measure in the _____ system.")

ENGLISH		METRIC		OTHER / BOTH
acre	pound	centimeter	meter	score
cubic yard	quart	gram	milligram	
cup	square foot	kilogram	milliliter	
dozen	square mile	kilometer	millimeter	
mile	square yard	liter		
ounce	ton			
pint	yard			

C-251
(Classified by machine type)

LEVER	SCREW	WEDGE	WHEEL/AXLE
bottle opener	airplane	chisel	door knob
crowbar	propeller	nail	electric mixer
hammer	clamp		pencil sharpener
pliers	nut		pulley

(Classified by machine function)

HOLD	MOVE	TURN	PUSH/DRIVE
clamp	bottle	airplane	chisel
nail	opener	propeller	hammer
nut	crowbar	door knob	
pliers	pulley	electric mixer	
		pencil	
		sharpener	

FOLLOW-UP REFERENT

When might you find it helpful or necessary to sort a list of items by specifying classes?

Examples: organizing daily activities by grouping into like categories; sorting or organizing tools, utensils, games, clothes, coupons, records, or books for storage and easy retrieval; organizing a shopping list; making lists for special projects or occasions, e.g., weddings, holidays, planning a party or school project; organizing or filing office records or letters; organizing or sorting items at work, e.g., for a department store or supermarket display or warehouse, shelving items in a library, bookstore, or record shop

CURRICULUM APPLICATION

Language Arts: comparing literary genre or works within a genre by determining common characteristics; classifying figures of speech, parts of speech, or paragraph types; choosing words that convey exact desired meaning; organizing and classifying articles and/or pictures for journalism projects, e.g., according to yearbook or newspaper sections, according to genre for creative writing publications

Mathematics: differentiating among number properties or problem types; grouping like terms in equations; organizing information for statistical analysis or probability studies; recognizing set-subset relationships

Science: determining common characteristics, then classifying plants or animals according to those characteristics; determining common properties among elements or compounds, then using those properties to classify

Social Studies: classifying types of dwellings, weapons, household articles, or tools according to era or culture; classifying items from psychological profiles according to specific behaviors; classifying social, economic, political, or governmental actions, behaviors, or processes within a given society

Enrichment Areas: classifying music, art, architecture, or dance according to era, culture, or type; selecting appropriate tools and materials for various steps in art, shop, or home economics projects; analyzing or sorting sports teams according to statistics, team, position, league, or other classifying criteria

OVERLAPPING CLASSES—MATRIX

STRAND: Verbal Classifications   **PAGES:** 271–273

ADDITIONAL MATERIALS
Transparency of TM #22
Washable transparency marker
Student copies of TM #22 (optional)

INTRODUCTION

In the preceding lesson you sorted items into classes of your own choosing. You also discovered that each word group could be correctly sorted several different ways.

OBJECTIVE

In these exercises you will use matrix diagrams to classify items having two characteristics in common.

DEMONSTRATION / EXPLANATION

Project the transparency of T.M. #22.

Remember working with matrices? Matrices are used to show relationships among items having two common characteristics. What characteristic do the rows in this matrix represent?

Answer: The rows name materials of which objects are made (PLASTIC, METAL, or OTHER).

What characteristic do the columns represent?

Answer: The columns name the object's function (FASTENERS, CLEANERS, or CONTAINERS). Indicate the Row 1-Column 1 (top left) cell.

What type of object would belong in this cell? How can you tell?

Answer: A plastic object used as a fastener would go in this cell; it must be plastic because it is in Row 1 and a fastener because it is in Column 1. Indicate the Row 2-Column 2 (center) cell.

What type of objects belong in this cell?

Answer: Metal objects used as cleaners. Indicate the Row 3-Column 3 (lower right) cell.

What type of objects belong in this cell?

Answer: Containers made of materials other than plastic or metal.

You are to classify each object named in the CHOICE BOX by placing it in the matrix cell or cells that best describe it. If an item is commonly made of more than one type of material, then list it in more than one cell. Would you classify the first item, <u>aluminum foil</u>, as a fastener, a cleaner, or a container?

Answer: Aluminum foil is most frequently used as a container.

So you know that aluminum foil would belong in the third column. Now you need to determine the proper row or cell in which to place the item. Of what is aluminum foil made?

Answer: Foil is made of metal.

So aluminum foil belongs in the middle cell of the FASTENER column, since it is made of metal (Row 2).

Write ALUMINUM FOIL in the proper cell of the third column. Continue this process until all items in the **CHOICE BOX** are sorted, or distribute copies of TM #22 for students to complete as a **GUIDED PRACTICE** exercise. Encourage them to consider various materials of which each item might be made.

	FASTENERS	CLEANERS	CONTAINERS
PLASTIC	button paper clip	brush mop paint scraper	jar trash bag
METAL	button nail paper clip safety pin staple wire	paint scraper steel wool	aluminum foil can jar kettle
OTHER	button cotton string glue masking tape rubber band	brush eraser mop rag	jar paper cup trash bag

GUIDED PRACTICE
EXERCISE: **C-252**
ANSWER:

C-252

	FLOWERS	FRUITS	VEGETABLES
ON TREES	magnolia	apricot lime plum tangerine	
ON VINES	morning glory	cantaloupe grape melon	cucumber squash
ON STALKS OR IN THE GROUND	carnation poppy daffodil tulip iris violet lily zinnia marigold	pineapple	cabbage spinach carrot turnip cauliflower celery

INDEPENDENT PRACTICE
Assign exercises **C-253** and **C-254**.

DISCUSSION TIPS
Classification exercises using matrices promote and reinforce such study skills as visualization, memory, observation, organization, and divergent analysis. Students should discuss and explain their answers, defend their classifications, and give specific examples.

Students may approach matrices in various ways. Some will begin with the first word on the list, determine its classification, and write it on the matrix before going to the next word, repeating this process until all items are placed. Others may proceed cell by cell, noting the characteristics of each cell, then choosing words from the list to fit those characteristics. Ask various students to explain how they approached the exercises. Such verbalization of analysis technique is helpful for students who need an organized approach. It is also useful for helping students realize that there is more than one way to arrive at a solution.

ANSWERS
C-253

	AREA	LENGTH	NUMBER	VOLUME	WEIGHT
ENGLISH SYSTEM	acre sq. foot sq. mile sq. yard	mile yard	dozen	cu. yard cup pint quart	ounce pound ton
METRIC SYSTEM		centimeter kilometer meter millimeter		liter milliliter	gram kilogram milligram
OTHER			score		

C-254

	TASTE	TOUCH	SOUND	APPEARANCE
GENERALLY FAVORABLE	*rich* delicious	balmy downy fluffy	cheerful harmonious	*rich* cheerful fluffy harmonious stylish
GENERALLY UNFAVORABLE	rotten stale	coarse irritating scratchy stinging	coarse irritating scratchy shrieking shrill	blinding coarse gaudy irritating rotten
SOMETIMES FAVORABLE/ SOMETIMES UNFAVORABLE	salty sour spicy tart	nudging	babble (+ brook, – chatter) humming (+ a tune, – a bee)	casual showy

FOLLOW-UP REFERENT

When might you use a matrix to understand, compare, or sort information?

Examples: reading matrix tables, e.g., bus, train, or airplane schedules; making or reading class schedules; interpreting sports data from scoreboard columns; organizing daily, study, or work schedules; reading product comparison charts; preparing study sheets for comparative items, e.g., comparing governments, economic systems, and military structures of several countries or eras

CURRICULUM APPLICATION

Language Arts: comparing or contrasting elements from or among works of literature, e.g., main character, point of view, symbolism; using a matrix to organize points or paragraphs for a compare/contrast composition; using matrices to compare similarities and differences among languages, grammatical structures, punctuation, or spelling

Mathematics: constructing and/or using probability, statistical, or arithmetic charts

Science: reading or constructing probability charts for experiments or genetics; depicting or presenting experiment results using a matrix; classifying objects using more than one characteristic; reading the periodic table

Social Studies: using a matrix to present survey results; interpreting comparative information presented on a matrix; using a matrix to organize information, e.g., responsibilities of various branches of government, types of juries, duties of club officers; job descriptions

Enrichment Areas: using a matrix to compare or contrast characteristics of multiple works of art, artists, music, dramatics, or dance; using a matrix to compare teams or types of sports; depicting the effects of specific variables, e.g., the effects of water, fertilizer, and temperature on experimental crops or plots of ground in agriculture; the effects of various ingredients, temperatures, or processing times on cooking and baking

BRANCHING DIAGRAMS

STRAND: Verbal Classifications   **PAGES:** 274–279

ADDITIONAL MATERIALS
Transparency of TM #23
Washable transparency marker
Student copies of TM #23 (optional)

INTRODUCTION
In previous lessons you sorted items into particular groups or classes by determining specific characteristics of each item.

OBJECTIVE
In these exercises you will sort a list of words into specific classes, then sort those classes into given subclasses. You will then depict these divisions and subdivisions on branching diagrams.

DEMONSTRATION/EXPLANATION
Project the transparency of TM #23.

For this exercise you are given a list of words designated RECREATIONAL ACTIVITIES. You are to sort them into two major classes, SPORTS and GAMES, then further classify each class into two subclasses. According to the partially completed diagram, what subclass labels will you use?

Answer: The SPORTS group is divided according to TEAM sports and INDIVIDUAL sports, and the GAMES group is divided according to TABLE games and MOVEMENT games.

First, classify each listed activity as either a SPORT or a GAME. Into which of these two general classes does the first word, <u>baseball</u>, fit?

Answer: Baseball is a sport. Write an S above the word baseball (or write BASEBALL on the left side of the transparency).

Does the next word, <u>checkers</u>, refer to a sport or a game?

Answer: Checkers is a game. Write a G above the word checkers (or write CHECKERS on the right side of the transparency). Continue this line of questioning until each word has been classified.

Answers: **SPORTS:** baseball, football, golf, gymnastics, hockey, skating, skiing, soccer; **GAMES:** checkers, chess, hopscotch, jump rope, tag.

Now look at the sports group and determine whether each is a team sport or an individual sport. How will you distinguish team sports from individual sports?

Answer: A team sport is one in which you cannot participate alone. An individual sport is one in which you can compete alone, even though that sport, such as swimming, may also have organized teams.

Is baseball a team sport or an individual sport?

Answer: A team sport. Write BASEBALL in the **TEAM** box.

Which of the words listed under SPORTS names an individual sport?

Possible Answer: Golf, gymnastics, skating, or skiing; write the selected answer in the **INDIVIDUAL** box.

Now look at the GAMES list. Which of these names a table game?
Possible Answer: Checkers or chess; write the selected answer in the **TABLE** box.
Which is an example of a movement game?
Possible Answer: Hopscotch, jump rope, or tag; write the selected answer in the **MOVEMENT** box, then continue the exercise by having student volunteers classify individual words and write them in the proper subclass box on the transparency. As an alternative, you may wish to distribute copies of TM #23 for students to complete as a **GUIDED PRACTICE** exercise.

GUIDED PRACTICE
EXERCISE: **C-255**
Give students sufficient time to complete the exercise. Then, using the demonstration methodology above, have them discuss and explain their choices.
ANSWER:
C-255

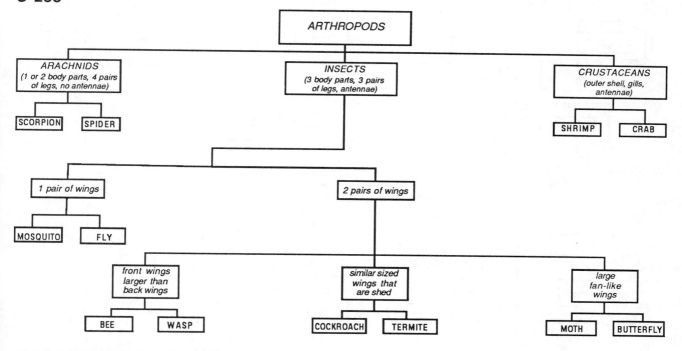

INDEPENDENT PRACTICE
Assign exercises **C-256** and **C-257**.

DISCUSSION TIPS
Classification activities such as these are useful tools for assimilating new information by extending existing categories. Students expand their memories by such connections, thereby retaining otherwise unconnected items or ideas. Recognition of these connected relationships is also necessary for analogy analysis.

Ask students to state the location of each item by tracing its "lineage," e.g., rather than allowing a student to specify the location of bass clarinet in **C-256** by saying, "The bass clarinet goes in the left hand box in the bottom row," require that they define the location by saying, "A *bass clarinet* is a *reed* instrument belonging to the *woodwind* branch of the *wind* family." Such statements will reinforce the interrelationships among the items.

ANSWERS
C-256

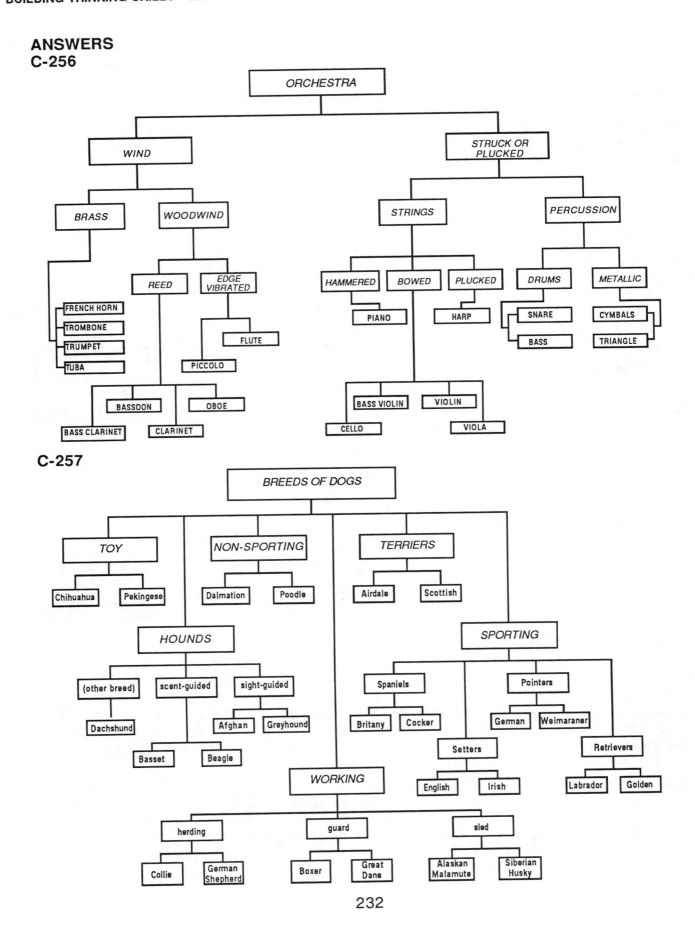

C-257

FOLLOW-UP REFERENT

When might you find it necessary or helpful to sort items into given classes and subclasses using branching diagrams?

Examples: organizing tools, utensils, clothes, coupons, records, or books for storage and easy retrieval; making a shopping list; organizing duties for projects or occasions according to committee, person, or type of activity; recording the organization of records or letters in an office or computer file; making or using a topic outline; classifying warehouse, stock, or business inventories

CURRICULUM APPLICATION

Language Arts: sorting literary works according to genre and types of works within genre; classifying figures of speech, parts of speech, or paragraph types; diagraming sentence structure; showing etymology of words or phrases; organizing information or steps for preparing written or oral presentations

Mathematics: differentiating among number properties and problem types; recognizing set-subset relationships; organizing multistep solutions to arithmetic, geometry, or algebra problems; organizing materials into classes and subclasses for statistical or probability analysis

Science: differentiating among classes and subclasses of plants, animals, food groups, soils, climatic conditions, gems, or rocks; classifying elements or compounds according to properties and subproperties; organizing and/or depicting steps in scientific experiments or demonstrations

Social Studies: organizing information for charts, maps, or graphs that depict class-subclass structures; using class-subclass distinctions in archeology to classify types of dwellings, weapons, household articles, or tools; using branching diagrams to show organizational structures of governments, political parties, or legislative and judicial systems

Enrichment Areas: differentiating among works of music, art, architecture, or dance by determining class-subclass relationships; chaining components of computer programs; depicting desired or existing organizational structures

DIAGRAMING CLASSES—SELECT

STRAND: Verbal Classifications

PAGES: 280–288

ADDITIONAL MATERIALS
Transparency of TM #24
Washable transparency marker

INTRODUCTION

In previous lessons you sorted words into groups, classes, and subclasses, then depicted the results on charts, matrices, or branching diagrams.

OBJECTIVE

In these exercises you will determine how specific items or descriptions relate to given classes, then identify the corresponding location on a circle diagram.

DEMONSTRATION / EXPLANATION

Project **EXAMPLE 1** from the transparency of TM #24.

> *Circle diagrams are frequently used to show relationships between classes and members of those classes. This particular diagram represents a class containing two distinctly different subclasses.*

Indicate the largest circle.

> *What general class does the large circle represent in this diagram?*

Answer: The large circle represents the general class "vehicles."

> *What subclasses do the two smaller circles represent?*

Answer: The smaller circles represent the two subclasses "bicycles" and "trucks."

> *According to the diagram, how are the two subclasses related to each other?*

Answer: They are separate and distinct, having no members in common. (They are a disjoint set.)

> *This relationship might be expressed in a sentence like "No bicycle is a truck, and no truck is a bicycle."*

Indicate the diagram again.

> *Again referring to the diagram, what relationship does it show between the two subclasses and the general class?*

Answer: All members of each subclass are also members of the general class.

> *How might you express the relationship shown in this particular diagram in a sentence?*

Answer: All bicycles and all trucks are vehicles.

NOTE: Make sure students use the word "all" in describing this particular class-subclass relationship. This becomes important when distinguishing among subclasses that overlap classes, subclasses that are included within classes, and separate classes.

> *How might you phrase a sentence to describe the entire class-subclass relationship shown in EXAMPLE 1?*

Answer: "All bicycles and all trucks are vehicles, but no bicycle is also a truck (or "…no truck is also a bicycle")." Project **EXAMPLE** 2 from the transparency.

> *This three-circle diagram shows the relationships among a general class, a subclass, and a more specific subclass. Remember when you learned to identify this type of relationship earlier in the classifications section?*

(See student workbook page 241.)

> *Which circle in this example diagram represents the most general class, and what is the name of that class?*

Answer: The largest (outside) circle represents the most general class, vehicles.

> *Which circle represents the first subclass, and which represents the more specific subclass?*

Answer: The medium-sized (middle) circle represents the first subclass, and the smallest (center) circle represents the more specific subclass.

> *What does each inner circle represent in this specific example?*

Answer: The medium-sized circle represents trucks; the smallest circle represents vans.

> *What relationship does this diagram show among vehicles, trucks, and vans?*
> *How could you state their relationships to each other in a sentence?*

Answer: All vans are trucks, and all trucks are vehicles.

> *According to this diagram, are all vans vehicles?*

Allow time for student discussion and reasoning. They should conclude that all vans are vehicles. If you have students who present arguments to the contrary by citing specific

examples, remind them that the only basis for a decision in this instance is the diagram presented in **EXAMPLE 2**.
Project **EXAMPLE 3** from the transparency.

> *This diagram pictures overlapping subclasses. Once again the most general class is vehicles. What are the names of the subclasses?*

Answer: The subclasses are bicycles, mopeds, and motorcycles.

> *The two smaller, overlapping circles represent bicycles*

Indicate the **B** circle.

> *...and motorcycles.*

Indicate the **C** circle.

> *The intersection, or overlapping area of the subclasses,*

Indicate the intersection (**M**).

> *...indicates that these subclasses have some, but not all, members in common. A moped can be peddled like a bicycle, so it is a member of the class "bicycles." It can also be powered by its engine like a motorcycle, so it is a member of the class "motorcycles," too. Can you think of a single sentence to describe the relationships shown in this diagram?*

Answer: Mopeds are vehicles that can be operated like either a bicycle or a motorcycle.
Project **EXAMPLE 4** from the transparency.

> *Nearly any relationship can be shown using circle diagrams. This diagram shows seven different class-subclass relationships among the three general classes of PARENTS, FEMALES, and EXECUTIVES. These relationship areas are numbered on the diagram. Where on the diagram would you located the three general classes?*

Answer: The general classes (PARENT, FEMALE, and EXECUTIVE) would go in the areas marked as **1**, **2**, or **3** on the diagram.

> *Does it make any difference which class goes in which location?*

Answer: No, as long as only one class is designated for each circle. Indicate the **P**, **F**, and **E** on the **DESIGNATION** blanks beside their corresponding numbers on the transparency. Point to each area you mention as you proceed with the lesson.

> *Area 4 indicates the overlapping members of the classes PARENT and FEMALE. This area has been designated PF to identify the members of that intersection. What subclass is indicated by area 5?*

Answer: Area **5** indicates the overlapping members of the classes FEMALE and EXECUTIVE.

> *How could this area be named or designated, and why?*

Answer: It could be designated **FE** or **EF** to identify the overlapping members of the classes FEMALE (F) and EXECUTIVE (E). Write the designation beside the **5** on the transparency.

> *What about area 6? What intersection does it indicate, and how could it be designated?*

Answer: It shows overlapping members of the classes PARENT (P) and EXECUTIVE (E) and could be designated either **PE** or **EP**. Write the designation on the appropriate line.

> *What intersecting area indicates members that all three classes have in common?*

Answer: Area **7** is the only area on the diagram that is part of all three classes. If necessary, trace each class circle with a different colored marker. Area **7** will be outlined with one side in each color.

> *How could you designate this area, and why would you designate it that way?*

235

Answer: It could be designated **PFE** (or any order of that letter combination) to indicate that it contains the overlapping members of the classes PARENT, FEMALE, and EXECUTIVE.

> *Now that you've designated the name for each class, let's see where some specific members would fit on this diagram. In which region or area would you classify a married female plumber with two children?*

Answer: In region **4**, the overlapping members of the classes PARENT and FEMALE.

> *Why couldn't you use region 1 or region 2? After all, this particular person is a parent (Area 1) and a female (Area 2). Couldn't you just list her in each class?*

Allow time for class discussion. Encourage arguments for and against the proposal. Students should realize that the purpose of a circle diagram is to show the relationships between and among class memberships. Listing a member in each area individually does not indicate relationship; it indicates membership.

> *Which region or class on the diagram would include a male professional athlete who has one child? Why?*

Answer: Area **1** contains people who are PARENTS, not FEMALES, and not EXECUTIVES. Continue giving specific examples such as the following for students to classify.

> ABRAHAM LINCOLN (executive, parent–Area 4); A THREE-YEAR-OLD BOY (does not fit any area under consideration–Outside); YOUR FATHER (parent–Area 1; possibly parent, executive–Area 6); A WOMAN WHO HAS NO CHILDREN AND WHO IS A CORPORATE PRESIDENT (female, executive–Area 5); INDIRA GANDHI (female, executive, parent–Area 7); MOTHER CAT (female, parent–Area 4); MALE CORPORATE VICE-PRESIDENT WHO HAS NO CHILDREN (executive–Area 3); A FIVE-YEAR OLD GIRL (female–Area 2)

GUIDED PRACTICE
EXERCISES: **C-258, C-259**
Give students sufficient time to complete these exercises. Then, using the demonstration methodology above, have them discuss and explain their choices.
ANSWERS: **C-258**   **C-259**

INDEPENDENT PRACTICE
Assign exercises **C-260** through **C-305**.
NOTE: Because of the length and complexity of this lesson, you may wish to divide it into two separate assignments or to extend the normally allotted time for completion. It is important that students have adequate time to determine the answers, to discuss their decisions, and to defend their reasoning.

DISCUSSION TIPS
Showing relationships through the use of circles is frequently used in mathematics (to show sets, subsets, overlapping sets, disjoint sets, and union of sets) and in logic (to diagram class arguments). Such circles may be referred to as *Venn diagrams* or *Euler circles*. As an extending activity, have students identify similar relationships in curricular areas and use the diagrams to depict class relationships. Encourage students to discuss their answers and defend their classifications.

ANSWERS

C-260

C-261

C-262

C-263

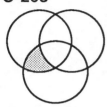

Female
Teacher

C-264

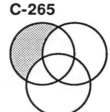

Female
Scientist

C-265

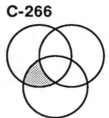

Male
English Teacher

C-266

Female
French Teacher

C-267

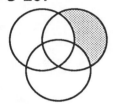

Male Industrial
Scientist

C-268

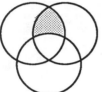

Science
Teacher

C-269

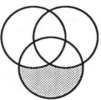

Female
Social Worker

C-270

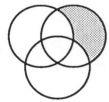

Short Female
Astronaut

C-271

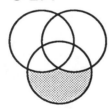

Short
Female Model

C-272

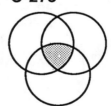

Tall Male
Basketball Player

C-273

Tall Male
Astronaut

C-274

Short
Female Gymnast

C-275

Tall Female
Astronaut

C-276

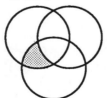

Short Male
Astronaut

C-277

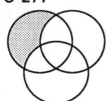

Slice of Beef

C-278

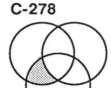

Plain Roast
Beef Sandwich

C-279

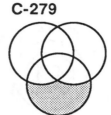

Biscuit

C-280

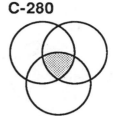

Bacon, Lettuce and
Tomato Sandwich

C-281

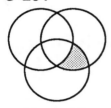

Vegetable
Sandwich

C-282

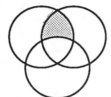

Beef Stew

C-283

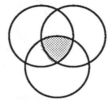

Hamburger with
"Everything"

C-284

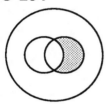

Ten of
Diamonds

C-285

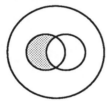

Ace
of Spades

C-286

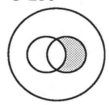

Queen
of Hearts

C-287

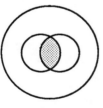

Ace
of Hearts

C-288

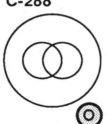

Red Checker

C-289

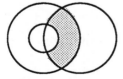

Female Computer
Maintenance Person

C-290

Female Computer
Salesperson

C-291

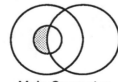

Male Computer
Programmer

C-292

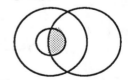

Female Computer
Programmer

C-293

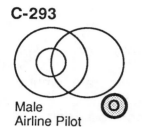

Male
Airline Pilot

C-294

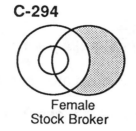

Female
Stock Broker

C-295

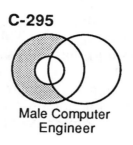

Male Computer
Engineer

C-296	F	C-297	E	C-298	B	C-299	C	C-300	E
C-301	B	C-302	D	C-303	M	C-304	I	C-305	J

FOLLOW-UP REFERENT
When might you use a circle diagram to illustrate or clarify class relationships?
Examples: interpreting or drawing diagrams in advertising, magazines, and newspapers; explaining, depicting, or clarifying class relationships in any area

CURRICULUM APPLICATION

Language Arts: reading comprehension involving *all, none, some, not, and,* and *or;* selecting diagrams to illustrate class relationships in an article, report, or presentation; depicting character relationships within a work of literature; clarifying etymological relationships

Mathematics: creating or interpreting mathematical diagrams, e.g., set-subset, disjoint sets, overlapping sets

Science: using diagrams to depict relationships within the plant or animal kingdoms

Social Studies: using diagrams to show relationships between or among ideas, groups, or organizations

Enrichment Areas: using diagrams to illustrate relationships between various works of an author, composer, or artist; creating or interpreting circle diagrams that show the relationships among authors, athletes, composers, artists, or architects who share at least one common characteristic; depicting business plans, trends, or organization

DIAGRAMING CLASSES—DESCRIBE

STRAND: Verbal Classifications

PAGES: 289–293

ADDITIONAL MATERIALS
Transparency of TM #24
Washable transparency marker

INTRODUCTION
In the previous lesson you determined how specific members were related to the classes shown in a circle diagram.

OBJECTIVE
In these exercises you will describe the class represented by each specific region in a circle diagram, then give an example of something that would belong in that class.

DEMONSTRATION / EXPLANATION

Project **EXAMPLE 4** from the transparency of TM #24.

> *Remember how you designated each area in this diagram and why you designated it that way?*

Allow time for students to discuss and reconfirm the various areas on the diagram, writing the designation beside each corresponding number.

> *Now that you've designated a name for each class, can you describe each class in general terms.*

Indicate the description beside Area **1**, designation **P** on the transparency.

> *Members of Area 1, for example, could be described as people who are* PARENTS, *but who have no characteristics of the other classes. In other words, they are not females, and they are not executives. Would the description "male parents who are not executives" apply to all members of class P?*

Allow time for the class to discuss and confirm the description.

> *Now think of some specific examples of members that would belong to this class. Remember that they must fit all the characteristics that have been ascribed to members of this particular area.*

List student answers beside the Area **1–P** on the chalkboard or transparency as they are given. Do not stop to confirm each answer, but rather treat them as brainstorming ideas. Encourage students to be creative. For example, a lion with a cub could be a member of this class (PARENT? yes; FEMALE? no—a female lion is a lioness; EXECUTIVE? no—"king of beasts" hardly qualifies him for executive status). When the list contains several suggestions, help the class determine whether each suggested answer fits the predetermined characteristics by asking the following questions.

> *Is this member a* PARENT?

The answer must be "yes" if the example is accepted as a member of Area 1.

> *Is this a* FEMALE? *An* EXECUTIVE?

The answer to each of these questions must be "no" if the example is accepted as a member of Area 1. When each suggestion has been evaluated, go on to Area 2 and follow the same procedure as above. Continue this line of questioning until all areas on the diagram have been described and examples have been given for each.

AREA-DESIGNATION	DESCRIPTION	MEMBER
1-P	male, parent, not executive	lion with cub
2-F	female, no children, not executive	5-year-old girl
3-E	male, executive, no children	childless man who is a corporate president
4-PF	female, parent, not executive	mother who works as a nurse
5-FE	female, executive, no children	childless woman who is a corporate president
6-EP	male, executive, parent	father who is vice-president of a corporation
7-PFE	female, executive, parent	mother who is vice-president of a corporation

GUIDED PRACTICE
EXERCISES: **C-306, C-307, C-308**

Give students sufficient time to complete these exercises. Then, using the demonstration methodology above, have them discuss and explain their choices.
ANSWERS:

REGION		DESCRIPTION OF CLASS	MEMBER
C-306	B	large dogs that do not hunt	*Great Dane
C-307	C	large animals that do not hunt	elephant
C-308	D	small hunting dogs	*Dachshund

*See exercise **C-257** in student workbook.

INDEPENDENT PRACTICE
Assign exercises **C-312** through **C-327**.

DISCUSSION TIPS
Insist that students give detailed descriptions of each class, specifying how that class relates to the other areas in the diagram. For example, describing the members of Region A on page 289 as "dogs" is insufficient, since some dogs can also be classified as members of Regions B, D, and E. Students should specify that the dogs belonging in Region A are those that are <u>not</u> large and do <u>not</u> hunt.

As an extending activity, have students name various animals, then identify the class and region for each. They might wish to create an oversized diagram for one wall of the classroom and add animals to the various classifications as they think of them. If the regions are not labeled on the chart, challenge students in other classes to determine the classifying characteristics.

ANSWERS

REGION		DESCRIPTION OF CLASS	MEMBER
C-309	E	large hunting dogs	*Afghan
C-310	F	large hunting animals	lion; tiger
C-311	G	small hunting animals	fox

*See exercise **C-257** in student workbook.

REGION		DESCRIPTION OF CLASS	MEMBER
C-312	B	berries that are not red	blueberry
C-313	C	red berries	strawberry
C-314	D	red fruit	red apple
C-315	E	red foods that are not fruit	beet; red cabbage

REGION		DESCRIPTION OF CLASS	MEMBER
C-316	B	electronic computers that are not games	business computers
C-317	C	electronic computer games	interactive video games
C-318	D	electronic games that are not computers	remote-control vehicles
C-319	E	games that are not electronic and not computers	card games; board games

REGION		DESCRIPTION OF CLASS	MEMBER
C-320	A	female professional athletes who are not professional tennis players	LPGA* member
C-321	C	male professional tennis players	winner of the men's singles at Wimbledon

C-322	D	male professional athletes who are not professional tennis players	MVP* of the Super Bowl
C-323	E	males who are not professional athletes	Little League team members who are boys

*LPGA—Ladies' Professional Golf Association; MVP—Most-valuable Player

REGION		DESCRIPTION OF CLASS	MEMBER
C-324	B	men who are entertainers	a male actor
C-325	C	entertainers who are neither men nor women	a circus animal
C-326	D	women who are entertainers	a female comedienne
C-327	E	women who are not entertainers	a female managing editor

FOLLOW-UP REFERENT

When might it be helpful or necessary for you to describe classification relationships, then name several members of each class?

Examples: explaining or describing something new by relating it to something known; using relationships as a mnemonic technique; describing something specific when you don't know its name, but do know several things about it; expanding descriptions by identifying additional members of specific classes

CURRICULUM APPLICATIONS

Language Arts: choosing reading materials by its relationship to some desired criteria, e.g., author, setting, character, type of literature; describing relationships among elements in a novel or short story and giving examples of each relationship; explaining, describing, or identifying etymological relationships; depicting the relationship between a root word and its derivatives

Mathematics: using set theory to describe classes; naming additional members to predetermined mathematical or geometrical classes

Science: explaining or describing diagrams of class arguments in logic; describing classification relationships among members of the plant or animal kingdoms; identifying and naming additional members of classes and/or subclasses in taxonomy; classifying new discoveries in astronomy, chemistry, oceanography, or other scientific areas

Social Studies: describing and diagraming relationships among cultures, eras, groups, economic systems, political parties, or governments; naming additional members of predetermined classes by identifying the classification characteristics

Enrichment Areas: describing classification relationships in any area of fine arts, sports, practical arts, business, or computer science

DIAGRAMING CLASSES—SELECT THE DIAGRAM

STRAND: Verbal Classifications

PAGES: 294–295

ADDITIONAL MATERIALS

Transparency of student workbook page 294
Washable transparency marker

INTRODUCTION

In the last several lessons you have used various arrangements of circle diagrams to represent relationships between or among specified classes. Some of these were separate classes, with no members in common; some were inclusive classes, with all members of one class included within another; and some were overlapping classes, with some members in common. In each lesson, however, you were given a specific arrangement of circles which identified the relationships of the classes.

OBJECTIVE

In these exercises you will be given several groups of related words and diagrams showing various types of relationships. You are to determine the relationships among the words in each group, locate the diagram that depicts those relationships, then label the location of each major group on the selected diagram.

DEMONSTRATION/EXPLANATION

Project the **EXAMPLE** word group from the transparency of page 294.

Each word group in these exercises includes one term that names the general class to which all the other terms belong. Remember how you determined the general class earlier in the classification exercises?

Allow time for students to discuss and remember the technique for determining general class identification. If necessary, refer to pages 234–236 in the student workbook and the corresponding lesson plan before continuing the lesson.

Which term in this word group names the general class to which all the other items belong?

Answer: The general class is SANDWICHES; CHEESE, EGG and HAM all name kinds of sandwiches.

Now you need to determine the relationships among the subclasses. There are three possibilities—separate classes, inclusive classes, or overlapping classes. You might also have a combination of relationships. How might CHEESE and EGG be related in connection with the general class SANDWICHES?

Answer: They are overlapping classes; some sandwiches might contain both cheese and eggs.

Why can't you say they are separate classes? In the first place, I would say that "no cheese is an egg," and in the second place, I would NEVER eat a cheese and egg sandwich!

Allow time for class discussion. Students should realize that although it is true that "no cheese is an egg" in generic terms, it is not true that "no cheese SANDWICH is also an egg SANDWICH." The general class is sandwiches, and all subclasses are related to that general class. Students should also conclude that relationships such as this show possible combinations, and do not reflect personal taste or preference. Since it is *possible* to have both cheese and an egg on a single sandwich, the two types are overlapping classes. Draw an intersecting circles diagram on the transparency under the word **EXAMPLE**, and label the regions.

How is the third class, HAM, related to these two classes?

Answer: It overlaps both classes. Add an overlapping circle to the bottom of the diagram and label it "H."

> ***How many types of sandwiches are represented in this diagram, and what are they?***

Answer: Seven different combinations (types) of sandwiches are possible. (1) cheese (2) egg (3) ham (4) cheese and egg (5) egg and ham (6) ham and cheese (7) cheese, egg, and ham. Project the **DIAGRAMS** column to confirm the answer.

GUIDED PRACTICE
EXERCISES: **C-328, C-329**
Give students sufficient time to complete these exercises. Then, using the demonstration methodology above, have them discuss and explain their choices.
ANSWERS:

C-328

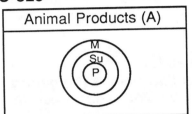

C-329

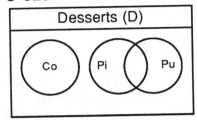

INDEPENDENT PRACTICE
Assign exercises **C-330** through **C-338**.

DISCUSSION TIPS
Have students discuss and explain the relationships within each given word list and defend their choice of diagram for each. They should also be able to say why other diagram choices are not correct for a given list. Encourage them to use the negation phrase "It is not true that ..." when explaining why certain diagrams do not represent the relationship within a word list.

ANSWERS
C-330

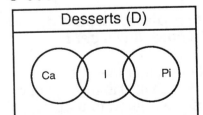

C-331

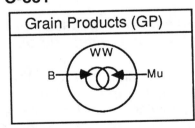

C-332

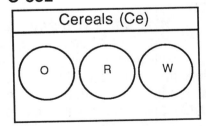

C-333

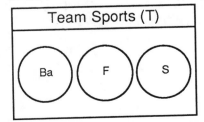

C-334

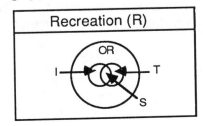

C-335

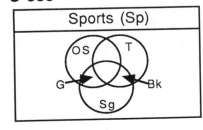

C-336

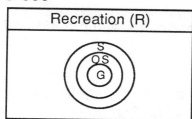

C-337

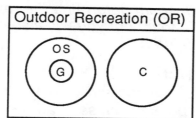

C-338

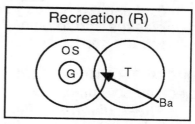

FOLLOW-UP REFERENT

When might you use the ability to determine and depict relationships among a group of items?

Examples: determining and depicting relationships among groups of people for social, educational, or entertainment purposes; determining relationships among materials for cross references; using relationships to locate items in an index, card catalogue, or store; organizing answers to identification questions on essay tests

CURRICULUM APPLICATIONS

Language Arts: identifying nouns according to class and distinguishing characteristics; determining related topics when researching papers or compositions; determining and depicting relationships among the characters or elements of a short story or novel; showing etymological relationships among languages

Mathematics: relating cue words in word problems to computational operations; using set theory and grouping or regrouping techniques

Science: determining and/or depicting relationships among members of the plant or animal kingdoms; using diagrams to show relationships between science and other areas, e.g., historical eras and scientific developments

Social Studies: using sociograms to determine relationships or preferences within a group of people; using diagrams to determine or depict historical, economic, cultural, geographic, or political relationships

Enrichment Areas: using diagrams to identify the most active participants in any area, e.g., most sports participation, most music competitions, most shop projects completed; determining relationships in any areas of fine arts, practical arts, sports, dramatics, or music; using diagrams to depict business plans, trends, or organizational structure

DIAGRAMING CLASSES—SELECT AND EXPLAIN

STRAND: Verbal Classifications

PAGES: 296–299

ADDITIONAL MATERIALS

Transparency of student workbook page 296

INTRODUCTION

In previous lessons you used circle diagrams to sort groups into classes and subclasses and identified the relationships among groups by selecting and labeling the correct diagram.

OBJECTIVE

In these exercises you will again determine the relationship between two classes and to label the diagram, but you will also describe the relationship and write a sentence that explains it.

DEMONSTRATION/EXPLANATION

Project the column of diagrams from the top section of the transparency of page 296.

These diagrams illustrate possible class relationships. What type of relationship is shown in the first two diagrams?

Answer: The first two diagrams show an inclusive relationship; all the members of one class are also members of the other class.

What is the difference between these two diagrams?

Answer: The labels on the classes are reversed.

In diagrams like these, it makes a difference which class goes in which circle. In the other diagrams, the classes are interchangeable.

Indicate the top diagram in the column.

This diagram can be described by saying "Class A includes class B." Does this mean that all members of class B are also members of class A?

Answer: Yes; the diagram supports this statement, since all of circle B is inside circle A.

Can you reverse this statement without changing the meaning? Can you say that all members of class A are also members of class B?

Answer: No, according to the diagram, some members of class A are outside of class B. Class B does not include all of class A, but class A includes all of class B.

A sentence that would express this relationship might be "All members of B are also members of A." How would you describe the second diagram so that someone else could visualize both the diagram and the labels?

Answer: Class A is included in class B.

NOTE: Students should keep the classes in their original order when describing relationships, being careful not to confuse which is "Class A" and which is "Class B."

What sentence could you use to express this relationship?

Answer: All members of A are members of B.

Who can think of an example of two classes that have the kind of relationship shown by these two diagrams?

Possible answers might include such classes as students in the school (A) and students in the class (B), store employees (A) and salespeople (B), dogs (A) and animals (B). For each suggested pair, ask the student to express the relationship in sentence form, e.g., "All students in this class (B) are students in this school (A)." OR "All dogs (A) are animals (B)." Again, remind students that it is important which class is designated class A and which is designated class B for the purposes of describing the relationship. It is not true, for example, that all store employees (A) are salespeople (B); stores also employ people as stock personnel, secretaries, managers, and many other positions.

How would you describe the relationship shown by the third diagram?

Answer: Class A overlaps class B.

Now, express that relationship in a sentence, and give some examples of two classes with this relationship.

Answer: Some members of class A are also members of class B. Examples might include combinations of school classes (band and chorus), social or special-interest groups (my friends and the chess club), gender analysis of groups (boys and art club), or physical characteristics and team or club membership (tall persons and track team).

How would you describe the relationship shown in the last diagram?
Answer: Class A is separate from class B.
Can you express that relationship in a sentence and give some examples of classes that have this relationship?
Answer: No members of class A are members of class B. Examples include classes that are mutually exclusive (if A, then not B), e.g., true-false; male-female; dogs-apes.
Project the **EXAMPLE** sentence from the center of the transparency, leaving the diagrams on the screen also. Indicate the top diagram.
This example is like those you will do in the exercises. Let's try the various phrases that describe relationships in the blank space in the sentence. Is it true that the class TEACHERS (class A) includes the class MEN (class B)? Are all men (B) teachers (A)?
Answer: No, it is not true that all men are teachers. Some men are not teachers. Indicate the second diagram.
Is it true that the class TEACHER is included in the class MEN? Why or why not?
Answer: No, it is not true that all teachers are men (all A are B); some are women.
Which phrase best describes the relationship between the two classes TEACHERS and MEN?
Answer: The class TEACHER overlaps the class MEN.
What sentence could you use to express this relationship?
Answer: Some teachers are men (or some men are teachers).
Why can't you use the last diagram to show the relationship between these classes?
Answer: The last diagram represents separate classes and cannot be used, since it is not true that no teachers are men. Project the solution from the transparency to confirm the answers.

GUIDED PRACTICE
EXERCISES: **C-339, C-340**
Give students sufficient time to complete these exercises. Then, using the demonstration methodology above, have them discuss and explain their choices.
ANSWERS:

C-339 *The class CHOCOLATE PRODUCTS (C)* **overlaps** *the class DRINKS (D).*

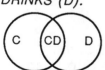

Some drinks are chocolate products; some chocolate products are drinks.

C-340 *The class HEROES (HMR)* **is separate from** *the class HEROINES (HMS).*

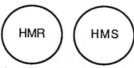

No hero is a heroine (and vice versa).

INDEPENDENT PRACTICE
Assign exercises **C-341** through **C-346**.

DISCUSSION TIPS
This lesson extends students' experience in using diagrams to depict class relationships. Help the students identify class relationships in other areas (see **FOLLOW-UP REFERENT**

and **CURRICULUM APPLICATIONS**), and encourage them to use diagrams to depict such relationships. Students should discuss all possibilities, defend their choices, and explain why the other choices are less correct.

ANSWERS

C-341
The class FICTION (F) **includes** *the class NOVELS (N).*

All novels are fiction (but not all fiction are novels).

C-342
The class SAXOPHONES (S) **is separate from** *the class CLARINET (C).*

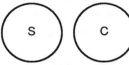

No saxophone is a clarinet; no clarinet is a saxophone.

C-343
The class AMPHIBIANS (A) **is separate from** *the class FISH (F).*

No amphibians are fish; no fish are amphibians.

C-344
The class ELECTED OFFICIALS (O) **includes** *the class STATE GOVERNORS (G).*

All state governors are elected officials (but not all elected officials are state governors).

C-345
The class ELECTRIC DEVICES (E) **overlaps** *the class SAWS (S).*

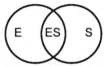

Some electric devises are saws; some saws are electric devises.

C-346
The class ATHLETES (A) **includes** *the class GYMNASTS (G).*

All gymnasts are athletes (but not all athletes are gymnasts).

FOLLOW-UP REFERENT

When might using a diagram help you understand or explain the relationship between classes or items?

Examples: using diagrams to clarify relationships referred to in advertising, magazine or newspaper articles, or news broadcasts; using diagrams to clarify or illustrate when explaining any class relationship

CURRICULUM APPLICATION

Language Arts: reading comprehension involving the adjectives *all*, *no*, and *some*; selecting, creating, or labeling diagrams to illustrate relationships referred to in an article, report, or presentation; using diagrams to depict complicated relationships among characters in a novel or short story

Mathematics: creating or interpreting mathematical diagrams; using diagrams to illustrate or explain sets or set theory

Science: using diagrams to understand or illustrate relationships within the plant or animal kingdoms, between elements in a compound or other mixture, or among various branches of science

Social Studies: using diagrams to show relationships between or among ideas, groups, or organizations

Enrichment Areas: using diagrams to illustrate relationships between various works of an author, composer, or artist; illustrating relationships between or among composers, artists, or authors who have at least one characteristic in common

DIAGRAMING CLASS STATEMENTS

STRAND: Verbal Classifications

PAGES: 300–305

ADDITIONAL MATERIALS
Transparency of student workbook page 300
Washable transparency marker

INTRODUCTION
In the previous lesson you depicted and explained class relationships by selecting and labeling a circle diagram that corresponded to the expressed relationships. Those exercises illustrated the class relationships indicated by the English adjectives "some," "all," and "no."

OBJECTIVE
In these exercises you will also select the diagram that illustrates a class relationship, but these relationships are expressed as standard English sentences.

DEMONSTRATION/EXPLANATION
Project the first **EXAMPLE** sentence from the transparency of page 300.
    What two classes are talked about in this example sentence?
Answer: The two classes are "cars" and "fast."
    What type of circle diagram would you use to show the relationship expressed in this sentence? Why?
Answer: An overlapping circles diagram would be used because the cue word "some" indicates that the two classes have some members in common.
    How would you label the diagram?
Answer: Mark one class circle "C" and the other class circle "F."
    Does it make any difference which circle is labeled C and which F?
Answer: No, the classes in this type of diagram are interchangeable.
    What area or region on the diagram would contain the members described by the sentence?
Answer: The overlapping area would contain the fast cars described in the sentence.
Project the solution for confirmation, asking students to explain why the alternate diagrams could not be used to depict the relationship expressed in the sentence.
Project the second **EXAMPLE** sentence, but keep the solution covered.
    This sentence refers to the same two classes, "cars" and "fast." Would you use the same type of circle diagram? Why or why not?
Answer: Yes, the same diagram would be used, since the cue word is still "some."
    Which region of the diagram would contain the members described in this sentence?
Answer: The circle labeled "C" would contain the cars that are not fast. Project the solution for confirmation and discussion, then project the third **EXAMPLE** sentence.

What class relationship is expressed in this sentence, and what are the classes?

Answer: The cue word "all" indicates that this is an inclusive relationship between the class "cars" and the class "vehicles."

What diagram would you use to show this relationship?

Answer: One class circle is completely inside the other class circle.

How would you label this diagram. Does it make a difference which circle is labeled cars and which vehicles?

Answer: The inner circle must be labeled "C," because the statement says that all members of the class "cars" are also members of the class "vehicles." It does not say that all vehicles are cars, so the class circle "V" cannot go on the inside.

What region of the diagram would be shaded to indicate those members described in the sentence?

Answer: The inner circle (C) should be shaded, since the sentence describes cars.. Project exercise **C-347**.

Read this sentence, then determine the proper diagrams, labels, and shading to reflect the members described by the sentence.

Allow time for discussion and decision making, then have a student write his/her answer on the transparency. Ask the class to confirm the answer and to state why any possible alternatives are or are not correct.

Remember that you are to diagram the classes and the relationship expressed in each statement. Some statements may not be true, but they can still be diagramed.

GUIDED PRACTICE
EXERCISES: **C-348, C-349**
ANSWERS:

C-348
No Ford (F) is a Dodge (D).

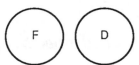

C-349
Some cars (C) are not produced in America (A).

INDEPENDENT PRACTICE
Assign exercises **C-350** through **C-365**.

DISCUSSION TIPS
This exercise provides students with experience using diagrams to depict class relationships. Identify similar relationships in other academic areas, and use the diagrams to clarify class relationships. Encourage students to discuss and explain their answers and to bring in examples of *some, all*, and *no* used as adjectives. Encourage students to find variations of *all* or *no* statements. Often the *all* is understood and omitted, such as in the statement "Dandelions are plants," which means "All dandelions are plants." *None* or

not are also sometimes substituted for *no*, e.g., "None of the plants are green" and "The plants are not green" and "No plant is green" would all have the same diagram in a class argument.

ANSWERS

C-350
All Dodges (D) are vehicles (V).

C-351
Some Dodges (D) are fast (F).

C-352
All intelligent beings (I) are people (P).

C-353
Some intelligent beings (I) are people (P).

C-354
No intelligent beings (I) are people (P).

C-355
Some people (P) are not intelligent (I).

C-356
Everyone (E) is intelligent (I).

C-357
Some people (P) are intelligent (I).

C-358
Not everyone (E) is intelligent (I).

C-359
No one (N) is intelligent (I).

*(NOTE: The overlapping section of **C-358** can be shaded instead of the E circle, a solution that indicates those members of E who are intelligent, as opposed to the unshaded circle E, indicating those members of E who are not intelligent.*

C-360
Some plants (P) are not green (G).

C-361
All marigolds (Ma) are flowers (F).

C-362
Some flowers (F) grow on vines (V).

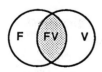

C-363
Both marigolds (Ma) and morning glories (Mg) are flowers (F).

C-364
Some flowers (F) do not grow on vines (V).

C-365
Marigolds (Ma) are flowers (F) that do not grow on vines (V), but morning glories (Mg) do.

*NOTE: Both the diagram and the sentence for **C-365** combine the previous three exercises.*

FOLLOW-UP REFERENT
When might you use a diagram for illustrating class relationships?
Examples: interpreting or drawing diagrams in advertising, magazines, and newspapers; explaining or clarifying class relationships in any area

CURRICULUM APPLICATION
Language Arts: reading comprehension involving *and*, *or*, *all*, *none*, *some*, and *not*; selecting diagrams for illustrating an article, report, or presentation
Mathematics: creating or interpreting mathematical diagrams
Science: using diagrams to understand relationships within phyla of plants and animals
Social Studies: using diagrams to show relationships between or among ideas, groups, or organizations
Enrichment Areas: using diagrams to illustrate relationships between various works of an author, composer, or artist who share at least one common characteristic

DIAGRAMING CLASS ARGUMENTS

STRAND: Verbal Classifications   **PAGES:** 306–312

ADDITIONAL MATERIALS
Transparencies of student workbook pages 306, 307, and 308

INTRODUCTION
In the previous lesson you selected the diagram which best described the class relationships indicated by the English adjectives "some," "all," and "no."

OBJECTIVE
In these exercises you will draw diagrams to illustrate three statements—two premises and a conclusion—to see if the conclusion is valid by determining if it must follow from the premises.

DEMONSTRATION / EXPLANATION
Project the **EXAMPLE ARGUMENT** from the top of the transparency of page 306.
Here you see an example of a simple argument. You are to assume that each premise is true and diagram it as you have done in earlier exercises. How would you diagram Premise 1, "All actors (A) are performers (P)"?
Allow time for class discussion and decision making, then project the diagram of Premise 1 for confirmation.
What is Premise 2, and how would you diagram it?
Answer: Premise 2 says, "All comedians (C) are actors (A)," and would use the inclusive circle diagram also. Be certain that students label the two circles to indicate that the class comedians is included in the class actors, and not vice versa.
Now you have a diagram of each premise on which the conclusion is based. Is it possible to combine the two premise diagrams into a single diagram?
Answer: Yes, the two can be combined into a three-circle diagram, with all of circle C (comedians) inside circle A (actors), and all of circle A (actors) inside circle P (performers). Remove the transparency of page 306, and project the conclusion diagram from the top of the transparency of page 307 to verify student responses.

Is it possible to combine the two premise diagrams in any way that shows any or all of the class, comedians, outside the class, actors?

Allow time for students to experiment with various diagram arrangements. They should conclude that there is no way to draw class C outside of class P.

Does the combined diagram support the stated conclusion?

Answer: Yes, since all of circle C (comedians) is inside circle P (performers), the conclusion is supported.

If the premise diagrams CAN be combined to support the conclusion, and if they CANNOT be combined in any way that does NOT support the conclusion, then the conclusion is shown, demonstrating its validity.

NOTE: The word "shown" is used throughout this demonstration section rather than "valid," a logic term used in more advanced books, such as **Critical Thinking** by Anita Harnadek. The more technical term may be used if you desire.

Project the **EXAMPLE 2** argument from the transparency.

Assuming that Premise 1 is true, how would you diagram it?

Students should describe the same diagram as was used for Premise 1 in the first argument, with circle A (actors) completely inside circle P (performers).

Premise 2 says, "No editors (E) are performers (P)." How should this premise be diagramed?

Answer: The cue word *no* suggests two separate circles that do not overlap. Students should describe two circles, labeled P and E, that do not touch.

Now you have a diagram of each premise. How would you draw a diagram that combined the two premise diagrams?

Answer: The two premise diagrams can be combined by drawing two separated circles, labeled P and E, then placing circle A (from Premise 1) entirely inside circle P (from Premise 2).

Since there is no other way to combine the two diagrams, is the stated conclusion shown or not shown (valid or invalid)?

Answer: Since the conclusion is supported by the only possible combination diagram, the conclusion is shown (valid). Project the transparency of page 308.

Remember that you are to assume that each premise is true. How would you diagram Premise 1?

Students should again describe the same diagram as was used for Premise 1 in the preceding examples.

Premise 2 says, "All actors (A) are talented people (T)." How should this premise be diagramed?

Answer: The cue word *all* suggests the inclusive-circle diagram again. All of circle A should be within circle T.

Can you combine the two premise diagrams into a single diagram that shows the conclusion?

Allow ample time for class discussion and decision making. Ask various students to draw their combined diagrams on the chalkboard, then encourage the class to evaluate the possible solutions. They should conclude that it is possible to combine the two premise diagrams into a three-circle diagram as shown here.

> *Is it possible to combine the two diagrams so that all of circle T (talented people) is NOT inside circle P (performers)?*

Answer: Yes, by using overlapping circles. Project the conclusion diagram from the bottom of the transparency.

> *The shaded area of this diagram indicates "talented people who are not actors." Since it is possible to combine the two premise diagrams so they do NOT support the conclusion, the conclusion is not shown (invalid).*

GUIDED PRACTICE
EXERCISES: **C-366, C-367, C-368**
Give students sufficient time to complete these exercises. Then, using the demonstration methodology above, have them discuss and explain their choices.
ANSWERS:

C-366 PREMISE 1	PREMISE 2	CONCLUSION
All friends of Maria (FM) are friends of Sarah (FS).	*Ruth (R) is a friend of Maria.*	*Ruth is a friend of Sarah.*

Since there is no way to draw R outside of FS and still describe the premises, the conclusion **is** shown. (It is valid.)

C-367 PREMISE 1	PREMISE 2	CONCLUSION
All friends of Maria (FM) are friends of Sarah (FS).	*Ruth (R) is a friend of Sarah.*	*Ruth is a friend of Maria.*

Since it is possible to draw R outside of FM and still describe the premises, the conclusion **is not** shown. (It is invalid.)

C-368 PREMISE 1	PREMISE 2	CONCLUSION
Maria (M) is a friend of Sarah (FS).	*Ruth (R) is a friend of Sarah.*	*Maria is a friend of Ruth (FR).*

Since it is possible to combine the diagrams into a diagram that does not show the conclusion, the conclusion **is not** shown. (It is invalid.)

INDEPENDENT PRACTICE
Assign exercises **C-369** through **C-377**.

DISCUSSION TIPS
This lesson provides students with experience using diagrams to depict and evaluate class arguments. Stress to the students that the object of each exercise is not to see if the class circles can be drawn to show that the conclusion **is** true, but rather to see if the

diagram can be drawn to show that the conclusion is **not** true. Allow ample time for this lesson, as students will need to develop and discard alternate solutions to make sure the premise diagrams cannot be combined in other ways.

You may need to remind students that they are not determining the "truth" of a statement; they are to accept each premise as a true statement and proceed from that assumption. The two books in the *Critical Thinking* series by Anita Harnadek (available from Midwest Publications) provides extensive information and student practice in logical argument, validity, and the probabilities of truth and falsity.

Help the students identify class arguments in other areas, and encourage them to use the diagrams to analyze the validity of conclusions drawn from such arguments. As an extending activity, have students bring or develop examples of simple arguments for their classmates to diagram and analyze.

ANSWERS

C-369 PREMISE 1
Ruth (R) is not a friend of Sarah (FS).

PREMISE 2
All friends of Maria (FM) are friends of Sarah.

CONCLUSION
Ruth is not a friend of Maria.

The conclusion is **valid**, since there is no way to combine the premise diagrams so that R is inside FM.

C-370 PREMISE 1
All cute creatures (C) are amusing (A).

PREMISE 2
All babies (B) are cute creatures.

CONCLUSION
All babies are amusing.

The conclusion is **valid**, since there is no way to combine the premise diagrams so that B is outside A.

C-371 PREMISE 1
All cute creatures (C) are amusing (A).

PREMISE 2
Some babies (B) are cute creatures.

CONCLUSION
All babies are amusing.

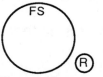

HOWEVER, it is *POSSIBLE* to combine the diagrams of the premises to show that *SOME* babies are not amusing (some part of B is not inside A).

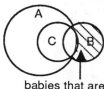

babies that are not amusing

Therefore, the conclusion is **invalid**, since there is a way to combine the premise diagrams so that at least part of B is outside A.

C-372 PREMISE 1
*All babies (B) are cute
creatures (C).*

PREMISE 2
*Some cute creatures
are amusing (A).*

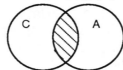

CONCLUSION
*Some babies are
amusing.*

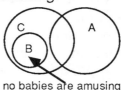

The conclusion is **invalid**, since there is a way to combine the premise diagrams so that
all of B is outside A.

C-373 PREMISE 1
*All babies (B) are cute
creatures (C).*

PREMISE 2
*Some cute creatures
are amusing (A).*

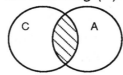

CONCLUSION
No babies are amusing.

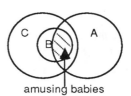

The conclusion is **invalid**, since there is a way to combine the premise diagrams so that at
least part of B is inside A.

C-374 PREMISE 1
*No babies (B) are
amusing (A).*

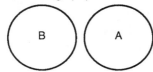

PREMISE 2
*Some babies are cute
creatures (C).*

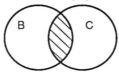

CONCLUSION
*No cute creatures
are amusing.*

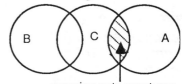

The conclusion is **invalid**, since there is a way to combine the premise diagrams so that at
least part of C is inside A.

C-375 PREMISE 1
*All babies (B) are
cute (C).*

PREMISE 2
*All amusing things
(A) are cute.*

CONCLUSION
*All babies are
amusing.*

The conclusion is **invalid**, since it is possible to combine the premise diagrams so that at
least part of B is outside A.

C-376 PREMISE 1
*All babies (B) are
cute (C).*

PREMISE 2
*All amusing things
(A) are cute.*

CONCLUSION
*No babies are
amusing.*

The conclusion is **invalid**, since it is possible to combine the premise diagrams so that at
least part of B overlaps A.

C-377 **PREMISE 1**
Some babies (B) are cute creatures (C).

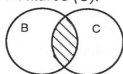

PREMISE 2
Some babies are amusing (A).

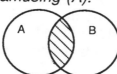

CONCLUSION
Some cute creatures are amusing.

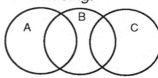

The conclusion is **invalid**, since it is possible to combine the premise diagrams so that no part of C is inside A.

FOLLOW-UP REFERENT
When might you use a diagram to reach a conclusion or evaluate the validity of a classification argument (class argument)?

Examples: recognizing and diagraming class arguments used in advertising or in magazine and newspaper articles or editorials; determining valid and invalid conclusions when explaining or clarifying class arguments; using a diagram to validate conclusions when using class arguments

CURRICULUM APPLICATION
Language Arts: recognizing and evaluating the validity of class arguments used in persuasive writing, essays, or other literary works; reading comprehension involving *and, or, all, none, some,* and *not;*using diagrams to illustrate conclusions in an article, report, or presentation

Mathematics: creating or interpreting mathematical diagrams, especially concerning sets and set theory

Science: using diagrams to illustrate relationships within the plant or animal kingdom, then basing conclusions on the diagrams; using diagrams to illustrate relationships between or among the various branches of science; using diagrams to evaluate class arguments in logic

Social Studies: using diagrams to illustrate and evaluate relationships between or among ideas, groups, or organizations

Enrichment Areas: using diagrams to illustrate relationships between or among various works of an author, composer, or artist

DEFINITIONS THAT CONTAIN CLASSES—SELECT/SUPPLY

STRAND: Verbal Classifications   **PAGES:** 313–318

ADDITIONAL MATERIALS
None

INTRODUCTION
Throughout this section you have identified the class to which something belongs.

OBJECTIVE
Now you will use this ability to analyze and write clear, concise definitions.

DEMONSTRATION/EXPLANATION

How would you define the word "definition"?

Allow time for students to discuss the problem and arrive at a consensus, then ask a volunteer to write the definition on the chalkboard. Answers will vary among students, but most should agree that a definition is a statement of the meaning of a word.

What would you say makes the difference between a "good" definition and a "poor" definition?

Again, allow time for students to discuss the question. Answers will vary, but they should include the concept that a "good" definition gives enough information for the listener to determine what the word means and what makes it different from similar things.

A complete definition of a noun should name the CLASS to which the item or concept belongs and the CHARACTERISTICS that set this particular noun apart from others. For example, suppose that I was not familiar with the word "bicycle," and someone defined a bicycle for me as "something that kids ride to school." Is this a true statement about a bicycle?

Answer: Yes, the statement is true.

Is it a good definition of a bicycle? Why or why not?

Answer: No, the definition implies that a bicycle is a form of transportation because it can be ridden to school, but it fails to separate it from other forms of transportation.

What are some identifying characteristics of a bicycle?

List the descriptive words and phrases on the chalkboard as they are suggested. You may need to help the students expand the definition by using a statement like the one that follows. Choose several of the listed descriptive terms to use in the sentence.

Now I know what a bicycle is! A bicycle is red and has two wheels and a handlebar. Sounds like a video game or a wheelbarrow. What is missing from this definition?

Answer: The general class to which the noun bicycle belongs is not mentioned and not enough distinguishing characteristics are given to completely identify the item.

Can you come up with a more complete definition of a bicycle?

Give the students time to make several descriptions of a bicycle, evaluating each suggestion as to its completeness. A possible definition might be "A bicycle is a <u>vehicle</u> consisting of <u>two wheels</u> connected by a <u>steel tubing framework</u> and that is <u>steered by handlebars</u> and <u>propelled by foot pedals</u>." (<u>class</u> and <u>identifying characteristics</u>)

As you read the definition for nouns in these exercises, you are to determine whether each is complete or incomplete. A complete definition contains both the class to which the noun belongs and enough distinguishing characteristics to differentiate it from other members of that class. If an exercise contains a complete definition, mark it C and leave the class and characteristics lines blank. If the definition does not provide enough information, mark it I for incomplete and supply the necessary missing information on the class or characteristics lines.

GUIDED PRACTICE

EXERCISES: **C-378, C-379, C-380**

Give students sufficient time to complete these exercises. Then, using the demonstration methodology above, have them discuss and explain their choices.

ANSWERS:

C-378 C

C-379 I *characteristics:* violent, accompanied by heavy rains, can cause great property damage

e.g., A hurricane is a violent wind storm which is frequently accompanied by heavy rains and can cause great property damage.

C-380 C

INDEPENDENT PRACTICE
Assign exercises **C-381** through **C-411**.

DISCUSSION TIPS
This lesson is intended to make students think about the classification skills they have practiced, apply the knowledge they have learned, and make well-reasoned statements of definition. Encourage students to use this criteria for definitions when they need oral or written definitions or identifications in any academic area. Students should discuss their definitions and explain the rationale behind their decisions. Encourage them to apply the class-characteristics test to definitions they find in newspapers or magazines, and to discuss the results.

ANSWERS
C-381 C

C-382 I *characteristics:* electronic, computerized

e.g., "A video game is an electronic, computerized game that can be played by one or more people." The characteristics stated in the original definition failed to identify the "video" part of the noun; thus it did not distinguish video game from any other game.

C-383 I *class:* personal feeling

e.g., "Satisfaction is a personal feeling that things are all right." Satisfaction is a personal feeling; while things may be all right for the satisfied person, another person in that same situation may be dissatisfied with the same results. For example, the winners and the losers of a baseball game may very well have two different feelings about the same game.

C-384 I *class:* chart

e.g., A graph is a chart that shows changes in conditions over a period of time.

C-385 C

C-386 I *class:* established time period; *characteristics:* can leave your seat

e.g., "Intermission is an established time period in the middle of a game or concert when you can leave your seat to go to the rest room or concession stand." The definition as stated implies that any time you get up (from where?) in the middle of a game or concert to go to the rest room or concession stand is an intermission. This is not only an incomplete definition, it is not true.

C-387 C

C-388 I *characteristics:* drawers for storage; flat surface for writing

e.g., "A desk is a piece of furniture with drawers for storage and a flat surface for writing." The definition as given contains no distinguishing characteristics.

C-389 I *class:* emotion

e.g., "Love is an emotion that includes tenderness, joy, and affection." It is possible to feel tenderness, joy, or affection without the emotion of love. As stated, tenderness, joy, and affection equal love.

C-390 C

C-391 I *characteristics:* caused by the threat or nearness of pain, danger, or evil

e.g., "Fear is an emotion caused by the threat or nearness of pain, danger, or evil." The definition given contains no characteristics that distinguish fear from any other emotion.

C-392 I *characteristics:* bright blue and green head feathers and white neckband of the male

e.g., "A mallard is a type of wild duck that is characterized by the bright blue and green head feathers and white neckband of the male." The definition given contains no characteristics to distinguish a mallard from any other wild duck.

C-393 C

C-394 I *class:* emotion; *characteristics:* expressed by loudness, violence, or the desire for revenge

e.g., "Anger is an emotion frequently expressed by loudness, violence, or the desire for revenge." Mad may be used as a synonym for anger; it supplies no additional information or characteristics for the noun.

C-395 C

C-396 I *class:* social concept; *characteristics:* all people are treated the same

e.g., "Equality is a social concept that means all people are accorded the same treatment." As the definition reads, there is no class identification. The characteristics stated are not accurate, for equality may also be unfair or unjust, so long as it is applied to all.

C-397 I *class:* vehicular congestion; *characteristics:* at the same time

e.g., "A traffic jam is vehicular congestion that results from too many cars and trucks being on a road at the same time." The original definition does not name a class. The time element is necessary to distinguish traffic jams from normally busy highways that, nevertheless, manage to flow smoothly.

C-398 I *characteristics:* with a fabric roof that can be raised and lowered

e.g., "A convertible is a kind of car that has a fabric roof that can be raised and lowered." No identifying characteristics are given in the original definition to distinguish a convertible from any other car.

C-399 A *refrigerator* is an <u>electric</u> (appliance) that is <u>used to keep food cold or frozen</u>.

C-400 A *week* is a (period of time) that is <u>equal to seven days or 1/52 of a year</u>.

C-401 *Jeans* are a kind of (pants) that <u>may be worn casually by either men or women</u>, are <u>made of heavy denim</u>, and usually <u>have double-stitched seams and pockets</u>.

C-402 *Seat belts* are <u>safety</u> (devices) that are <u>used to strap a person into a seat</u>, such as those in an airplane, automobile, or amusement-park ride.

C-403 A *rose* is a (flower) that is <u>known for its fragrance</u>, its <u>delicacy</u>, and its <u>thorns</u>.

C-404   A *postage stamp* is a <u>small</u>, <u>rectangular</u> (piece of paper) that is <u>attached to letters or packages to tell that the sender has paid the amount shown to have the item delivered to the addressee</u>.

C-405   An *automobile* is a <u>four-wheeled</u> (vehicle) <u>powered by a gasoline engine</u> and <u>driven by one person using a steering wheel, a brake, and a gas pedal</u>.

C-406   *Resentment* is a (feeling) <u>of anger or displeasure</u> that is <u>the result of a specific action</u>.

C-407   A *dollar bill* is a type of <u>United States</u> (currency) <u>printed on 2 1/2" by 6" paper</u>, <u>worth 100 cents</u>, and <u>used as a medium of exchange</u>.

C-408   *Education* is the (process) of <u>training skills or gaining information by practice and instruction</u>.

C-409   *Lettuce* is a (vegetable) <u>commonly used in salads</u> and <u>identified by its edible green leaves</u>.

C-410   A *sister* is a <u>female</u> (sibling) with <u>the same mother and father as another child in the family</u>.

C-411   A *calculator* is an <u>electronic</u> (device), <u>commonly small enough to hold in your hand</u> and <u>battery or solar operated</u>, <u>used to perform mathematical operations</u>.

FOLLOW-UP REFERENT

When might you need to recognize or provide a complete definition that contains both identifying class and distinguishing characteristics?

Examples: finding items in a supermarket, hardware store, mall directory, telephone book yellow pages, or classified ads; answering identification or definition questions on essay tests; using the Dewey Decimal System to locate sources in a library; locating related topics in books, reference sources, or card catalogs; differentiating among tools or utensils for specific jobs; writing job descriptions; providing written specifications for a blueprint; providing accurate descriptions of vehicles, people, or events in case of an accident or a crime; organizing an office or business operation, e.g., storage facilities or a production line

CURRICULUM APPLICATION

Language Arts: recognizing and using proper form when defining nouns, i.e., stating the word, the general class, and the characteristics that distinguish the word within that class; organizing, recognizing, and writing descriptive paragraphs; organizing topic or passage outlines

Mathematics: using cue words to determine correct operations for solving word problems; recognizing and using set theory

Science: describing phyla; identifying natural objects in the same manner as nouns, e.g., name, general class, distinguishing characteristics; establishing research procedures; stating an experimental hypothesis

Social Studies: defining social studies terms or identifying people, events, artifacts, groups, or eras; recognizing specific examples of general social science categories, e.g., geography includes the study of maps, physical features, climates, and natural resources

Enrichment Areas: classifying music according to type and characteristics, art by style and characteristics, and dance by type and characteristics; describing architectural styles or recognizing styles from descriptions

VERBAL ANALOGIES

ANTONYM OR SYNONYM ANALOGIES—SELECT

STRAND: Verbal Analogies

PAGES: 320–321

ADDITIONAL MATERIALS
Transparency of TM #25, top section
Washable transparency marker

INTRODUCTION
In previous lessons you examined how words were alike and how they were different, arranged words into various sequential orders, and separated words into classes.

OBJECTIVE
In these exercises you will apply all of those skills to determining the relationship between a given pair of words. Then you will choose a word that is related to a third word in the same way. These similarly related word pairs are referred to as an analogy. In this particular lesson, all word pairs will have either an antonym or synonym relationship.

DEMONSTRATION / EXPLANATION
Project the **EXAMPLE** analogy from the top section of the transparency of TM #25.
Who remembers how to read an analogy? How would you read this one?
Answer: "COMPLEX is to SIMPLE as EXTRAORDINARY is to _blank_." Project the sentence from the transparency to confirm students' answer.
You complete analogies by determining the relationship between the given pair of words, then applying that relationship to the second pair of words. Each pair of words must be related in the same way. This lesson concerns only two types of analogies. Each word pair must have either a synonym relationship, that is, the two words must mean the same thing; or they must have an antonym relationship, that is, the two words must be opposite in meaning.
Project the analogy form statements from the transparency, indicating the appropriate form as you talk.
These analogies will take the form of "word is to synonym as word is to synonym" or "word is to antonym as word is to antonym." In the example, the given word pair is COMPLEX and SIMPLE. How is COMPLEX related to SIMPLE?
Answer: COMPLEX is an antonym for (the opposite of) SIMPLE. Project the Relationship 1 statement from the transparency.
Look at the answer choices you have, and think about which answer is related to EXTRAORDINARY in the same way.
Project the Relationship 2 statement.
You need a word that will correctly complete the statement, "EXTRAORDINARY is an antonym for _blank_." Try each answer choice, starting with AVERAGE. Is EXTRAORDINARY an antonym for AVERAGE?
Answer: Possibly, but there might be a better answer. Encourage students to examine the other choices before they accept any choice as an answer.
Now try FANCY. Is EXTRAORDINARY an antonym for FANCY?
Answer: No, EXTRAORDINARY and FANCY have similar meanings ("not normal"), although they may differ in degree.
Now try WORTHY. Is EXTRAORDINARY an antonym for WORTHY?

263

Answer: No, a worthy person is frequently a person of outstanding importance or significance; in other words, someone who is extraordinary.

Which word choice, then, is most nearly an opposite to EXTRAORDINARY?

Answer: AVERAGE is most nearly opposite EXTRAORDINARY. Write AVERAGE in the answer blank, then project the next analogy example from the transparency.

How would you read this analogy?

Answer: "GORGEOUS is to STUNNING as CLUMSY is to blank ."

What relationship do you see between the word pair GORGEOUS and STUNNING?

Answer: GORGEOUS is a synonym for STUNNING.

Which word in the choice column completes the analogy? Which comes closest to correctly completing the sentence, "CLUMSY is a synonym for blank"?

Allow time for individual decision making. Answer: CLUMSY is a synonym for AWKWARD.

Why doesn't ELEGANT complete the synonym analogy?

Answer: ELEGANT is closer to a synonym for GORGEOUS. It refers to tastefulness of dress or behavior, rather than grace or skill.

Why doesn't GRACEFUL complete the synonym analogy?

Answer: GRACEFUL is an antonym for CLUMSY. It would show an antonym, rather than a synonym, relationship.

GUIDED PRACTICE
EXERCISES: **D-1, D-2, D-3**
Give students sufficient time to complete these exercises. Then, using the demonstration methodology above, have them discuss and explain their choices.
ANSWERS:

D-1   *cautious : careful :: daring :* reckless (S)

D-2   *import : export :: interior :* exterior (A)

D-3   *conceive : invent :: manufacture :* produce (S)

INDEPENDENT PRACTICE
Assign exercises **D-4** through **D-17**.

DISCUSSION TIPS
After students have completed the exercises independently, assign them to small groups to consider and discuss each individual exercise, then conduct a total-group discussion. Encourage students to discuss and defend their answer for each exercise by stating the relationship shown in each word pair and explaining why the other answer choices do not complete the analogy. Class discussion of similarities and differences between words can be fun and interesting if students present their varying points of view.

As an extending activity, ask students to create their own analogies which would make each unchosen answer correct. For example, alternate analogies for exercise **D-1** might include *reckless : cautious :: daring :* timid (A), or *daring : reckless :: cautious :* timid (S), or *daring : careful :: reckless :* watchful (A), or *reckless : daring :: careful :* watchful (S).

ANSWERS

D-4   *fore : front :: hind :* rear (S)

D-5   *excess : surplus :: lack :* shortage (S)

D-6   *essential : required :: unnecessary :* needless (S)

D-7   *important : significant :: minor :* trivial (S)

D-8   *safety : security :: danger :* _peril_ (S)

D-9   *construct : build :: function :* _operate_ (S)

D-10   *prospect : expectation :: reality :* _fact_ (S)

D-11   *explore : search :: locate :* _discover_ (S)

D-12   *compose : create :: destroy :* _wreck_ (S)

D-13   *enroll : enlist :: resign :* _quit_ (S)

D-14   *include : exclude :: superior :* _inferior_ (A)

D-15   *front : anterior :: rear :* _posterior_ (S)

D-16   *frontier : border :: interior :* _heartland_ (S)

D-17   *frugal : thrifty :: extravagant :* _wasteful_ (S)

FOLLOW-UP REFERENT

When might it be helpful to recognize and duplicate an antonym or synonym relationship in an analogous form?

Examples: explaining family relationships; teaching someone to use a tool or construct a model; recognizing different items that can be used for similar purposes or functions; explaining or understanding something new by relating it to something known

CURRICULUM APPLICATION

Language Arts: recognizing and using word analogies; using context clues to infer meaning of unfamiliar words; using paraphrasing skills; identifying and stating the relationship shown by pairs or groups of words, sentences, passages, or selections; recognizing analogous relationships used in literary images, metaphors, or similes; using analogies to develop compare-contrast writing; recognizing, interpreting, and stating analogous relationships in literature, e.g., symbolism, relationships between or among characters, relationship between mood and setting

Mathematics: changing numerical information to graphic or verbal information and vice versa; recognizing and using part-to-whole analogies in measurements of time, weight, size, or volume; identifying analogous relationships between fractional parts and fractions; stating numerical ratios; using analogies to compare statistics

Science: comparing members of the plant or animal kingdoms; conducting and reporting the results of laboratory experiments; understanding or comparing various uses of chemical elements, laboratory instruments, or measuring devices

Social Studies: recognizing historic, geographic, or cultural parallels; comparing or contrasting societies, behaviors, events, people, or governments

Enrichment Areas: recognizing and using comparative note values in music; comparing styles in music, art, dance, or drama; comparing individual or team statistics in sports

ANTONYM OR SYNONYM ANALOGIES—SELECT MORE THAN ONCE

STRAND: Verbal Analogies   **PAGES:** 322–325

ADDITIONAL MATERIALS

Transparencies of student workbook pages 322 and 325

Washable transparency marker

Dampened cloth to use as transparency eraser

INTRODUCTION

In the previous lesson you determined the relationship between a pair of words, then selected the correct word to complete an antonym or synonym analogy.

OBJECTIVE

Although these exercises are similar in that they also concern antonym or synonym analogies, they ask you to think of several different ways the same word can be used and defined.

DEMONSTRATION / EXPLANATION

Project the instructions and exercise **D-18** from the transparency of page 322.

What differences do you see between this exercise and those you did in the previous lesson?

Possible answers: No choice column is provided for individual exercises; a **CHOICE BOX** is shown above the exercise.

How is this exercise similar to those in the last lesson?

Possible answers: The first three words are given in the analogy; the first word pair is complete; the second word in the last word pair is the unknown; each blank has three possible answer choices; each analogy shows either an antonym or synonym relationship between the words in each pair.

How would you read the partial analogy in exercise D-18?

Answer: "REACH is to ARRIVE as EXIT is to blank ."

What is the first step in completing an analogy?

Answer: Determine the relationship between the given or complete word pair.

What relationship—antonym or synonym—do you see between the word pair REACH and ARRIVE?

Allow time for class discussion and student decision making. The most common answer is that the words have a synonym relationship, with both meaning "to get to a destination."

What word in the CHOICE BOX can you use to complete the analogy and why?

Answer: LEAVE; EXIT is a synonym for LEAVE, just as REACH is a synonym for ARRIVE. Write the choice on the transparency, then ask students to defend their answer by telling why the unchosen words would be less correct.

Remove the transparency from the projector, then project the top section, including the **EXAMPLE**, from the transparency of page 325.

These exercises also concern antonym and synonym analogies, except that this time you will need two words to complete each analogy. What words from the CHOICE BOX were chosen to complete the EXAMPLE analogy, what type of analogy have they created, and why were those two words chosen?

Answers: COMPLETELY and NEARLY were chosen to complete the synonym analogy. Each is a synonym for the given word in its word pair.

Project exercise **D-55**.

Which word in the CHOICE BOX could you use as a synonym or antonym for the first given word in D-55?

Allow adequate time for covert thinking, then ask for choices. Students should always be asked to explain why they chose a particular word over the other possibilities. Possible answers: COMPLETELY might be used as a synonym; SCARCELY might be used as an antonym. Underline each chosen word in the **CHOICE BOX**, then write COMPLETELY in the first answer blank on the transparency.

If you use the word COMPLETELY as the second word in the first pair, what relationship does that word pair have?

Answer: DEFINITELY is a synonym for COMPLETELY.

What word in the CHOICE BOX could you now use to complete the second word pair and the analogy?

Answer: SOMEWHAT is closest to a synonym for NEARLY. Write NEARLY in the second answer blank.

How would you read the completed analogy?

Answer: "DEFINITELY is to COMPLETELY as SOMEWHAT is to NEARLY."

Does each word pair in the analogy have the same relationship?

Answer: Yes, each word in the pair is a synonym for the other word.

So, the analogy is complete.

Erase the answer from **D-55** on the transparency, then write SCARCELY in the first answer blank and COMPLETELY in the second.

What happens to the analogy when I do this?

Allow time for class discussion. Students should realize that the analogy is still complete, but that an antonym relationship now exists between the words in each pair rather than a synonym relationship.

Some exercises in this section have more than one correct answer, depending upon how you choose to complete the first pair of each analogy. As long as the second word pair completes the analogy by showing the same relationship as the first pair, the answer is correct.

GUIDED PRACTICE
EXERCISES: **D-19, D-20; D-56, D-57**
Give students sufficient time to complete these exercises. Then, using the demonstration methodology above, have them discuss and explain their choices.

*NOTE: Synonym answers are given for **D-56** and **D-57**. Antonym analogies may be written by reversing the words between the two answer blanks.*

ANSWERS:

D-19   *pursue : follow :: guide :* <u>lead</u> (S)

D-20   *place : set :: remove :* <u>take</u> (S)

D-56   *exactly :* <u>completely</u> *:: almost :* <u>nearly</u> (S)

D-57   *exceedingly :* <u>completely</u> *:: moderately :* <u>usually</u> (S)

INDEPENDENT PRACTICE
Assign exercises **D-21** through **D-54** and **D-58** through **D-67**. These exercises may easily be divided into two assignments.

DISCUSSION TIPS
This makes an excellent small-group discussion and decision-making lesson. When the smaller groups have considered, discussed, and determined their answer for each exercise, conduct a total-group discussion. Maintain a nonjudgmental environment to encourage voluntary student participation. Such discussions of the similarities and differences between words can be fun and interesting if students present their varying points of view. Encourage them to discuss and defend their answers for each exercise by stating the relationship shown in each word pair and explaining why the other answer choices do not complete the analogy.

ANSWERS

D-21   *permit : allow :: control :* lead (S)

D-22   *join : unite :: detach :* leave (S)

D-23   *enroll : join :: resign :* leave (S)

D-24   *govern : manage :: direct :* lead (S)

D-25   *trace : track :: guide :* lead (S)

D-26   *present : confer :: acquire :* take (S)

D-27   *achieve : attain :: abandon :* leave (S)

D-29   *there : here :: forth :* back (A)

D-30   *former : before :: latter :* after (S)

D-31   *forward : backward :: future :* past (A)

D-32   *present : here :: past :* back (S)

D-33   *former : latter :: before :* after (A)

D-34   *forward : present :: backward :* past (S)

D-35   *forward : backward :: forth :* back (A)

D-36   *here : there :: near :* far (A)

D-37   *forward : forth :: backward :* back (S)

D-38   *first : last :: front :* back (A)

D-39   *despise : detest :: cherish :* value (S)

D-40   *confess : admit :: forgive :* pardon (S)

D-41   *approve : decline :: agree :* reject (A)

D-42   *question : approve :: doubt :* accept (A)

D-43   *resist : oppose :: acknowledge :* accept (S)

D-44   *scorn : appreciate :: degrade :* value (A)

D-45   *trust : suspect :: believe :* reject (A)

D-46   *exclude : eliminate :: include :* accept (S)

D-47   *authorization : permission :: assessment :* value (S)

D-48   *sentence : excuse :: condemn :* pardon (A)

D-49   *reserve : discard :: retain :* reject (A)

D-50   *ideal : perfection :: esteem :* value (S)

D-51   *deny : admit :: refuse :* accept (A)

D-52   *store : deposit :: rid :* reject (S)

D-53   *appreciation : gratitude :: merit :* value (S)

D-54   *choose : select :: decline :* reject (S)

---

*NOTE: Synonym answers are given for **D-58** through **D-67**. Antonym analogies may be written by reversing the words between the two answer blanks.*

D-58   *perfectly :* completely *:: partly :* nearly (S)

D-59   *extremely :* completely *:: barely :* scarcely (S)

D-60   *rarely :* scarcely *:: frequently :* usually (S)

D-61   *thoroughly :* completely *:: hardly :* scarcely (S)

D-62   *totally :* <u>completely</u> *:: just :* <u>scarcely</u> (S)
D-63   *infrequently :* <u>scarcely</u> *:: often :* <u>usually</u> (S)
D-64   *definitely :* <u>completely</u> *:: commonly :* <u>usually</u> (S)
D-65   *commonly :* <u>usually</u> *:: seldom :* <u>scarcely</u> (S)
D-66   *finally :* <u>completely</u> *:: practically :* <u>nearly</u> (S)
D-67   *uniquely :* <u>scarcely</u> *:: often :* <u>usually</u> (S)

FOLLOW-UP REFERENT

When might it be helpful to recognize, duplicate, or create an antonym or synonym relationship in an analogous form?

Examples: explaining family relationships; teaching someone to use a tool or construct a model; recognizing different items that can be used for similar purposes or functions; explaining or understanding something new by relating it to something known

CURRICULUM APPLICATION

Language Arts: recognizing and using word analogies; using context clues to infer meaning of unfamiliar words; using paraphrasing skills; identifying and stating the relationship shown by pairs or groups of words, sentences, passages, or selections; recognizing analogous relationships used in literary images, metaphors, or similes; using analogies in compare-contrast writing; recognizing and stating analogous relationships in literature, e.g., interpreting symbolism, relationships between or among characters, relationship between mood and setting

Mathematics: changing numerical information to graphic or verbal information and vice versa; recognizing and using part-to-whole analogies in measurements of time, weight, size, or volume; identifying analogous relationships between fractional parts and fractions; stating numerical ratios; using analogies to compare statistics

Science: comparing members of the plant or animal kingdoms; conducting and reporting the results of laboratory experiments; understanding or comparing uses of chemical elements, laboratory instruments, or measuring devices; formulating hypotheses

Social Studies: recognizing and explaining historic, geographic, or cultural parallels

Enrichment Areas: recognizing and using comparative note values in music; comparing styles in music, art, dance, or drama; comparing individual or team statistics in sports

ASSOCIATION ANALOGIES—SELECT

STRAND: Verbal Analogies   **PAGES:** 326–328

ADDITIONAL MATERIALS
Transparency of TM #25, lower section
Washable transparency marker

INTRODUCTION

In the previous lessons you completed antonym and synonym analogies by determining the relationship between pairs of words.

OBJECTIVE

These exercises concern a different type of analogy. The word pairs in these analogies are related by a similar association.

DEMONSTRATION / EXPLANATION

Project the explanation and **EXAMPLE** analogy from the transparency of TM #25.

> *In association analogies you also look at the relationship between two pairs of words, but they are not related as synonyms or antonyms. As in the previous analogies, however, both word pairs must be related in the same way. How would you read this example analogy?*

Answer: "FLOUR is to BAKING as FABRIC is to blank ."

> *How are FLOUR and BAKING related?*

Answer: FLOUR is used (an ingredient) in most BAKING products. Project the Relationship 1 statement to confirm student answer.

> *Think about which of the answer choices is related to FABRIC in the same way. How do you know?*

Allow time for discussion and decision making. Answer: SEWING; the relationship is the same. FABRIC is used in most SEWING products.

> *Notice that the technique you used for antonym or synonym analogies also works for association analogies. If you write out the relationship shown by the given word pair, then you should be able to substitute the words from the second pair into the same statement.*

Project the statement for Relationship 2, indicating the substituted words.

> *Why do cloth or material not complete the analogy?*

Answer: Both cloth and material are synonyms for fabric; neither names a product made from fabric, nor can either be considered an ingredient of fabric.

Project the next analogy from the transparency.

> *How would you read this analogy, and how might you state the relationship between the terms in the given word pair?*

Answer: "BEACH is to DUNES as OCEAN is to blank ." The relationship might be stated as "A BEACH contains DUNES (sand whipped into piles by the wind)."

> *Which answer choice gives you that same relationship to OCEAN?*

Answer: WAVES; "An OCEAN contains WAVES (water whipped into peaks by the wind)."

> *Why can't you use SHIP or WATER to complete the analogy. An ocean also contains ships and water?*

NOTE: This should elicit some student responses, but it may take them awhile to put their reasons into words. Have patience.

Possible answers: The most direct relationship is that of wind-whipped particles that form peaks. Both DUNES and WAVES meet that definition. SHIPS are not a part of the ocean; they use the ocean. An ocean is made up of particles of WATER, of which waves are created. An analogous relationship for ocean–water would be beach–sand.

GUIDED PRACTICE

EXERCISES: **D-68, D-69, D-70**

Give students sufficient time to complete these exercises. Then, using the demonstration methodology above, have them discuss and explain their choices.

ANSWERS:

D-68   *scale : weight :: compass :* direction
   A *scale* is used to determine *weight*; a *compass* is used to determine *direction*.

D-69   *closet : clothes :: warehouse :* merchandise
   A *closet* is used to store *clothes*; a *warehouse* is used to store *merchandise*.

D-70   *garment : alteration :: house :* remodeling
   A *garment* is changed by *alteration*; a *house* is changed by *remodeling*.

INDEPENDENT PRACTICE
Assign exercises **D-71** through **D-92**.

DISCUSSION TIPS
Association analogies are difficult for many students because, unlike synonym or antonym analogies, the relationships change with each analogy. Although it is time consuming, insist that students state the relationship they used to complete each analogy and explain why the alternate answer choices are less correct. The elimination procedure may prove more difficult than the relationship statement for students to verbalize, especially if the teacher plays "devil's advocate." Since it greatly increases student understanding of analogous relationships and leads to more discriminating decision-making, however, it is an extremely important part of the discussion process. Accept alternative answers if students can explain the reasoning that led to their decision

Teachers frequently use analogies to relate new information to prior knowledge in most curriculum areas. Calling attention to such usage—and inviting students to draw analogies from their own experiences—will help transfer the skill into academic areas.

ANSWERS
D-71   *can : bottle :: shell :* <u>pod</u>
Can and *bottle* are types of containers; *shell* and *pod* are types of coverings.

D-72   *lake : reservoir :: river :* <u>canal</u>
A *reservoir* is a man-made *lake*; a *canal* is a man-made *river*.

D-73   *appetizer : dessert :: introduction :* <u>summary</u>
An *appetizer* precedes and a *dessert* follows the main part of a meal; an *introduction* precedes and a *summary* follows the main part of an oral or written presentation.

D-74   *speedometer : velocity :: thermometer :* <u>temperature</u>
A *speedometer* is used to measure *velocity*; a *thermometer* is used to measure *temperature*.

D-75   *product : multiply :: quotient :* <u>divide</u>
A *product* is the result when you *multiply*; a *quotient* is the result when you *divide*.

D-76   *plus : add :: less :* <u>minus</u>
Plus is a cue to use an *add* sign; *less* is a cue to use a *minus* sign.

D-77   *quotient : product :: difference :* <u>sum</u>
The *quotient* results from division, and the *product* results from multiplication (opposite operations); the *difference* results from subtraction, and the *sum* results from addition (opposite operations).

D-78   *times : multiply :: plus :* <u>add</u>
Times is a name for the sign used when you *multiply*; *plus* is a name for the sign used when you *add*.

D-79   *dividend : divide :: factor :* <u>multiply</u>
A *dividend* is a number in a problem you *divide*; a *factor* is a number in a problem you *multiply*.

D-80   *factor : product :: addend :* <u>sum</u>
You use a *factor* to determine a *product*; you use an *addend* to determine a *sum*.

D-81   *factor : dividend :: multiply :* <u>divide</u>
Factor is related to *dividend* in the same way as *multiply* is related to *divide*. Each word pair contains one word related to multiplication and one related to division.

D-82   *product : times :: difference :* _minus_
           Product is a cue word to use a *times* sign in an operation; *difference* is a cue word
           to use a *minus* sign in an operation

D-83   *factor : multiply :: addend :* _add_
           A *factor* is used to *multiply*; an *addend* is used to *add.*

D-84   *fawn : buck ::* colt *:* _stallion_
           A *fawn* and a *buck* have the relationship of young to adult male of the same
           species; *colt* and *stallion* have the same relationship.

D-85   *buck : ram ::* doe *:* _ewe_
           A *buck* and a *ram* have the relationship of adult male deer to adult male sheep;
           doe and *ewe* have the same development-gender-species relationship.

D-86   *ram : lamb ::* stallion *:* _colt_
           A *ram* and a *lamb* have the relationship of adult male to young of the same
           species; *stallion* and *colt* have the same relationship.

D-87   *stallion : mare ::* ram *:* _ewe_
           A *stallion* and a *mare* have the relationship of adult male to adult female of the
           same species; *ram* and *ewe* have the same relationship.

D-88   *mare : colt ::* doe *:* _fawn_
           A *mare* and a *colt* have the relationship of adult female to young of the same
           species; *doe* and *fawn* have the same relationship.

D-89   *fawn : lamb ::* doe *:* _ewe_
           A *fawn* and a *lamb* have the relationship of young deer to young sheep; *doe* and
           ewe are the only two choices that have the same development-species
           relationship, i.e., adult deer to adult sheep.

D-90   *doe : buck ::* ewe *:* _ram_
           A *doe* and a *buck* have the relationship of adult female to adult male of the same
           species; *ewe* and *ram* have the same relationship.

D-91   *mare : ewe ::* stallion *:* _ram_
           A *mare* and a *ewe* have the relationship of adult female horse to adult female
           sheep; *stallion* and *ram* show the same relationship on the male side.

D-92   *buck : stallion ::* fawn *:* _colt_ [OR doe *:* _ewe_ OR ram *:* _stallion_]
           A *buck* and a *stallion* have the relationship of adult male deer to adult male
           horse; *fawn* and *colt* have the closest similar relationship, i.e., young deer to
           young horse. [If the relationship between the first word pair is seen as adult-male-
           species to adult-male-different species, then either *doe : ewe* or *ram : stallion*
           may be acceptable completers.]

FOLLOW-UP REFERENT

   ***When might you need or want to recognize or duplicate a specific relationship
   between two items?***

Examples: explaining family relationships; teaching someone to use a tool or construct
a model; recognizing different items that can be used for similar purposes or functions;
relating new information to prior knowledge

CURRICULUM APPLICATION

Language Arts: recognizing and using word analogies; using context clues to infer
   meaning of unfamiliar words; using paraphrasing skills; identifying and stating
   relationships shown by pairs or groups of words, sentences, passages, or selections;

using analogies in compare-contrast writing; recognizing and stating analogous relationships in literature, e.g., interpreting symbolism, relationships between or among characters, relationship between setting and mood; establishing or identifying etymological relationships

Mathematics: changing numerical information to graphic or verbal information and vice versa; recognizing and using part-to-whole analogies in measurements of time, weight, size, or volume; identifying the relationship between fractional parts and fractions; interpreting, understanding, or comparing ratios

Science: comparing like relationships in the plant or animal kingdoms; developing and reporting on laboratory experiments; using analogous relationships to develop working hypotheses; establishing or identifying biological or chemical relationships

Social Studies: recognizing historic, geographic, or cultural parallels; using analogous situations to predict outcomes, changes, or future needs

Enrichment Areas: recognizing and using comparative note values in music; comparing styles in music, art, dance, or drama; comparing team or individual statistics in sports; using analogy to compare or contrast competitive performances

"KIND OF" AND "PART OF" ANALOGIES—SELECT

STRAND: Verbal Analogies

PAGES: 329–331

ADDITIONAL MATERIALS
Transparency of TM #26
Washable transparency marker

INTRODUCTION
So far you have studied three specific types of analogies: antonym, synonym, and association. You have also learned that analogies must contain two word pairs that share a common relationship.

OBJECTIVE
In this lesson you will study two other specific relationships that can be expressed as analogies. These analogy types—"kind of" and "part of"—require you to use skills you learned in the sequencing and classification sections.

DEMONSTRATION/EXPLANATION
Project the "kind of" definition from the top of the transparency of TM #26.
Remember how you distinguished between a class and its members? You learned to apply "kind of" statements to determine which items named the members and which named the class. For example, if you were given a group of items like dog, cat, animal, and dinosaur, you would ask, "Is a dog a kind of cat? A kind of animal? A kind of dinosaur?" When the answer was affirmative, you used the same technique to confirm each member of the class. You can also use this method to analyze and complete "kind of" analogies.
Read the definition from the transparency, then project analogy 1.
How would you read this incomplete analogy?
Answer: "MALLARD is to DUCK as TABBY is to _blank_."

Using the class-subclass statement, how would you explain the relationship between the words in the first word pair?

Answer: "A MALLARD is a kind of DUCK." Project the first relationship statement to confirm the answer.

What is the next step in completing this analogy?

Answer: See which answer choice shows the same relationship to the given word in the second word pair by substituting the second word pair into the relationship statement.

How would you phrase the relationship statement for the second word pair?

Answer: "A TABBY is a kind of _blank_."

Which word choice best completes the analogy?

Allow time for student discussion and decision-making before accepting a final answer. Write the answer in the blank.

Why won't either of the other choices provide a closer analogy?

Listen to student rationale, questioning individuals who make statements that are too general or that show faulty reasoning. If students fail to mention it, point out that a TABBY is also a kind of ANIMAL, but that the relationship shown by the first word pair is species–family, as is the relationship between tabby and cat. The tabby–animal relationship, on the other hand, is a breed–kingdom relationship.

Project analogy 2 from the transparency.

How would you complete this analogy?

Allow ample time for discussion, then write the answer choice in the blank. Ask students to confirm the answer by following the steps demonstrated above. Answer: METAL.

Why doesn't either of the other choices fit the analogy better?

Answer: Although GOLD may be a part of JEWELRY, it is not a kind of jewelry. (A pin or a ring would be a kind of jewelry.) SILVER, like gold, is a member of the class METAL.

Project the "part of" definition and read it from the transparency.

How can you distinguish between a "kind of" and a "part of" analogy?

Allow time for discussion and distinctions. You may wish to list the differences students state in two columns on the chalkboard.

Project analogy 3 from the transparency.

Who can read this analogy and make a relationship statement about the words in the first pair?

Answer: "NOSE is to FACE as FINGER is to _blank_." A NOSE is part of a FACE.

Which word in the CHOICE COLUMN would you use to complete the analogy, and why would you use it?

Answer: HAND; a FINGER is part of a HAND, so the relationship is the same as that in the first word pair.

Why are the other choices less precise or less correct?

Answer: TOE is part of a foot, not a hand; it is a digit of the foot like a finger is a digit of the hand. A KNUCKLE is a joint of a finger or toe. It also has a part-whole relationship to finger, but it is not in the given order of the analogy. A FINGER is not part of a KNUCKLE.

Project analogy 4 from the transparency.

How would you complete this analogy?

Allow time for class discussion and group decision making, then write the chosen answer in the answer blank.

Let's test your answer. Does the same relationship exist between the words in each word pair? State the relationship.

If students have chosen an incorrect answer, let them discover it at this point and choose another word to complete the analogy. Continue testing the answers until the same relationship can be stated, i.e., "A SENATE is part of a LEGISLATURE and a SUPREME COURT is part of a JUDICIARY."

> *Now confirm your answer by eliminating the alternate choices.*

Answer: A SUPREME COURT is not part of a JUDGE (although if the terms were reversed the analogy would be true, i.e., a JUDGE is part of a SUPREME COURT). A STATE COURT is another member of the class JUDICIARY.

Project analogy 5 from the transparency.

> *This is an example of another type of exercise you will do in this lesson. Notice that you do not need to complete this analogy; you are given both word pairs. What analogy type is this?*

Answer: It is an example of a "part of" analogy. A JACKET is part of a BOOK as an ENVELOPE is part of a LETTER.

> *You do, however, have a CHOICE COLUMN. The words you have to choose from all name general parts of things. Which of the answer choices best names the specific "part of" relationship shown in this analogy?*

Answer: COVERING.

> *Check your answer by substituting the chosen relationship for "part of" in the relationship statement. Is a jacket a CENTER of a book? A COVERING for a book? An EDGE of a book?*

Answer: A jacket is a covering for a book.

> *Does the same specific relationship work for the other word pair?*

Answer: Yes; an envelope is a covering for a letter.

> *Remember as you do these analogy exercises to develop relationship statements. Keep the analogy words in order as you state the relationships.*

GUIDED PRACTICE
EXERCISES: **D-93; D-100; D-107, D-108**

Give students sufficient time to complete these exercises. Then, using the demonstration methodology above, have them discuss and explain their choices.

ANSWERS:

D-93   *oxygen : gas :: water :* _liquid_
Oxygen is a kind of *gas*; *water* is a kind of *liquid*.
[Although water can be used to produce fuel and can be broken down to produce hydrogen, which is a kind of fuel, water itself is not a kind of fuel. Water is a kind of compound, not a kind of mixture.]

D-100   *tuner : television set :: valve :* _pipeline_
[*Dial* and *gauge* are related to each other in the same way as the other two word pairs; neither can be used to complete the original analogy.]

D-107   *plaster : wall :: varnish : furniture* covering
[*Plaster* covers *walls* as *varnish* covers *furniture*.]

D-108   *fringe : shawl; :: hem : skirt* edge
[*Fringe* is at the edge of a *shawl* as *hem* is at the edge of a *skirt*.]

INDEPENDENT PRACTICE
Assign exercises **D-94** through **D-99**, **D-101** through **D-106**, and **D-109** through **D-122**.

NOTE: These exercises may easily be divided into two or three assignments if students find it difficult to distinguish between the types of analogy or if it is too lengthy.

DISCUSSION TIPS

Analogies invite students to compare similarities between two things that are not the same. As such, they are often confusing. Make sure the students understand the vocabulary. Group discussion and decision making are especially valuable in expanding vocabulary and in adding to the general knowledge of the students. Encourage alternative answers, but require students to defend their analysis of the exercise and the reasoning behind their choice.

Encourage students to use the process of elimination to narrow their answer choices and to express each relationship in the form of a statement. Stress that they should maintain the original word order when substituting words from the incomplete word pair into any relationship statement.

ANSWERS

D-94 *iron : metal :: granite :* _rock_
Iron is a kind of *metal*; *granite* is a kind of *rock*.
[Granite is *made of* atoms, not a *kind of* atom. Decomposed granite may *be a part of* soil, but granite is not a *kind of* soil.]

D-95 *zucchini : squash :: cantaloupe :* _melon_
Zucchini is a kind of *squash*; *cantaloupe* is a kind of *melon*.
[Although it is true that cantaloupe is a kind of fruit, melon is closer to expressing the relationship shown by zucchini-squash. A cantaloupe *grows from* a seed and a cantaloupe *produces* seeds, but it is not a *kind of* seed.]

D-96 *tissue : paper :: silk :* _fabric_
Tissue is a kind of *paper*; *silk* is a kind of *fabric*.
[Silk is a kind of dress *fabric*, not a kind of dress. Silk is not a kind of synthetic; it is a natural fabric.]

D-97 *ballpoint : pen :: watercolors :* _paint_
Ballpoint is a kind of *pen*; *watercolors* are a kind of *paint*.
[Watercolors cannot be considered as either a kind of clay or a kind of crayons.]

D-98 *dictionary : reference book :: magazine :* _periodical_
A *dictionary* is a kind of *reference book*; a *magazine* is a kind of *periodical*.
[Newspaper is another kind of periodical, not an example of a magazine. Most periodicals are identified by issue number.]

D-99 *movement : activity :: depression :* _mood_
Movement is a kind of *activity*; *depression* is a kind of *mood*.
[Depression is neither a kind of effort nor a kind of noise.]

D-101 *brim : hat :: bill :* _cap_
[*Cuff* and *coat* are related to each other in the same way as the other two word pairs; neither can be used to complete the original analogy.]

D-102 *eyelid : eye :: shutter :* _camera_
[*Nerve* and *film* name additional parts of the eye and camera respectively; neither can be used to complete the original analogy.]

D-103 *officer : army :: manager :* _company_
[*Employees* and *stockholder* name additional parts of a company; neither can be used to complete the original analogy.]

D-104 *ribs : chest :: rafters :* _roof_
[*Beams* and *joists* name additional parts that, like rafters, support the roof; neither can be used to complete the original analogy.]

D-105   *lapel : jacket :: collar :* <u>shirt</u>
[*Tie* and *apron* are related to each other in the same way as the other two word pairs; neither can be used to complete the original analogy.]

D-106   *film : camera :: magnetic tape :* <u>cassette recorder</u>
[*Projector* and *record player* name other audio-visual equipment, but neither utilizes magnetic tape as a storage-retrieval system and therefore cannot be used to complete the original analogy.]

D-109   *crust : pie :: shell : taco*   <u>covering</u>
[*Crust* covers *pie* as *shell* covers *taco.*]

D-110   *perimeter : rectangle :: circumference : circle*   <u>edge</u>
[*Perimeter* is the length of the outside edge of a *rectangle* as *circumference* is the length of the outside edge of a *circle.*]

D-111   *axis : earth :: diameter : circle*   <u>center</u>
[The *axis* runs through the center of the *earth* as the *diameter* runs through the center of a *circle.*]

D-112   *shoulder : road :: rim : tire*   <u>edge</u>
[A *shoulder* is the edge of a *road* as a *rim* is the edge of a *tire.*]

D-113   *peel : orange :: pod : pea*   <u>covering</u>
[A *peel* is the covering of an *orange* as a *pod* is the covering of a *pea.*]

D-114   *cob : corn :: core : apple*   <u>center</u>
[A *cob* is in the center of an ear of *corn* as a *core* is in the center of an *apple.*]

D-115   *lip : bottle :: rim : cup*   <u>edge</u>
[A *lip* is the outside edge of a *bottle* opening as a *rim* is the outside edge of a *cup* opening.]

D-116   *railing : stair :: fence : field*   <u>edge</u>
[A *railing* is found at the edge of *stairs* as a *fence* is found at the edge of a *field.*]

D-117   *upholstery : furniture :: pillowcase : pillow*   <u>covering</u>
[*Upholstery* covers *furniture* as a *pillowcase* covers a *pillow.*]

D-118   *nucleus : atom :: sun : solar system*   <u>center</u>
[The *nucleus* is the center of an *atom* as the *sun* is the center of the *solar system.*]

D-119   *border : country :: coast : continent*   <u>edge</u>
[A *border* is the edge of a *country* as a *coast* is the edge of a *continent.*]

D-120   *median : road :: bisector : line*   <u>center</u>
[A *median* marks the center of a *road* as a *bisector* marks the center of a *line.*]

D-121   *coat : person :: blanket : horse*   <u>covering</u>
[A *coat* covers a *person* as a *blanket* covers a *horse.*]

D-122   *eye : hurricane :: crater : volcano*   <u>center</u>
[The *eye* is the center of a *hurricane* as the *crater* is the center of a *volcano.*]

FOLLOW-UP REFERENT

When might it be helpful to recognize or complete a parallel comparison expressing "kind of" or "part of" relationships?

Examples: evaluating or developing arguments; recognizing the distinction between a part of something and a kind of something, e.g., tools, engines, fuels, constructions; relating new information to prior knowledge; recognizing parallel circumstances in social or business situations; recognizing or stating the relationships among military ranks, business titles or offices, and job descriptions

277

CURRICULUM APPLICATIONS

Language Arts: distinguishing between main ideas and supporting ideas in critical reading; drawing correct inferences from literary or etymological relationships; using context clues to infer word meaning; recognizing or identifying parallel construction and development in compositions; recognizing the effect of common prefixes or suffixes on root words

Mathematics: recognizing the relationship among fractional parts, fractions, decimals, and ratios; recognizing or verbalizing figural parallels; using relationships to project probabilities; using ratio comparisons in statistics

Science: recognizing or constructing logical arguments or hypotheses; using analogies to illustrate class-subclass or part-whole relationships within the plant or animal kingdoms; using analogous characteristics to classify stars, galaxies, rocks, minerals, plants, or animals; using knowledge of use or parts to classify archaeological finds; distinguishing among compounds, mixtures, elements, rocks, and minerals

Social Studies: recognizing or illustrating parallel developments in governments, societies, economics, or politics; recognizing parallel effects of geography on the development of specific world areas; recognizing the distinction between supporting statements that are examples of a concept and statements that list components of a concept; using analogous relationships to draw conclusions from anthropological discoveries; using analogous relationships to distinguish among economic terms

Enrichment Areas: recognizing the parallel effects of social, political, geographic, and cultural changes on the arts and entertainments of an era or a country; distinguishing between a style representative of a school of dance or art and a component of the particular dance or work of art

"USED TO"/ACTION/"DEGREE OF" ANALOGIES—SELECT

STRAND: Verbal Analogies   **PAGES:** 332–335

ADDITIONAL MATERIALS
Transparency of TM #27
Washable transparency marker

INTRODUCTION
In previous lessons you completed several different types of analogies, including antonym, synonym, association, kind of, and part of relationships.

OBJECTIVE
The exercises in this lesson will introduce you to three additional types of relationships that can be expressed as analogies. These analogy types are referred to as "used to," action, and "degree of" analogies.

DEMONSTRATION/EXPLANATION
Project the transparency of TM #27.
> *"Used to" analogies involve noun–verb relationships and must be in the form of "A (noun) is used to B (verb) as C (noun) is used to D (verb)." Look at EXAMPLE 1 on the screen. How would you read the analogy?*

Answer: "CALCULATOR is to COMPUTE as PEN is to WRITE."

How could you make a relationship statement from the first word pair in this analogy?

Answer: "A CALCULATOR is used to COMPUTE."

Can you substitute the second word pair for the first in the relationship statement?

Answer: Yes; "A PEN is used to WRITE." Project the two relationship statements to confirm the answers, then indicate **EXAMPLE 2.**

Read this analogy as it is written, make a relationship statement for the first word pair, then substitute the words from the second pair to test the relationship.

Answer: "FICTION is to ENTERTAIN as FACT is to INFORM." The relationship statements would be "FICTION is used to ENTERTAIN" and "FACT is used to INFORM."

Action analogies also involve noun–verb relationships, but the "used to" relationship statement cannot be applied to the word pairs. The relationship is subject–action verb, as in example 3 on the transparency. These analogies are read like all the others.

Indicate the analogy parts from **EXAMPLE 3** as you read.

POSTMAN is to DELIVERS as ANNOUNCER is to BROADCASTS. How would you make a relationship statement from the first word pair in this analogy?

Answer: "A POSTMAN DELIVERS something."

Can you substitute the words from the second word pair into your relationship statement?

Answer: Yes; "an ANNOUNCER BROADCASTS something."

What do you notice about these relationship statements that is different from the other statements you have formed?

Allow time for student discussion and discovery. Answer: The given words in these statements follow each other rather than being separated by the relationship words.

Look back at EXAMPLE 2 on the transparency. We said that it was a "used to" analogy, yet it looks like an action analogy to me. "FICTION ENTERTAINS and FACT INFORMS." Isn't that an action analogy?

Allow students ample time to discuss this problem. Answer: To make it into an action analogy, the verb form had to be changed. One cannot say, for example, "FICTION ENTERTAIN." Since one cannot change the given words in an analogy, even by adding an —s, this cannot be an action analogy. The relationship must be stated as a "used to" relationship.

Read EXAMPLE 4, then make a relationship statement from the first word pair.

Answer: "SECRETARIES is to TYPE as ARTISTS is to DRAW." The relationship statement would be "SECRETARIES TYPE things," or "SECRETARIES TYPE."

Since you can substitute the second word pair for the first in the relationship statement—ARTISTS DRAW—you know that the relationship is true of both word pairs and that the two word pairs form an analogy.

Indicate the definition of "degree of" analogies on the transparency.

The final analogy type that you will identify in these exercises is known as a "degree of" analogy. You have used this relationship before in sequencing exercises. These word pairs have a direct relationship involving degree, rank, size, or order of the common characteristic. The relationship is either HIGHER : LOWER, MORE : LESS, LARGER : SMALLER, LATER : EARLIER (in order), or the reverse of these relationships. For example, look at EXAMPLE 5. The analogy reads, "MORNING is to AFTERNOON as APRIL is to OCTOBER." What relationship statement could you make about the first word pair? Remember that this is an example of a "degree of" analogy.

Answer: MORNING is earlier (in the day) than AFTERNOON (or MORNING comes before AFTERNOON).

Can you substitute APRIL for MORNING and OCTOBER for AFTERNOON in the relationship statement?

Answer: Yes, APRIL is earlier (in the year) than OCTOBER (or APRIL comes before OCTOBER).

Since the second word pair can be substituted; it has the same relationship. Read the analogy in EXAMPLE 6, make a relationship statement from one word pair, then substitute the other pair into the statement to test the relationship you found. Since you are given all the words in this analogy, it doesn't matter which word pair you use to form the relationship statement.

Answer: "PINT is to QUART as INCH is to FOOT." "A PINT is less than a QUART." "An INCH is less than a FOOT."

Project analogies **A** through **C** from the bottom of the transparency.

These are examples of the three analogy types we have just discussed. Determine the type of each analogy, form a relationship statement from the given pair, then choose the answer that best completes each analogy. Test your answer choice by substituting the new word pair into the relationship statement. Notice that the position of the unknown word changes in each analogy, so be careful how you form your relationship statements.

Provide ample time for the students to complete the analogies, then discuss each one using the techniques demonstrated above. Always ask students to tell why the unchosen answer choices are not as appropriate or not correct. The answers given below include analogy type, relationship statements, and rationale for eliminating unchosen answers.

A   *surgeon : operates :: mechanic : _repairs_* (Action)

A SURGEON OPERATES and a MECHANIC <u>REPAIRS</u>. Although a mechanic may cut things and remove things in the process of repairing, the primary task is to repair.

B   *bulldozer : _push_ :: crane : lift* (Used to)

A CRANE is used to LIFT and a BULLDOZER is used to <u>PUSH</u>. A bulldozer can stop, and it can be used to drive, but its primary task is to push earth or debris from one place to another.

C   *_warm_ : hot :: cool : cold* (Degree of)

COOL is a lesser degree of COLD and <u>WARM</u> is a lesser degree of HOT. Sizzling and flaming are both higher degrees of temperature and closer to being synonyms of hot.

GUIDED PRACTICE
EXERCISES: **D-123, D-124; D-139; D-146**
Give students sufficient time to complete these exercises. Then, using the demonstration methodology above, have them discuss and explain their choices.
ANSWERS:

D-123 *rudder : steer :: brake : _stop_*

D-124 *gauge : measure :: gear : _drive_*

D-139 *sheriff : arrests :: fugitive : _flees_*

D-146 *irritated : furious :: pleased : _overjoyed_* (**A** is a lesser degree of **B**)

INDEPENDENT PRACTICE
Assign exercises **D-125** through **D-138**, **D-140** through **D-145**, and **D-147** through **D-152**.

DISCUSSION TIPS
Analogies invite students to find similarities between two things that are not the same. As such, they are often confusing. Make sure the students understand the vocabulary. Group discussion and decision making are especially valuable for extending vocabulary development and adding to the students' general knowledge. Encourage them to use the process of elimination to narrow their answer choices and to express each relationship in the form of a statement. Stress that they should maintain the original word order when they substitute words from the incomplete word pair into a relationship statement.

Students may confuse "action" analogies with "used to" analogies. Remind them that the given words in each analogy cannot be changed in any way and that one purpose of making relationship statements is to see if they "sound right."

ANSWERS
D-125 *clamp : hold :: crank :* _turn_
D-126 *strap : bind :: hoist :* _lift_
D-127 *seal : close :: valve :* _stop_
D-128 *wrench : twist :: jack :* _lift_
D-129 *needle : pierce :: plug :* _stop_
D-130 *bolt : fasten :: shaft :* _turn_
D-131 *pipe : connect :: engine :* _drive_

D-132 *vault : safeguard :: gallery :* _exhibit_
D-133 *exclamation : emphasize :: statement :* _inform_
D-134 *falsehood : deceive :: evidence :* _prove_
D-135 *imagination : create :: reason :* _decide_
D-136 *stilts : elevate :: foundation :* _support_
D-137 *valve : regulate :: gauge :* _indicate_
D-138 *radar : locate :: lens :* _observe_

D-140 *pharmacist : dispenses :: librarian :* _circulates_
D-141 *dilemma : confuses :: solution :* _resolves_
D-142 *adjective : modifies :: conjunction :* _connects_
D-143 *dictator : rules :: conductor :* _directs_
D-144 *guard : protects :: signal :* _warns_
D-145 *flask : contains :: levee :* _protects_

D-147 *loudness : sound :: brightness :* _light_ (**A** is a high degree of **B**)
D-148 *dynamic : activity :: expert :* _ability_ (**A** reflects a high degree of **B**)
D-149 *timid : confidence :: lazy :* _motivation_ (**A** reflects a low degree of **B**)
D-150 *positive : certainty :: undeniable :* _proof_ (**A** is the highest degree of **B**)
D-151 *inaudible : blaring :: dim :* _glaring_ (**A** is much less than **B**, nearly opposite)
D-152 *emergency : urgency :: continuously :* _frequency_ (**A** is a high degree of **B**)

FOLLOW-UP REFERENT
When might it be helpful to recognize or complete a parallel comparison expressing action, "used to," or "degree of" relationships?
Examples: evaluating or developing arguments; recognizing the distinction between active and passive voice; relating new information to prior knowledge; recognizing parallel relationships in social or business situations; recognizing or stating the relationships among military ranks, business titles or offices, and job descriptions; choosing proper words when expressing degrees, orders, ranks, or sizes

CURRICULUM APPLICATIONS
Language Arts: distinguishing between active and passive voice in critical reading, compositions, and foreign languages; using context clues to infer word meaning; recognizing or identifying parallel construction and development in compositions

Mathematics: recognizing the relationship among mathematical tools and their purposes, especially in geometry; recognizing or verbalizing parallel changes in figural sequences; using analogous relationships to project probabilities; using ratio comparisons in statistics

Science: recognizing or constructing logical arguments or hypotheses; using analogies to illustrate comparative rank within the plant or animal kingdoms; using analogous characteristics to classify movements of stars, galaxies, or animals; using knowledge of use or development to classify archaeological finds

Social Studies: recognizing or illustrating parallel actions or degrees of change in governments, societies, economics, or politics; recognizing the distinction between active and passive causes of change in any area of social studies; using analogous relationships to draw conclusions from anthropological discoveries; using analogous relationships to distinguish among degrees of economic effect or change

Enrichment Areas: recognizing the parallel effects of social, political, and cultural actions on the arts and entertainments of an era or a country; distinguishing between action and purpose of tools and machinery, i.e., a screw machine turns (its action), but it is used to lift (its purpose), tools have no action of their own, but they have various uses

MIXED ANALOGIES—SELECT

STRAND: Verbal Analogies   **PAGES:** 336–337

ADDITIONAL MATERIALS
Transparency of student workbook page 336
Transparency of TM #28 (optional)
Washable transparency marker

INTRODUCTION
In previous lessons you examined eight different types of analogies, learning to identify and complete antonym, synonym, association, "kind of," "part of," "used to," "degree of," and action relationships expressed in analogy form.

OBJECTIVE
In these exercises you will distinguish among three types of relationships. You will also have to choose two words to complete each analogy.

DEMONSTRATION/EXPLANATION
Project the transparency of page 336.

Look at the EXAMPLE analogy. You will notice that these analogies have two blanks that need to be filled in, one in each word pair, and that the second word is missing in each pair. The instructions also tell you that each analogy you create must be one of three types: action, association, or synonym. How would you read this EXAMPLE analogy, and what relationship statement can you make from the first word pair?

Answer: "SPEECH is to <u>hear</u> as LETTER is to <u>read</u>." The relationship might be stated as "The object of a SPEECH is to <u>hear</u> what is being said."

Is it possible to substitute the words from the second word pair into your relationship statement?

Answer: Yes; "The object of a LETTER is to <u>read</u> what is being said."

What type of analogy has been created in this EXAMPLE?

Answer: Association; SPEECH is associated with <u>hear</u> in the same way as LETTER is associated with <u>read</u>.

Now look at exercise D-153. The first step to completing these exercises is to determine what kind of relationship it is possible to create. Do you see any relationship between the first given word in this exercise, WRITING, and the first word in the CHOICE BOX?

Answer: No, there is no apparent relationship between WRITING and HEAR.

What relationship, if any, do you see between the given word in the second word pair, SOUNDS, and the first answer choice?

Answer: SOUND is recognized because you HEAR it. There is an association between the two words.

Is there a word in the CHOICE BOX that is related to WRITING in the same way as HEAR is related to SOUNDS?

Answer: Yes, SEE. WRITING is recognized because you SEE it. Write the answers in the appropriate blanks.

Take time to look at the other answer choices. Other than SEE, which you have already paired with WRITING, do any of the other choices have any relationship with WRITING?

Answer: Yes, READ.

What relationship do you see between WRITING and READ?

Answer: The purpose of (some) WRITING is so that someone can READ it. The two words are associated.

Is there another answer choice that is related to SOUND in this same way?

Answer: Yes, HEAR. The purpose of (some) SOUND is so that someone can HEAR it.

Do these two answer choices work as well in completing the analogy? Is one set of answers better than the other?

Allow time for class discussion. Students should agree that either answer set will work equally well. The correctness of answers for these exercises should be judged by two criteria: 1) Do the answer choices represent parallel relationships? and 2) Are the analogies created representative of one of the three assigned types (action, association, or synonym).

NOTE: As an optional aid, you may wish to project the definitions of analogy types from TM #28 as a reference while students complete the assignments in this lesson.

GUIDED PRACTICE
EXERCISES: **D-154, D-155, D-156**
Give students sufficient time to complete these exercises. Then, using the demonstration methodology above, have them discuss and explain their choices.
ANSWERS:
D-154 *oral :* talk *:: visual :* see
[Association; One *talks* orally, and one *sees* visually.]

D-155 *glimpse :* see *:: skim :* read
[Synonym; Glimpse is a more specific term for *see*, and skim is a more specific term for *read*. Some students may see this as a "degree of" analogy. Remind them that that analogy type is not one of their choices.]

D-156 *stare :* see *:: chatter :* talk
[Synonym; Stare is a more specific term for *see*, and chatter is a more specific term for *talk*.]

INDEPENDENT PRACTICE
Assign exercises **D-157** through **D-180**.

DISCUSSION TIPS
Provide ample time for the students to determine the possible relationships and complete the analogies, then discuss each exercise using the techniques demonstrated above. Encourage alternate answers for the analogies, but make certain that students state the relationship and the reasoning they used to create the analogy.

ANSWERS
D-157 *correspondence :* read *:: conversation :* hear
[Association; One *reads* correspondence, and one *hears* conversation.]

D-158 *listeners :* hear *:: speakers :* talk
[Action; Listeners *hear*, and speakers *talk*.]

D-159 *television :* see *:: stereo :* hear
[Association; One *sees* television, and one *hears* stereo. Although a television may also be listened to (heard), its primary enjoyment comes from sight.]

D-160 *orator :* hear *:: dancer :* see
[Association; One *hears* an orator, and one *sees* a dancer.]

D-161 *debate :* hear *:: movie :* see
[Association; One *hears* a debate, and one *sees* a movie. Although a movie may also be listened to (heard), its primary enjoyment comes from sight.]

D-162 *lecture :* hear *:: encyclopedia :* read
[Association; One *hears* a lecture to gain knowledge, and one *reads* an encyclopedia for the same purpose.]

D-163 *observers :* see *:: editors :* read
[Action; Observers *see*, and editors *read*.]

D-164 *book :* read *:: recorded music :* hear
[Association; One *reads* a book, and one *hears* recorded music.]

D-165 *apparent :* seems *:: real :* is
[Synonym; Reversing the word choices will result in an antonym analogy.]

D-166 *get :* have *:: learn :* know
[Association; When you get something, you *have* it, and when you learn something, you *know* it.]

D-167 *realize :* know *:: obtain :* have
[Synonym]

D-168 *fact :* is *:: hint :* seems
[Synonym (or action); A fact *is*, and a hint *seems* to be. Reversing the word choices will result in an antonym analogy.]

D-169 *learning :* know *:: possession :* have
[Association; Through learning you *know* things, and through possession you *have* things.]

D-170 *object :* is *:: image :* seems
[Association (or action); An object *is* real, and an image *seems* real.]

D-171 *heirloom :* have *:: memory :* know (or seems)
[Association; One *has* an heirloom, and one *knows* (remembers) a memory.]

D-172 *forget :* know *:: lose :* have
[Antonym]

D-173 *keep :* have *:: remember :* know
[Synonym]

D-174 *proof :* is *:: theory :* seems
[Association; A proof *is* true, and a theory *seems* true.]

D-175 *wealthy :* have *:: wise :* know
[Association (or action); The wealthy *have* a lot, and the wise *know* a lot.]

D-176 *existence :* is *:: appearance :* seems
[Synonym (or action)]

D-177 *understand :* know *:: own :* have
[Synonym]

D-178 *person :* is *:: ghost :* seems
[Association (or action); A person *is* (exists), and a ghost *seems* (appears). See **D-176.**]

D-179 *collection :* have *:: education :* know
[Association; A collection enables one to *have* things, and an education enables one to *know* things.]

D-180 *genuine :* is *:: counterfeit :* seems
[Association; A genuine item *is* real, and a counterfeit item *seems* real.]

FOLLOW-UP REFERENT
When might you need or want to recognize or complete a specific relationship between two items?

Examples: explaining family relationships; teaching someone to use a tool or construct a model; recognizing different items that can be used for similar purposes or functions

CURRICULUM APPLICATION
Language Arts: recognizing and using word analogies; using context clues to infer meaning of unfamiliar words; using paraphrasing skills; identifying and stating the relationship shown by pairs or groups of words, sentences, passages, or selections; choosing words that indicate the exact desired relationship

Mathematics: changing numerical information to graphic or verbal information and vice versa; recognizing and using part-to-whole analogies in measurements of time, weight, size, or volume; identifying the relationship between fractional parts and fractions; using cue words when solving word problems

Science: comparing phyla of plants or animals; conducting laboratory experiments and writing reports on them; establishing sensible hypotheses

Social Studies: recognizing historic, geographic, or cultural parallels

Enrichment Areas: recognizing and using comparative note values in music; comparing styles in music, art, dance, or drama; comparing sports statistics or teams; recognizing and explaining parallels and contrasts in any area

ANALOGIES—EXPLAIN

STRAND: Verbal Analogies   **PAGES:** 338–341

ADDITIONAL MATERIALS
Transparency of student workbook page 338
Transparency of TM #28 (optional)

INTRODUCTION
In previous lessons you identified and completed eight kinds of analogies.

OBJECTIVE
In these exercises you are given complete analogies. You are to determine what type each analogy is an example of and explain your reasoning.

DEMONSTRATION/EXPLANATION
Project the transparency of page 338.
At the top of this transparency, you see a list of the eight different types of analogies you have studied. As you do these exercises, keep these types in mind to determine the relationships between the word pairs.
Indicate exercise **D-181.**
How would you read this analogy?
Answer: LACE is to TIE as BUTTON is to FASTEN.
Which of the analogy types listed at the top of the page seems to best identify the relationship between the first word pair in the analogy?
Answer: Probably "used to," possibly action, "kind of," or synonym.
Can you make a relationship statement using a "used to" relationship?
Answer: Yes; "A LACE is used to TIE."
What about an action statement, a "kind of" statement, or a synonym statement?
Answers: An action statement would have to be "A LACE TIES." Since ties is not the second word of the word pair, the relationship is not an action relationship. A "kind of" statement would be "A LACE is a kind of TIE." This relationship is still a possibility. LACE may also be used as a synonym for TIE (a cord used to fasten shoes), so a synonym statement would also be possible (A LACE is the same as a TIE.)

Now try substituting the words from the second pair into your relationship statements. Which relationship is true of both word pairs?

Answers: Used to—A BUTTON is used to FASTEN; Kind of—A BUTTON is a kind of FASTEN; Synonym—A BUTTON is the same as a FASTEN. Only the "used to" relationships works for both word pairs in the analogy without changing any of the words. Write USED TO on the answer line, then write the relationship sentences as explanation.

D-182 reads "BARREN is to VEGETATION as PARCHED is to MOISTURE. Which of the eight types of analogies best identifies the relationship in this analogy? How might BARREN and VEGETATION be related?

NOTE: *Make certain that students understand the vocabulary in each analogy before proceeding with analysis. Class discussion should be used to determine word meanings.*

Answers: The two words might have an antonym, association, or "degree of" relationship.

Try making statements using these different possible relationships.

Answers: Antonym—BARREN is the opposite of VEGETATION; Association—BARREN is the lack of VEGETATION; Degree of—BARREN is the lowest degree of VEGETATION. Of these three possible relationships, only antonym doesn't seem to work. The word barren cannot be substituted for the word vegetation, since barren in an adjective and vegetation is a noun.

Of the two possible relationships between BARREN and VEGETATION, which also can be applied to the word pair PARCHED and MOISTURE?

Answer: Degree of; since parched is not a "lack" of moisture, but rather the lowest degree of moisture. Write DEGREE OF and the relationship statements on the answer lines.

NOTE: *As an optional aid, you may wish to project the definitions of analogy types from TM #28 as a reference while students complete the assignments in this lesson.*

GUIDED PRACTICE
EXERCISES: **D-183, D-184, D-185**
Give students sufficient time to complete these exercises. Then, using the demonstration methodology above, have them discuss and explain their choices.
ANSWERS:

D-183 *crane : machinery :: bus : vehicle*
[KIND OF; A *crane* is a KIND OF *machinery*, and a *bus* is a KIND OF *vehicle*.]

D-184 *heart : blood :: pump : water*
[ASSOCIATION; A *heart* CIRCULATES *blood* and a *pump* CIRCULATES *water*. Both provide actions that circulate a fluid.]

D-185 *silk : worm :: honey : bee*
[ASSOCIATION; *Silk* IS PRODUCED BY *worms* as *honey* IS PRODUCED BY *bees*.]

ALTERNATE: [KIND OF; *Silk* is A KIND OF *worm* (silkworm) and *honey* is A KIND OF *bee* (honeybee).]

INDEPENDENT PRACTICE
Assign exercises **D-186** through **D-206**.

DISCUSSION TIPS
Encourage class discussion of each analogy, questioning students closely on the possible relationships between the words and the word pairs in each analogy. Some exercises have more than one possible relationship. Do not, however, let students confuse "association" analogies with the other types. Only those that cannot easily be categorized as any other relationship should be identified as association analogies.

ANSWERS

D-186 *always : occurrence :: doubtless : probability*
[DEGREE OF; *Always* is the HIGHEST DEGREE OF *occurrence* as *doubtless* is the HIGHEST DEGREE OF *probability*.]

D-187 *mask : costume :: vest : suit*
[PART OF; A *mask* is PART OF a *costume* as a *vest* is PART OF a *suit*.]

D-188 *right : privilege :: duty : responsibility*
[SYNONYM; *Right* MEANS THE SAME AS *privilege* and *duty* MEANS THE SAME AS *responsibility*.]

D-189 *know : understand :: ignore : overlook*
[ASSOCIATION; *Know* indicates INTENTIONALLY *understanding* in the same way as *ignore* indicates INTENTIONALLY *overlooking*.]

ALTERNATE: [SYNONYM; *Know* MEANS THE SAME AS *understand* and *ignore* MEANS THE SAME AS *overlook*.]

D-190 *bottle : contains :: sponge : absorbs*
[ACTION; A *bottle contains* (liquid) and a *sponge absorbs* (liquid).]

D-191 *rind : watermelon :: shell : peanut*
[PART OF; The *rind* is the OUTER PART OF a *watermelon* as the *shell* is the OUTER PART OF a *peanut*.]

D-192 *enamel : paint :: posterboard : paper*
[KIND OF; *Enamel* is a KIND OF *paint* as *posterboard* is a KIND OF *paper*.]

D-193 *ready : preparation :: alert : awareness*
[DEGREE OF; *Ready* is a HIGH DEGREE OF *preparation* as *alert* is a HIGH DEGREE OF *awareness*.]

D-194 *aspirin : medication :: cider : beverage*
[KIND OF; *Aspirin* is a KIND OF *medication* as *cider* is a KIND OF *beverage*.]

D-195 *moon : month :: sun : year*
[ASSOCIATION; The *moon* IS ASSOCIATED WITH *month* and the *sun* IS ASSOCIATED WITH *year*. It takes the moon about a month to orbit the earth and it takes the earth about a year to orbit the sun.]

D-196 *gate : entrance :: aisle : passageway*
[KIND OF; A *gate* is a KIND OF *entrance* as an *aisle* is a KIND OF *passageway*.]

D-197 *dictionary : spell :: calculator : compute*
[ASSOCIATION; A *dictionary* HELPS ONE *spell* and a *calculator* HELPS ONE *compute*.]

ALTERNATE: [USED TO; A *dictionary* is USED TO *spell* and a *calculator* is USED TO *compute*.]

D-198 *exhibit : museum :: painting : gallery*
[ASSOCIATION; An *exhibit* is DISPLAYED AT a *museum* as a *painting* is DISPLAYED AT a *gallery*.]

ALTERNATE: [PART OF; An *exhibit* is PART OF a collection at a *museum* and a *painting* is PART OF a collection at a *gallery*.]

D-199 *newspaper : periodical :: novel : book*
[KIND OF; A *newspaper* is a KIND OF *periodical* and a *novel* is a KIND OF *book*.]

D-200   *never : frequency :: none : amount*
[DEGREE OF; *Never* is the LOWEST DEGREE OF *frequency* as *none* is the LOWEST DEGREE OF *amount*.]

D-201   *pat : butter :: bar : soap*
[ASSOCIATION; A *pat* is an INDIVIDUAL PORTION of *butter* and a *bar* is an INDIVIDUAL PORTION of *soap*.]

D-202   *span : bridge :: lane : highway*
[PART OF; A *span* is PART OF a *bridge* as a *lane* is PART OF a *highway*.]

D-203   *mirrors : reflect :: lenses : focus*
[ACTION; *Mirrors reflect* and *lenses focus*.]

ALTERNATE: [USED TO; *Mirrors* are USED TO *reflect* and *lenses* are USED TO *focus*.]

D-204   *pasture : ranch :: lawn : yard*
[ASSOCIATION; A *pasture* is ASSOCIATED WITH the grassy part of a *ranch* as a *lawn* is ASSOCIATED WITH the grassy part of a *yard*.]

ALTERNATE: [PART OF; A *pasture* is a PART OF a *ranch* and a *lawn* is a PART OF a *yard*.]

D-205   *drift : float :: glide : fly*
[ASSOCIATION; *Drift* and *float* have the relationship of passive : active movement in water, and *glide* and *fly* have the relationship of passive : active movement in air. Drift and glide are more at the mercy of the elements than are float and fly, which require more activity on the part of the participant.]

ALTERNATE: [SYNONYM; *Drift* MEANS THE SAME AS *float* and *glide* MEANS THE SAME AS *fly*.]

D-206   *composer : symphony :: sculptor : statue*
[ASSOCIATION; A *composer* is the CREATOR OF a *symphony* as a *sculptor* is the CREATOR OF a *statue*.]

FOLLOW-UP REFERENT
> *When might you need or want to explain or verbalize the relationship between two items or two groups of items?*

Examples: explaining family relationships; explaining possible tool, machine, or construction techniques by comparison or contrast with existing models or techniques; recognizing different items that can be used for similar purposes or functions; comparing and contrasting job descriptions, business or social relationships, or characters in a drama; understanding the effect of various ingredients or ingredient combinations on a recipe; answering compare-contrast test questions

CURRICULUM APPLICATION
Language Arts: recognizing and using word analogies; using context clues to infer meaning of unfamiliar words; using paraphrasing skills in reports or research papers; identifying and stating relationships between or among words, sentences, passages, or selections; recognizing comparative elements in works of literature; interpreting or stating the meaning of imagery, symbolism, metaphors, or similes in a work of literature; organizing, writing, or evaluating compare-contrast presentations

Mathematics: changing numerical information to graphic or verbal information and vice versa; recognizing and using part-to-whole analogies in measurements of time, weight, size, or volume; identifying the relationship between fractional parts and fractions; using, understanding, or completing ratios

Science: comparing or contrasting members, classes, or families of the plant or animal
    kingdom; conducting and reporting laboratory experiments; comparing and/or
    contrasting machines and their purposes in physics or elements, mixtures, and
    compounds in chemistry; formulating inductive hypotheses

Social Studies: recognizing and stating historical, geographical, political, economic, or
    cultural parallels; comparing or contrasting eras, people, places, or events

Enrichment Areas: recognizing and using comparative note values in music; comparing
    and/or contrasting elements of style, artist, director, or creator in music, art, dance, or
    drama; comparing or contrasting team or individual sports statistics; understanding
    and stating the effects of various elements of design in architecture, engineering,
    decorating, or graphic arts

ANTONYM AND SYNONYM ANALOGIES—SUPPLY

STRAND: Verbal Analogies   **PAGES:** 342–343

ADDITIONAL MATERIALS
Transparency of student workbook page 342
Washable transparency marker

INTRODUCTION
*In the previous exercises you classified and explained different types of
analogies.*

OBJECTIVE
*In these exercises you will supply the missing antonym or synonym to
complete an analogy.*

DEMONSTRATION / EXPLANATION
Project the directions and the **EXAMPLE** from the transparency of page 342.

*These exercises are similar to the antonym and synonym analogies you did
earlier, except this time you will have to think of your own word to complete
the analogy, rather than choosing from a list of possible answers. The
EXAMPLE analogy reads "FORMER is to LATTER as BEFORE is to AFTER. What
relationship exists between the words in the first word pair, FORMER and
LATTER?*

Answer: FORMER means the first of two items or people, and LATTER means the last of two,
so the words have an antonym relationship. (FORMER is an antonym for LATTER.)

*Is BEFORE an antonym for AFTER? Does the analogy created fit the parallel
relationship test?*

Answer: Yes, the created word pair can be substituted for the given word pair in the
relationship statement, so the analogy is complete.

Project exercise **D-207**.

*How would you read the incomplete analogy in this exercise, and what
statement would identify the relationship between the given word pair?*

Answer: BEACH is to SHORE as OCEAN is to _blank_. BEACH is a synonym for SHORE.

*What words can you think of for the second word pair that would complete
the analogy?*

Write all student answers on the transparency without judging or commenting on their correctness. Give students adequate time to think of alternate answers, then as them to evaluate each suggested answer by substituting the new word pair into the relationship statement for the given pair. Possible answers might include sea, gulf, or water.

> ***Look at D-208. Read the analogy to yourself, then form a relationship statement and think of a word to complete the analogy.***

Answer: INTERIOR is to EXTERIOR as ENTRANCE is to _blank_. INTERIOR is a antonym for EXTERIOR. Possible answers include exit, departure, egress, withdrawal, escape.

GUIDED PRACTICE
EXERCISES: **D-209, D-210, D-211**
Give students sufficient time to complete these exercises. Then, using the demonstration methodology above, have them discuss and explain their choices.
ANSWERS:
D-209 *sheer : bulky :: thin :* _thick_, _plump_, _substantial_ (A)
D-210 *carve : slice :: shear :* _fleece_, _cut_, _trim_, _shave_ (S)
D-211 *inhale : exhale :: inflate :* _deflate_, _empty_, _contract_ (A)

INDEPENDENT PRACTICE
Assign exercises **D-212** through **D-228**.

DISCUSSION TIPS
"Supply" activities, especially those requiring antonyms or synonyms, provide an excellent opportunity for vocabulary development. Ask students to provide as many alternative answers as they can from memory, but be certain they can defend their selections. Since the words in an analogy have no context, sometimes the supplied antonym or synonym will depend upon how the individual student defines the word. For example, antonyms given for ENTRANCE (**D-208**) will differ depending upon whether students interpret the given word as the avenue by which a place may be entered ["The entrance was blocked."], as the act of entering [The actress made a grand entrance.], or as the power to enter [The burglars gained entrance to the house through an open window.]. Some students may also interpret the word as a verb meaning "the act of putting into a trance" or "enchanting." Antonyms for this interpretation would obviously differ from those provided.

These exercises may be easily extended into work with a thesaurus or dictionary by asking students to search out additional meanings or terminology as a homework or library assignment. Asking students to form their own analogies using currently popular advertising or curriculum terminology will also extend the application into other fields and make it more applicable to daily life. For example, instead of asking students to look up and write out definitions for social studies terms, ask them to form an analogy with each term and to write a relationship statement for each analogy they form.

ANSWERS
D-212 *occasional : continual :: temporary :* _permanent_, _durable_, _persistent_ (A)
D-213 *humility : modesty :: vanity :* _pride_, _conceit_, _egotism_ (S)
D-214 *bureau : dresser :: cupboard :* _sideboard_, _cabinet_, _buffet_ (S)
D-215 *casual : informal :: courteous :* _polite_, _mannerly_, _considerate_ (S)
D-216 *waste : conserve :: squander :* _save_, _guard_, _preserve_ (A)

D-217 *graph : diagram :: navigation chart :* _map_ (S)

D-218 *advance : retreat :: promote :* _diminish_ , _undermine_ , _prevent_ (A)

D-219 *choose : select :: reject :* _refuse_ , _dismiss_ , _decline_ (S)

D-220 *preserve : maintain :: alter :* _change_ , _modify_ , _revise_ (S)

D-221 *hamper : hinder :: aid :* _help_ , _assist_ , _promote_ (S)

D-222 *recess : adjourn :: assemble :* _meet_ , _congregate_ , _convene_ (S)

D-223 *assemble : construct :: demolish :* _destroy_ , _wreck_ , _raze_ (S)

D-224 *significant : petty :: major :* _minor_ , _unimportant_ , _trivial_ (A)

D-225 *submit : yield :: resist :* _oppose_ , _defy_ , _withstand_ (S)

D-226 *repair : mend :: shatter :* _break_ , _smash_ , _pulverize_ (S)

D-227 *disperse : distribute :: gather :* _assemble_ , _collect_ , _accumulate_ (S)

D-228 *bow : stern :: front :* _back_ , _rear_ (A)

FOLLOW-UP REFERENT

*NOTE: Refer to **pages 289** and **290** in this manual for suggested **FOLLOW-UP REFERENTS** and **CURRICULUM APPLICATIONS**. Although this lesson, and those that follow, contain mixed analogies on various skill levels, the skill applications are similar.*

ASSOCIATION/"KIND OF"/"PART OF" ANALOGIES—SUPPLY

STRAND: Verbal Analogies

PAGES: 344–346

ADDITIONAL MATERIALS
Transparency of student workbook page 344
Washable transparency marker
Transparency of TM #28 (optional)

INTRODUCTION
In the previous lesson you supplied words to complete analogies that had either an antonym or a synonym relationship between the words in each pair.

OBJECTIVE
The exercises in this lesson are in a similar form, but this time they have different relationships. The words you will need to supply for these analogies must be related in association, kind, or part.

DEMONSTRATION/EXPLANATION
Project the directions and exercise **D-229** from the transparency of page 344.
It is especially important, although more difficult, to form relationship statements to test association analogies. Read the analogy in D-229 to yourself, then try to think of a relationship statement that would reflect the association between the given word pair.
Allow ample time for students to read the analogy and form their statement before asking for verbalization. Students will sometimes create and discard several relationship statements before arriving at one they like. This process is to be encouraged. As students

state their relationships, write them on the transparency or the chalkboard, then ask students to evaluate each, concluding with one or more relationship statements with which the entire class agrees. Possibilities include such statements as "A line of TREE(s) is called a ROW," or "One plants a TREE in a ROW of trees."

> ***Now think of as many words as you can that would be associated with MOUNTAIN in the same way. Check your suggested words by putting them into the relationship statements you formed.***

Give students enough time to think of and accept or reject relationships statements or words before calling for answers, then write down all suggested answers, asking the class to evaluate each as you go along. Some of the suggested relationship statements will not work with the second word pair. Possible answers: RANGE, CHAIN, RIDGE; "A line of MOUNTAIN(s) is called a _RANGE_ (or chain or ridge).

> ***Some of the exercises in this lesson are association analogies, like the one you just did. Others are "kind of" or "part of" analogies. Whatever type you are doing, however, remember that the same relationship must apply to both word pairs in the analogy.***

NOTE: As an optional aid, you may wish to project the definitions of analogy types from TM #28 as a reference while students complete the assignments in this lesson.

GUIDED PRACTICE
EXERCISES: **D-230; D-240; D-252**
Give students sufficient time to complete these exercises. Then, using the demonstration methodology above, have them discuss and explain their choices.
ANSWERS:
D-230   *oak : acorn :: pine :* _(pine) cone_
            [The fruit of an *oak* is an *acorn*; the fruit of a *pine* is a *cone*.]

D-240   *cabin : house :: sedan :* _car_, _automobile_

D-252   *map : atlas :: word :* _dictionary_, _thesaurus_

INDEPENDENT PRACTICE
Assign exercises **D-231** through **D-239**, **D-241** through **D-251**, and **D-253** through **D-261**. These exercises may be easily divided into two shorter assignments.

DISCUSSION TIPS
"Supply" activities provide an excellent opportunity for vocabulary expansion and development. Ask students to provide as many alternative answers as they can from memory, but be certain they can defend their selections. Since the words in an analogy have no context, sometimes the supplied antonym or synonym will depend upon how the individual student defines the word.

These exercises may be easily extended into work with a thesaurus or dictionary by asking students to search out additional meanings or terminology as a homework or library assignment. Asking students to form their own analogies using currently popular advertising or curriculum terminology will also extend the application into other fields and make it more applicable to daily life.

ANSWERS
D-231   *scripture : minister :: script :* _actor_, _actress_
            [*Scripture* is read by a *minister*; a *script* is read by an *actor* or *actress*.]

D-232　*map : city :: blueprint :* <u>building</u>
[A *map* is a diagram of a *city*; a *blueprint* is a diagram of a *building*.]

D-233　*model : airplane :: globe :* <u>earth</u> , <u>world</u>
[A *model* is a small representation of an *airplane*; a *globe* is a small representation of the *earth* or *world*.]

D-234　*fever : degrees :: pulse :* <u>beats</u> , <u>rate</u>
[*Fever* is measured by *degrees*; *pulse* is measured by *beats* or *rate*.]

D-235　*doctor : infection :: dentist :* <u>decay</u>
[A *doctor* treats *infection*; a *dentist* treats (tooth) *decay*.]

D-236　*meter : yard :: liter :* <u>quart</u>
[A *meter* is a metric measure slightly larger than the English measure *yard*; a *liter* is a metric measure slightly larger than the English measure *quart*.

D-237　*shortcut : route :: discount :* <u>price</u>
[A *shortcut* is a reduced *route*; a *discount* is a reduced *price*.]

D-238　*charter : club :: constitution :* <u>country</u> , <u>nation</u>
[A *charter* grants powers, rights, and privileges to a *club*; a *constitution* grants the same to a *country* or *nation*.]

D-239　*area code : telephone :: zip code :* <u>mail</u>
[An *area code* directs your *telephone* calls to the right area; a *zip code* directs your *mail* to the right area.]

D-241　*novel : book :: pun :* <u>joke</u>

D-242　*bomber : plane :: destroyer :* <u>ship</u>

D-243　*prune : plum :: raisin :* <u>grape</u>

D-244　*cheddar : cheese :: wheat :* <u>grain</u> , <u>bread</u> , <u>flour</u>

D-245　*vinyl : plastic :: silk :* <u>fabric</u> , <u>material</u>

D-246　*milk : liquid :: butter :* <u>solid</u>

D-247　*tumbler : glass :: carton :* <u>box</u> , <u>container</u>

D-248　*basketball : sport :: chess :* <u>game</u>

D-249　*dictionary : book :: auditorium :* <u>room</u> , <u>building</u>

D-250　*expressway : road :: boulevard :* <u>street</u> , <u>avenue</u>

D-251　*enamel : paint :: gasoline :* <u>fuel</u>

D-253　*base : statue :: foundation :* <u>house</u> , <u>building</u>

D-254　*singer : choir :: musician :* <u>band</u> , <u>orchestra</u>

D-255　*summit : mountain :: scalp :* <u>head</u> , <u>body</u>

D-256　*shell : nut :: husk :* <u>corn</u>

D-257　*branch : trunk :: arm :* <u>body</u> , <u>torso</u> , <u>frame</u> (of a chair)

D-258　*curtain : stage :: shade :* <u>window</u>

D-259　*teeth : comb :: bristles :* <u>brush</u>

D-260　*net : tennis court :: goal posts :* <u>football field</u> , <u>soccer field</u> , <u>hockey rink</u>

D-261　*telescope : observatory :: microscope :* <u>laboratory</u>

FOLLOW-UP REFERENT

*NOTE: Refer to **pages 289** and **290** in this manual for suggested **FOLLOW-UP REFERENTS** and **CURRICULUM APPLICATIONS**. Although this lesson, and those that follow, contain mixed analogies on various skill levels, the skill applications are similar.*

"USED TO"/ACTION/"DEGREE OF" ANALOGIES—SUPPLY

STRAND: Verbal Analogies

PAGES: 347–350

ADDITIONAL MATERIALS
Transparency of TM #28 (optional)

INTRODUCTION

In the previous lessons you determined the relationship shown between a given pair of words, then supplied a word that had that same relationship to a third word. You worked with synonym and antonym relationships, with specific association relationships, and with "kind of" and "part of" relationships.

OBJECTIVE

The exercises in this lesson are similar to those in the previous lesson, but this time you will be working to complete different types of analogies.

DEMONSTRATION/EXPLANATION

You will need to supply words that have "used to," action, or "degree of" relationships to a given word, and that match the relationship shown in the other word pair of the analogy. Supply as many words as you can think of for each answer, but be certain that each expresses the relationship you need to complete the analogy. The final part of this lesson asks you to create analogies of your own for each type of analogous relationship you have studied.

NOTE: As an optional aid, you may wish to project the definitions of analogy types from TM #28 as a reference while students complete the assignments in this lesson.

GUIDED PRACTICE
EXERCISES: **D-262; D-274; D-286**
Give students sufficient time to complete these exercises. Then, using the demonstration methodology above, have them discuss and explain their choices.
ANSWERS:

D-262 *makeup : beautify :: mask :* _hide_, _disguise_

D-274 *jet engine : propels :: magnet :* _holds_, _attracts_

D-286 *compact : sedan :: inn :* _hotel_, _motel_, _resort_

INDEPENDENT PRACTICE
Assign exercises **D-263** through **D-273**, **D-275** through **D-285**, and **D-287** through **D-298**. These exercises may be easily divided into three shorter assignments.

DISCUSSION TIPS

"Supply" activities provide an excellent opportunity for vocabulary expansion and development. Ask students to provide as many alternative answers as they can from memory, but be certain they can defend their selections. Since the words in an analogy have no context, sometimes the supplied antonym or synonym will depend upon the individual's inferences and definitions.

These exercises may be easily extended into work with a thesaurus or dictionary by asking students to search out additional meanings or terminology as a homework or library assignment. Asking students to form their own analogies using currently popular advertising or curriculum terminology will extend the skill into other fields and make it more applicable to daily life.

ANSWERS

D-263 *styrofoam : insulate :: copper wire :* _conduct_

D-264 *splint : support :: adhesive tape :* _bind_, _wrap_, _bandage_

D-265 *lecture : inform :: movie :* _entertain_

D-266 *conveyor : move :: brake :* _stop_

D-267 *building : shelter :: vehicle :* _move_, _transport_

D-268 *needle : puncture :: blade :* _cut_, _slice_, _saw_, _carve_

D-269 *notice : inform :: souvenir :* _remind_

D-270 *lamp : illuminate ::* _telephone_, _telegraph_, _modem_, _letter_ *: communicate*

D-271 *monument : commemorate ::* _sign_, _notice_, _mark_, _underline_ *: indicate*

D-272 *graph : display ::* _map_, _chart_, _index_, _file_ *: locate*

D-273 *animal coloration : conceal :: shell :* _protect_

D-275 *archaeologist : digs :: chemist :* _experiments_, _mixes_

D-276 *lawyer : defends :: jury :* _tries_, _decides_, _convicts_, _acquits_

D-277 *doctor : prescribes :: counselor :* _advises_, _guides_, _counsels_

D-278 *insult : offends :: compliment :* _pleases_, _flatters_, _praises_

D-279 *clerk : sells :: donor :* _gives_, _contributes_, _bequeaths_

D-280 *argument : divides :: treaty :* _binds_, _unites_, _regulates_

D-281 *saver : deposits :: spender :* _withdraws_, _borrows_

D-282 *lotion : soothes :: treatment :* _cures_, _heals_, _relieves_

D-283 *traitor : betrays :: patriot :* _safeguards_, _defends_, _upholds_

D-284 *dictator : rules :: general :* _orders_, _commands_, _leads_

D-285 *blood : circulates :: water :* _flows_, _streams_, _courses_

D-287 *nibble : bite :: glimpse :* _glare_, _stare_, _gaze_

D-288 *pat : slap :: poke :* _punch_, _hit_, _wallop_

D-289 *heavy : weight :: far :* _distance_, _interval_

D-290 *pitch : darkness :: glare :* _lightness_, _brightness_, _reflection_

D-291 *inaudible : loudness :: dim :* _brightness_, _brilliance_, _distinctness_

D-292 *bitter : taste :: stench :* _smell_, _odor_, _scent_

D-293 *tropical : heat :: polar :* _cold_

D-294 *perfume : fragrance :: harmony :* <u>sound</u> , <u>music</u> , <u>balance</u>

D-295 *fury : anger :: delight :* <u>pleasure</u> , <u>happiness</u> , <u>enjoyment</u>

D-296 *trivial : importance :: worthless :* <u>value</u> , <u>significance</u> , <u>usefulness</u>

D-297 *remote : distance :: antique :* <u>age</u> , <u>time</u>

D-298 Answers will vary.

FOLLOW-UP REFERENT

*NOTE: Refer to **pages 289** and **290** in this manual for suggested **FOLLOW-UP REFERENTS** and **CURRICULUM APPLICATIONS**. Although this lesson contains mixed analogies on various skill levels, the applications are similar to those in previous lessons.*

TRANSPARENCY MASTERS

for

BUILDING THINKING SKILLS LESSON PLANS

TM # refers to **Transparency Master Number**. These are referenced by number under **ADDITIONAL MATERIALS** in applicable individual Lesson Plans.

HEADINGS for the transparency masters match the bold-type lesson titles at the top of the corresponding page(s) in the student workbook and the individual Lesson Plan to which each TM applies. The page number included in the heading refers to the student workbook page, not the Lesson Plan book page.

INSTRUCTIONS to the teacher appear in parentheses on the TM. Instructions to students appear in bold type.

DOTTED LINES indicate places where the transparency is to be cut apart or figures that are to be cut out.

SOLID LINES across the transparency indicate that the sections above and below the line are to be used with different lessons.

Please note that it is possible to make reproduced transparencies and copies of these master sheets, as well as the pages of the student workbook, without removing the pages from either book. Such reproductions can be made on most copy machines. See specific instructions for your copy machine or check with a firm which supplies transparency masters for directions.

TRANSPARENCY MASTER (TM) #1

STACKING SHAPES—SUPPLY, p. 49

A.   **Shade the final figure to show that the triangle is on the circle.**

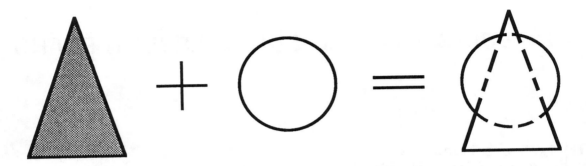

B.   **Shade the final figure to show that the triangle is on the circle.**

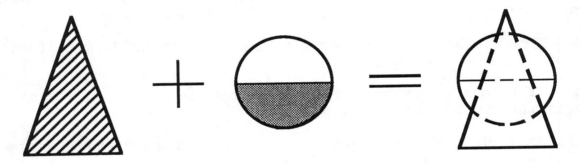

C.   **Shade the final figure to show that the circle is on the triangle.**

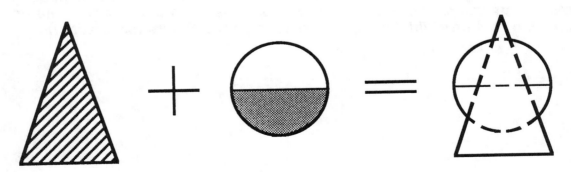

TM #2

STACKING SHAPES—SUPPLY, p. 51

A   Darken parts of the figure so that it looks as if the white square is on both the black circle and the black triangle.

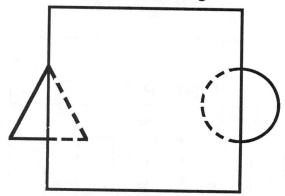

B   Darken parts of the figure so that it looks as if both the black circle and the black triangle are on the white square.

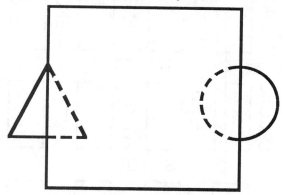

C   Darken parts of the figure so that it looks as if the black triangle is on the white square and the white square is on the black circle.

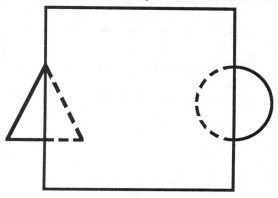

TM #3

MINI–OPOLIS

TM #4

DESCRIBING LOCATIONS AND DIRECTIONS, p. 75

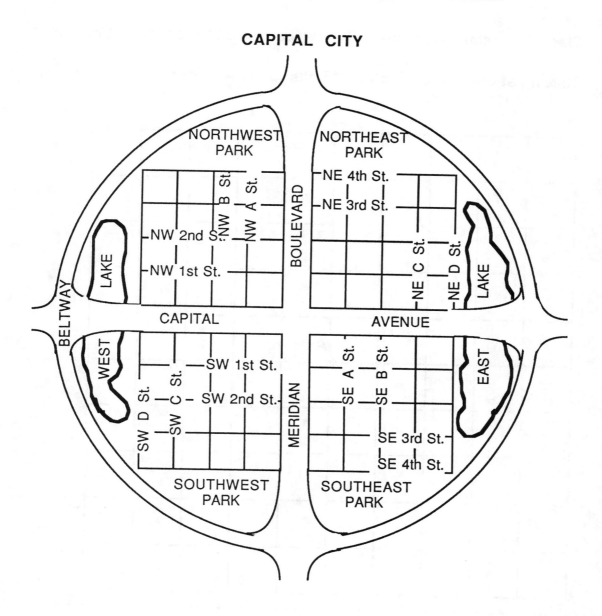

TM #5

DEPICTING DIRECTIONS, p. 82

1.   Place the rectangle on the grid using point A as the southeast corner.

2.   Starting at point A, draw a line 3 units to the east, then turn south and continue for 4 units.

A

(Cut out rectangle.)

NW		NE
SW		SE

TM #6

TRANSITIVITY—FAMILY TREE, p. 111

CLUES:
A. Juan and Rosita have the same names as their grandparents.
B. Marie has the same name as her mother.
C. One of Jose's daughters has the same name as Jose's mother.

DIAGRAM:

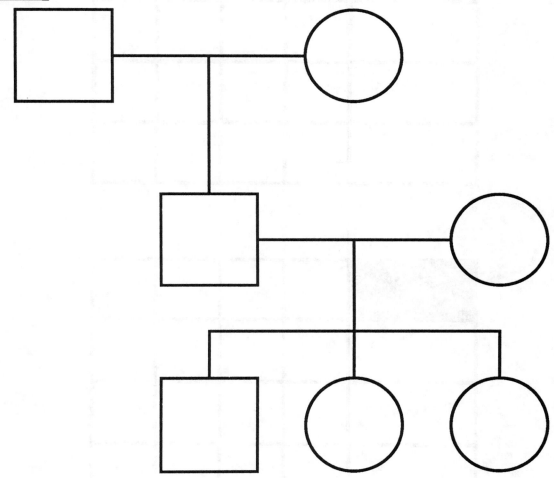

TM #7

DEDUCTIVE REASONING GRID, pp. 117–121

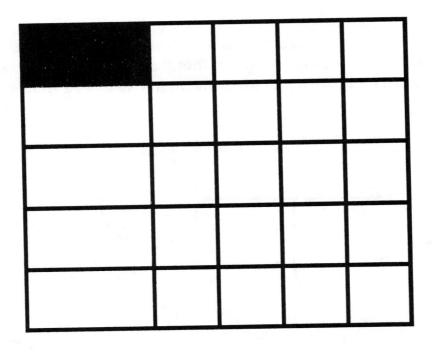

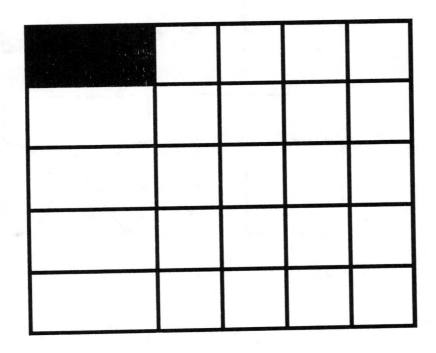

TM #8

NEGATION—FOLLOWING YES-NO RULES, pp. 123

> Rule: YES–color is the same; NO–color is not the same

Follow the arrows from START to FINISH.
Write YES or NO on each arrow according to the YES-NO rule above.

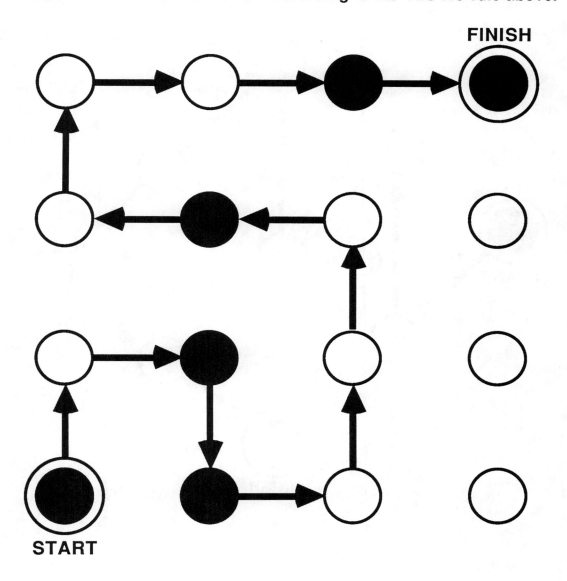

TM #9

NEGATION—FOLLOWING YES-NO RULES, pp. 125

Rule:　YES–color is the same;　NO–color is not the same

Mark the circles along the path from START to FINISH so that the path shown follows the YES-NO rule.

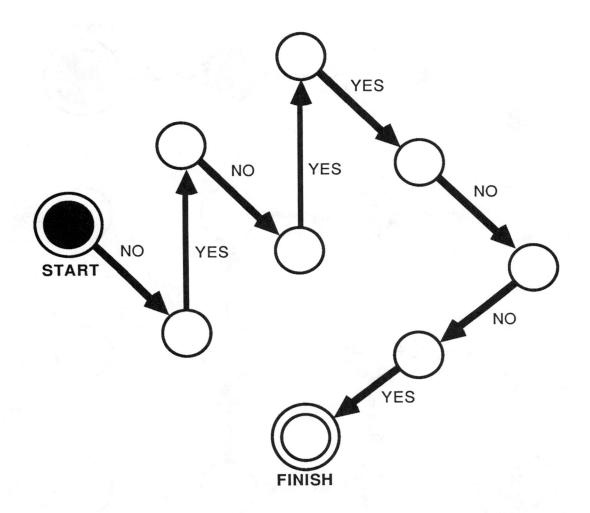

TM #10

NEGATION—COMPLETING TRUE-FALSE TABLES, p. 128

		Column 1	Column 2	Column 3
		IT IS STRIPED	IT IS CHECKED	IT IS SQUARE
Row 1	▨			
Row 2	▦			
Row 3	◉			

NEGATION—GRID FOR TRUE-FALSE TABLES, pp. 130–136

Use these shades only ↓	☐	☐	⬡	⬡	◯
▨					
▨					
▦					

TM #11

FOLLOWING "AND" RULES, p. 137

Write YES if the statement is true, and NO if the statement is false.

USING "AND"

        A   B   C   D

1. Figure A is large and checked.   ——————————

2. Figure B is small and checked.   ——————————

3. Figure C is round and large.   ——————————

4. Figure D is small and s quare.   ——————————

USING "AND" and "NOT"

        E   F   G   H

5. Figure E is small and not white.   ——————————

6. Figure F is gray and not small.   ——————————

7. Figure G is large and not checked.   ——————————

8. Figure H is triangular and is not gray.   ——————————

TM #12

CONJUNCTION—FOLLOWING "AND" RULES, p. 139

Refer to these ten squares to solve the exercises below.

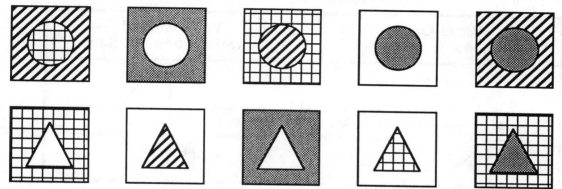

1. **Draw the squares that are gray and contain a white figure.**

2. **Draw the squares that contain a checked figure and are not gray.**

3. **Draw the squares that are not white and do not contain a gray figure.**

TM #13

CONJUNCTION—FOLLOWING "AND" RULES, p. 140

The following symbols represent valves that control the flow of water.

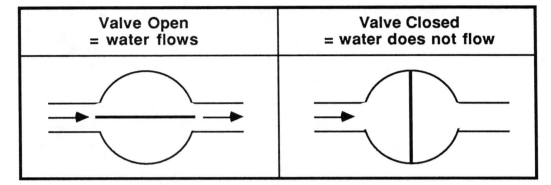

Valve Open = water flows	Valve Closed = water does not flow

1. **Valve A = Open**   **Valve B = Open**   **Does water flow?**

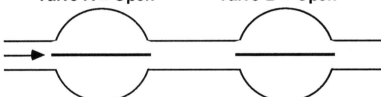

_____

2. **Valve A = Open**   **Valve B = Closed**   **Does water flow?**

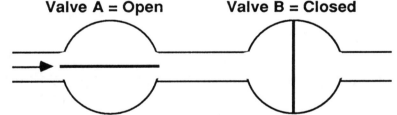

_____

3. **Valve A = Closed**   **Valve B = Open**   **Does water flow?**

_____

TM #14

DISJUNCTION—FOLLOWING "AND/OR" RULES, p. 146

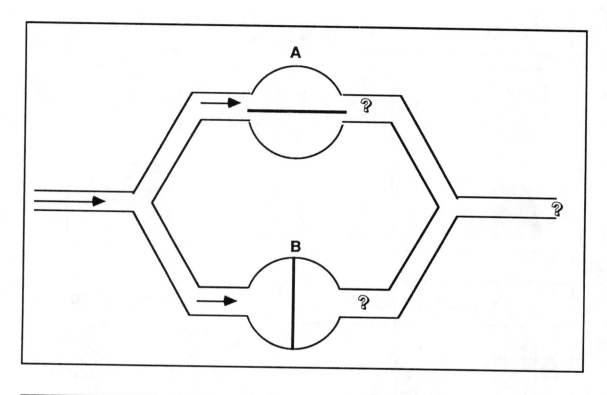

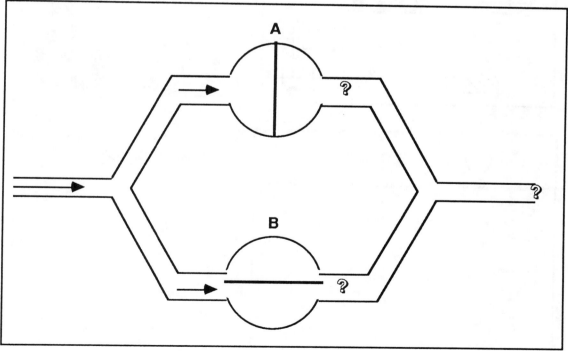

TM #15

DISJUNCTION—FOLLOWING "AND/OR" RULES, p. 149

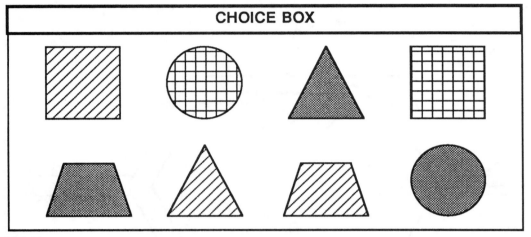

EXAMPLE:

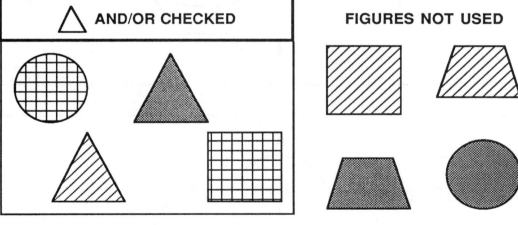

A.

⬡ **AND/OR CHECKED**	**FIGURES NOT USED**

TM #16

IMPLICATION—FOLLOWING "IF-THEN" RULES, pp. 156–160

A.   If the shape is square, then it is checked.

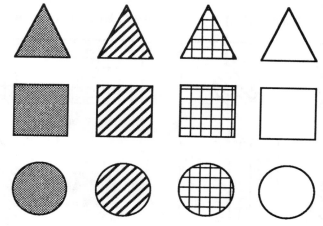

B.   If the shape is square,...

C.   ... then it is checked.

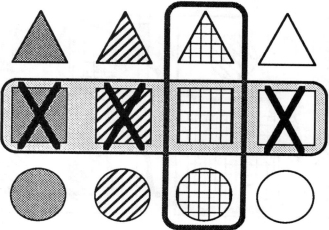

TM #17

IMPLICATION—FOLLOWING "IF-THEN" RULES, p. 161

Which group of shapes—a and/or b, or neither—follows the rule?

RULE: If the shape is checked, then it is a square.

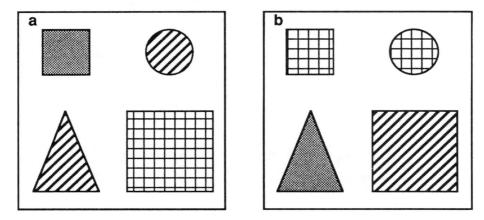

If the shape is checked,...

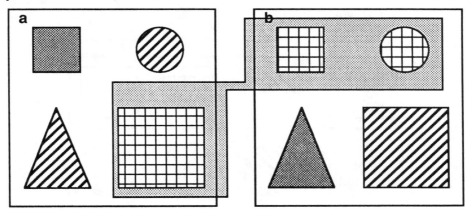

...then it is a square.

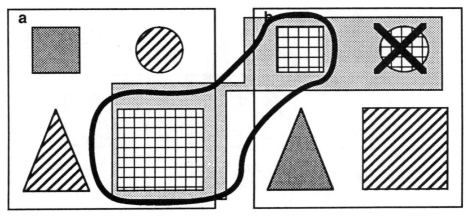

TM #18

Shade the shapes in the box so that they all follow the given rule.

RULE: If the shape is not a circle, then it is checked.

If the shape is not a circle,...

...then it is checked.

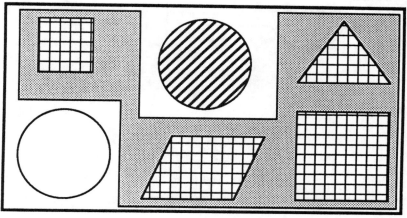

TM #19

A.   **A ∧ (B ∨ C)**

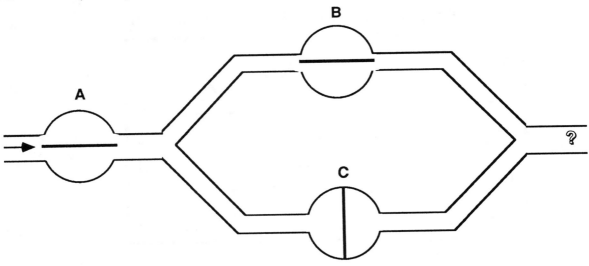

B.   **A ∨ (B ∧ C)**

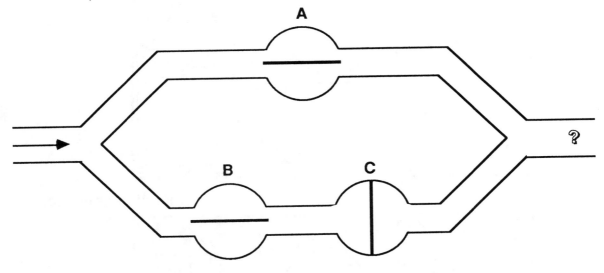

TM #20

THREE CONNECTIVES, p. 175

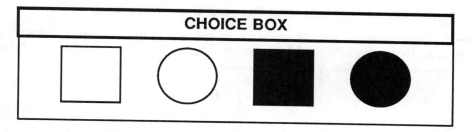

Draw the figures from the CHOICE BOX for which the first statement is true.
The next two statements help you discover the one figure for which all three sentences are true.

EXAMPLE:

1. It is black ∨ it is a circle.

2. It is white ∨ it is a square.

3. It is black ∨ it is a square.

PRACTICE:

1. It is white and/or a square.

2. It is black and/or a circle.

3. It is white and/or a circle.

Draw answers below.

TM #21

THREE CONNECTIVES, p. 179

Find the shortest path to the ecit that follows the given rule.

> **RULE: If you are on a white field, then the next field you enter is striped.**

A.

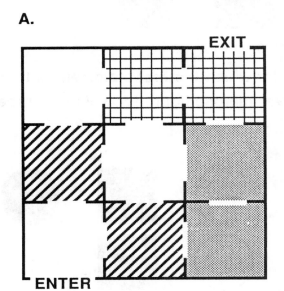

B.

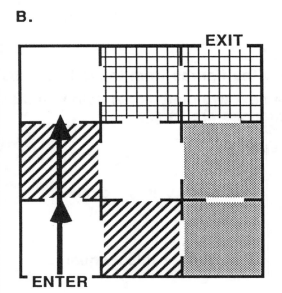

C.

D.

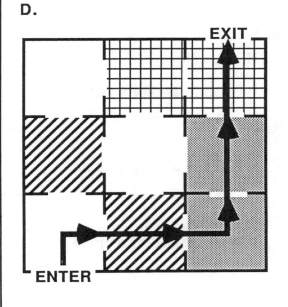

TM #22

OVERLAPPING CLASSES—MATRIX, p. 271

- Sort the items listed in the CHOICE BOX according to material and use.
- Items may be listed more than once.

CHOICE BOX
aluminum foil, button, brush, can, cotton string, eraser, glue, jar, kettle, masking tape, mop, nail, paint scraper, paper cup, rag, rubber band, safety pin, staple, steel wool, trash bag, wire

		Column 1 FASTENERS	Column 2 CLEANERS	Column 3 CONTAINERS
Row 1	PLASTIC			
Row 2	METAL			
Row 3	OTHER			

TM #23

BRANCHING DIAGRAMS, p. 274

Use the branching diagram to classify the following activities.

RECREATIONAL ACTIVITIES
baseball, checkers, chess, football, golf, gymnastics, hockey, hopscotch, jump rope, skating, skiing, soccer, tag

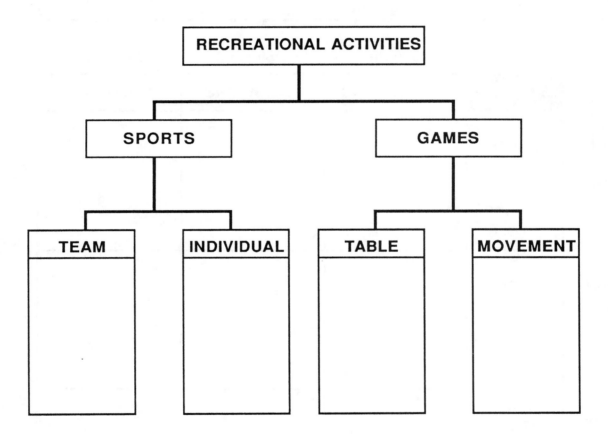

TM #24

EXAMPLE 1: bicycles, trucks, vehicles
   B = bicycles
   T = trucks
   V = vehicles

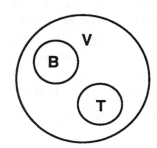

EXAMPLE 2: trucks, vans, vehicles
   T = trucks
   Va = vans
   V = vehicles

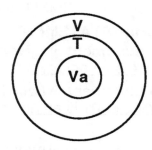

EXAMPLE 3: bicycles, mopeds, motorcycles, vehicles
   B = bicycles
   Mp = mopeds
   Mc = motorcycles
   V = vehicles

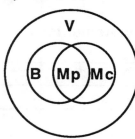

EXAMPLE 4: parents (P), females (F), executives (E)

Area	Designation
1	P
2	F
3	E
4	
5	
6	
7	

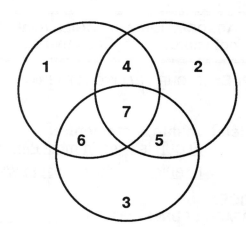

TM #25

ANTONYM AND SYNONYM ANALOGIES—SELECT, p. 320

- **ANTONYM ANALOGIES** relate the words in each word pair as antonyms.
- **SYNONYM ANALOGIES** relate the words in each word pair as synonyms.

FORM: A is a synonym for B as C is a synonym for D.
A is an antonym for B as C is an antonym for D.

EXAMPLE: COMPLEX : SIMPLE :: EXTRAORDINARY : _____   **average**
fancy
remarkable

READ: "COMPLEX is to SIMPLE as EXTRAORDINARY is to <u>BLANK</u>."

MAKE RELATIONSHIP STATEMENT:

Relationship statement 1 (given word pair):
<u>COMPLEX is an antonym for (the opposite of) SIMPLE.</u>

Relationship statement 2 (word pair with unknown):
<u>EXTRAORDINARY is an antonym for (the opposite of) BLANK.</u>

PRACTICE:
A.   GORGEOUS : STUNNING :: CLUMSY : _____   **awkward**
elegant
graceful

Relationship statements:

_____

_____

ASSOCIATION ANALOGIES— p. 326

- **ASSOCIATION ANALOGIES** relate the words in each word pair in a way not expressed by the other specific relationships you will study.

EXAMPLE: FLOUR : BAKING :: FABRIC : _____   **cloth**
material
sewing

Relationship statements:
<u>FLOUR is used in most BAKING products.</u>
<u>FABRIC is used in most SEWING products.</u>

PRACTICE:
A.   BEACH : DUNES :: OCEAN : _____   **ship**
water
waves

TM #26

"KIND OF" AND "PART OF" ANALOGIES—SELECT, pp. 329–330

> • **"KIND OF" ANALOGIES** involve member-class relationships.

FORM: **A** is a kind of **B** as **C** is a kind of **D**.
             A is a member of the Class **B** as **C** is a member of the Class **D**.

EXAMPLE: MALLARD : DUCK :: TABBY : _____

animal
cat
Siamese

Relationship statements:
A MALLARD is a kind of DUCK.
A TABBY is a kind of CAT.

PRACTICE:

A.   IGNEOUS : ROCK :: GOLD : _____

jewlery
metal
silver

Relationship statements:

_____

_____

> • **"PART OF" ANALOGIES** involve part-whole relationships.

FORM: **A** is a part of **B** as **C** is a part of **D**.

EXAMPLE: NOSE : FACE :: FINGER : _____

hand
knuckle
toe

Relationship statements:
A NOSE is a part of a FACE.
A FINGER is a part of a HAND.

PRACTICE:

B.   SENATE : LEGISLATURE :: SUPREME COURT : _____

judge
judiciary
state court

Relationship statements:

_____

_____

C.   JACKET : BOOK :: ENVELOPE : LETTER

center
covering
edge

TM #27

> • **"USED TO" ANALOGIES** involve noun-verb relationships.

FORM: **NOUN A** is used to **VERB B** as **NOUN C** is used to **VERB D.**

EXAMPLE 1:   CALCULATOR : COMPUTE :: PEN : WRITE

   Relationship statements:
       A CALCULATOR is used to COMPUTE.
       A PEN is used to WRITE.

EXAMPLE 2:   FICTION : ENTERTAIN :: FACT : INFORM

> • **"ACTION" ANALOGIES** also involve noun-verb relationships.

FORM: A **NOUN A VERB B** something as a **NOUN C VERB D** something.

EXAMPLE 3:   POSTMAN : DELIVERS :: ANCHORMAN : BROADCASTS

   Relationship statements:
       A POSTMAN DELIVERS something.
       An ANCHORMAN BROADCASTS something.

EXAMPLE 4:   SECRETARIES : TYPE :: ARTISTS : DRAW

> • **"DEGREE OF" ANALOGIES** involve degree, rank, size or order relationships.

FORM: **A** is (a comparative degree) of **B** as **C** is (a comparative degree) of **D.**

EXAMPLE 5:   MORNING : AFTERNOON :: APRIL : OCTOBER

   Relationship statements:
       MORNING is earlier (in the day) than AFTERNOON.
       APRIL is earlier (in the year) than OCTOBER.

EXAMPLE 6:   PINT : QUART :: INCH : FOOT

PRACTICE:

A. **surgeon : operates :: mechanic : _____**	cuts removes repairs
B. **bulldozer : _____ :: crane : lift**	drive push stop
C. **_____ : hot:: cool : cold**	drive push stop

TM #28

ANALOGY TYPES

> • **ANTONYM ANALOGIES** relate the words in each word pair as antonyms.
> • **SYNONYM ANALOGIES** relate the words in each word pair as synonyms.

FORM: **A** is a synonym for **B** as **C** is a synonym for **D**.
               A is an antonym for **B** as **C** is an antonym for **D**.

> • **ASSOCIATION ANALOGIES** relate the words in each word pair in a way not expressed by the other specific relationships you will study.

FORM: **A** is related to **B** as **C** is related to **D**.

> • **"KIND OF" ANALOGIES** involve member-class relationships.

FORM: **A** is a kind of **B** as **C** is a kind of **D**.
               A is a member of the Class **B** as **C** is a member of the Class **D**.

> • **"PART OF" ANALOGIES** involve part-whole relationships.

FORM: **A** is a part of **B** as **C** is a part of **D**.

> • **"USED TO" ANALOGIES** involve noun-verb relationships.

FORM: **NOUN A** is used to **VERB B** as **NOUN C** is used to **VERB D**.

> • **"ACTION" ANALOGIES** also involve noun-verb relationships.

FORM: A **NOUN A VERB B** something as a **NOUN C VERB D** something.

> • **"DEGREE OF" ANALOGIES** involve degree, rank, size or order relationships.

FORM: **A** is a (comparative) degree of **B** as **C** is a (comparative) degree of **D**.